Praise for *Implementing Service Level Objectives*

"SLIs and SLOs are core practices of the discipline of SRE, but they're trickier than they look. Alex and his merry band of SRE luminaries have a metric ton of experience and are here to help."

—*David N. Blank-Edelman, Curator/Editor of* Seeking SRE *and Cofounder of SREcon*

"Practical examples of software reliability are hard to come by, but this book has done it...A must-read for ensuring that your end users are happy and successful."

—*Robert Ross, CEO at FireHydrant*

"An approachable, clear guide that enables 'normal' companies to achieve Google SRE quality monitoring. I can't recommend this book enough!"

—*Thomas A. Limoncelli, SRE Manager, Stack Overflow, Inc.*

Implementing Service Level Objectives

A Practical Guide to SLIs, SLOs, and Error Budgets

Alex Hidalgo

Beijing · Boston · Farnham · Sebastopol · Tokyo

Implementing Service Level Objectives

by Alex Hidalgo

Printed in the United States of America.

Published by O'Reilly Media, Inc., 1005 Gravenstein Highway North, Sebastopol, CA 95472.

O'Reilly books may be purchased for educational, business, or sales promotional use. Online editions are also available for most titles (*http://oreilly.com*). For more information, contact our corporate/institutional sales department: 800-998-9938 or *corporate@oreilly.com*.

Acquisitions Editor: John Devins	**Indexer:** nSight, Inc.
Development Editor: Corbin Collins	**Interior Designer:** David Futato
Production Editor: Deborah Baker	**Cover Designer:** Karen Montgomery
Copyeditor: Rachel Head	**Illustrator:** O'Reilly Media, Inc.
Proofreader: Piper Editorial, LLC	

September 2020:   First Edition

Revision History for the First Edition

2020-08-04:   First Release
2020-09-04:   Second Release

See *http://oreilly.com/catalog/errata.csp?isbn=9781492076810* for release details.

978-1-492-07681-0

[LSI]

Table of Contents

Part III.   SLO Culture

Foreword

Reliability is a conversation.

It is a conversation we have with our infrastructure, our systems, and our services as we attempt to operate them. It is a conversation we have with complexity, security, scalability, and velocity in the hopes they will emerge in the way we need them. It is a conversation we have with ethics, privacy, and justice as we attempt to do the right thing for the people who depend on us. And finally, it is a conversation we have with our colleagues so we can work together to build what matters to us.

If there is anything the world needs right now (either the now of this writing or the now when you are reading this), it is better conversations. They are not easy. We can use all of the help we can get with them.

And that's where SLIs and SLOs come into the picture. For me, they offer a tool, a practice, a model—whatever you want to call it—for having better reliability conversations. Conversations that put the humans first. SLIs and SLOs help us think about, communicate, and interact with reliability in a new way. They aren't actors' scripts for some David Mamet-esque play telling us exactly what to say—where to speak or where to put the pauses. I'm pretty sure we wouldn't want them if they were.

Instead, SLIs and SLOs give us a little guidance when we need it. "Hmm, your customer's latency might be a bit better if you zigged there instead of zagging" or "Are you *sure* you want to deploy a new version now?" or "Oh, so that's what is important to our users; maybe we'd better start paying attention to that..." And given all of the different conversations mentioned earlier that we are responsible for navigating, this guidance is gold.

If we were to play the old good news/bad news game, the bad news is just as conversations about reliability can be hard at times, conversations about conversations about reliability can be less straightforward than we'd like. SLIs and SLOs in theory are potentially easy, but in practice, not always so much.

The other piece of soggy news is that just as reliability conversations (at least the good ones) never really end, so too it is with SLIs and SLOs. They don't finish. As Rilke said: "Live the questions now."

The good (albeit slightly less poetic) news is that you have this book. Alex and the other contributors have already lived some of the questions, and they are ready to share what they've learned with you. This can help you mine the gold and get the most from what SLIs and SLOs have to offer.

I don't want to keep you any longer from reading the rest of this book, but I will use up the free "Dear reader" card you get when you agree to write a book foreword:

Dear reader, please use all of the advice in this book (and any other tool you encounter) to have better conversations. I'm counting on you.

— David N. Blank-Edelman
Curator/Editor of Seeking SRE
and Cofounder of SREcon

Preface

On the surface, this book is about service level objectives (SLOs). But on a deeper level, this book is about people. All the theory, philosophy, and approaches outlined in the pages that follow really only exist to make people's lives easier, and therefore hopefully better.

We're going to be discussing a lot of topics. Some of them are going to be fairly philosophical, and some will be heavy with math and formulae. Some will focus on software, while others will focus on processes. But all of them are ultimately about people, and I want to start with a true story about that.

You Don't Have to Be Perfect

Shortly after agreeing to write this book, I was getting a haircut in New York City. My stylist was someone who had lived in Richmond, Virginia, at the same time I had. We never met while we lived there, but we quickly realized we both used to hang out at all the same places. It only took us about three minutes before we realized we also knew many of the same people. We hit it off immediately.

Molly is a great stylist, and I always had a good time catching up while getting my hair cut. The haircut relevant to this story, however, was the last one I'd get from her before she moved away from New York to open a coffee shop in Detroit. I had built so much trust in her, I didn't find another stylist or get another haircut for four months.

During this final haircut, I told her that I had signed a book deal, and she asked me to tell her what it was about. So I laid it out in the same simple terms I do in the first chapter: you can't be perfect, no one needs you to be perfect anyway, it's too expensive to try to be perfect, and everyone is really happier at the end of the day if you accept those facts.

She responded with an anecdote of her own. When she first started cutting hair, she was so focused on making sure everything was absolutely perfect that it would sometimes take her an hour to do a simple men's haircut that should have taken 30 minutes. Cosmetology school had ingrained in her that everything had to be as even and measured as possible. Trying to be perfect caused too many haircuts to run over in time, which upset the clients that had later appointments booked.

Eventually, as she progressed through her career, she realized that trying to be perfect didn't really do much for anyone involved. It was more stressful for her, it was more time-consuming for everyone, and it didn't actually improve anyone's life. She learned that it was fine to only be a certain amount of perfect—a certain *percentage* of perfect, if you will. Spending less time on each customer meant that the haircuts weren't always quite as symmetrical or even as they could have been. It meant that sometimes, technically, mistakes were made. But even if she had continued to try and be perfect, she knew that slight mistakes would have been made anyway. The important lesson is that none of her customers cared when she changed what her goal, her target, was.

This is because her haircuts were incredibly good. They got the job done—and more! I never had any complaints in the many years that she cut my hair. I always loved how I looked when I left, even if from her perspective she knew that she could have done just *slightly* better if she had concentrated just a little more or had spent a little more time.

She told me about becoming a little more lax in her standards as I explained this book to her. She didn't make these changes in her approach because she was lazy. She changed how stringent she was because she realized it actually allowed her to provide a better experience for her customers—and that it was better for her own bottom line, as well. Her customers were happier with the shorter time the haircuts took, and she subsequently made more money in tips because everyone was in and out the door without having to wait too long. The owners of the shop were happier, too, since this new efficiency led to more positive reviews of the business. It turned out that every human involved was happier when perfection wasn't being aimed for.

In a way, this story sums up what this book is about: it's about how to make people happy by not trying to be perfect, and only making sure you're being *good enough*.

Learn from Molly. The primary philosophies that are covered in this book are lessons she learned organically from her own business: nothing is perfect all the time, and it turns out that people don't actually expect things to be. So, instead, think about what your customers—your users—actually need from you. It might be something entirely different than what you currently think it is, or what you were taught; however, everyone involved could end up much happier by accepting this fact.

For complex computer systems, there can be a lot that goes into this idea. You might have to perform very complicated math. You might have to architect and deploy entirely new services to provide you with the correct telemetry. You might have to conduct interviews with users, both internal and external. You might have to spend exhausting amounts of time convincing leadership that trying to be 100% reliable isn't the right goal. There are many, many things you might have to do, and I'm not trying to say that all of this is necessarily easy. There is a reason why there is an entire book here for you to learn from.

People are happy when their haircut is good enough, it doesn't cost too much, and they can get in and out the door in a reasonable amount of time. If you think about it, your computer services probably don't have to be much different. SLOs, and everything that comes with them, give you a way of measuring exactly what your users need from you, provide you with powerful data to have better discussions and make better decisions, and ultimately can make everyone's lives easier.

How to Read This Book

The most important thing that I want you to know when you start reading this book is that this is all only a model. SLO-based approaches to reliability are exactly that—they're approaches, not some magic tincture that will immediately solve all of your problems. They're a way to have better discussions and develop measurements that should allow for you to make better data-driven decisions. But there is no one-size-fits-all approach to this. Everything we talk about in this book is only a model. (For a great set of resources about how to think about things as being models, check out *https://www.itsonlyamodel.com*, maintained by John Allspaw.)

The book has been split into three parts.

Part I, SLO Development
> This should be considered mandatory reading if you're going to implement an SLO-based approach to reliability—it outlines the concepts, philosophies, and definitions you need to be familiar with to take your first steps. The chapters in this part explain what the various components of SLOs are, how to use them successfully, why they work, and how you can make them work for you.

Part II, SLO Implementation
> Here you'll start to hear from some of my brilliant friends from across the industry. While Part I helps you learn how things work, Part II is much more practical in nature. Together we'll help you tackle some of the more complicated aspects of implementing an SLO-based approach, including the math you need to have meaningful service level indicators (SLIs) and accurate SLO targets, the most useful alerting for your team, as well as how to get buy-in company-wide.

Part III, SLO Culture
> This part discusses how you can make sure that adoption of an SLO-based approach to reliability for your team, organization, or entire company can be engaged with in the most efficient manner. Too many people think of implementing SLOs as "something you do," in the sense that it's a singular goal you can

check off a list. That isn't how all of this actually works. SLO-based approaches encourage thinking about the reliability of your services in a different and more accurate way. The chapters in this section ensure that you can implement SLOs in the best possible way, and use the concepts behind them for better communications across teams.

Additionally, the final chapter, Chapter 17, *Reliability Reporting*, brings everything to a close and contains some of the most useful advice in the entire book. Make sure you don't skip over that.

To make the most out of the book, I truly hope you read every chapter. The chapters in the first section should be read in order, but the last two sections can be read in whatever order best addresses the needs of your situation. You don't need to read every chapter consecutively; I hope this book will be as much of a reference for you in the future as it is an educational tool to get you started. It was designed to be both a primer and a source for you to return to again and again.

No matter what your situation is, or what your goals are, I hope at the very least you can walk away from this text remembering the lessons Molly taught us. While this book is mostly about computer systems, the general philosophies are broadly applicable: you can't be perfect, no one needs you to be perfect anyway, it's too expensive to try to be perfect, and everyone is happier at the end of the day if you embrace this.

Conventions Used in This Book

The following typographical conventions are used in this book:

Italic
: Indicates new terms, URLs, email addresses, filenames, and file extensions.

`Constant width`
: Used for program listings, as well as within paragraphs to refer to program elements such as variable or function names, databases, data types, environment variables, statements, and keywords.

`Constant width bold`
: Shows commands or other text that should be typed literally by the user.

`Constant width italic`
: Shows text that should be replaced with user-supplied values or by values determined by context.

This element signifies a tip or suggestion.

 This element signifies a general note.

 This element indicates a warning or caution.

O'Reilly Online Learning

 For more than 40 years, *O'Reilly Media* has provided technology and business training, knowledge, and insight to help companies succeed.

Our unique network of experts and innovators share their knowledge and expertise through books, articles, and our online learning platform. O'Reilly's online learning platform gives you on-demand access to live training courses, in-depth learning paths, interactive coding environments, and a vast collection of text and video from O'Reilly and 200+ other publishers. For more information, visit *http://oreilly.com*.

How to Contact Us

Please address comments and questions concerning this book to the publisher:

O'Reilly Media, Inc.
1005 Gravenstein Highway North
Sebastopol, CA 95472
800-998-9938 (in the United States or Canada)
707-829-0515 (international or local)
707-829-0104 (fax)

We have a web page for this book, where we list errata and any additional information. You can access this page at *https://oreil.ly/Implementing_SLOs*.

Email *bookquestions@oreilly.com* to comment or ask technical questions about this book.

For news and information about our books and courses, visit *http://oreilly.com*.

Find us on Facebook: *http://facebook.com/oreilly*

Follow us on Twitter: *http://twitter.com/oreillymedia*

Watch us on YouTube: *http://www.youtube.com/oreillymedia*

Acknowledgments

Wow. I wrote a book. I have an incredible number of people to thank for this. I'm going to miss someone who deserves to be in this section—please know that if I did, it was purely accidental.

First, I have to start with all of the contributing authors. It's not so much that *I* wrote a book as that *we* wrote a book. When I first started thinking about this project, I had a few people in mind to cover certain topics. At first this was probably two or three chapters, and I figured I'd write the rest. But as word got around people started volunteering all over the place, and we ended up with eight chapters written by contributing authors. This is amazing, because there is almost nothing more important than having a bunch of voices speaking about the same topic.

Thank you Daria Barteneva, Blake Bisset, Toby Burress, Polina Giralt, Niall Murphy, Eva Parish, Dave Rensin, Ben Sigelman, Harold Treen, Salim Virji, and Jaime Woo. The readers of this book are much better off due to your contributions and to your telling this story with me. Please go read all about who they are and what they do in the Contributors section of this book.

But contributing to a book is about more than just writing the words.

I'd like to thank my acquisitions editor, John Devins, for believing in the very idea of this book, and my content editor, Corbin Collins, and my production editor Deborah Baker: without your support and patience along the way this book would never have happened. We did all of this during a global pandemic, after all.

Rachel Head, my copyeditor: you were amazing, insightful, and comprehensive. After months of putting this book together, it was brought to a whole new level once you were involved.

David Blank-Edelman: thank you for taking the time to answer a random email and getting me started on this entire journey. Without your response and your assistance this book could have ended up a forgotten pipe dream.

Gabe Ochoa: thank you for accidentally pushing me to do this. In the summer of 2019 I was lamenting that there wasn't an entire book about this subject. I had gotten tired of repeating the same things to people over and over again. When I mentioned this to you, you said I should write the book. I started to protest, explaining that an expert should be the one to write it, and you responded with, "You *are* the expert." Those four words are some of the most meaningful I've ever heard, and we can blame the entire existence of this book on them.

Eva Parish and John Turner: thank you for bowls of ramen and helping me find a home when I needed one the most.

To all of my reviewers and other helpers: thank you, thank you, thank you! Once chapters started getting sent off to O'Reilly, I got the following note back:

> You guys are amazing. Hard to believe the pitiful pickiness I've been reduced to. Really good writing and careful quality control. Super refreshing.

Y'all kicked ass, and I thank every single one of you for that. Thank you to William Banfield, Abby Bangser, Betsy Beyer, Danyel Fisher, Liz Fong-Jones, Heinrich Hartmann, Marke Howell, Matt LeMay, Matthias Loibl, Christian Long, Ben Lutch, Charity Majors, Ben Picolo, Isobel Redelmeier, John Reese, Shelby Spees, Daniel Spoonhower, Emil Stolarsky, Tim Tischler, Amy Tobey, and Scott Wilson. Some of you I've known for a long time and some of us met just for this project, but I now consider every single one of you my friends.

And, I would be remiss if I didn't call out a few of y'all specifically...

Jacob Scott, you reviewed more of the book than almost anyone and did so with your expert curiosity and skepticism. Thank you for making this book better, and I'm glad we don't always agree.

Štěpán Davidovič, you showed up when we needed you most, and several chapters owe so much to your magnificent talent with your second language. You're up next. You have things to say and you have a talent for saying them.

And, finally: Kristina Bennett. You were an absolute rockstar that stepped in at just the right moments and went way above and beyond with your reviews. I miss working with you, and this book would not exist in the state it does today without you. You helped start things off and you helped finish things, too. Thank you.

To Molly van Tassel: thanks for letting me share your story in the preface. I miss your haircuts.

To Denise Yu: thank you for the amazing wiener dog pictures in Chapter 12.

To Pizzachat: thank you for literally everything. Every day you help me feel connected, grounded, and loved.

To Prodigy Coffee: thank you for all of your pre-pandemic coffees, smiles, and daily inquiries into how the book was going. You have no idea how much your encouragement helped.

To The Gate and Skylark: a lot of this book was written within your walls and with one of your drinks by my side. It's a shame I couldn't finish it the way it started, but thank you for being there while you could. On the other side of this, thank you to Lucey's Lounge for the encouragement and to-go margaritas I drank amongst lonely warehouses once the pandemic arrived.

To Jimmy Eat World: playing *Clarity* on repeat is how I've done all of my writing—big and small—for over two decades now. Thank you for recording my favorite album. It is seared into my soul.

Tanya Reilly, thank you for being there for me on my first day at Google, thank you for being there for me on my last day, thank you for always being the exemplar of both an SRE and a good human, and thank you for encouraging me to put more of my thoughts out into the wider world.

Niall Murphy, I cannot figure out how to say thank you enough. You were more important to the success of this project than anyone. No one could ask for a better mentor or friend. Thank you, thank you, thank you.

To my mother, brother, sister, and the rest of my family back home: thank you for indulging me as a child when I forced you to read my "books." I always wanted to be an author. Turns out it happened.

To six-year-old me, I know it's not a high fantasy tale filled with dragons and magic, but: We did it! We're an author after all!

And, finally, and most importantly: thank you to my partner Jen and my rescue dog Taco. You are my soulmates; you are the reasons I do the things I do. I love you.

Black lives matter. We only have this one planet. Adopt, don't shop. Take care of each other.

PART I

SLO Development

CHAPTER 1

The Reliability Stack

Alex Hidalgo

We live in a world of services. There are vendors that will sell you Network as a Service or Infrastructure as a Service. You can pay for Monitoring as a Service or Database as a Service. And that doesn't even touch upon the most widely used acronym, *SaaS*, which in and of itself can stand for Software, Security, Search, or Storage as a Service.

Furthermore, many organizations have turned to a microservice approach, one where you split functionality out into many small services that all talk to each other and depend on each other. Our systems are becoming more complex and distributed and deeper with every passing year.

It seems like everything is a service now, to the point that it can be difficult to define exactly what a service even is. If you run a retail website, you might have microservices that handle things like user authentication, payments systems, and keeping track of what a user has put in their shopping cart. But clearly, the entire retail website is itself also a service, albeit one that is composed of many smaller components.

We want to make sure our services are reliable, and to do this with—and within—complex systems, we need to start thinking about things in a different way than we may have in the past. You might be responsible for a globally distributed service with thousands of moving parts, or you might just be responsible for keeping a handful of VMs running. In either case, you almost certainly have human users who depend on those things at some point, even if they're many layers removed. And once you take human users into account, you need to think about things from their perspective.

Our services may be small or incredibly deep and complex, but almost without fail these services can no longer be properly understood via the logs or stack traces we have depended on in the past. With this shift, we need not just new types of telemetry, but also new approaches for using that telemetry.

This opening chapter establishes some truths about services and their users, outlines the various components of how service level objectives work, provides some examples of what services might look like in the first place, and finally gives you a few additional points of guidance to keep in mind as you read the rest of this book.

Service Truths

Many things may be true about a particular service, but three things are always true.

First, a proper level of reliability is the most important operational requirement of a service. A service exists to perform reliably enough for its users, where reliability encompasses not only availability but also many other measures, such as quality, dependability, and responsiveness. The question "Is my service reliable?" is pretty much analogous to the question "Is my service doing what its users need it to do?" As we discuss at great length in this book, you don't want your target to be perfect reliability, but you'll need your service to do what it is supposed to well enough for it to be useful to your users. We'll discuss what reliability actually means in much more detail in Chapter 2, but it always comes back to doing what your users need.

Because of this, the second truth is that how you appear to be operating to your users is what determines whether you're being reliable or not—not what things look like from your end. It doesn't matter if you can point to zero errors in your logs, or perfect availability metrics, or incredible uptime; if your users don't think you're being reliable, you're not.

 What do we mean when we say "user"? Simply put, a *user* is anything or anyone that relies on your service. It could be an actual human, the software of a paying customer, another service belonging to an internal team, a robot, and so on. For brevity this book refers to whatever might need to communicate with your service as a user, even if it's many levels removed from an actual human.

Finally, the third thing that is always true is that nothing is perfect all the time, so your service doesn't have to be either. Not only is it impossible to be perfect, but the costs in both financial and human resources as you creep ever closer to perfection scale at something much steeper than linear. Luckily, it turns out that software doesn't have to be 100% perfect all the time, either.

The Reliability Stack

If we accept that reliability is the most important requirement of a service, users determine this reliability, and it's okay to not be perfect all the time, then we need a way of thinking that can encompass these three truths. You have limited resources to spend, be they financial, human, or political, and one of the best ways to account for these resources is via what I've taken to calling the *Reliability Stack*. This stack is what the majority of this book is about. Figure 1-1 shows the building blocks—we'll begin with a brief overview of the key terms so we're all on the same page.

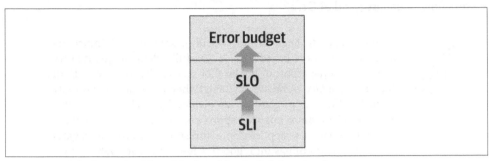

Figure 1-1. The basic building blocks of the Reliability Stack

At the base of the Reliability Stack you have *service level indicators*, or SLIs. An SLI is a measurement that is determined over a metric, or a piece of data representing some property of a service. A good SLI measures your service from the perspective of your users. It might represent something like if someone can load a web page quickly enough. People like websites that load quickly, but they also don't need things to be instantaneous. An SLI is most often useful if it can result in a binary "good" or "bad" outcome for each event—that is, either "Yes, this service did what its users needed it to" or "No, this service did not do what its users needed it to." For example, your research could determine that users are happy as long as web pages load within 2 seconds. Now you can say that any page load time that is equal to or less than 2 seconds is a "good" value, and any page load time that is greater than 2 seconds is a "bad" value.

Once you have a system that can turn an SLI into a "good" or "bad" value, you can easily determine the percentage of "good" events by dividing it by the total number of events. For example, let's say you have 60,000 visitors to your site in a given day, and you're able to measure that 59,982 of those visits resulted in pages loading within 2 seconds. You can divide your good visits by your total visits to return a percentage indicating how often your users' requests resulted in them receiving a web page quickly enough:

$$\frac{59982}{60000} = 0.9997 = 99.97\%$$

At the next level of the stack we find *service level objectives*, or SLOs, which are informed by SLIs. You've seen how to convert the number of good events among total events to a percentage. Your SLO is a target for what that percentage should be. The SLO is the "proper level of reliability" targeted by the service. To continue with our example, you didn't hear any complaints about the day when 99.97% of page loads were "good," so you could infer that users are happy enough as long as 99.97% of pages load quickly enough. There is much more at play than that, however. Chapter 4 covers how to choose good SLOs.

 In *Site Reliability Engineering* (O'Reilly), service level indicators were defined fairly broadly as "a carefully defined quantitative measure of some aspect of the level of service that is provided." In *The Site Reliability Workbook* (O'Reilly), they were more commonly defined as the ratio of good events divided by total events. In this book we take a more nuanced approach. The entire system starts with measurements, applies some thresholds and/or aggregates them, categorizes things into "good" values and "bad" values, converts these values into a percentage, and then compares this percentage against a target. Exactly how you go about this won't be the same for every organization; it will heavily depend on the kinds of metrics or measurements available to you, how you are able to store and analyze them, their quantity and quality, and where in your systems you can perform the necessary math. There is no universal answer to the question of where to draw the line between SLI and SLO, but it turns out this doesn't really matter as long as you're using the same definitions throughout your own organization. We'll discuss these nuances in more detail later in the book.

Finally, at the top of the stack we have *error budgets*, which are informed by SLOs. An error budget is a way of measuring how your SLI has performed against your SLO over a period of time. It defines how unreliable your service is permitted to be within that period and serves as a signal of when you need to take corrective action. It's one thing to be able to find out if you're currently achieving your SLO, and a whole other thing to be able to report on how you've performed against that target over a day, a week, a month, a quarter, or even a year. You can then use that information to have discussions and make decisions about how to prioritize your work; for example, if you've exhausted your error budget over a month, you might dedicate a single engineer to reliability improvements for a sprint cycle, but if you've exhausted your error budget over an entire quarter, perhaps it's time for an all-hands-on-deck situation where everyone focuses on making the service more reliable. Having these discussions is covered in depth in Chapter 5.

You may have also heard of *service level agreements*, or SLAs (Figure 1-2). They're often fueled by the same—or at least similar—SLIs as your SLOs are, and often have their own error budgets as well. An SLA is very similar to an SLO, but differs in a few important ways.

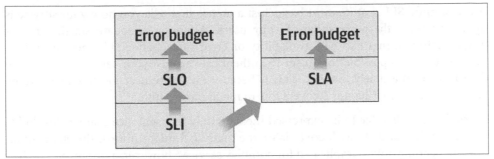

Figure 1-2. Service level agreements are also informed by service level indicators

SLAs are business decisions that are written into contracts with paying customers. You may also sometimes see them internally at companies that are large enough to have charge-back systems between organizations or teams. They're explicit promises that involve payment.

An SLO is a target percentage you use to help you drive decision making, while an SLA is usually a promise to a customer that includes compensation of some sort if you don't hit your targets. If you violate your SLO, you generate a piece of data you use to think about the reliability of your service. If you violate an SLO over time, you have a choice about doing something about it. If you violate your SLA, you owe someone something. If you violate an SLA over time, you generally don't have much of a choice about how and when to act upon it; you need to be reactive, or you likely won't remain in business for very long.

SLAs aren't covered here in much depth. Developing and managing SLAs for an effective business is a topic for another book and another time. This book focuses on the elements of the Reliability Stack that surround service level objectives and how you can use this data to have better discussions and make better decisions within your own organization or company.

Service Level Indicators

SLIs are the single most important part of the Reliability Stack, and may well be the most important concept in this entire book. You may never get to the point of having reasonable SLO targets or calculated error budgets that you can use to trigger decision making. But taking a step back and thinking about your service from your users' perspective can be a watershed moment for how your team, your organization, or your company thinks about reliability. SLIs are powerful datasets that can help you with everything from alerting on things that actually matter to driving your debugging efforts during incident response—and all of that is simply because they're measurements that take actual users into account.

A meaningful SLI is, at its most basic, just a metric that tells you how your service is operating from the perspective of your users. Although adequate starting points might include things like API availability or error rates, better SLIs measure things like whether it is possible for a user to authenticate against your service and retrieve data from it in a timely manner. This is because the entire user journey needs to be taken into account. Chapter 3 covers this in much more depth.

A good SLI is also able to be expressed meaningfully in a sentence that all stakeholders can understand. As we'll cover later, the math that might inform the status of an SLI can become quite complicated for complex services; however, a proper SLI definition has to be understandable by a wide audience. Chapter 15 talks much more about the importance of definitions, understandability, and discoverability.

Service Level Objectives

As has been mentioned, and will be mentioned many more times, trying to ensure anything is reliable 100% of the time is a fool's errand. Things break, failures occur, unforeseen incidents take place, and mistakes are made. Everything depends on something else, so even if you're able to ensure that you're reliable 99.999% of the time, if something else you depend on is any less than that, your users may not even know that your specific part of the system was operating correctly in the first place. That "something" doesn't even have to be a hard dependency your service has; it can be anything in the critical path of your users. For example, if the majority of your users rely on consumer-grade internet connections, nothing you can do will ever make your services appear to be more reliable than what those connections allow a user to experience. Nothing runs in a complete vacuum—there are always many factors at play in complex systems.

The good news is that it isn't the case that computer systems actually need to be perfect. Computer systems even employ error detection and correction techniques at the hardware level. From their inception, the networking protocols we use today have had built-in systems to handle errors and failures, because it's understood that those errors and failures are going to happen no matter what you try to do about them.

Even at the highest levels, such as a human browsing to a web page and expecting it to load, failures of some sort are expected and known to occur. A web page may load slowly, or parts of it won't load at all, or the login button won't register a click. These are all things humans have come to anticipate and are usually okay with—as long as they don't happen too often or at a particularly important moment.

And that's all SLOs are. They're targets for how often you can fail or otherwise not operate properly and still ensure that your users aren't meaningfully upset. If a visitor to a website has a page that loads very slowly—or even not at all—once, they'll probably shrug their shoulders and try to refresh. If this happens every single time they visit the site, however, the user will eventually abandon it and find another one that suits their needs.

You want to give your users a good experience, but you'll run out of resources in a variety of ways if you try to make sure this good experience happens literally 100% of the time. SLOs let you pick a target that lives between those two worlds.

 It's important to reiterate that SLOs are *objectives*—they are not in any way contractual agreements. You should feel free to change or update your targets as needed. Things in the world will change, and those changes may affect how your service operates. It's also possible that those changes will alter the expectations of your users. Sometimes you'll need to loosen your SLO because what was once a reasonably reachable target no longer is; other times you'll need to tighten your target because the demands or needs of your users have evolved. This is all fine, and the discussions that take place during these periods are some of the most important aspects of an SLO-based approach to reliability. Chapter 4 and Chapter 14 explore a wide variety of strategies for how to pick SLO targets and when you should change these targets.

Error Budgets

Error budgets are, in a way, the most advanced part of the Reliability Stack. This is not only because they rely on two other parts of the stack both existing and being meaningful, but also because they're the most difficult to implement and use in an effective manner. Additionally, while error budgets are incredibly useful in explaining the reliability status of your service to other people, they can sometimes be much more complicated to calculate than you might expect.

There are two very different approaches you can take in terms of calculating error budgets: *events-based* and *time-based*. The approach that's right for you will largely depend on the fidelity of the data available, how your systems work, and even personal preference. With the first approach, you think about good events and bad events. The aim is to figure out how many bad events you might be able to incur during a defined error budget time window without your user base becoming dissatisfied.

The second approach focuses on the concept of "bad time intervals" (often referred to as "bad minutes," even if your resolution of measurement is well below minutes.) This gives you yet another way of explaining the current status of your service. For example, let's say you have a 30-day window, and your SLO says your target reliability is 99.9%. This means you can have 0.1% failures or bad events over those 30 days before you've exceeded your error budget. However, you can also frame this as "We can have 43 bad minutes every month and meet our target," since 0.1% of 30 days is approximately 43 minutes. Either way, you're saying the same thing; you're just using different implementations of the same philosophy.

Error budget calculation, and the decisions about which approach to use, can get pretty complicated. Chapter 5 covers strategies for handling this in great detail.

At their most basic level, error budgets are just representations of how much a service can fail over some period of time. They allow you to say things like, "We have 30 minutes of error budget remaining this month" or "We can incur 5,000 more errors every day before we run out of error budget this month." However, error budgets are useful for much more than communication. They are, at their root, very important decision-making tools. While there is much more nuance involved in how this works in practice, Figure 1-3 illustrates the fundamental role they play in decision making.

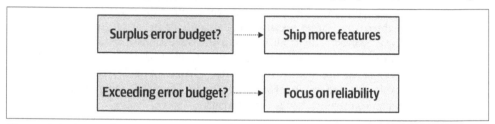

Figure 1-3. A very basic representation of how you can use error budgets to drive decisions

The classic example is that if you have error budget remaining, you can feel free to deploy new changes, ship new features, experiment, perform chaos engineering, etc. However, if you're out of error budget, you should take a step back and focus on making your service more reliable. Of course, this basic example is just that: an example. To inform your decisions, it's important to have the right discussions. We'll look at the role of error budgets in those discussions in much more detail in Chapter 5.

What Is a Service?

The word *service* is used a lot in this book, and that probably isn't too much of a surprise since it's in the title. But what do we mean when we talk about a service? Just as we defined a *user* as anything or anyone that relies on a service—be it a paying customer, an internal user, or another service—a *service* is any system that has users! Now that we've outlined the basic ideas around how to think about measuring the reliability of a service, let's discuss some common examples of what services are.

This book sometimes uses the word *system* in place of *service*. This is because computer services are almost always complex systems as well.

Example Services

This section briefly outlines a number of common service types. This list is by no means exhaustive, since complex systems are generally unique in one way or another. This is just a starting point for thinking about what constitutes a service, and hopefully you'll see something that resembles your service in one of the following. Example SLIs and SLOs are presented for various different service types throughout this book, and in particular in Chapter 12.

Web services

The most accessible way to describe a service is to think about a web-based service that humans interact with directly—a website, a video streaming service, a web-based email provider, and so on. These kinds of systems serve as great examples to base discussions around, for a few reasons. First, they are often much more complicated and have many more uses than you might first suspect, which means that they're useful for considering multiple SLIs and SLOs for a single service. Second, just about everyone has interacted with a service like this and likely does so many times every day. This means that it's easy for anyone to follow along without having to critically think about a type of service they may not be familiar with. For these reasons, we'll frequently return to using services that fall into this category as examples throughout the book. However, that does not mean to imply in any sense that these are the only types of services out there, or the only types of services that can be made more reliable via SLO-based approaches.

Request and response APIs

Beyond web-based services, the next most common services you'll hear discussed when talking about SLOs are request and response APIs. This includes any service that provides an API that takes requests and then sends a response. In a way, almost every service fits this definition in some sense, if only loosely. Essentially, every service takes requests and responds to them in some way; however, the term "request and response API" is most commonly used to describe services in a distributed environment that accept a form of remote procedure call (RPC) with a set of data, perform some sort of processing, and respond to that call with a different set of data.

There are two primary reasons why this kind of service is commonly discussed when talking about SLOs. First, they're incredibly common, especially in a world of microservices. Second, they're often incredibly easy to measure in comparison with some of the service types we'll discuss. Establishing meaningful SLIs for a request and response API is frequently much simpler than doing so for a data processing pipeline, a database, a storage platform, etc.

If you're not responsible for a web service or a request and response API, don't fret. Some additional service types are coming right up, and we discuss a whole variety of services in Chapter 12. We'll also consider data reliability in depth in Chapter 11.

Data processing pipelines

Data processing pipelines are similar to request and response APIs in the sense that something sends a request with data and processing of this data occurs. The big difference is that the "response" after the processing part of a pipeline isn't normally sent directly back to the original client, but is instead output to a different system entirely.

Data processing pipelines can be difficult to develop SLIs and SLOs for. SLIs for pipelines are complicated because you generally have to measure multiple things in order to inform a single SLO. For example, for a log processing pipeline you'd have to measure log ingestion rate *and* log indexing rate in order to get a good idea of the end-to-end latency of your pipeline; even better would be to measure how much time elapses after inserting a particular record into the pipeline before you can retrieve that exact record at the other end. Additionally, when thinking about SLIs for a pipeline, you should consider measuring the correctness of the data that reaches the other end. For lengthy pipelines or those that don't see high volumes of requests per second, measuring data correctness and freshness may be much more interesting and useful than measuring end-to-end latency. Just knowing that the data at the end of the pipeline is being updated frequently enough and is the correct data may be all you need.

SLOs are often more complicated with data processing pipelines because there are just so many more factors at play. A pipeline necessarily requires more than a single component, and these components may not always operate with similar reliability. Data processing pipelines receive much more attention in Chapter 11.

Batch jobs

Even more complicated than data processing pipelines are batch jobs. Batch jobs are series of processes that are started only when certain conditions are met. These conditions could include reaching a certain date or time, a queue filling up, or resources being available when they weren't before. Some good things to measure for batch jobs include what percentage of the time jobs start correctly, how often they complete successfully, and if the resulting data produced is both fresh and correct. You can apply many of the same tactics we discussed for data processing pipelines to many batch jobs.

Databases and storage systems

At one level, databases and storage systems are just request and response APIs: you send them some form of data, they do some kind of processing on that data, and then they send you a response. In terms of a database, the incoming data is likely very structured, the processing might be intense, and the response might be large. On the other hand, for storage system writes, the data may be less structured, the processing might mostly involve flipping bits on an underlying hardware layer, and the response might simply be a true or false telling you whether the operation completed successfully. The point is that for both of these service types, measuring things like latency and error rates—just like you might for a request and response API—can be very important.

However, databases and storage systems also need to do other, more unique things. Like processing pipelines and batch jobs, they also need to provide correct and fresh data, for example. But, one thing that sets these service types apart is that you also need to be measuring data availability and durability. Developing SLIs for these types of systems can be difficult, and picking SLO targets that make sense even more so. Chapter 11 will help you tackle these topics in the best possible way.

Compute platforms

All software has to run on something, and no matter what that platform is, it's also a service. Compute platforms can take many forms:

- Operating systems running on bare-metal hardware
- Virtual machine (VM) infrastructures
- Container orchestration platforms
- Serverless computing
- Infrastructure as a Service

Compute platforms are not overly difficult to measure, but they're often overlooked when organizations adopt SLO-based approaches to reliability. The simple fact of the matter is that the services that run on top of these platforms will have a more difficult time picking their own SLO targets if the platforms themselves don't have any. SLIs for services like these should measure things like how quickly a new VM can be provisioned or how often container pods are terminating. Availability is of the utmost importance for these service types, but you also shouldn't discount measuring persistent disk performance, virtual network throughputs, or control plane response latencies.

Hardware and the network

At the bottom of every stack you will find physical hardware and the network that allows various hardware components to communicate with each other. With the advent of cloud computing, not everyone needs to care about things at this level anymore, but for those that do, you can use SLO-based approaches to reliability here too.

Computing proper SLIs and setting appropriate SLOs generally requires a lot of data, so if you're responsible for just a few racks in a data center somewhere, it might not make a lot of sense to expend a lot of effort trying to set reasonable targets. But if you have a large platform, you should be able to gather enough data to measure things such as hard drive or memory failure rates, general network performance, or even power availability and data center temperature targets.

Physical hardware, network components, power circuits, and HVAC systems are all services, too. While services of these types might have the biggest excuse to aim for very high reliability, they, too, cannot ever be perfect, so you can try to pick more reasonable targets for their reliability and operations as well.

Things to Keep in Mind

SLO-based approaches to reliability have become incredibly popular in recent years, which has actually been detrimental in some ways. *Service level objective* has become a buzzword: something many leadership teams think they need just because it is an important part of Site Reliability Engineering (SRE), which itself has unfortunately too often devolved into a term that only means what its users want it to mean. Try to avoid falling into this trap. Here are some things about successful SLO-based approaches that you should keep in mind as you progress through this book.

The key question to consider when adopting an SLO-based approach to reliability is, "Are you thinking about your users?" Using the Reliability Stack is mostly just math that helps you do this more efficiently.

SLOs Are Just Data

The absolute most important thing to keep in mind if you adopt the principles of an SLO-based approach is that the ultimate goal is to provide you with a new dataset based on which you can have better discussions and make better decisions. There are no hard-and-fast rules: using SLOs is an approach that helps you think about your service from a new perspective, not a strict ideology. Nothing is ever perfect, and that includes the data SLOs provide you; it's better than raw telemetry, but don't expect it to be flawless. SLOs *guide* you, they don't *demand* anything from you.

SLOs Are a Process, Not a Project

A common misconception is that you can just make SLOs an Objective and Key Result (OKR) for your quarterly roadmap and somehow end up at the other end being "done" in some sense. This is not at all how SLO-based approaches to reliability work. The approaches and systems described in this book are different ways of thinking about your service, not merely tasks you can complete. They're philosophies, not tickets you can distribute for a sprint or two.

Iterate Over Everything

There are no contracts in place with SLOs or any of the things that surround them. This means that you can, and should, change them when needed. Start with just trying to develop some SLIs. Then, once you've observed those for a while, figure out if you can pick a meaningful SLO target. Once you have one of those, maybe you can pick a window for your error budget. Except maybe you've also realized your SLI isn't as representative of the view of your users as you had hoped, so now you need to update that. And now that you've changed your SLI, you realize you need to pick a different SLO target, which completely negates the error budget window you had picked. And all of this has to be done working hand-in-hand with not just the developers of the service but those that maintain it, those responsible for the product roadmap, the leadership chain, and so forth. This is all fine. It's a journey, not a destination. The map is not the territory.

The World Will Change

The world is always changing, and you should be prepared to update and change your SLIs and SLOs to take account of new developments. Maybe your users now have different needs; maybe your dependencies have made your service more robust; maybe your dependencies have made your service more brittle. All of these things, and many more, will happen during the lifecycle of a service. Your SLIs and SLOs should evolve in response to such changes.

It's All About Humans

If you ever find when trying to implement the approaches outlined in this book that the humans involved are frustrated or upset with things, take a step back and reflect on the choices you've made so far. Service level objectives are ultimately about happier users, happier engineers, happier product teams, and a happier business. This should always be the goal—not to reach new heights of the number of nines you can append to the end of your SLO target.

Summary

Many of our services today are complex, distributed, and deep. This can make them more difficult to understand, which in turn can make it more difficult to figure out if they're doing what they're supposed to be doing. But by taking a step back and putting yourself into your users' shoes, you can develop systems and adopt approaches that let you focus on things from their perspective. At the same time, you can make sure you're not overexerting yourself and spending resources on things that don't actually matter to your users.

An SLO-based approach to service management gives you the great benefit of being able to pick a reasonable target for a service, write that down in a relatively easily consumable way, and run that service toward that target. This might not sound like much, but if you've ever tried to do it any other way you'll know the incredible virtue that underpins simplicity, in service-, organization-, and user-based terms. These are the things an SLO-based approach to reliability can give you.

Measure things from your users' perspective using SLIs, be reasonable about how often you need to be reliable using SLOs, and use the results of these measurements to help you figure out how and when to become more reliable using error budgets. Those are the basic tenets of the Reliability Stack.

CHAPTER 2

How to Think About Reliability

Alex Hidalgo

The tech industry has a habit of becoming enamored with certain terms, phrases, or philosophies and overusing them to the point that they become just meaningless marketing jargon. One well-known recent example of this is the term *DevOps*, which was coined to describe a certain approach to getting things done. DevOps as originally formulated was intended to be a *philosophy* that could help shorten development release cycles and provide quicker feedback loops, but today it's often used as a job title or assigned to a category of vendor tools. Another closely related example is the term *Site Reliability Engineering*, and along with it, the word *reliability* itself.

Reliability has far too often come to mean only *availability* in the tech world. Although availability and reliability are closely linked, availability doesn't tell the whole story. Words like *reliability*, *robustness*, and *resilience* have all, unfortunately, strayed from their original meanings when used to talk about computer services. Common terms like *uptime* and *downtime* further complicate the matter, because when people say, "Is it up?" they don't always mean, "Is the binary running?" Much more often, they mean something more nuanced.

The truth of the matter is that none of these things is new. Reliability engineering as a discipline is not a new invention or idea. SLOs are an approach that is most often tied to the tech world, but building systems and models to think about, measure, or predict the reliability of systems is a practice that has existed across many engineering disciplines for a very long time. Reliability for systems means that a system is doing what its users need it to do, and reliability engineering principles can help us figure out how to accomplish this for computer systems as well.

This chapter introduces the concept of reliability engineering, goes through a worked example that should look familiar to you, and finally discusses why being perfect isn't possible (or necessary). Hopefully spreading this understanding can help prevent the term *service level objectives* from suffering the same fate so many other tech terms have.

Reliability Engineering

Reliability engineering as a discipline has been around for decades. It's a subset of systems engineering, which is the study of how to properly build complex systems (and has itself also been around for decades). The phrase *complex systems* is one you may have heard when discussing computer systems, and specifically microservice-based architectures—but if you've only heard it in those contexts, it's just another example of the tech industry partially adopting or overloading something that has a more concrete meaning and history. Complex systems are everywhere, from the building you live in and the cars that drive on our streets, to our political or ecological environs. In fact, it is in these sorts of things that the majority of analysis of complex systems has taken place.

In addition to reliability engineering, there are many other closely related disciplines you may have heard about: safety engineering, resilience engineering, requirements engineering, and so on. None of these is unique to the tech world, even if you've only heard them discussed in that context. They are all heavily studied and older than modern computer systems.

We should be grateful for this, because things like reliability engineering and safety engineering are the reasons we can traverse a bridge and feel confident that it won't collapse under our feet. I don't mean to imply that if you work with software you don't know these things; just that this knowledge isn't as widely dispersed as maybe it should be.

Reliability engineering and its peers are studied disciplines, but they don't necessitate the same approach every time. There are lessons you can learn and concepts you can adopt from fields like these, but there isn't a single concrete set of steps to follow in order to "engineer reliably." This is because complex systems are not just complex, they're also generally unique. How you build a reliable complex system, whether it is a bridge, the International Space Station, or a computer service, will depend on the details of that system itself.

What an SLO-based approach to reliability gives you is additional data to use to make decisions in order to make your systems more reliable. The concepts we'll be discussing throughout this book are not the only ones involved in making complex systems reliable, or in making those systems resilient, robust, or safe. SLOs are a way to gather data to help you have discussions and make decisions that will allow you to take a better approach to improving your systems. They facilitate data-driven decision making and help system designers be more effective.

At the end of the day, being reliable is highly dependent on what your system or service actually is and what it needs to do. While the actual changes you'll need to make to improve reliability may not be the same for every system, ensuring that you're thinking about reliability in the correct way likely is. Computer systems provide a wide variety of services, but thinking about reliability in terms of "Is this service doing what it needs to be doing?" is a great approach to take across the board. Using an SLO-based approach to service reliability is just one step in turning software engineering into a true engineering discipline.

Reliable performance of a service could mean many things to many people, but if your goal is to have happy users, good service performance has to encompass your service doing what your users need it to do. This might not seem like too far-fetched a claim, but it's also true that it's not always easy to figure out everything your users need. What's more, what your users need and expect will change over time, often in ways that are unpredictable.

Past Performance and Your Users

There is no such thing as a perfect predictor. No one can tell the future. There may be lots of mathematical formulae we can use to predict things when we have enough data, but that often doesn't matter to other humans. People have a habit of expecting things to remain the same; that is to say, for most people, past performance predicts future performance. Or, at the very least, past performance predicts how people *expect* future performance to be.

As you start to think about the reliability of your service, you have to begin with its history. It doesn't really matter if your users have been happy or upset with your service in the past: the important thing is to understand where you've been and where you are today. This is because users expect things from you, and you've probably already made implicit agreements to them even if you don't have formal and published SLOs or SLAs today.

 If your service doesn't exist yet, don't worry! Chapter 10 covers how to use these approaches to build a reliable system from the ground up.

Implied Agreements

When a service has been operating at a certain level for a certain amount of time, your users will see this as an agreement with them—it won't matter if you're lacking documentation or a contract stating as much. The level of reliability your users are used to is generally what they're going to expect moving forward in time. Your users are going to trust you to operate in this way.

This does not mean that your current state is what you should be striving for in the future. It could be the case that you're losing users, or that your users are generally unhappy even if they're not yet looking for greener pastures. Sometimes you're the only option available, and users may have nowhere else to go.

It also does not mean that you shouldn't be better. You might gain many more users, and have happier supporting engineers, if you were more reliable.

The point is that when you are starting to think about the reliability of your service, you need to know where you've been and acknowledge that there is a good chance people will expect you to be similar moving into the future. SLOs are not contracts, but you've still likely promised something about your reliability to your users, even if it's just from their perspective. You can't properly measure your reliability without keeping that in mind.

Making Agreements

Setting an SLO may not be a guarantee in the way a contractually obligated SLA is, but you also shouldn't hide your SLOs from your users. People, whether paying customers or internal teams, should be able to understand and discover what your goals and targets are. We'll go into much more detail about why this is later in the book, but be aware that your goals are only partially as useful as they could be if they're not discoverable by other people. Transparency with your users is a powerful tool.

If others cannot find out how reliable you intend to be, they cannot voice if they're happy or upset about this target. Additionally, if users that depend on your service cannot find out how reliable you intend to be, they cannot accurately set their own reliability targets.

By adopting an SLO-based approach to reliability, you are in some sense promising that you're going to do your best to provide service at a certain level. You might sometimes miss that target level, and you might change what it is over time, but there is still a level of agreement in place. You're at least striving to make your service as reliable as your published target. SLOs may not be binding SLAs, but you cannot start to think about the reliability of your service without acknowledging that your users will read your reliability targets as a type of agreement with them.

A Worked Example of Reliability

As an example, let's consider the reliability requirements of a large digital media streaming service. This service has many movies, documentaries, TV shows, and other types of content available for people to watch. You're probably subscribed to one or more of these kinds of services today.

What makes this service reliable to you, the user? What do you need, and what do you expect? What sorts of implicit or explicit agreements are there between this service and those who use it?

The first things you might think about are things like, "When I start a movie, does it play?" This is a great starting point and absolutely a part of the story. A digital streaming service needs to be able to stream things, or it's clearly not reliable.

But the service doesn't only need to be able to stream to your device. For example, it also needs to stream in a timely manner. A great example of not striving for perfection is the buffering time you might expect when you start a new streaming movie or TV show. Most people are going to be totally fine with several seconds of buffering time at the beginning of a viewing. The concept that the content needs to "load" is a thing users are used to, so it's fine if starting things off takes a little while. It just can't consistently take *way too* long, or people won't consider the service reliable anymore and might move to a different service. On the other hand, you may not lose any users if it takes "too long" occasionally, as long as it doesn't take that long every single time.

While people are accustomed to buffering time at the beginning, they don't want buffering to interrupt things in the middle of their viewing. So, while you can be reliable and buffer for a fair amount at one point in time, you might not be able to do so at other points in time and still be seen as reliable.

However, there is much more to the reliability of a video stream than just starting in a reasonable amount of time and not stopping to buffer in the middle of the action. You also need the video stream to be the correct one. If you select the movie *Anchorman*, you'd better not get delivered an episode of *Seinfeld*. And this is true not only for how the stream starts—you also can't have your selection switch right in the middle, even if the switch is otherwise seamless.

Additionally, you need the stream to be of a certain quality. For most people a streaming service doesn't have to be 100% perfect all the time, but other people specifically pay for guarantees of higher resolutions. So, in order to be reliable, the service needs to deliver good enough video quality for some people and very good video quality for others.

Seeing the images on the screen is great, but most people will also need audio. And not only does the audio need to be present, but it needs to be synced to the video. If the audio lags behind the video by even a second or two the video might be unwatchable to some people. Additionally, the audio needs to be for the correct movie, in the correct language, and at an understandable quality and volume.

Other users may not need audio at all, but in that case they'll probably need for subtitles to be present, synced to the video, in the correct language, and in a font and size that are readable.

When you search for a movie, relevant results should show up. When you add something to your queue, it should stay there. When you select a movie, the preview text should match the movie you've selected. If you're on season 3, episode 8 of *Lost*, the next thing to start playing should be season 3, episode 9 of *Lost*, not *Mad Max: Fury Road*. Or perhaps there is a setting users can select to decide whether the next episode of a TV show should automatically start playing or not. If this setting exists, it should be honored, or you're not being reliable in yet another way.

If the service has a kids-friendly login option, the available choices should be child-friendly and not R-rated movies.

Subscribers to the service should be charged the amount they're supposed to be charged, and they should be charged that amount at the right time. The subscription package they have selected should also persist and not change on them without warning. On the other hand, if they do opt to upgrade or downgrade their package, that change should actually take place.

I could go on and on and on. I've barely scratched the surface of the things that need to be true for a complex video streaming service to be reliable to a user. (For example, we haven't considered the quality of a user's streaming device or internet connection.) But hopefully this can serve as a good example of how you need to place yourself in your users' shoes to make sure you're measuring the things they actually care about. It's not just about being "up" or "available"; the service needs to be doing what users need it to do. With so many things at play, hopefully it is also clear why it's pretty unrealistic to assume that every single one of them will be reliable all the time, or at the same time.

How Reliable Should You Be?

The example discussed in the preceding section showed that you often have many things to think about when you're thinking about reliability, and things can get even more complicated when you're trying to figure out exactly how reliable each of these components needs to be. This is not necessarily an easy process. Chapter 4 talks in much more depth about how to pick good SLO targets once you have SLIs. But before you have this data—or your best attempt at it—there are still some reliability concepts that you'll have to internalize.

If we can agree that it's users that determine what reliability means for your service, then it's users that you need to think about when choosing the correct targets. This means that you'll have to figure out some way to determine how your users feel and what they need. For customer-facing services, you could just look at adoption rates or data points like the reviews left about your product. For internal services many layers removed from humans this can be more involved, but likely will still end up relying on measuring or asking people how they feel about your reliability performance. Asking people, however, can be a complicated task.

One of the most important things to keep in mind when soliciting user feedback is that approaches like surveys often provide noisy data. If you allow respondents to self-select, you have no idea how biased your sample set could be. Further, users often view surveys as an annoyance, and they won't spend a lot of time really thinking about their responses, if they even choose to fill them out at all. People have a tendency to just select "good" or "bad" without any real nuance in place.

While much more resource-intensive, a better option is something like an interview process. Actually sit down with your users, whether they are paying customers or other internal teams, and have a conversation about how they currently view the reliability of your service. If you have a dedicated customer support organization or UX team, you have more great resources that you can sit down and have a chat with: they likely have these kinds of conversations with and think about your external users every single day. Chapter 14 covers talking to your users in more depth.

Chances are that you can't just guess about how reliable you need to be, unless you already have very clear business analysis guiding expectations of what that should look like. And chances are that you won't know how reliable your users need you to be until you ask them directly. We'll cover a lot of the math you can use to help you figure this out in various sections later in the book. But first, there are a few other things you need to keep in mind besides your users' hopes, dreams, and desires.

100% Isn't Necessary

A primary mantra of this book is that *100% is impossible*. Nothing is ever 100% perfect 100% of the time. We can even get pedantic if we want to and point to the problem of induction: even if something has been 100% reliable since time immemorial, you really have no logical case to make that it will continue to be so. Even things like pacemakers are designed with a certain failure rate being considered acceptable.[1]

And because 100% isn't possible, humans are actually very used to this fact. Lots of the things we purchase or otherwise interact with either occasionally fail or are expected to fail after a certain amount of time. There is no reason your software services have to be any different or any better.

An example many people might be familiar with is that sometimes cars don't start on the first attempt. You turn the key, you hear the engine start to turn over, but it just chugs a little bit and a full combustion cycle never actually begins. If this is a permanent problem, it'll be seen as a true failure; you'll have to take action such as replacing the fuel pump. But sometimes this just happens. As long as the car starts on the second attempt *most* of the time, people aren't going to rush out and buy a new car. This is an example of the availability of a feature—the feature of being able to start—not being perfect at all times.

If your car doesn't start quickly and on the first attempt every single time, it's not being 100% reliable; however, as long as it starts on the first or second attempt most of the time, it's being reliable *enough*. There aren't many reasons a car manufacturer should be spending resources developing a better fuel pump if they aren't losing current or future business with their current setup.[2]

Let's consider another example. Perhaps you have a watch that you really like. It's stylish and it fits well, but one of the primary ways that a watch needs to be reliable is that it needs to tell the time correctly. This watch is prone to falling behind in time,

---

1 Maisel, William H. 2006. "Pacemaker and ICD Generator Reliability." *Journal of the American Medical Association* 295 (16): 1929–1934. doi: 10.1001/jama.295.16.1929 *https://www.researchgate.net/deref/http%3A%2F %2Fdx.doi.org%2F10.1001%2Fjama.295.16.1929*.

2 An argument could be made that spending resources on developing a new, better fuel pump that is *so* reliable that it makes people switch companies is an investment worth making. However, it's not immediately clear that fuel pumps in cars as of the time of this writing are unreliable enough for this to be the case.

but maybe it only falls behind by about one minute every few months or so. By falling behind, the watch isn't being perfectly reliable, but if you only have to update the time on your watch by a minute every few months, you'll probably still be happy with it.

Another way a watch could be unreliable is that it is behind the true time by a minute or two, but holds steady at that state. The watch isn't being perfectly reliable in the sense that it has a feature that could be described as "let the user discover the correct time," and it isn't completely fulfilling that. But as long as the watch is unreliable in more or less the same way all the time, its owner might not be bothered by this too much. They'll simply learn to add a minute or two to whatever their watch says, and that result is good enough for most people most of the time. This is an example of how synchronicity of data across multiple things doesn't have to be perfect all of the time.

One more? Sometimes when you order food, it doesn't come out exactly how you expected it to, or how you asked for it. If you're in a restaurant, you might just send it back to be corrected, but that's not as easy to do if you're ordering delivery. Let's say you order some pizza from your favorite local pizza joint. You have a pretty simple order: a large pie with pepperoni. When the delivery shows up, it turns out to be a plain cheese pizza with no toppings.

Luckily, you also like plain cheese pizza, so you just accept this as a failure that some-times occurs, and the pizza is enjoyed anyway. This kind of mistake might bother you slightly in the moment, but it probably won't make you stop ordering from your favorite pizza place—unless it happens too often. As long as the ratio of correct orders to total orders remains high, you'll still be a happy customer. This is an exam-ple of how data quality or correctness doesn't have to be perfect at all times, especially if you can ensure you merely degrade into a state that is still acceptable to the user when these failures do occur. Or, following the example of being in the restaurant and sending the order back, you can fail on occasion as long as the user can retry their request easily enough.

Similarly, suppose that most of the time when you order from this pizza place, the order shows up in about 30–40 minutes, which makes you very happy. However, every tenth order or so takes up to an hour to arrive. You don't particularly love it when you have to wait a full hour, but because the pizza is so good, and it arrives quickly the other 90% of the time, at the end of the day you don't really care that much. You, as the user, just come to expect this as part of how things work. This is an example of how service latency doesn't have to be reliable at all times, either.

 This book is about how to keep computer systems reliable, but the concepts really apply to almost everything. It's not just software that fails: everything fails at some point. So, build expectations and a culture that is ready for this, and aim to fail only as often as is acceptable to your users.

Reliability Is Expensive

Not only is being perfect all the time impossible, but trying to be so becomes incredibly expensive very quickly. The resources needed to edge ever closer to 100% reliability grow with a curve that is more steep than linear. Since achieving 100% perfection is impossible, you can spend infinite resources and never get there.

Reliability is expensive in many different ways. The first and most obvious one is financially. To build systems that are able to tolerate failure, you need many things. You need your system to be distributed, so that a problem in one location doesn't mean your entire service stops operating. It doesn't matter if you run your service on your own hardware in your own data centers, via a cloud provider, or both. If you need your service to be highly available, you're going to incur more expenses in pursuit of that goal, because you'll need a presence in more than just one physical or logical location.

Additionally, you'll need your systems to have rigorous testing infrastructures. You're much more likely to encounter failures and unreliability if you're not properly vetting your changes before they go out. This could mean everything from QA and testing teams to staging environments and proper canarying techniques. All of these things are good, and should exist in any mature engineering organization, but they also cost money. The more comprehensive you want them to be, the more people and computing resources you'll need.

Beyond financial costs, there are also human ones. For example, let's say you want to hit a common reliability target of 99.99% over a 30-day window. This target implies that you can only be unreliable for 4 minutes and 32 seconds during those 30 days.[3] This further implies that anyone on call for this service needs to have a response time on the order of seconds. You can't have a service that is 99.99% reliable if it takes your on-call engineers five minutes just to get in front of their laptops and start diagnosing things. People who are on call for a service that is aiming for 99.99% will need to always be within arm's reach of a laptop, they'll have to coordinate their commutes with their secondaries or backups, and they won't be able to do the little things like go to a movie or take their dog on a walk during their shifts.[4]

Depending on your service, it might actually be totally fair to ask this of your engineers. But the only way you can do it in a humane manner is to ensure you have many engineers in your on-call rotation so they don't have to adhere to a very strict

---

3 This math was done based upon a 365.25-day year to account for leap years. Later chapters cover approaches to this in much more detail.

4 There are techniques you can use to build your services to reach these kinds of targets without requiring humans to respond within seconds that are covered later in this book, but the point here is that people don't often stop to think about what they're actually asking of their engineers when they set these sorts of targets.

response time too often. This kind of overload is how you get engineers to quit. Additionally, you'll almost certainly need a follow-the-sun approach, where you have people spread out across the world, so they only have to be on call during their waking hours. This leads to needing globally distributed offices and lots of employees to pay.

In addition to all of these factors, there's some simple math we can rely on to help drive this point home. For example, when you think about going from 99.9% to 99.95% reliable, your intuition might tell you that it's about the same increase as going from 99.95% to 99.99% reliable—but that's not how the math actually works out.

99.9% reliable implies an unreliability of 0.1%, whereas 99.95% reliable implies an unreliability of 0.05%. Moving from 0.1% to 0.05% is a change factor of 2:

$$\frac{0.1}{0.05} = 2$$

Meanwhile, 99.99% reliable implies an unreliability of 0.01%. That means you're moving from 0.05% to 0.01% if you're going from 99.95% to 99.99%. This is a change factor of 5:

$$\frac{0.05}{0.01} = 5$$

Moving from 99.95% to 99.99% is thus 2.5 times more of a change than moving from 99.9% to 99.95%. The resources you'll need to achieve this will need to increase proportionally, if not more so. This is why chasing a target that forever approaches, but never reaches, 100% will end up costing you more than you could plan for.

We'll get much more into the math of how this all works later in the book, but for now the takeaway should be that it gets more and more expensive in many different ways as you try to get closer to a 100% reliable system. Your users don't need you to be 100% reliable anyway, so don't spend too many of your resources trying to get there.

How to Think About Reliability

With all of that said, we're still left with the primary question: "How should you think about reliability?" Overall, there isn't a single answer here—it depends on a variety of factors.

We could say something like, "Be as reliable as your users need you to be." That statement isn't wrong. The problem is that it's incredibly difficult to know exactly what that level is, especially because users will vary in their acceptable limits, and those limits will rise and fall with time.

Taking this further, we could say something like, "Just be reliable enough that your business is growing." But I'm not sure that's quite correct, either. There doesn't exist a perfect formula for making sure that you're both reliable enough to be a growing and profitable business, and growing and being profitable at the rate you could be. Additionally, you can only ever be as reliable as your upstream services, which often include things like the internet and the reliability of consumer connections.

The answer to that question is something much more nuanced. SLOs are meant to be changing things that can be adapted to your current reality and your current situation. There will be times when it is true that you should hold fast and enforce your error budget strongly. There will be other times where you experience a black swan event and have to temporarily ignore what the numbers tell you. No matter what happens, looking at the data will spark discussions.

Never forget that the entire SLO-based approach is just a way of collecting new data in a new way, and using this data to make good decisions. There will never be a single answer to the question of how reliable you should be.

Summary

Reliability can be a complicated subject when talking about complex systems. There are people who have spent their entire lives studying just that. But that doesn't mean you have to do the same in order to make your services reliable *enough*. When thinking about reliability, all you really need to do is take a step back and put yourself in the shoes of your users. What are the things that they need from you? How often do they need those things to be performant? How performant do they need them to be in the first place?

Ask yourself these kinds of questions, and you're well on your way to thinking about reliability in a way that will make everyone happier. Your users will be happier because you're thinking about them first, your engineers and operational teams will be happier because you won't be asking them to do the impossible, your product teams will be happier because you'll be focused on what the service is supposed to be doing, and your leadership will be happier because this will likely lead to a better bottom line, as well.

CHAPTER 3

Developing Meaningful Service Level Indicators

Alex Hidalgo

The single most important aspect of adopting an SLO-based approach to reliability doesn't even involve SLOs at all. SLIs are the most vital part of this entire process and system. There are several reasons for this, all of which boil down to the fact that human happiness is the ultimate end goal of using SLO-based approaches to running reliable services.[1] You can make lots of lives better if you take the time to develop meaningful SLIs.

SLIs are the foundation of the Reliability Stack. You can't have reasonable SLO targets or useful error budgets if your SLIs aren't meaningful. The entire stack becomes useless if it hasn't been built upon something solid. You want to be able to have meaningful discussions and make meaningful decisions with the data an SLO-based approach can give you, and you won't have good data to use if the measurements at the bottom of your stack aren't good ones. Remember we defined a meaningful SLI as "a metric that tells you how your service is operating from the perspective of your users" in Chapter 1. It is this kind of meaningfulness that needs to travel up through the rest of your stack so you can make the most meaningful data-driven decisions with the data you produce.

Furthermore, your service isn't reliable if your users don't think it is. While many services only directly have users that are other services, there are still humans

---

[1] There are, unfortunately, many computer-based services that do harm to our world. Weapons systems, mass surveillance systems, machine learning algorithms biased against nonwhite people, and many more do little to improve the human condition while they remain reliable. The ethical concerns about how to address all of this are out of the scope of this book, but important enough to mention here.

involved at every step along the way. Even if you're responsible for just a single micro-service that is depended upon by just a single other service, those two services both still have humans that maintain them and are responsible for them.[2] Taking a step back and measuring what your users need you to measure is an important step to understanding reliability. Even if you never end up with SLO target percentages or decision making based upon error budgets, you can still think about your users.

Sometimes you might say that the user is simply wrong in terms of what they expect from a service. You might have financial or technological constraints they aren't aware of, or you may have miscommunicated what it is that your service intends to do. This is an unfortunate reality, but even here meaningful SLIs can help you. By exposing how you're measuring the reliability of your service, you can communicate to users what they can expect. This could come with an implicit promise that you'll try to meet their needs at some point, or it could simply communicate to your users that they are trying to fit a square peg into a round hole. In either case, you're helping humans have a better understanding of the state of the world and the direction it might be headed in.

At some level all computer systems exist to perform some sort of task for people, and you can help ensure the operators, the maintainers, and the users of these systems have a better experience and view of things if your system measurements are built from the ground up considering what they need.

This chapter talks about the concepts behind developing meaningful SLIs. Chapters 7 and 9 discuss the technology and math behind measuring them.

What Meaningful SLIs Provide

Though some of the benefits of meaningful SLIs may seem self-evident, we haven't really spent much time talking about why they can be so important to you, your users, and your business. Measuring things from your users' perspective might be an intuitive thing to aim for, but there are many benefits to adopting such an approach. Using an SLI-based approach to measuring your service reliability has multiple perks.

Happier Users

It's not a difficult argument to make that positioning your users as your primary focus may mean that your users end up happier. It can be easy to get caught up in the day-to-day, quarterly OKRs, or various other business needs while forgetting about what it is that your service actually needs to do. Some engineering teams are very far

---

2 There are definitely cases where services get lost in the shuffle and suddenly no one knows who is responsible for them, but that just leads to humans having to scramble around trying to figure stuff out, so people are still involved.

removed from the users of their services, to the point that it can be easy to forget that users even exist at all. The people writing the code or running the operations for software services haven't traditionally been closely involved with conversations that involve the needs of users, whether these are internal or external.

By shifting your thinking away from what you think your service needs to do and toward what the users of the service need it to do—and encouraging others to do the same—you can build and observe better telemetry about these user needs. It doesn't matter if the users are represented by a single other internal service maintained by a team across the hall, or if there are hundreds of thousands of external, paying customers—by making any kind of user the focus of how you think about your service's reliability, you're almost certainly going to make those users happier. You're now thinking about them, which is a great first step.

Happier Engineers

Figuring out how to properly measure user-focused SLIs is often more complicated than just relying on traditional system resource metrics. This means that being able to expose or collect the metrics you do need might require nontrivial amounts of code to be written. It might mean standing up entire new services that exist only to help determine what this telemetry looks like. But even if you initially have to ask for more work to be performed, at the end of the SLI adoption process you'll likely end up with happier engineers, as well.

One of the primary ways that this can happen is that you can stop alerting on almost everything else you have in the past. You should absolutely still continue to collect metrics and other telemetry about the basic status of the services you run, such as the state of the jobs that back your service, their error rates and stack traces, their response latencies, and even their resource utilization. These are all incredibly important pieces of data to have access to—but they're not always good pieces of data to alert or page off of.

If you can develop meaningful SLIs, the only reason you have to wake someone up at 03:00 is when that SLI isn't performing correctly. It doesn't matter how many errors are in your logs, what latencies your database queries are currently experiencing, or how many of your jobs are currently crash-looping. If your service is still able to perform its job reliably as determined by comprehensive SLIs, then those are all problems that can wait until normal work hours—if they even have to be addressed at all.

 Develop good SLIs so your engineers have a single thing to point at in order to determine what constitutes an emergency.

A Happier Business

Your business could have many goals, or just one. Your business may not even be a business in the traditional capitalist sense. Maybe your analogue to what we're talking about is an open source project, or something provided not for profit or entirely for free. Regardless of how it's defined, however, there is always some other actor involved besides the people writing and maintaining the service and the people using the service—the people determining what the service should be in the first place.[3]

Developing meaningful SLIs will make your business happier. Primarily, this is because your engineering organizations can now better align with your product, business, and QA organizations. Remember that at a philosophical level, an SLI is essentially a user journey, which is often just a key performance indicator (KPI), which is often similar to an interface test. Different organizations may place different weights on these, and they'll certainly use different language to describe them, but it's important to remember that all of these efforts work better together.

If you can bring about alignment across many organizations about what should be measured, you can also generate new and more meaningful data that allows you to better communicate across these organizations. With a representative SLI you can power an SLO. Then you can use the status of that SLO to report to the product, business, executive, and other teams in your company about exactly how reliable a service has been. Chapter 17 discusses how to do this in great depth.

Developing meaningful SLIs will not only make your business units happier, but can also improve the very health of your business. By making sure you are thinking about your customers—no matter who they may be—from the ground up, you can also make sure that your customers are as happy as they can be. Happy customers and happy employees mean a happy business.

Caring About Many Things

In order to develop meaningful SLIs, it turns out that you often have to care about many things. To best leverage an SLO-based approach to reliability, you need to make sure that you're measuring a lot of different levels of interaction with your service. Individual metrics about things like system-level resources or error rates are not always enough, even if that's how you've been measuring or monitoring your service in the past. Things could be worse than you realize if you're just measuring error rates, since those don't matter if requests aren't even reaching your service in the first place. Alternatively, the situation could be better than you realize if your focus is on

---

3 At smaller organizations, the people who write the code, the people who maintain it, the people who use it, and the people who determine what it should be may all be the same people, or even the same individual. The general philosophies as described here all still stand.

high memory or CPU usage, since those things don't matter to your users if requests are completing successfully at a high rate anyway.

In many organizations, setting monitoring for a service is a one-and-done task. You make sure you have system resource metrics, maybe some HTTP response code counts, some access logs, a place to store stack traces, and so forth; then you build some dashboards you can look at when you get paged, which can be for any number of situations, none of which may actually map onto what your service needs to do for its users. Chances are you should instead be looking at the complex interactions between the many different components of your systems.

Another example is that people often conflate reliability, availability, and uptime, even though they're all entirely different things. A service can be running yet not be available to your users. Additionally, it could be available but not operating in a reliable manner. These are all important measures of your service, and you should care about all of them.

 There are a few terms that people frequently blend together when talking about how computer services operate. The three most common of these will benefit from concrete definitions to avoid confusion:

Uptime
    A measurement of the time an individual service is
    actually running on a platform

Availability
    A measurement of the time an individual service is
    actually able to respond to requests by users

Reliability
    A measurement of the time an individual service is
    actually able to perform the duties it was designed to do

In addition, you have to care about many people. These include the people responsible for actually operating your service, the product managers that help define your services, the customer operations staff that have to handle end-user inquiries and complaints, and those end users themselves.

We've barely scratched the surface here, but if you want to think about your service from your users' point of view, you have to care about many things. Luckily, it turns out there are some simple logic tricks you can employ to narrow down what you ultimately need for meaningful SLIs. That is to say, you can care about many things by caring about just a few. Let's look at a simple example.

A Request and Response Service

Imagine that you're responsible for a simple request and response API. It doesn't really matter what this service does, but it has to accept calls from across the network, and then return some data based upon these calls. How do you start to think about the reliability of such a simple service? How do you begin to put yourself into the shoes of your users? Let's compile a list of questions you need to answer in order to determine the reliability of this service.

The first thing you have to care about is if your service is actually up. If your service isn't up and running, it clearly can't do what your users need it to do. So, you should probably have some kind of metric that tells you if things are actually running. If your service is in a crash loop or has been accidentally stopped, it almost certainly can't do what it needs to be doing. So, the first question on your list is, "Is the service up?"

Asking if the service is up is a fine starting point; however, that doesn't really matter to your users if the service isn't also available. Being *available* and being *up* might seem like very similar things, but there are important differences. You could have 100 instances of your service all running, but if they aren't actually available for your users to communicate with, they're not really doing much at all. So now you have to ask yourself two questions: "Is the service up?" and "Is the service available?"

Moving on, you can now answer two questions that your users need you to, but even if you're both up and available, it doesn't matter if you can't send a response in a timely manner. Exactly what a response time needs to look like depends a lot on what it is that your service does, but no matter what that is, it needs to be in a time frame that's acceptable to your users. Now you have three questions to ask: "Is the service up, is it available, and is it responsive?"

With these three things under your belt it might seem like you're getting close to developing a meaningful SLI—but there are still a few more things that are vitally important for the reliability of even the most simple request and response service. For example, even if the service is up, available, and responsive to the user, it's not a useful service if it only returns errors. Even if those errors are delivered consistently and quickly, too high an error rate cannot be a feature of a reliable service. Add, "Is the service returning an acceptable number of good responses?" to the list.

You've now established four things to care about: is the service up, is it available, is it responsive, and is it returning an acceptable number of good responses? Your telemetry needs to be able to report on all four of these, or you can't be sure your service is being reliable. But even if you can ensure all of that, it doesn't matter much if the service can't provide responses in an understandable data format. If someone performs a request call against the API and they receive a response in a timely manner and free of errors, they still are not going to be happy if they can't understand what that response is. For example, if the user is expecting a response in JSON but gets a protobuf instead, that response isn't going to be very useful to them. Therefore, you need to add a fifth item to the list of things you need to care about: is the service up, is it available, is it responsive, does it return an acceptable number of good responses, and are these responses in the correct format?

If the service is up, available, responsive, and sending good responses in the correct format, you're probably pretty close to ensuring the reliability of a request and response API. Except none of that matters if the data being returned is from yesterday when today's data is expected. So now you also need to ask yourself, "Is the correct data being returned?"

 We could continue this thought experiment for a while, but these initial six questions are a great place to start. Conduct this same sort of experiment for your own services.

Measuring Many Things by Measuring Only a Few

It may seem like there are quite a number of things you need to care about in order to determine the reliability of even a simple service. In one way, this is true: you need to be collecting at least six metrics so that they can be analyzed and examined when needed. However, not all of these metrics help inform a meaningful SLI directly, even if they're all important things to know about. Even if you have many things to measure, you can often get to meaningful SLIs by measuring only a few of them.

Here is the list of things you know you should care about:

- Is the service up?
- Is the service available?
- Is the service responsive?
- Are there enough good responses when compared to errors?
- Are the responses in the correct data format?
- Are the payloads of the responses the data actually being requested?

Looking at this list again, it turns out that while there should probably be metrics for all of these, you only need a few of them in order to inform a meaningful SLI.

To explain how this works, let's start with the question at the bottom of this list: "Are the payloads of the responses the data actually being requested?" It turns out that if you can figure out a way to measure this, you're also measuring "Are the responses in the correct data format?" From a user's perspective, you can't possibly be receiving the correct data if the data isn't formatted in the way you expect it to be.

And if you know that the data is both the data you need and in the correct format, you can also be sure that the responses you're receiving are good, and not just errors. If you're receiving responses at all, you also know that the service is both up and available. You've just gone from measuring one thing to measuring five.

It might be the case that you'll have to calculate latency via a secondary metric, but even if that's true, you're still measuring six things by measuring only two of them.

A Written Example

What might the description of an SLI for measuring a service like the one we were discussing earlier look like? In simple English, it might read:

> The 95th percentile of requests to our service will be responded to with the correct data within 400 ms.[4]

This is simple and understandable by most people, which is an incredibly important part of having meaningful SLIs. Chapter 15 goes into much more detail about this, but it is crucial that your written and defined SLIs and SLOs are easily understood by any and all stakeholders, even if the underlying process that delivers the data is complex. Chapter 7 covers how to actually measure SLIs at a technical level.

This is also a great description because it informs a binary state. As written, this can result in an outcome that is either true or is not: "Yes, this service is currently doing what it needs to be doing," or "No, this service is currently not doing what it needs to be doing." When measuring things that are either true or not, trivial math can be used to convert the results into a percentage, which makes it much easier to set an SLO target percentage later.

SLI Measurements and Metrics

SLIs are metrics that eventually need to be able to be sorted into binary values, often by applying thresholds or aggregations or performing other math. That doesn't mean the metrics that back them have to literally be ones or zeros, just that in order to inform a percentage, you need to be able to separate out the "good" values from the total values.

This isn't always straightforward. Your service might have variable or diurnal traffic patterns, your metrics systems may only provide insight into your system at set intervals or via aggregates, you could have a significant long tail in the distribution of your

---

4 Measuring "correct data" can be incredibly difficult and sometimes fraught with problems, and it is often the case that you are measuring things "well enough" even if you don't get all the way to this point. This example serves to try and cover all of the bases, but don't worry if this isn't a realistic possibility for measuring your service.

metrics, or your events might only occur at a very low frequency. In such situations, it might make sense to only look at certain percentiles or to consider your time window as "good" when there are no recorded events and "bad" only when you explicitly have an error. The key is to have metrics that enable you to make statements that are either true or not, which will allow you to easily inform a percentage down the road.

Don't worry if the simplified terms in which we talk about service status in this chapter don't totally match up with the reality of your metrics or your service. We discuss how this all works in much more detail in various chapters in Part II of this book.

But now you might be thinking, "My service is much more complicated than just a simple request and response API. How can I measure that?"

Something More Complex

Our thought experiment involving a request and response API gave us a great starting point for some of the most important aspects of developing meaningful SLIs. By taking a step back and ensuring you're measuring the things your users actually care about, instead of looking only at all the intermediary metrics that might exist, you're well on your way to ensuring your service can be made more reliable for those users. But most modern services aren't just a single API. So, let's define something a little more complex.

Imagine you are in charge of a retail website. Like before, the details don't really matter. It's not of particular consequence for our discussion what this website sells; it's just a starting point for describing a service that is itself composed of many other services and components.

Figure 3-1 shows a very oversimplified example of what a retail website's architecture might look like. It's missing many components you might find in the real world, but we wouldn't gain much from trying to architect an entire solution here. We just need an example of a service that is composed of more than a single microservice.

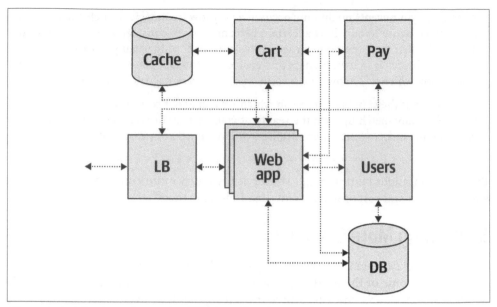

Figure 3-1. A basic and oversimplified retail website architecture

The setup here is pretty simple. At the center we have a web app that acts as our site server. This is where user requests enter, and where the corresponding web pages are constructed for rendering in the user's browser. This site server web app is likely the busiest part of the infrastructure, so it's distributed across multiple instances. It has to talk to a database in order to get accurate data about what to actually display for a user, and it also relies on a caching service layer to better handle serving frequently accessed assets such as the front page, images that exist on most pages such as the company logo, and information about the most popular items for sale.

Because there are multiple instances of this site server, there also needs to be some kind of load balancing solution. This load balancer sits in front of the web app and routes user requests from the internet to the site server app.

Behind the primary web app live a number of microservices. One handles things like user information, which also then requires a database that stores data like usernames, password hashes, and payment and shipping information.

There is also a shopping cart microservice, since something needs to be responsible for keeping track of what a user wants to purchase. This service probably relies on a database too, but it also likely has some kind of cache setup since shopping cart information is often more transient than other bits of data about a user, and that cache will ensure quicker responses as well.

The final piece of our simple retail website is a payment gateway microservice. Handling sensitive information like credit card numbers and actually charging them is a thing most people don't want to have to think about, so the primary purpose of this microservice is to interact with a third-party vendor that does the payment processing for us.

Now that we have this basic architecture defined, how might we think about the ways it needs to be reliable?

Measuring Complex Service User Reliability

This more complicated service has many more components, so we have many more things we need to measure. Let's go through some possible user interactions with this retail website service, and see how they might inform a meaningful SLI.

Just like with our simple web API example, the first thing you need to care about is if your service is both up and available. No matter what your service looks like or how it is architected, it won't do much for your users if they can't access it. Similarly, the service needs to respond in a timely manner, send an acceptable number of good responses compared to errors, and include the correct data in its responses. What "correct" data for a service like this looks like is where things start to diverge a bit.

Measuring correct data becomes more difficult for a more complex service for two separate but related reasons: because there are more ways to interact with multicomponent systems, user requests will have to travel through more logical routes in order for the service to appropriately respond to these interactions. Just to start off with, Table 3-1 identifies a number of these paths and the components such requests will have to interact with.

Table 3-1. Some example service interactions

Interaction	Components
Visit home page	Load balancers, web app, cache
Browse items	Load balancers, web app, database
Add/remove cart item	Load balancers, web app, cart service, cache, database
Edit shipping address	Load balancers, web app, user service, database
Purchase item	Load balancers, web app, payment gateway, third-party payment vendor

While all of these interactions rely on the load balancers (and the network in general) and the primary site serving app, every user journey follows a different logical service path. You'll have to make sure you develop a way to measure all of these different interactions, and all of them will require different ways of determining whether the response is correct or not.

You can likely get a lot of the way there by watching responses from the site server that aren't errors, and there is nothing wrong with using this as a starting point as it's a metric you likely already have available to you. But in order to get even better insight, you'll have to measure in a way that follows the entire logical service path from start to finish. As an example, let's imagine what it's like to attempt to log in to this service.

To determine if users are reliably able to log in, we could look at something like the error rate between the web app and the user microservice—but, this metric doesn't really mean much if most user login requests aren't reaching the user microservice in the first place. It also might not mean much if users are able to log in, but they're logged in as the wrong user. It might be a good idea for the team responsible for the login service to be monitoring and maybe even using login success/failure as the basis for their own SLI in order to determine how they are doing in terms of what other internal teams need. However, that's not a very representative or meaningful basis for an SLI for the external customers actually trying to buy things on this site.

 This chapter is focused on stopping what you're currently doing so you can make sure that you're examining all of the things that are required for a service to be reliable, so our examples have often been broad. However, it might also be the case that your service is very simple and only relied upon by a small number of other services. In a case like that, there is *nothing wrong* with having a simple SLI that only measures a few things. The point, as always, is just to make sure that you're thinking about what your users need. If all they need is responses that aren't errors, then that might be all you need, as well.

That being said, measuring the error rate between the site server web app and the user microservice isn't the worst way to start, because it does already encompass a different layer as well. Unless some strange error handling has been set up, looking at errors at that location in the service mesh should also expose errors when the user service tries to query or update the database. So, at least a few things are being measured at the same time. This could very well be a great starter SLI, especially since it's entirely possible you already have the data you need to power this sort of measurement.

But it's nowhere close to representing the entire user experience. If you want to have an SLI for your actual human customers that encompasses how they experience logging into your site, it has to start at the edge. (Or even beyond—remember that these users have internet connections that will not operate reliably at all times, as well!) You need to be able to say that requests that hit your load balancers are received, not rejected, and properly forwarded to a working instance of your web app, which then knows what to do with them. It should properly forward each request to the login microservice, which is able to talk to the database and verify that the username and password combination is correct. It then relays this information back to the site server web app, which is able to present a page that can be rendered correctly in the user's browser of choice. That is how you make sure you're measuring many things by measuring only a few. Complex systems don't make the actual measurement easy, but it shouldn't be too difficult to figure out what you should be trying to measure.

Our example up to this point doesn't include user journeys like adding things to the shopping cart or being able to pay, check out, and receive an order, but the concepts for those are the same. These sorts of user journeys are complex and complicated, and it would be next to impossible to accurately measure every single possible user interaction or data flow. But the closer you can get to what your users are actually doing and what they actually need, the more meaningful and representative your SLIs are going to be.

Just as your services can never be perfect, your measurements of them can never be perfect either. Things like latency or error rates are often easy to measure and calculate, especially when you only have a single component at play. As your systems get more complex and deeper, measuring everything correctly gets more difficult at some rate that is almost certainly steeper than linear. For many services it might make more sense to just ensure that each component is performing reliably enough in relation to the others, as opposed to capturing the entire user journey with a single measurement. You can use these individual measurements to inform an approximate view of the entire flow, and often that is more than good enough. Meaningful SLIs are about capturing data in a way that you might not be doing today, and it is of the utmost importance that that is being done from a user's perspective—but you don't have to entirely mimic their interactions to do so.

Another Written Example

What might the description for how to measure a slightly more complex service such as this one look like? In simple English, it might read like this:

> When clients external to our network provide a valid username and password combination, the site will reload in a logged-in state.

Again, this is a simple sentence that most people should be able to understand, even if the underlying technology that measures this is nontrivial and complex. Measuring this sort of thing is not always going to be easy. It might require a lot of custom code, standing up black box monitors in remote data centers, or very clever math using the white box metrics you already have. Even better is introducing a service tracing solution that allows you to measure every actual incoming user request instead of generating artificial ones (Chapter 7 covers how to do this kind of measurement in detail). But no matter how complicated the underlying approaches are, the best SLIs are always able to be used to write easy-to-explain sentences.

Business Alignment and SLIs

Once you take the time to take a step back and think about how to measure your service from your users' perspective, you're well on your way to adopting an SLO-based approach to reliability. There is even a fair argument to be made that this single step gets you most of the way through the story this book is trying to tell. One of the reasons why is that this step is one that's already kind of expected by other organizations in your business, even if no one else has noticed it yet.

Engineers want to work on fun new projects and write new code more than they want to clean up technical debt or fix bugs to make things more reliable; however, if those bugs pile up enough, they'll never actually have any time to work on those new projects. Product managers and the business want to ship new features and might not like seeing an entire month or quarter dedicated to just making things more reliable; however, if you let reliability out of your sight for too long, those new features may never work at all. It turns out that it's likely that all of these groups already want meaningful SLIs that inform reliability—they just think about things in a slightly different manner.

For example, let's think about our SLI measurement from the previous section. If you were to put that sentence in front of a product manager, they might say: "Sure, but that's not an SLI, that's a user journey." They very well may already have a document literally titled "User Journeys" that has your exact SLI defined in slightly different language. And if you took that SLI description and put it in front of the business aspect of your organization, they might say: "Sure, but that's not an SLI, that's a KPI." Taking this a step further, if you described your SLI to your QA or test engineering team, they might respond with: "We agree, but that's not an SLI, it's an interface test."

Chances are that many people at your company or in your organization are already entirely aligned in terms of what aspects of your service need to be measured and how important those are to users. It's just likely that the language you've all been using doesn't line up exactly. We'll cover how to ensure everyone is on the same page in various future chapters, but as you start your journey in developing SLIs, make sure you're thinking about how various aspects of your organization are thinking about these same things—because they probably already are.

Summary

Service level indicators are the single most important part of an SLO-based approach to reliability. You can use SLIs even if you don't have SLOs, and you have to have SLIs before you can have SLOs.

No matter what your service does, it isn't doing much if it isn't doing what its users need it to do, and the only way you can make sure that's true is by measuring things from that angle. In some cases, simple service level metrics might be all you need.

Maybe you can measure reliability just from locally reported error rates. Or perhaps you can use the throughput of various components of a pipeline to determine if things are running well enough. Sometimes you might have to write a brand new service that exists only to explore other services and see what they look like from the outside. But no matter which of these things might be true for your own service, they all require some moments of reflection as you stop thinking about what *you* need and instead place what *your users* need first.

Achieving everything outlined in this book isn't easy. It can take a lot of time, but you also might be surprised at how quickly you can ship out your first SLI/SLO—and how addicting it can be to continue that process. You might need to convince a lot of people of the usefulness of this approach. You might need to spend a lot of time developing documents, tooling, and workshops. You might have to ask people to think about things in a different way than they've ever done in the past. But don't let any of that discourage you. Get started with your first SLI today, then refine it over time. Pick an SLO target, and see how you perform against it. You don't need buy-in from everyone to get started. Achieving everything outlined in this book isn't easy, but you can often see value quickly by tackling the low-hanging fruit yourself.

That all being said, eventually you'll want to get buy-in from the entire organization to best utilize SLO-based approaches. Chapter 6 covers strategies for how to do that. In the meantime, even if you can't or haven't yet reached all of your goals, you can always develop meaningful SLIs. Thinking about your users first is never a bad idea.

CHAPTER 4

Choosing Good Service Level Objectives

Alex Hidalgo

Every system will fail at some point. Sometimes systems will fail in catastrophic ways, and other times they can fail in ways that are barely noticeable. System failures can be lengthy or last just fractions of a second. Some system failures require human intervention in order to get things back into a good state, while in other cases the system may start operating correctly again all by itself.

Chapter 3 discussed how to think about measuring if a service is doing what it is supposed to be doing, and from that framing we can define failure as when a service is *not* doing what it is supposed to be doing. A service failure does not have to mean there is an emergency. Things as simple as an API not sending a response quickly enough or the click of a button on a web form not registering are both failures. Failure happens all the time, because complex systems are fallible. This is all totally fine and expected and shouldn't stress you out.

Problems only arise when failures occur *too often* or *last too long*, and that's what service level objectives are all about. If a service level indicator gives you a good way to think about whether your service is performing in the manner it should be, a service level objective gives you a good way to think about whether your service is doing so often enough.

We've established that you can't be perfect, but how good should you try to be instead? This chapter looks to help you figure that out. First, we'll talk about what SLO targets really are and why it's important to choose them to the best of your ability. Second, we'll spend a little bit of time talking about service components and dependencies and how to take these into consideration when setting SLOs. After that, we'll get into some of the ways you can use data to help you pick these targets, including an introduction to the basic statistics you'll need in order to do so.

Reliability Targets

Fundamentally, SLOs are targets: they're a defined set of criteria that represent an objective that you're trying to reach. Good SLOs generally have two traits in common:

1. If you are exceeding your SLO target, your users are happy with the state of your service.

2. If you are missing your SLO target, your users are unhappy with the state of your service.

But what exactly do we mean by *user happiness*?

User Happiness

When we talk about user happiness in terms of service reliability, we're mostly appealing to the contentment aspect of happiness. It's not necessarily the case that the users of your service have to be actively and consciously overjoyed with their experience in order for them to be happy. For some people, it might be easier to think about it in terms of your users *not* being *unhappy*.

At some level, these ideas come from the concept that you need satisfied users in order to have a growing business. Reliability is a service feature that will often determine if people will choose to use yours as opposed to another one. Chances are that one of the goals of your service is to attract more users, even if you aren't strictly a business. Being reliable, and thinking about the happiness of your users, is a major component of this.

This is also applicable to services that do not strictly serve customers. For example, if you're in charge of the database offering for your organization, and your offering is seen as too unreliable by other engineers, they're going to find ways to work around this. They might spin up their own database instances when they really shouldn't, or they might try to solve data storage problems in a suboptimal manner that doesn't involve a database at all.

We could also imagine an internal service that users can't find a workaround for. Perhaps you maintain the Kubernetes layer at your organization. If users of this service (your fellow engineers) are too unhappy about its reliability, they'll eventually get fed up and find *some* way to move to a different service—even if that means actually leaving the company.

You want to make sure that you're reliable, and you want to make sure that your users are happy. Whatever targets you choose, they have to be ones that keep this in mind.

The Problem of Being Too Reliable

That all being said, you also don't want to be *too* reliable. There are a few reasons for this.

Imagine, for example, that you've chosen an SLO target percentage of 99.9%. You've done a lot of due diligence and followed the advice in this book in order to determine that this is the right objective for you. As long as you're exceeding this 99.9%, users aren't complaining, they aren't moving elsewhere, and your business is growing and doing well.

Additionally, if you miss this target by just a little bit, you likely won't immediately hemorrhage users. This is ideal, since it gives you time to say, "We've missed our target, so now we need to refocus our efforts to ensure we stay above it more often." You can use the data that your SLO provides you in order to make decisions about the service and the work you're performing.

However, let's now imagine that you're routinely being 99.99% reliable instead of just hitting your 99.9% target. Even if your SLO is published and discoverable, people are going to end up expecting that things will continue to be 99.99% reliable, because humans generally expect the future to look like the past.[1] Even if it was true that in the past everyone was actually happy with 99.9%, their expectations have now grown. Sometimes this is absolutely fine. Services and products can mature over time, and providing your users with a good experience is never a bad idea.

So maybe you make your official target more stringent, and now you aim for 99.99%. By doing so you're giving yourself fewer opportunities to fail but also fewer opportunities to learn. If you're being too reliable all the time, you're also missing out on some of the fundamental features that SLO-based approaches give you: the freedom to do what you want. If you're being too reliable, you're missing out on opportunities to experiment, perform chaos engineering, ship features quicker than you have before, or even just induce structured downtime to see how your dependencies react—in other words, a lot of ways to learn about your systems.

Additionally, you need to think about the concept of operational underload. People learn how to fix things by doing so. Especially in complex systems, you can learn so much from failures. There is almost no better way to learn about how systems work than to respond to them when they aren't performing how they're supposed to. If things never fail, you'll be missing out on all of that.

---

[1] Think, for example, about Hyrum's law, discussed in Chapter 2. There's also a great story about Chubby, a dependency for many services at Google, in Chapter 5.

Chapter 5 goes into much more detail about how to use error budgets, but ensuring you don't lose insight into how your services work by inducing failure or allowing it to occur is one of the main components at play. If your users and your business only need you to be 99.9% reliable, it is often a good idea to make sure you're not far beyond that. You'll still want to make sure that you're able to handle unforeseen issues, but you can set appropriate expectations as well as provide useful learning opportunities if you make sure you're not too reliable all the time. Pick SLO target percentages that allow for all of this to be true when you can.

The Problem with the Number Nine

In addition to the desire to be too reliable, there is another problem you can run into when picking the correct SLO for your service. When people talk about SLOs and SLAs, they most often think about things in terms of "nines."

Even if you don't want to aim for 100% reliability, you do almost always want to be fairly reliable, so it's not surprising that many common reliability targets are very close to 100%. The most common numbers you might run into are things like 99%, 99.9%, 99.99%, or even the generally unattainable 99.999%.[2] These targets are so common, people often even refer to them as just "two nines," "three nines," "four nines," and "five nines."

Table 4-1 shows what these targets actually look like in terms of acceptable bad time.[3]

Table 4-1. SLO targets composed of nines translated to time

Target	Per day	Per month	Per year
99.999%	0.9 s	26.3 s	5 m 15.6 s
99.99%	8.6 s	4 m 23 s	52 m 35.7 s
99.9%	1 m 26.4 s	43 m 49.7 s	8 h 45 m 57 s
99%	14 m 24 s	7 h 18 m 17.5 s	3 d 15 h 39 m

Not only can hitting these long strings of nines be much more difficult and expensive than people realize, but there is also a general problem where people only think about SLO targets as comprising series of the number nine, when in reality this doesn't

---

2 Trying to be 99.999% reliable over time means you can be operating unreliably for less than one second per day and only about 5 minutes and 15 seconds over the course of an entire year (Chapter 5 discusses how to do this math). This is an incredibly difficult target to reach. Even if your services are rock solid, everything depends on something else, and it is often unlikely that all of those dependencies will also consistently operate at 99.999% for extended periods of time.

3 These numbers were calculated via an excellent tool (*https://uptime.is/*) written by Kirill Miazine and are based upon calculations that assume a year has 365.25 days in order to account for leap years.

make any sense at all. Picking the right target for your service involves thinking about your users, your engineers, and your resources—it shouldn't be arbitrarily constrained in this way.

You might also see targets such as 99.95% or 99.98%, and including these is certainly an improvement over using only the number nine, but even here you're not always allowing yourself enough nuance to describe the requirements of your exact service.

There is absolutely nothing wrong with having an SLO defined as having a target of something like 99.97%, 98.62%, or even 87%. You can address having low target percentages by using percentiles in your definition—we'll talk more about that later in this chapter—but you should also make sure you aren't tied to thinking about these targets just in terms of the number nine.

Table 4-2 shows some other options and what amounts of bad time those translate into.

Table 4-2. SLO targets composed of not-just-nines translated to time

Target	Per day	Per month	Per year
99.95%	42.2s	5m2.4s	4h22m58.5s
99.7%	4m19.2s	30m14.4s	1d2h17m50.9ss
99.3%	10m4.8ss	5h6m48.2s	2d13h21m38.7s
98%	28m48s	14h36m34.9s	7d7h18m59s

That's not to say you should be aiming at a lower target if you don't have a reason to do so, but the difference between 99.9% and 99.99% (or something similar) is often much greater than people realize at first. You should be looking at the numbers in between as well.

Sometimes it's helpful to start with a time rather than a percentage. For example, it might be reasonable (or even required due to the daily downtime of your dependencies, locking backups taking place, and so on) to want to account for about two hours of unreliability per month. In that case 99.7% would be the correct starting point, and you could move on from there after seeing how you perform at that target for some time. Some of the most useful SLOs I have personally worked with have been set at carefully measured numbers like 97.2%, and there is nothing wrong with that. Later in this chapter we'll discuss in more depth how to do this math and make these measurements.

The Problem with Too Many SLOs

As you start on your journey toward an SLO-based approach to reliability, it might be tempting to set a lot of SLOs for your services. There is no correct number of SLOs to establish, and the number that will be correct for you will heavily depend on both how complex your services are and how mature the SLO culture in your organization is.

While you do want to capture the most important features of your system, you can often accomplish this by measuring only a subset of these features. Always ask yourself what your users need, and start by observing the most important and common of these needs. SLOs are a process, and you can always add (or remove!) them at any point that makes sense.

When the number of SLOs you have grows to be too large, you'll run into a few particular problems. First, it will be more difficult to make decisions using your data. If you view SLOs as providing you with data you can use to make meaningful choices about how to improve your service, having too many divergent data points can result in these decisions being harder to make. Imagine for example a storage service with a simple caching layer. It might not be necessary to have separate SLOs for both cache miss latency and cache hit latency for reads. You'll certainly still want to be collecting metrics on both, but you might just be adding noise if you have entirely independent SLOs for each. In this situation you could just have an SLO for general read latency, and if you start performing badly against your target, you can use your separate metrics to determine where the problem lies—hits, misses, or both—and what you need to address to make things better.

The second problem you can run into is that it becomes more complicated to report to others what the reliability status of your service has been. If you can provide someone outside of your team with the status of three to five SLOs over time, they can probably infer from that data both how your service has been running and how they could set their own targets if they depend on it. If they have to sort through dozens of SLOs, perhaps all with different target percentages and histories, you're not benefiting from one of the elements that this whole process is about: communicating your reliability to others in an easy-to-understand way.

More generally, there are statistical issues that arise with too many measurements. The *multiple comparison problem*, at its most basic, is one that arises due to the fact that if you have many different measurements of the same system, there are greater chances of incorrect measurements taking place. And even if the measurements are actually correct, if you're looking at too many things you'll always find something that looks just *slightly* off, which can just waste your time by sending you down endless rabbit holes.

Every system is unique, and there is no perfect answer to the question of how many SLOs you should define for any particular service. As with everything, try to be reasonable. SLOs are about providing you data to have discussions about, and you can't do that if you have too many data points to discuss.

Service Dependencies and Components

No service stands alone; everything depends on something else. Downstream, microservices often have dependencies that look like other microservices and databases. Services that appear to be mostly standalone will always have upstream dependencies, such as load balancers, routers, and the network in general. In both of these situations, these services will be dependent upon a compute layer of some sort, be that a container orchestration layer, a virtual machine infrastructure, or an operating system running on a bare-metal physical machine.

And we can go much deeper than that. An operating system running on a physical machine is dependent on that physical machine, which is dependent on things like power circuits, which are dependent on delivery from an electrical substation, and so forth. We could continue down this path virtually infinitely.

Because everything has many dependencies, it also turns out that services often have many components. Complex computer systems are made up of deep interwoven layers of service dependencies, and before you can set appropriate SLO targets, you need to understand how the various components of your services interact with each other.

Service Dependencies

When thinking about what kind of objective you can set for your service, you have to think about the dependencies your service has. There are two primary types of service dependencies. First are the hard dependencies. A *hard dependency* is one that *has* to be reliable for your service to be reliable. For example, if your service needs to read from a database in order to do what it is supposed to do, it cannot be reliable if that database isn't. Second are soft dependencies. A *soft dependency* is something that your service needs in order to operate optimally but that it can still be reliable without. Converting your hard dependencies into soft ones is one of the best steps you can take to make your service more reliable.

To choose a good service level objective, you have to start by examining how reliable your dependencies are. There's some simple math you can do to calculate the effect they have on the reliability your service can offer; I'll show you that after we dig a little more deeply into the issues of hard and soft dependencies.

Hard dependencies

Understanding the effect your known hard dependencies have on your service is not an overly complicated ordeal.[4] If the reliability of your service directly depends on the reliability of another service, your service cannot be any more reliable than that one is. There are two primary ways you can determine the reliability of a hard dependency.

The first is just to measure it. To continue with our database example, you can measure how many requests to this database complete without a failure—whether that be without an error or timeout, or quickly enough—directly from your own service. You don't have to have any kind of administrative access to the database to understand how it works from your perspective. In this situation, you are the user, and you get to determine what reliable means. Measure things for a while, and use the result to determine what kind of reliability you might be able to expect moving into the future.

The second, and more meaningful, way is to look at the published SLOs and reliability history of your dependencies, if they have them and they're shared with users. If the team responsible for the database you depend upon has internalized the lessons of an SLO-based approach, you can trust them to publish reasonable SLO targets. You can trust that team to take action if their service starts to exceed its error budget, so you can safely set your target a little lower than theirs.

Soft dependencies

Soft dependencies are a little more difficult to define than hard dependencies, and they also vary much more wildly in how they impact the reliability of your service. Hard dependencies are pretty simple to define and locate, and if a hard dependency isn't being reliable—whether it's entirely unavailable or just responding slowly—your service isn't being reliable during that time frame, either.

Soft dependencies, however, don't have this same one-to-one mapping. When they're unreliable the reliability of your service may be merely impacted, not nullified. A good example is services that provide additional data to make the user experience most robust, but aren't strictly required for it to function.

For example, imagine a maps application on your phone. The primary purpose of such an application could be to display maps of your immediate surroundings, show what businesses or addresses are located where, and help you orient yourself. The application might *also* allow you to overlay additional data such as traffic congestion,

---

4 Actually *identifying* all of your dependencies, however, *is* a complicated ordeal. This is why you need to measure the actual performance of your service, and not just set your targets based upon what your known dependencies have published. You almost certainly have dependencies you don't know about, and your known dependencies aren't all going to have perfectly defined SLOs.

user reviews of restaurants, or a satellite view. If the services that provide this traffic, user review, or satellite maps data aren't operating reliably, it certainly impacts the reliability of the maps application, but it doesn't make it wholly unreliable since the application can still perform its primary functions.

Turning hard dependencies into soft dependencies

One of the best things you can do in terms of making your service more reliable is to remove the hard dependencies it might have. Removing hard dependencies is not often a viable option, however, so in those situations you should think about how you might at least be able to turn them into soft dependencies instead.

For instance, going back to our database example, you might be able to introduce a caching layer. If much of the data is similar—or it doesn't necessarily have to be up-to-date to the second—using a cache could allow you to continue to operate reliably from the perspective of your users even if there are failures happening on the backend.

The topic of turning hard dependencies into soft ones is way too large for this book, but remember to think about this as you determine your SLO targets and use this as an example of the kind of work you could perform to increase the reliability of your service.

Dependency math

Perhaps the most important part of thinking about your service dependencies is understanding how to perform the math you need in order to take their reliability into account. You cannot promise a better reliability target than the things you are dependent on.

Most services aren't just individual pieces that float around in an empty sea. In a world of microservices where each might have a single team assigned to it, these services work together as a collective to comprise an entirely different service, which may not have a dedicated team assigned to it. Services are generally made up of many components, and when each of those components has its reliability measured—or its own SLO defined—you can use that data to figure out mathematically what the reliability of a multicomponent service might look like.

An important takeaway for now is how quickly a reasonable reliability target can erode in situations such as this. For example, let's say your service is a customer-facing API or website of some sort. A reasonably modern version of a service such as this could have dozens and dozens of internal components, from container-based microservices and larger monoliths running on virtual machines, to databases and caching layers.

Imagine you have 40 total components, each of which promises a 99.9% reliability target and has equal weight in terms of how it can impact the reliability of the collective service. In such situations, the service as a whole can only promise much less than 99.9% reliability. Performing this math is pretty simple—you just multiply 99.9% by itself 40 times:

$$0.9999^{40} = 0.96077021$$

So, 40 service components running at 99.9% reliability can only ensure that the service made up of these components can ever be 96% reliable. This math is, of course, overly simplistic compared to what you might actually see in terms of service composition in the real world, and Chapter 9 covers more complicated and practical ways to perform these kinds of calculations. The point for now is to remember that you need to be reasonable when deciding how stringent you are with your SLOs—you often cannot actually promise the reliability that you think or wish you could. Remember to stay realistic.

Service Components

As we've seen (for example, in the case of the retail website discussed in the previous chapter), a service can be composed of multiple components, some of which may themselves be services of different types. Such services generally fall into two categories: those whose components are owned by multiple teams, and those whose components are all owned by the same team. Naturally, this has implications when it comes to establishing SLIs and SLOs.

Multiple-team component services

When a service consists of many components that are owned by multiple teams, there are two primary things to keep in mind when choosing SLIs and SLOs.

The first is that even if SLOs are set for the entire service, or a subset of multiple components, each team should probably have SLIs and SLOs for its own components as well. The primary goal of SLO-based approaches to reliability is to provide you with the data you need to make decisions about your service. You can use this data to ask questions like: Is the service reliable enough? Should we be spending more time on reliability work as opposed to shipping new features? Are our users happy with the current state of the world? Each team responsible for a service needs to have the data to consider these questions and make the right decisions—therefore, all the components of a service owned by multiple teams should have SLOs defined.

The second consideration about services owned by many teams is determining who owns the SLOs that are set for the overarching service, or even just subsets of that service. Chapter 15 addresses the issue of ownership in detail.

Single-team component services

For services that consist of multiple components that are all owned by a single team, things can get a bit more variable. On the one hand, you could just apply the lessons of the multiple-team component services and set SLOs for every part of your stack. This is not necessarily a bad idea, but depending on the size or complexity of the service, you could also end up in a situation where a single team is responsible for and inundated by SLO definitions and statuses for what realistically is just a single service to the outside world.

When a single team owns all the components of what users think of as a service, it can often be sufficient to just define meaningful SLIs that describe enough of the user journeys and set SLOs for those measurements. For example, if you're responsible for a logging pipeline that includes a message queue, an indexing system, and data storage nodes, you probably don't need SLOs for each of those components. An SLI that measures the latency between when a message is inserted and when it is indexed and available for querying is likely enough to capture most of what your users need from you. Add in another SLI that ensures data integrity, and you've probably got most of your users' desires covered. Use those kinds of SLIs to set the minimum number of SLO targets you actually need, but remember to also use telemetry that tells you how each component is operating to help you figure out where to apply your reliability efforts when your data tells you to do so.

Reliability for Things You Don't Own

The classic example of how SLOs work involves a dichotomy between a development team and an operational team, both responsible for the same service in different ways. In this prototypical example, the development team wants to move fast and ship features, and the operations team wants to move slowly to ensure stability and reliability. SLOs are a way to ease this tension, as they give you data specifically aimed at determining when to move fast and when to move slow. This is the basic foundation of Site Reliability Engineering.

If your team or service doesn't fit into this model, however, that doesn't mean you can't adopt an SLO-based approach. If the service your team supports is open source, proprietary from a vendor, or hardware, you can't really use the primary example of "stop shipping features and focus on reliability code improvements instead"—but that doesn't mean you can't shift your focus to reliability. You just have to do it in a slightly different manner.

Open Source or Hosted Services

If you're relying on open source software for your infrastructure, as many companies do, you can still make changes to improve reliability—it's just that the changes you make are not always directly applicable to the code at the base of things. Instead, they're likely things like configuration changes, architecture changes, or changes to in-house code that complements the service in some way. This isn't to say that these sorts of changes don't also apply to services for which you own the entire codebase— just that the classic examples of how SLO-based approaches work often overlook them.

Additionally, you might be reliant on software that is entirely hosted and managed. This can make reliability approaches even more difficult, because in these situations there may not be many configuration or architecture changes you can make. Instead, when thinking about SLOs for these sorts of services, you might start with a baseline that represents the amount of failure a user can tolerate and use this data to justify either renewing a contract or finding a new vendor that can meet your needs.

Measuring Hardware

Chances are there are many different hardware components you might like to observe and measure, but it's not often worth your time unless you're operating at a certain scale. Commercial and enterprise-grade computer hardware is generally already heavily vetted and measured by the manufacturers, and you often cannot develop a system of measurement with enough meaningful data points unless you are either a hardware development company, a telco/internet service provider, or one of the largest web service providers. Remember that unless you introduce complicated math to normalize your data, you generally need quite a few data points in order to ensure that your SLIs aren't triggered only by outliers.

That all being said, you don't *have* to operate at the scale of a telco or one of the largest tech companies to meaningfully measure the failure rates or performance of your hardware. For example, imagine you're responsible for 2,000 servers in various data centers across the planet. Though the number 2,000 isn't necessarily very large when it comes to statistical analysis, the numbers derived from it could be. You might have 8 hard drives or DIMMs per server, which gives you 16,000 data points to work with. That might be enough for you to develop meaningful metrics about how long your hardware operates without a fault.

Another option is to get aggregated data from other sources, and then apply those same metrics to your own hardware. It can be difficult to get failure rate data from vendors directly, but many resellers collect this data and make it available to their paying customers. You can use this sort of information to help you anticipate the potential failure rates of your own hardware, allowing you to set SLOs that can inform you when you should be ordering replacements or when you should be retiring old systems.

In addition to reseller vendors, there are other aggregated sources of data about hardware failure. For example, Backblaze, a major player in the cloud storage space, releases reports every year about the failure rates of the various hard drive makes and models it employs.

The point is that if you don't have a large enough footprint to use your own measurements to develop statistically sound numbers, you can rely on those who have done this aggregation for you. We'll also be discussing statistical models you can use to meaningfully predict things you only have sporadic data for in Chapter 9.

But I am big enough!

Of course, you might work for a company that operates at such a scale that you can measure your own hardware failure rates easily. Perhaps you're even a hardware manufacturer looking to learn about how you can translate failure data into more meaningful data for your customers!

If you have a lot of data, developing SLO targets for your hardware performance doesn't really deviate from anything discussed elsewhere in this book. You need to figure out how often you fail, determine if that level is okay with the users of your hardware, and use that data to set an SLO target that allows you to figure out whether you're going to lose users/customers due to your unreliability or not.

If your SLO targets tell you that you're going to lose users, you need to immediately pivot your business to figuring out how to make your components more reliable or you are necessarily going to make less money.

The point is that even as the provider of the bottom layer of everything computers rely upon, you're likely aware that you can't be perfect. You cannot deliver hardware components to all of your customers that will function properly all of the time. Some of these components will eventually fail. Some will even be shipped in a bad state. Know this and use this knowledge to make sure you're only aiming to prevent the correct amount of failures. You'll never prevent 100% of them, so pick a target that doesn't upset your users and that you won't have to spend infinite resources attempting to attain.

Beyond just hardware

In an absolutely perfect world, all SLOs would be built from the ground up. Since anything that is dependent on another system cannot strictly be more reliable than the one it depends on, it would be most optimal if each dependency in the chain had a documented reliability target.

For example, power delivery is required for all computer systems to operate. So, perhaps the first step in your own reliability story is knowing how consistently reliable levels of electricity are being delivered to the racks that your servers reside in. Then you have to consider if those racks have redundant circuits providing power. Then you have you consider the failure rates of the power supply units that deliver power to the other components of your servers. This goes on and on.

 Don't be afraid of applying the concepts outlined in this book to things that aren't strictly software-based services. In fact, remember from the Preface that this same approach can likely be applied to just about any business. Chapter 5 covers some of the ways in which you can use SLOs and error budgets to address human factors.

Choosing Targets

Now that we've established that you shouldn't try to make your target too high, and that your target doesn't have to be comprised of just the number nine many times in a row, we need to talk about how you can pick the correct target.

The first thing that needs to be repeated here is that SLOs aren't SLAs—they aren't agreements. When you're working through this process, you should absolutely keep in mind that your SLO should encompass things like ensuring your users are happy and that you can make actionable decisions based upon your measured performance against this SLO; however, you also need to remember that you can change your SLO if the situation warrants it. There is no shame in picking a target and then changing it in short order if it turns out that you were wrong. All systems fail, and that includes humans trying to pick magic numbers.[5]

Past Performance

The best way to figure out how your service might operate in the future is studying how it has operated in the past. Things about the world and about your service will absolutely change—no one is trying to deny that. But if you need a starting point in order to think about the reliability of your service, the best starting point you'll likely have is looking at its history. No one can predict the future, and the best alternative we have is extrapolating from the past.

---

5 Chapter 14 discusses how to evolve your SLO targets in great detail.

You may or may not want to discount previous catastrophes here. Severe incidents are often outlier events that you can learn important lessons from, but are not always meaningful indicators in terms of future performance. As always, use your own best judgment, and don't forget to account for the changes in the robustness of your service or the resilience of your organization that may have come from these lessons learned.

All SLOs are informed by SLIs, and when developing your SLIs, it will often be the case that you'll have to come up with new metrics. It will sometimes be the case that you might need to collect or export data in entirely new ways, but other times you might determine that your SLI is a metric you've already been collecting for some amount of time.

No matter which of these is true, you can use this SLI to help you pick your SLO. If it's a new metric, you might have to collect it for a while first—a full calendar month is often a good length of time for this. Once you've done that, or if you already have a sufficient amount of data available, you can use that data about your past performance to set your first SLO. Some basic statistics will help you do the math.

 Even if you have a solid grasp of basic statistics, you might still find value in reading about how to use these techniques within an SLO-specific context. Chapter 9 covers more advanced statistical techniques.

Basic Statistics

Statistical approaches can help you think about your data and your systems in incredibly useful ways, especially when you already have data you can analyze. We'll go into much more depth on the math for picking SLO targets in various chapters in Part II, but this section presents some basic and approachable techniques you can use to analyze the data you have available to you for this purpose. For some services, you might not even need the more advanced techniques described in future chapters, and you might be able to rely mostly on the ones outlined here.

That being said, while we'll tie basic statistical concepts to how they relate to SLOs in the next few pages, those who feel comfortable with the building blocks of statistical analysis can skip ahead to "Metric Attributes" on page 61.

The five Ms

Statistics is a centuries-old discipline with many different uses, and you can leverage the models and formulae developed by statisticians in the past to help you figure out what your data is telling you. While some advanced techniques will require a decent amount of effort to apply correctly, you can get pretty good insight into how an SLI is performing, and therefore what your SLO should look like, with basic math.

The building blocks of statistical analysis are five concepts that all begin with the letter *M*: min, max, mean, median, and mode. These are not complicated concepts, but they can give you excellent insight into time series–based data. In Table 4-3 you can see an example of a small time series dataset (known as a *sample*, indicating that it doesn't represent all data available but only some portion of it).

Table 4-3. Time series sample

Time	16:00	16:01	16:02	16:03	16:04	16:05	16:06	16:07	16:08	16:09
Value	1.5	6	2.4	3.1	21	9.1	2.4	1	0.7	5

When dealing with statistics it's often useful to have things sorted in ascending order, as shown in Table 4-4, so while the time window from which you've derived your sample is important for later context, you can throw it out when performing the statistics we're talking about here.

Table 4-4. Time series sample in ascending order

Value	0.7	1	1.5	2.4	2.4	3.1	5	6	9.1	21

The *min* value of a time series is the minimum value observed, or the lowest value. The *max* value of a time series is the maximum value observed, or the highest value. These are pretty easily understood ideas, but it's important that you use them when looking at SLI data in order to pick proper SLOs. If you don't have a good understanding of the total scope of possibilities of the measurements you're making, you'll have a hard time picking the right target for what these measurements should be. Looking at Table 4-4, we can see that the min value of our dataset is 0.7 and the max value is 21.

The third M word you need to know is *mean*. The *mean* of a dataset is its average value, and the words *mean* and *average* are generally interchangeable. A mean, or average, is the value that occurs when you take the sum of all values in your dataset and divide it by the total number of values (known as the *cardinality* of the set). We can compute the mean for our time series via the following equation:

$$\frac{(0.7 + 1 + 1.5 + 2.4 + 2.4 + 3.1 + 5 + 6 + 9.1 + 21)}{10} = 5.52$$

There is nothing terribly complicated about computing a mean, but it provides an incredibly useful and simple insight into the performance of your SLI. In this example, we now know that even though we had a min value of 0.7 and a max value of 21, the average during the 10 minutes of data that we're analyzing was 5.52. This kind of data can help you pick better thresholds for your SLOs. Calculating the mean value for a measurement is more reliable than looking at a graph and trying to eyeball what things are "normally" like.

The fourth M word is *median*. The *median* is the value that occurs right in the middle. In our case, we are looking at a dataset that contains an even number of values, so there is no exact middle value. The median of the data in situations like this is the mean of the two middle values. In our case this would be the 5th and 6th values, or 2.4 and 3.1, which have a mean of 2.75.

The median gives you a good way to split your data into sections. It'll become clearer why that is useful when we introduce percentiles momentarily, but what should hopefully be immediately clear is that the mean for this data is higher than the median value. This tells you that you have more values below your average than you have above it—in this case, 7 values compared to 3—which lets you know that the higher-value observations happen less frequently, and that they contain outliers. Knowing about outliers can help you think about where to set thresholds in terms of what might constitute a good observation versus a bad one for your service. Sometimes these outliers are perfectly fine in the sense that they don't cause unhappy users, and other times they can be indicative of severe problems, but at all times outliers are worth investigating more to know which category they fit into.

The fifth and final M word is *mode*. The *mode* of a dataset is the value that occurs most frequently. In our example dataset the mode is 2.4, because it occurs twice and all the other values occur only once. When no value occurs more than once, there is no mode. When multiple values occur at the same frequency, the dataset is said to be *multimodal*. The concept of counting the occurrences of values in a sample is very important, but is much better handled via things like frequency distributions and histograms, which are introduced in Chapter 9. The mode is only included here for the sake of completeness in our introduction to statistical terminology.

Ranges

Another important basic statistical concept is that of a *range*, which is simply the difference between your max value and your min value, which lets you know how widely distributed your values are. In our sample (Table 4-4), the min value is 0.7 and the max value is 21. The math to compute a range is just simple arithmetic:

$$21 - 0.7 = 20.3$$

Ranges give you a great starting point in thinking about how varied your data might be. A large range means you have a wide distribution of values; a small range means you have a slim distribution of values. Of course, what wide or slim could mean in your situation will also be entirely dependent on the cardinality of the values you're working with.

While ranges give you a great starting point in thinking about how varied your dataset is, you'll probably be better served by using the concept of *deviations*. Deviations are more advanced ways of thinking about how your data is distributed; Chapter 9 talks about how to better think about the distribution, or *variance*, of your data.

Percentiles

A percentile is a simple but powerful concept when it comes to developing an understanding of SLOs and what values they should be set at. When you have a group of observed values, a *percentile* is a measure that allows for you to think about a certain percentage of them. In the simplest terms, it gives you a way of referring to all the values that fall at or below a certain percentage value in a set.

For example, for a given dataset, the 90th percentile will be the threshold at which you know that all values below the percentile are the bottom 90% of your observations, and all values above the percentile are the highest 10% of your observations.

Using our example data from earlier, values falling within the 90th percentile would include every value except the 10th one. When working with percentiles you'll often see abbreviations in the form PX, where X is the percentile in question. Therefore, the 90th percentile will often be referred to as the P90. If you wanted to isolate the bottom 50% of your values, you would be talking about values below the 50th percentile, or the P50 (which also happens to be the median, as discussed previously). While percentiles can be useful at almost any value, depending on your exact data, there are also some common levels at which they are inspected. You will commonly see people analyzing data at levels such as the P50 (the median), P90, P95, P98, and P99, and even down to the P99.9, P99.99, and P99.999.

When developing SLOs, percentiles serve a few important purposes. The first is that they give you a more meaningful way of isolating outliers than the simpler concept of medians can. While both percentiles and medians split your data into two sets— below and above—percentiles let you set this division at any level. This allows you to look at your data split into many different bifurcations. You can use the same dataset and analyze the P90, P95, and P99 independently. This kind of thinking allows you to address the concept of a *long tail*, which is where your data skews in magnitude in one direction or the other, but perhaps not with a frequency that is meaningful.

The second way that percentiles are useful in analyzing your data for SLOs is that they can help you pick targets in a very direct manner. For example, let's say that you calculate the P99 value for a month of data about successful database transaction times. Once you know this threshold, you now also know that if you had used it as your SLO target, you would have been reliable 99% of the time over your analyzed time frame. Assuming performance will be similar in the future, you could aim for a 99% target moving forward as well.

 Calculating common percentiles based upon your current data is a great starting point in choosing an initial target percentage. Not only do they help you identify outliers that don't reflect the general user experience, but your metrics data will sometimes simply be more useful to analyze with those outliers removed. Another common way to achieve these results and better understand your data involves histograms, which we'll discuss in Chapter 9.

Metric Attributes

A lot of what will go into picking a good SLO will depend on exactly what your metrics themselves actually look like. Just like everything else, your metrics—and therefore your SLIs—will never be perfect. They could be lacking in resolution, because you cannot collect them often enough or because you need to aggregate them across many sources; they could be lacking in quantity, since not every service will have meaningful data to report at all times; or they could be lacking in quality, perhaps because you cannot actually expose the data in the exact way that you wish you could.

Chapter 1 talked about how an SLI that allows you to report good events and total events can inform a percentage. Though this is certainly not an incorrect statement, it doesn't always work that way in the real world—at least not directly. While it might be simplest to think about things in terms of good events over total events, it's not often the case that your metrics actually correlate to this directly. Your "events" in how this math works might not really be "events" at all.

Resolution

One of the most common problems you'll run into when figuring out SLO target percentages revolves around the resolution of your metrics. If you want a percentage informed by good events over total events, what do you do if you only have data about your service that is able to be reported—or collected—every 10, 30, or 60 seconds?

If you're dealing with high-resolution data, this is probably a moot point. Even if the collection period is slow or sporadic, you can likely just count aggregate good and total events and be done with it.

But not all metrics are high resolution, so you might have to think about things in terms of windows of time. For example, let's say you want a target percentage of 99.95%. This means that you're only allowed about 43 seconds of bad time per day:

$$(1 - 0.9995) \times 24 \times 60 \times 60 = 43.2$$

To work this out, you first subtract your target percentage from 1 to get the acceptable percentage of bad observations. Then, to convert this into seconds per day, you multiply that value by 24 (hours per day), then by 60 (minutes per hour), then by 60 again (seconds per minute).

In this case, you would exceed your error budget with just a single bad observation if your data exists at a resolution of 60 seconds, since you would immediately incur 60 seconds of bad time. There are ways around this if these bad observations turn out to be false positives of some sort. For example, maybe you need for your metric to be below (or above) a certain threshold for two consecutive observations before you count even just one of them against your percentage. However, this also might just mean that 99.95% is the wrong target for a system with metrics at that resolution. Changing your SLO to 99.9% would give you approximately 86 seconds of error budget per day, meaning you'd need two bad observations to exceed your budget.

Exactly what effect your resolution will have on your choice of reliability target is heavily dependent on both the resolution and the target at play. Additionally, the actual needs of your users will need to be accounted for. While we will not enumerate more examples, because they're potentially endless, make sure you take metric resolution into consideration as you choose a target.

Quantity

Another common problem you could run into revolves around the quantity of your metrics. Even if you are able to collect data about your service at a one-second interval, your service might only have an event to report far less frequently than that. Examples of this include batch scheduler jobs, data pipelines with lengthy processing periods, or even request and response APIs that are infrequently talked to or have strong diurnal patterns.

When you don't have a large number of observations, target percentages can be thrown for a loop very quickly. For example, if your data processing pipeline only completes once per hour, a single failure in a 24-hour period results in a reliability of 95.83% over the course of that single day. This might be totally fine—one failure every day could actually be a perfectly acceptable state for your service to be in—and maybe you could just set something like a 95% SLO target to account for this. In situations like this, you'll need to make sure that the time window you care about in terms of alerting, reporting, or even what you display on dashboards is large enough to encompass what your target is. You can no longer be 95% reliable at any given moment in time; you have to think about your service as being 95% reliable over a 24-hour period.

Even then, however, you could run into a problem where two failures over the course of two entire days fall within 24 hours of each other. To allow for this, you either have to make the window you care about very large or set your reliability target down to 90%, or even lower. Any of these options might be suitable. The important thing to remember is that your target needs to result in happy users over time when you're meeting it, and mark a reasonable point to pivot to discussing making things more reliable when you're not.

For something like a request and response API that either has low traffic at all times or a diurnal (or other) pattern that causes it to have low traffic at certain times, you have a few other options in addition to using a large time window.

The first is to only calculate your SLO during certain hours. There is nothing wrong with saying that all time periods outside of working hours (or all time periods outside of 23:00 to 06:00, or whatever makes sense for your situation) simply don't count. You could opt to consider all observations during those times as successes, no matter what the metrics actually tell you, or you could just ignore observations during those times. Either of these approaches will make your SLO target a more reasonable one, but could make an error budget calculation more complicated. Chapter 5 covers how to better handle error budget outliers and calculations in more detail.

The other option available to you is using some advanced probability math like confidence intervals. Yes, that is a complicated-sounding phrase. Yes, they are not always easy to implement. But don't worry, Chapter 9 has a great primer on how this works.

Services with low-frequency or low-quantity metrics can be more difficult to measure, especially in terms of calculating the percentages you use to inform an SLO target, but you can use some of these techniques to help you do so.

Quality

The third attribute that you need to keep in mind for the metrics informing your SLIs and SLOs is quality. You don't have quality data if it's inaccurate, noisy, ill-timed, or badly distributed. You could have large quantities of data available to you at a high resolution, but if this data is frequently known to be of a low quality, you cannot use it to inform a strict target percentage. That doesn't mean you can't use this data; it just means that you might have to take a slightly more relaxed stance.

The first way you can do this is to evaluate your observations over a longer time window before classifying them as good or bad. Perhaps you measure things in a way that requires your data to remain in violation of your threshold in a sustained manner for five or more minutes before you consider it a bad event. This lowers your potential resolution, but does help protect against noisy metrics or those prone to delivering false positives. Additionally, you can use percentages to inform other percentages. For example, perhaps you require 50% of all the metrics to be in a bad state over the five-minute time window before you consider that you have had a single bad event that then counts toward your actual target percentage.

 Using the techniques we've described here, as well as those covered in Chapters 7 and 9, you can even make low-quality data work for you—though you just might need to set targets lower than what your service actually performs like for your users. As long as your targets still ensure that users are happy when you exceed them and aren't upset until you miss them by too much for too long, they're totally reasonable. It doesn't matter what the percentage actually is. Don't let anyone trick you into thinking that you have to be close to 100% in your measurements. It's simply not always the case.

Percentile Thresholds

When choosing a good SLO, it's also important to think about applying percentile thresholds to your data. It's rarely true that the metrics that you're able to collect can tell you enough of the story directly. You'll often have to perform some math on them at some point.

The most common example of this is using percentiles to deal with value distributions that might skew in one direction or the other in comparison with the mean. This kind of thing is very common with latency metrics (although not exclusive to them!), when you're looking at API responses, database queries, web page load times, and so on. You'll often find that the P95 of your latency measurements has a small range while everything above the P95 has a very large range. When this happens, you may not be able to rely on some of the techniques we've outlined to pick a reliable SLO target.

Let's consider the example web page load time again, since it's a very easy thought experiment everyone should be familiar with. You're in charge of a website, and you've done the research and determined that a 2,000 ms load time keeps your users happy, so that's what you want to measure. But once you have metrics to measure this, you notice that your web pages take longer than 2,000 ms to load a full 5% of the time, even though you haven't been hearing any complaints. You could just set your target at 95%—and this might not be the wrong move—but you gain a few advantages by using percentiles instead. That is, you could say that you want web pages to load within 2,000 ms at the 95th percentile, 99.9% of the time.

The primary advantage of this approach is that you can continue to monitor and care about what your long tail actually looks like. For example, let's say that your P95 observed values generally fall below 2,000 ms, your P98 values fall below 2,500 ms, and your P99 values fall below 4,000 ms. When 95% of page loads complete within 2 seconds, your users may not care if an additional 4% of them take 4 seconds; they may not even care if 1% of them take 10 seconds or time out entirely. But what users *will* care about is if suddenly a full 5% of your responses start taking 10 seconds or more.

By not just caring about the bottom 95% of your latency SLI by setting an SLO target of 95%, and instead caring about a high percentage of your P95 completing quickly enough, you free yourself up to look at your other percentiles. Based on the preceding examples, you could now set additional SLOs that make sure your P98 remains below 2,500 ms and your P99 remains below 4,000 ms. Now you have three targets that help you tell a more complete story, while also allowing you to notice problems within any of those ranges independently, instead of just discarding some percentage of the data:

1. The P95 of all requests will successfully complete within 2,000 ms 99.9% of the time.

2. The P98 of all requests will successfully complete within 2,500 ms 99.9% of the time.

3. The P99 of all requests will successfully complete within 4,000 ms 99.9% of the time.

With this approach, you'll be able to monitor if things above the 95th percentile start to change in ways that make your users unhappy. If you try to address your long tail by setting a 95% target, you're discarding the top 5% of your observations and won't be able to discover new problems there.

Another advantage of using percentiles is a reporting one. This book preaches an idea that may have been best summarized by Charity Majors (*https://open.nytimes.com/ talking-technology-nick-rockwell-charity-majors-2acad1690dcf*): "Nines don't matter if users aren't happy." While this is true, a long tail accommodated by a lower target percentage can be misleading to those newer to SLO-based approaches. Instead, you can use percentiles to make your written SLO read more intuitively as a "good" one. You shouldn't set out to purposely mislead anyone, of course, but you can always choose your language carefully so as to not alarm people.

What to Do Without a History

What should you do if you're trying to set SLOs for a service that doesn't yet exist, or otherwise doesn't have historical metrics for you to analyze? How can you set a reasonable target if you don't yet have any users, and therefore may not know what an acceptable failure percentage might look like for them? The honest answer is: just take an educated guess!

SLOs are objectives, they're not formal agreements, and that means you can change them as needed. While the best way to pick an SLO that might hold true into the future is to base it on data you've gathered, not every SLO *has* to hold true into the future. In fact, SLO targets should change and evolve over time. Chapter 14 covers this in depth.

There may be other sources of data you can draw upon when making your educated guess—for example, the established and trusted SLOs of services that yours might depend on, or ones that will end up depending on yours. As you've seen, your service can't be more reliable than something it has a hard dependency on, so you need to take that into account when picking an initial target.

It's also true that not every service has to have an SLO at launch—or even at all. An SLO-based approach to reliability is a way of thinking: are you doing what you need to do, and are you doing so often enough? It's about generating data to help you ask those questions in a better way. If your service doesn't yet have the metrics or data you need to be able to ask those questions in a mathematical way, you can always make sure you're thinking about these things even without that data.

However, there are ways to make sure you're thinking about SLIs and SLOs as you architect a service from the ground up. Chapter 10 discusses some of these techniques.

Summary

Every system will fail at some point. That's just how complex systems work. People are actually aware of this, and often okay with it, even if it doesn't always seem obvious at first. Embrace this. You can take actions to ensure you don't fail too often, but there isn't anything you can do to prevent every failure for all time—especially when it comes to computer systems.

But if failures don't always matter, how do you determine when they *do* matter? How do you know if you're being reliable enough? This is where choosing good SLOs comes in. If you have a meaningful SLI, you can use it to power a good SLO. This can give you valuable insight into how reliable your users think you are, as well as provide better alignment about what "reliable" actually means across departments and stakeholders. You can use the techniques in this chapter to help you start on your journey to doing exactly that.

CHAPTER 5

How to Use Error Budgets

Alex Hidalgo

Error budgets are the final part of the Reliability Stack, and it takes a lot of effort and resources to use them properly. Not every team, organization, or company always gets to this part. It's not that thinking about error budgets is necessarily difficult or complicated, but actually using them as data to drive decisions will change how things work for many people.

In a software-based work environment, systems are often already in place to coordinate and mandate how work is done—including reliability work. You might follow some version of Agile and have sprints, you might simply have quarterly OKRs you work toward, or you might be an operational team that staffs a 24/7 control center that is tasked primarily with responding to customer requests or tickets. There are many ways that your organization may go about trying to keep things reliable.

Despite seeming straightforward, adopting an error budget approach to reliability can be a shocking change for some people, and it often doesn't align with the methods and processes you already have in place. This is all fine; remember that the aim of this book is to present a new way of thinking about your users, a new way of collecting data about their experiences, and a new way of having discussions about the state of your services. You don't have to subscribe to everything described in these pages. Crafting user-focused SLI measurements and using those to decide how to prioritize your work is your actual end goal; it's just that setting SLO targets and using error budgets can make having discussions about this prioritization easier. They're ways of performing math that better surface what your priorities might be.

Getting the cultural buy-in you need to use error budgets to drive monitoring, alerting, and decision making is often a long road, but if you can get there you'll find yourself with all kinds of great new data you can use for these purposes.

Error Budgets in Practice

The basic premise of error budgets was described in Chapter 1 as "Release new features when you have budget; focus on reliability when you don't," but this is a very simplistic view. For example, it's often by shipping features that you improve your reliability. Remember that reliability isn't just uptime; it's doing what your users need you to do. Shipping new features is often a part of that story.

 As already stated, SLOs are about collecting data regarding the reliability of your service in a different (and hopefully more meaningful) way. You can use this data for many things, including the following:

- Discovering reliability problems you weren't aware of before
- Communicating with other teams or users about how reliable you aim to be
- Alerting based upon a user-centric view of service performance
- Reporting to others how reliable you've been over a time period
- Establishing error budgets

An error budget is a way of measuring SLO performance over time. We've already discussed the concepts of either having an allowed number of errors or an allowed amount of bad minutes, and error budgets are a formal measurement of that. They allow you to say things like, "We are burning through our budget at the rate of 1% per day" or "We have 15 minutes of error budget remaining." These statements make it easier for people to understand the current situation you find yourself in, and they make it easier to have discussions about where your work should be focused: "Are we free to proceed as normal, or do we need to stop and examine the reliability of our service?"

 In many ways error budgets are primarily a communications framework. They give you a common language to use in order to have discussions with others—either on your own team or across your organization or company.

Using error budgets to make decisions is a sign that the maturity of the SLO culture in your organization is reaching high levels. Getting to this point is not easy. If there were some official hierarchy, the only more advanced part of an SLO-based approach would likely be abandoning all of your alerts and only paging on error budget burn rate (discussed in Chapter 8). But once you do get to this point, you'll find that error budgets give you a lot of freedom and a great new data source.

 It should be stressed again that the most important thing at play here is that this is a different kind of data, allowing you to have different and better conversations to make decisions. You can fall into a dangerous trap if you consider error budget status and how you respond to it as a hard-and-fast rule. A primary tenet of SLO-based approaches to reliability is that nothing is ever perfect. That means your measurements and your error budgets won't be either. Remain reasonable (and at times even skeptical) about what the numbers are telling you.

Before we delve into how to measure error budgets, let's talk about what benefits you'll get once you do so.

To Release New Features or Not?

The most common example is using your budget to decide whether you should ship new features. As normally described, this implies that there is a development team and an operational or SRE team that work in some kind of opposition to each other. This dichotomy does exist, and does serve as a great starting point for our conversation, even if it doesn't look exactly like your organization.

Budgets Are Budgets

Rarely under this system should you actually stop releasing things. This is a frequent misconception about properly using error budgets. I have seen way too many examples where all releases are frozen when the error budget is burned, causing an immediate, difficult-to-resolve incident when all the changes that queued up during the freeze are released at once. Don't freeze your pipeline unless you only have one product and believe it to be truly the best choice. You need to continue to work on your product, and at the *very least* you'll need your release cycle to help you address potential reliability concerns.

You should think of your budget as exactly that: a budget. Just as maybe you shouldn't book an expensive vacation when you're low on cash and your household budget won't allow it, maybe you shouldn't release brand new features that could fundamentally change how your service works if your error budget is low.

Or maybe you should! Maybe you really need a vacation, and having it on your calendar will be reinvigorating. In this same manner, perhaps you do want to ship a brand new feature when you're low on error budget, because you know your users have been waiting for it, and maybe their delight with the feature they've been waiting for will help them forget about your recent unreliability issues.

Even with all of these caveats, stopping deploys is not *necessarily* a bad thing, especially if your organization doesn't have a robust and trusted testing and release pipeline. In some cases it may be prudent to halt all releases for some amount of time.

As always, this data is just a model to help you think about things from your users' point of view.

In this stereotypical setup, you have a development team that works with a product team to develop and ship features. These teams want to ship features as fast as possible, since their entire goal is to make these features available to users. On the other side of the fence you have a team that is responsible for actually keeping the service up and running. This operational team doesn't love shipping features at a high rate, because changes cause failures. Some changes are out of people's control—a server experiences hardware problems, a dependency fails on you, and so forth—but every single release of a new binary is also a change, and these can be gated or slowed down. Naturally, a tension builds because one side wants to ship features, and the other side wants things not to change too often.

This is the classic example of where error budgets come into play. By developing meaningful SLIs that inform well-chosen SLOs, you can then establish useful error budgets that provide you with data you can point to in order to allow both sides to remain happy.[1] If your service remains reliable, you can push new releases whenever you want; if it becomes too unreliable, maybe you need to stop all releases except for those that directly address the reliability of the service.

Project Focus

Beyond just deciding whether new features should be shipped or not, you can use error budgets to drive the entire focus of your project work. This kind of scenario is more applicable to a situation where the development team is also the team responsible for keeping the service up and running, or for teams that support software they don't own the source code for. For example, it is incredibly common to use open source tooling for things like infrastructure: logging systems, metrics platforms, databases, load balancers, pub/sub systems, and so on. If you're responsible for keeping something like that running, you can't say "Don't release features!" unless you're willing to fork the codebase.

In both of these situations—singular teams responsible for writing the code and operations or teams that support open source solutions—you can use error budgets to

---

1 Do note that you can also run into issues with backpressure if development work is allowed to continue but you just aren't releasing features. We'll discuss this in more detail when we talk about calendar-bound time windows later in this chapter.

change the focus of your project work instead of using a strict "features versus reliability" dichotomy.

For single teams, this might mean dropping all of your current project work—even if you're in the middle of a sprint—and picking up tickets that address reliability-focused issues instead. Or perhaps your error budget hasn't been entirely depleted—in this case your policies might state that you just pivot your entire next sprint to reliability instead of dropping everything on the floor right then and there, or that a single engineer is assigned to reliability improvements while the rest of the team continues as normal. The point, as always, is that error budgets give you additional data with which you can have better discussions and make better decisions.

For teams that are responsible for open source infrastructure, error budget policy violations could result in a very long list of potential actions. Perhaps you need to spin up more instances of your databases, or introduce an additional piece of infrastructure that does a better job of load balancing or that provides a caching layer. There might be configuration changes you could make, or perhaps a version upgrade will fix the bug you're running into that's causing the error budget burn. The options here are numerous, but the underlying concept is the same as in the case of a single team responding: if your error budget is giving you meaningful data, drop some amount of your current work and pivot to reliability-focused project work instead.

Examining Risk Factors

Measuring error budgets over time can give you great insight into the risk factors that impact your service, both in terms of frequency and severity. By knowing what kinds of events and failures are bad enough to burn your error budget, even if just momentarily, you can better discover what factors cause you the most problems over time.

For example, by analyzing your error budget over a year, you might determine that approximately one in every five releases causes some amount of error budget burn. This could help point you to the fact that you need a smoother release process or better testing.[2] Even if your budget is never exceeded or impacted too much during these events, you can proactively earmark these items as problems that could be pivoted to when you do exceed the budget and need reliability features to focus on. Having a dedicated queue or tag in your ticketing system to keep track of these sorts of items is a great idea.

---

2 Do not confuse this with assuming that 20% of your releases will continue to cause you problems into the future—the important point is that if 20% of your releases have caused you problems in the past, perhaps you need to examine what has contributed to that being the case. We'll go into great detail about why using mean time measurements is problematic in Chapter 17.

Additionally, if you can tie events to error budget burn periods, you can also discover things that might surprise you about the reliability of your service. For example, you might have an issue that occurs monthly that causes your service to not be available for about 30 minutes. This could be seen as a very big deal. But after examining your error budget, suppose you also determine that your latency performs at an unreliable rate for five minutes every single day. That 30 minutes multiplied by 12 months is 360 minutes of unreliability per year; but the 5 minutes multiplied by 365 days is 1,825 minutes of unreliability per year. The 30-minute unavailability periods might be easier to spot via your normal monitoring, but adopting an error budget allows you to determine that your daily latency problems actually cause more of a headache for your users, especially when extrapolated over time. This gives you direction in performing a stack rank of what issues you should be applying resources to before others.

Don't forget that as you examine these sorts of risk factors you should also be asking yourself if your SLI, SLO, and even error budget time windows are defined correctly, or if you could collect even better data and measurements if you changed them—even if only by a tiny amount.

Experimentation and Chaos Engineering

If you have a lot of error budget remaining over a long period of time, you should feel free to experiment with your architecture and infrastructure in production. Some of this is a form of chaos engineering,[3] and a way to discover failure modes you may not have been familiar with before. Having an established and properly measured error budget allows you to have better data you can use to drive alignment across departments and with stakeholders about performing this sort of work. This gets especially important once you have SLOs defined for your entire user-facing product, and not just for the individual components that individual teams are responsible for.

The next sections cover things like load tests and blackhole exercises, and these are aspects of chaos engineering when done in production, but you should also be testing and experimenting with many things besides just increasing the stress on your production systems.

For example, you might have a long-standing cache-aside caching strategy that holds data for an hour before it expires. Your production traffic is fairly varied, so you can't be entirely sure what would happen if you increased this expiry time to two hours instead. Perhaps the extra overhead of storing more data in the cache would slow things down overall, or perhaps the extra hour of caching would lead to better

---

3 The discipline of chaos engineering is too broad and detailed to delve into in this text, but it is highly recommended that all readers of this book also read *Chaos Engineering* by Casey Rosenthal and Nora Jones (O'Reilly). Purposefully burning error budgets and performing chaos engineering are closely related ideas.

performance for clients. If you have enough error budget, twist this configuration knob and find out!

Error injection is another great option in this space. There are many tools and vendors available that allow you to inject problematic—or at least unusual—data into your application's workflows. This sort of work allows you to uncover all sorts of edge cases you might otherwise not discover during normal operations. "Normal" operations are never guaranteed, and inducing these situations early enables you to learn about your service's behavior during these times; you can share the valuable knowledge you gain with your entire organization. Error budgets provide data points that can act as strong justification for *when* to perform this kind of work, especially for organizations that have traditionally been averse to it.

Another example of experimentation might involve cutting down on a manual review process that you've had in place, and just relying on automated tooling instead. If you've slowly been converting from a human-observed testing system to a computer-observed testing system, it can be difficult to know when to flip the switch. Try it when you have lots of error budget, so if things go wrong, you can revert the system before you've been too unreliable in the eyes of your users.

Finally, feel free to do things like completely swapping out a library or other configuration you've been using to perform certain tasks. Maybe you've always wondered what would happen if you used Java's G1 garbage collection instead of the CMS collection? Give it a try. See what it looks like in production. Maybe it's an improvement, maybe it's a degradation, or maybe your service looks basically the same. Feel free to run experiments like this if you have enough error budget.

Load and Stress Tests

Load testing and stress testing are great ways to learn more about the reliability and robustness of your systems, but they are also by design procedures that could break your service. By applying additional load or stress to your systems you are, at some level, hoping to learn where things break down and cause your systems to fail. How to perform good load testing and stress testing is outside the scope of this book, but error budgets give you a great data point to use in deciding if you *should* be performing such tests, or when you can perform your next one.

If you have copious error budget remaining, it's a great time to perform a well-designed load test—even if it's against your production environment!—provided you have built processes to ensure that you can roll back and halt the test before you actually exceed your entire error budget. Load and stress tests are also great ways to find out if you are calculating your burn rate correctly and if your SLI measurements are accurate.

Blackhole Exercises

In order to remain reliable, many services run distributed. Your service might be distributed across two data centers, or many more. These data centers could be your own, or regions within a cloud provider. They could even be a combination of the above: you might have multiple physical data centers under your own control and a multicloud presence across multiple regions per cloud. No matter how you're architected, if you rely on more than a single location, it can be eye-opening to find out what happens if you lose access to one of these locations, and it's often better to find out on purpose than by accident!

A *blackhole exercise* is where you turn off an entire location for either a single service, a single environment, or all of your services. Like with load testing and stress testing, error budgets give you the best possible data point to use to figure out whether you should be performing this kind of exercise, or when you can perform your next one in the event that things went badly with the last one.

Performing blackhole exercises can help you discover dependencies and failure modes you never knew about before, but can also be disruptive to your users when performed in your production environment.[4] These kinds of experiments can cause you to burn or exceed your error budget very quickly. This is fine, and it's why you have error budgets in the first place. If you have a large surplus of error budget, feel free to do things like shutting off half of your entire infrastructure to see how you survive.

This process, of course, works better if you have confidence in your ability to roll back your changes quickly. If you're currently not at that level, use your surplus error budget and the very *desire* to be able to perform these sorts of experiments as your motivation to develop the required levels of confidence in your architecture. Much like how having a rule about not deploying on Fridays is often indicative that you don't trust your testing infrastructure, deploy pipeline, or the general reliability of your systems, not having the confidence to shut off redundant services means you likely have work to do to make them more robust. Use your error budget data to drive these efforts.

 Conversely, if there isn't much room in your error budget, you should postpone this kind of work. The important point to remember is that you can learn valuable lessons via these procedures, and you can use error budgets to help you figure out the right times to perform them.

---

4 Or disruptive to internal users in any environment!

Purposely Burning Budget

Perhaps the most advanced technique described in this entire book is the concept of burning your error budget on purpose. While experimenting on your service when you have a healthy error budget might make sense, it's an additional mental hurdle to leap to say that you should purposely make your service unreliable, not just hypothetically or accidentally, but explicitly by shutting it down.

Burning error budget on purpose is not recommended for services that have a newly established error budget policy; however, if you've been measuring things via SLOs and error budgets for an extended period of time and feel comfortable with your error budget policies, purposely burning the rest of your error budget can be incredibly helpful to other teams. If you consistently perform more reliably than you've documented yourself to be, dependent teams cannot rely on the measurements of their own services to be accurate.

There is a famous, and true, story told in the book *Site Reliability Engineering* by Betsy Beyer et al. about Chubby, a distributed lock service at Google. The service only promised a certain target of reliability over any given quarter, and users were warned that the global version of Chubby should not be depended upon—but every quarter new services would end up establishing a hard dependency on Chubby anyway. So every quarter, when this service had error budget remaining, things would just get shut down: global Chubby would not be available for however many minutes remained. And every single quarter, some team would discover they were more dependent on this service than they thought they were. Once the fires were put out, this actually led to positive outcomes as teams were able to learn more about their own services and work to fix the hard dependency issues that had been exposed.

It's an advanced step to get to this point in your SLO culture, but once you get to the point that you trust your SLIs, your SLO targets, and your error budgets, there is nothing wrong with strictly enforcing them every so often to see what happens.

Error Budgets for Humans

We've already established that the concepts behind SLO-based approaches can really be applied to almost anything, with Molly's story in the Preface being a great example: you can't be perfect, so don't try to be perfect, but do try to be good enough. Because of this, you can apply error budgets to all sorts of things that aren't computer services.

For example, you could track how many tickets are opened in your queue and set an SLO for response time, or even how many are closed as "Working as Intended" or "Won't Fix" or something similar. Using an error budget, you could then have a discussion at the end of a month or a quarter. Are there too many tickets being opened in the wrong queue? Are engineers on the team not aware of all components of the system they're supposed to be responsible for and closing tickets they shouldn't be?

Maybe you just didn't properly predict how many tickets would appropriately be closed with these statuses, so your SLO target for this was just wrong.

You could also track the amount of time pull requests (PRs) sit open in various repositories, and use this data to determine if people are being either too lax or too strict in their reviews. Perhaps you notice that PRs in repositories with code written in a certain language linger for much longer than others, which could lead you to realize that engineers in your organization need better training in that language—or maybe that a different language should be used altogether.

One approach that many of my teams have used is deciding to examine and reflect on our current sprint cycle's retrospective meeting discussion prompts once a quarter at the least. The idea is that the way retrospective meetings are conducted can be discussed at any time, and the error budget is exceeded if that discussion hasn't happened when a full quarter has passed. Then the discussion is a mandated one, even if the results of that discussion are "change nothing."

A final example I like is that you can use this to help ensure people are at least thinking about taking time off. You could set an error budget for vacation days used over a time window to make sure you're at least checking in on those who aren't using their days on occasion. No one should ever be *forced* to take time off, but using some simple budgeting math to check in with those who haven't is likely not a bad idea. Breaks from work are important.

The potential here is endless, and the examples here are just a few I've seen used in practice. SLO-based approaches are all about making humans happier, and you need to make sure that includes your own engineers.

Error Budget Measurement

Now that we've established some of the ways you can use error budget measurements, let's talk about how you actually establish and calculate them. None of the math is necessarily complicated, but it also generally isn't built into your metrics collection systems. While this is changing with more and more vendors and solutions arriving on the scene, it's still worth taking the time to talk about all of this from first principles.

Establishing Error Budgets

Just like everything else involved with an SLO-based approach to reliability, you need to make sure that your error budget windows, status, and policy are documented and discoverable. You should have a default time window defined for your services, so that you have a baseline for having discussions with stakeholders at all levels and so that those stakeholders can examine your reliability status without having to bother you or request a formal report.

You can also apply the same math you use for error budgets to historical SLO performance, for any time range in the past. This can be useful for reporting on a particular time period. Use your default time window to ensure you have data to examine about historical reliability at the ready; use malleable time windows to report on time periods that you've otherwise deemed important (for example, to examine a particularly rough week, to determine the exact impact of a nasty bug pushed to production, or to provide quarterly reporting to leadership). No matter what kind of window you're using, error budget math allows you to say, "Over X period of time, our service performed at Y level in terms of our SLI and SLO target."

As noted previously, there are two main approaches to thinking about error budgets. These are roughly grouped into "events-based" and "time-based." Events-based approaches just mean that you believe you can tolerate $X\%$ of bad events over time, while time-based approaches mean that you believe you can tolerate X amount of bad minutes (or seconds, and so on) over time.

Some people prefer one over the other, but the truth is that they both expose essentially the same data, just in different ways. In fact, I personally prefer that both are calculated for any given SLO, and I include the status of both in any SLO dashboard I build (much more about SLO reporting and dashboards is discussed in Chapters 15 and 17).

But even if they both really expose the same data, they do each have their own benefits and detriments. Events-based calculations are much simpler to calculate, and your monitoring software may already allow you to do this math natively even if it isn't advertised as an "error budget calculation" feature. On the other hand, events-based calculations can lead to issues for any metrics without a high resolution or cardinality. If you only have a few data points per hour, just a single failure can completely overwhelm your target percentages. Using a time-based approach is more complicated, but also accounts for both high- and low-resolution or -quantity measurements.

Additionally, events-based error budgets make it easier to perform the math you need to do error budget burn rate calculations (covered in detail in Chapter 8), but time-based error budgets make it easier to communicate your status to others. The former is because it's more difficult to perform math with times than with raw numbers, and the latter is because it is much easier for other people to understand a statement like "We can have 20 more minutes of bad operation this month before we're out of error budget" than one like "We have 7.3% of our error budget left."

Finally, events-based budgets are often more intuitive for concepts like latency measurements, since latency problems are often exposed as individual "bad" hits among many good ones, while time-based budgets are often more intuitive for concepts like availability measurements or the end-to-end state of a data processing pipeline, since those often manifest themselves over periods of time instead of as individual measurements of unreliability in a sea of reliable ones.

Which approach you use is up to you, and as I've stated I actually prefer both for different use cases. Using events-based approaches for your monitoring and time-based approaches for your human-driven decision making and reporting gives you the best of both worlds, even if it means more work to get there. No matter what, you'll have to pick a time window in which to apply to your SLO to get an error budget.[5]

Events-based error budget math

Events-based error budget math is often fairly simple. You've already worked through the process of defining an SLI and an SLO, so you already have both a percentage ratio of good events over total events and a target percentage that you want that ratio to exceed when everything is running reliably. Now you just have to compare those percentages to each other. I discuss how to pick time windows for your error budgets later in the chapter, but for simplicity let's stick with a common 30-day rolling window for our purposes right now.

For example, let's say that you have an SLO target of 99.8%. This gives you an error budget of 0.2% of all total requests. Looking back over the last month, you see that you've recorded a total of 20,000,000 good observations, with 36,513 failures during that same time period. First you need to calculate what percentage of your total requests those failures represent:

$$\frac{36513}{20000000} = 0.00182565 = 0.18\%$$

Since your error budget allows for you to tolerate up to 0.2% total failures, you can now subtract your actual failure percentage from your error budget:

$$0.2 - 0.18 = 0.02$$

This tells you that you can tolerate 0.02% more failures in your current time window before you've exhausted your budget.

---

5 It is also conceivable that you do not care about time in any way, and that you really just want 99.5% out of 100,000 requests to complete successfully, no matter whether those 100,000 requests happen over the course of an hour or a day or a week. In practice I have not often seen this sort of approach used, but if it's right for you, don't shy away from it. It's the philosophies that matter, not the exact implementation!

There are a few terms unique to how people talk about error budgets worth defining here:

Error budget surplus
A situation where you have time remaining out of your total error budget.

Error budget deficit
A situation where you exceeded your error budget and are now calculating negative time.

Error budget burn
Any time you are subtracting from your error budget. For example, "We're burning three minutes per hour right now."

Error budget recovery
Any time you are adding to your error budget as bad observations drop out of your time window.

However, it can be more useful to actually calculate what percent of your total error budget that represents, instead of just what percent of total requests are in your time window. Knowing what percentage you have remaining is more intuitive for determining if you need to take action or not. To do this, just divide your remaining budget by your total budget:

$$\frac{0.02}{0.2} = 0.01 = 10\,\%$$

Now you know that you have exactly 10% of your error budget remaining for the window in question.

Next, let's look at an example where the error budget has been exhausted. The math is all the same, but it can be useful to see some example numbers. We'll stick with our original 20,000,000 observations and 99.8% SLO, but now let's say we observed 153,872 failures during that time. First, we again calculate what percent of our total observations those failures represent:

$$\frac{153872}{20000000} = 0.0076936 = 0.76\,\%$$

Subtracting our failure percentage from our error budget, we now have a negative number, which indicates that the budget has been exhausted:

$$0.2 - 0.76 = -0.56$$

We can take one final step and divide how much the budget has been exceeded by the original error budget:

$$\frac{-0.56}{0.2} = -2.8$$

This number tells us that we've exhausted the error budget a total of 2.8 times during our time window. In this situation pretty immediate action should probably be taken.

Time-based error budget math

For time-based error budget math, you'll still need to pick a time window, but you'll also have to determine a base time unit for how precise you want your error budget calculations to be. This precision will be dependent on the precision of your metrics data. For most people, calculating things on the order of seconds or even minutes should be suitable; however, if you have very precise measurements and an SLO target percentage of 99.99% or above, you might consider subseconds.

In order to compute how much budget a particular window gives you, start with your base time unit and multiply this with the next time unit until you get to your time window. For example, to calculate how many seconds there are in a day:

$$1 \times 60 \times 60 \times 24 = 86400$$

The first number is your base unit, which is always 1, which is multiplied by 60 because there are 60 seconds in a minute, then by 60 because there are 60 minutes in an hour, and finally by 24 because there are 24 hours in a day. This results in you having 86,400 total potential data points that can represent good or bad values. This might seem pretty straightforward, but not everyone can have a base time unit of a single second. For example, if the best resolution you have in your metrics is every 30 seconds, you could perform the following math instead:

$$1 \times 2 \times 60 \times 24 = 2880$$

You still start off with 1, since that represents your base unit, even if it happens to be 30 seconds this time. You multiply this by 2, because there are two 30-second periods in a minute, then by 60 because there are 60 minutes in an hour, and finally by 24 because there are 24 hours in a day. This results in you having 2,880 data points over the course of your one-day time window.

This approach also lets you have fractional values for your time units. There are 365 days in a non-leap year, so while businesses often discuss quarters as being 90 days, the real math shows that a true quarter is a little longer than that:

$$\frac{365}{4} = 91.25$$

If there is value in having a year split exactly into four quarters for your reporting purposes (and this very well may be the case for SLOs with a large number of nines), you would compute the total number of data points with a 30-second resolution as follows:

$$1 \times 2 \times 60 \times 24 \times 91.25 = 262800$$

Once you have calculated the total number of data points for your time window, you can use your SLO target percentage and your base unit to determine what your error budget for this window is. We'll use our 91.25 days at a 30-second resolution and a 99.99% target as an example:

$$(1 - 0.9999) \times 262800 = 26.28$$

This tells us that a total of 26.28 of our base units are available to us before we exceed our error budget. To finally reach the most human-readable format, we can take this total and multiply it by the value of our base unit:

$$26.25 \times 30 = 787.5$$

Now we know we have 787.5 seconds—or 13 minutes and 7.5 seconds—of total error budget every 91.25-day quarter.

> Your math does not have to be this complex. For many purposes just using a base unit of a single second and whole-value time units makes the most sense, but these more complicated examples ensure you're armed to make these calculations in any way that your business or your users might need you to.

Once you've done the math for establishing what your error budget window looks like in terms of data points, you can also calculate your current error budget status. Let's take a moment and compute a very common error budget, 1-second-resolution metrics over a 30-day period:

$$1 \times 60 \times 60 \times 24 \times 30 = 2592000$$

With an error budget time window like this, we have a total of 2,592,000 data observations that could be either good or bad in terms of our SLO. Next, let's say that we have an SLO target percentage of 99.7% for this service. We can now calculate what our total error budget for this time period is:

$$(1 - 0.997) \times 2592000 = 7776$$

That gives us 7,776 observations, which with our base unit translates directly to seconds. Put another way, 7,776 seconds is 2 hours, 9 minutes, and 36 seconds.

Now that we know our total error budget in terms of individual units for this time window, we can use our SLO data to determine how much of an error budget we have remaining. Let's say that for this time period, we know that we had 3,888 bad observations. First, we subtract that number from the total events to get a count of good events:

$$2592000 - 3888 = 2588112$$

Remember that no matter what other steps and math exist along the way, at some point an SLO has to be informed by a percentage, which is just a ratio with a scale from 0 to 100. We calculate this percentage by dividing good events by total events:

$$\frac{2588112}{2592000} = 0.9985$$

This lets us know that our metrics tell us that we were reliable 99.85% of the time, which is greater than our SLO target of 99.7%. For the hypothetical time period we're currently analyzing, our service reliability wasn't perfect, but in terms of our SLO it was good enough. This means that out of an error budget of 2 hours, 9 minutes, and 36 seconds, we have some remaining. At this point it might be nice to calculate what our remaining budget is, so we have a better sense of how much additional "bad time" we might be able to incur.

We already know the number of observations informing our error budget (7,776) as well as how many bad observations we had (3,888). All we have to do next is subtract the bad events from the total events possible within our budget:

$$7776 - 3888 = 3888$$

Now we see that we've exhausted exactly half of our total error budget, leaving us with the other half remaining. Our base unit is seconds, so 3,888 events translates to 3,888 seconds, or 1 hour, 4 minutes, and 48 seconds of error budget remaining. These results indicate that if our SLI is a meaningful qualifier of our reliability, and our SLO target percentage accurately reflects what our users need from us, we probably don't need to take any drastic actions to improve the reliability of our service at this time.

It also might be the case that things have been unreliable and that you have actually exceeded your error budget. The math is all the same, it's just that you'll end up with a negative number of events to convert into time. For example, let's say that instead of 3,888 bad observations, we had 30,888 of them. First, we'd subtract those from the total number of observations in our time window:

$$7776 - 30888 = -23112$$

Then we'd follow the same steps as before and convert the number of negative events into time units. In our case, we're already dealing with seconds, so we know that we've exceeded our error budget by 23,112 seconds, which is 6 hours, 25 minutes, and 12 seconds. We can also figure out by what factor the error budget has been exceeded by dividing the bad observations by the total error budget allotment:

$$\frac{30888}{7776} = 3.97$$

In this case, the error budget has been exceeded by about 4 times total, which probably isn't ideal and indicates either a serious reliability problem or issues with how the measurements manifest themselves.

Rolling versus calendar-bound windows

When selecting the proper time window for your service, you'll have a decision to make on top of just how large it should be. Should you use a rolling window or one tied to the calendar?

A rolling window is one that moves as time progresses. If you have a 30-day window and a 10-second resolution, your error budget will be updated every 10 seconds as time moves into the future. This allows for bad event observations to fall off and no longer be involved in your computations as they expire beyond that 30-day window.

The other option is to use time windows that are bound to exact moments on a calendar. For example, instead of using a seven-day window, you might only calculate your error budget starting at the beginning of the week. This in itself could be considered a different time, depending on your culture: in some places 00:00 on a Sunday is when a new week starts, and in others it's 00:00 on a Monday.

You could also choose to tie your error budget to calendar months. In this case, instead of using a 28-day, 30-day, or 31-day window to calculate your error budget status, you'd do so starting from the very first second of the current month you're in. The math as described earlier is essentially still the same, it's just that when determining the events portions of the equations—total events, bad events, or good events—you need to ensure you're computing this from the beginning of your calendar-bound time period.

There are advantages to using calendar-based time windows. The primary benefit is that you have an easier time reporting to people what the state of your service is. When you tie your error budget to something like a calendar month, people will know exactly when the error budget returns in full. This can allow engineering teams to better plan their projects, and it can allow product teams to have a better idea of when new features may be shipped. If your error budget is tied to an SLA, it can also make it easier to calculate what kind of recompense you owe to your paying customers. Many services are billed on a monthly basis, and an error budget tied to that same month can make it easier to figure out what credits, discounts, or other types of remuneration are required for that particular month.

However, there are also downsides. The first is that time windows that are calendar-bound can obscure the impact of failures. If you're a public-facing product and your service is down for an entire day close to the end of the month, chances are your customers aren't going to have forgotten about this just a few days later, even if your error budget says you can incur more unreliability as soon as the calendar flips from one month to the next. In fact, it is for this very reason that, while it might make sense for internal services that talk to each other to have an error budget window of something like a month, for services viewed as entire products delivered to external and paying customers time windows of a quarter or more might make more sense. If you're letting your failures drop out of your decision making before your users can tolerate more failures, you're not picking the right time window.

Additionally, this kind of approach can lead to a repetitive problem. In a particular month, you run out of error budget. Your error budget policy (covered in more detail in "Error Budget Policies" on page 88) says that when you've exceeded your budget, you stop shipping new features and focus on improving the reliability of the service as your primary goal. However, this rarely means that people actually stop working on new features in the background; they just don't send them to production.

So, the rest of the month proceeds smoothly, and then on the first day of the following month suddenly everyone starts shipping their new features. Due to the sheer quantity of changes the service is suddenly subjected to, with changes being the most common source of failures, you again exceed your error budget very quickly. In order to deal with this, all feature releases are frozen again, and once again the product and engineering teams have several weeks to queue up a bunch of new releases. The calendar flips over, all of these releases hit production at the same time, and you're back to square one. This self-perpetuating cycle is one I've witnessed many times, and it's often forced upon teams responsible for the SLO for a service that also has a contractually obligated SLA for external customers. You might not have a choice about the window you can choose in this scenario, but it's useful to know about this particular failure pattern ahead of time so you can try and head it off by ensuring the releases are carefully vetted and perhaps staggered during any month that follows one where your budget was exhausted.

 As with everything else in this book, you need to determine what works best for you, your users, and your organization. In some situations time windows bound to a calendar could be the correct choice—but be aware of the potential detrimental effects of doing so.

Excluding time

Another way that your time window might differ from a standard one is that you might not always want it to be active. Some services only have to be reliable during certain hours or even days. Examples of this could be things like point of sales systems in retail stores, batch processing jobs that might run multiple times per month but only have to actually be reliable for the end-of-month financials, or systems that have some kind of lengthy and mandatory downtime every day. A good example of the latter is that older databases can sometimes take hours to perform a backup every day, and aren't accessible while doing so. If it's already been determined that everything is within your users' requirements if this system is down from 02:00 to 04:00 every day to perform this work, you could account for this when choosing your overall SLO target percentage—or you could just not let any measurements during this time count against your SLO or error budget at all.

If you have a service with these kinds of requirements, all you have to do is remove the events that would occur during those time frames from your error budget calculations. For example, you might recall that we calculated that a single day has 86,400 seconds. If your service doesn't have to be reliable for 2 hours overnight every day, you can just subtract 2 hours—or 7,200 seconds—of events from your calculations, and make sure that any metrics collected during this time are discarded. Nothing else about the math has to change.

An even simpler solution, if your metrics collection systems allow it, is just to not measure things at all during these periods of time.

Choosing a time window

Now that we've discussed exactly how time windows inform error budgets, and how to do all of the math associated with this, we also have to discuss how you can choose the one that's right for you in the first place. Your time window has to be one that allows for you, your team, or your organization to pivot their focus when the data tells them they should.

Don't discount that humans often think in terms of the units of time they're used to. Therefore, a seven-day—or one-week—window is going to be more understandable and relatable than a nine-day one would be. You might be tempted to be extra accurate and define your time window to be something like 30.41666 days, since that's what 365 (days in a non-leap year) divided by 12 (months in a year) equals out to. But chances are whatever benefits you might gain from being that pedantic will be outweighed by the confusion of your coworkers and users. Using a 30-day time window is something people are already used to. Use familiar time windows unless you have a very good excuse to do otherwise.

The most common time windows are 28 or 30 days, the first representing 4 weeks and the other an approximation of 1 month. There are a few reasons for this.

The first is that many things already occur on a monthly basis, and people are used to this fact. People generally have to pay bills on a monthly basis, and contracts are often signed with this billing cycle. Humans long ago decided that a month is a reasonable division of time, and that's not a bad reason to think about your reliability reporting in the same way. You have to start somewhere, and there is nothing wrong with borrowing a time frame from various other aspects of how businesses work.

While I advocate for something like a 30-day window for most services, it's often more useful to have a larger one when establishing goals for components of services that are very visible. Humans remember things for much longer than 30 days, and it might not be sustainable for your business to almost exceed your budget every single month without ever taking action to fix things. Do this by choosing a stricter SLO target, but a larger time window. For things like "total site/product availability," you'll want to have the data to help your entire company pivot to reliability work without bad events falling out of your calculations too soon. Consider something like a 90-day or yearly error budget for this, instead.

As always, these are all just tools to help you think about the reliability of your services in the most accurate way you can. Pick the time windows that work best for you.

Decision Making

Now that we've covered all the nitty-gritty of calculating error budgets, it's time to talk in more depth about how to actually use them. Although there is a very simple answer to use as a starting point, it doesn't come close to telling the entire story. The real world and the failures your services will experience are too varied and unique to adopt just a single rule.

Figure 5-1 revisits how we described error budget decision making all the way back in Chapter 1.

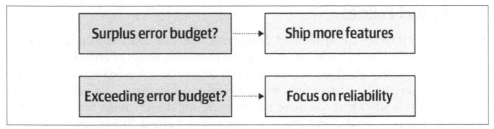

Figure 5-1. A very basic version of how you can use error budgets to drive decisions

The basic idea is straightforward. If you have error budget remaining, ship new features and push to production as often as you'd like; once you run out of it, stop pushing feature changes and focus on reliability instead. Changes—whether to code, configuration, datasets, or the underlying supporting systems—are the primary cause of failures. Computers are actually pretty good at continuing to do things correctly if nothing changes. It's when something new or different is introduced that things can, and will, go wrong.

If you have an SLI that meaningfully measures the reliability of your service, and an SLO that meaningfully tracks how much of the time your service has to be reliable, an error budget gives you a meaningful way of determining when you need to make it *more* reliable. Error budget surplus versus deficit is a great rudimentary starting point.[6]

However, this isn't a rule you can concretely follow every single time; as we just said, the world is too varied for that. It may not make sense for your team or company to drop feature work every time you exceed your error budget. Feature work is often reliability work! In fact, it's not even the case that everyone looking to adopt this kind of approach has feature work at play in the first place. You can use error budgets for much more than software for which you own the codebase.

In the next section we'll discuss setting error budget policies, which define how your team intends to respond to the status of your error budget. Having these policies in place is important, because without them you might never get around to actually taking action based on your error budget status. It's important to have an agreed-upon time at which to take action before you run out of error budget in the first place. You can use the data you're collecting to inform the discussions you have and the decisions you make—that's why you're collecting it, after all!

---

6 This does not mean that you can or should ever assume that SLOs or error budget status tell the whole story. They should be considered additional datasets you can use to inform discussions about reliability, which should be fueled by any and all relevant data humans have available to them.

Error Budget Policies

Error budget policies are formalized documents that you can use to establish rules and guidelines for how your team will respond to various levels of error budget burn. So far we've mostly talked about error budgets in a very simplified sense: things are okay if you have budget remaining, but you need to take action if you don't. Neither of these things is strictly true in many situations. It might make more sense to say that you need to take a certain kind of action once you've burned 20% of your budget, or another kind of action if you've burned through it entirely. Perhaps your team needs to do something if you're burning through your error budget at a certain *rate*, even if you've only spent a small percentage of it. These (and more) are all real-world possibilities, and a good way to make sure everyone is on the same page is to document them. The following subsections go over some of the important items to include in your error budget policy, and by extension the kinds of things you need to be thinking about when you create one.

Owners and stakeholders

An important feature of an SLO-based approach to reliability is that others can use the defined SLIs, SLOs, and error budgets of other services to help them think about their own. When establishing an error budget policy, it needs to be clear to everyone who owns it and who they can contact if they have questions or concerns. The owner could be a single person or a team.

For individual microservices, this will often just be the team responsible for that service. Even at that level, however, it's common to have development, operations, and product teams that all have to agree on these processes and policies together. Make this clear to an outside observer; don't expect that everyone at your company understands who is responsible for a certain set of microservices in the same way you might.

Things can become less clear as you move to services that are composed of many other services, or perhaps even your entire business product considered as a single service. This is why getting buy-in across your company is so important.[7] For services composed of many other services, there might be many teams involved. In that case, you should be looking to managers of managers or directors to own these policies. As things get larger and larger, and made up of more and more components, you should move on to getting VPs or even the C-level involved. Ownership of the SLO definition and error budget policy for an entire web-facing business should be by someone like the CTO or the CEO. This does not mean that this person has to be responsible

---

7 Getting buy-in is covered extensively in Chapter 6.

for implementation or calculation, but they need to be responsible for starting the conversations that changes in error budget status demand.

Error budget burn policies

You shouldn't just take action when you've completely exceeded your error budget, especially if you have evidence that you'll exceed it if you continue at your current rate. In your documented error budget policy, you should make sure that you have outlined what actions you will take under certain conditions. Exactly what these actions or conditions should look like are entirely dependent on the nature of your service, but following are some common examples.

First, it might make sense for you to take action once you've spent a given percentage of your total error budget. A great example of this is assigning a certain number of engineers to focus on reliability work at certain thresholds. For instance, if you have a team of six people supporting a single service, you could say that two (33%) of the team members will drop their other work and focus on making things more reliable once you've burned 33% of your error budget for any given window. If you recover, one or both of these engineers could return to their regularly scheduled work. Additionally, as the next step you could say that four (66%) of the team members will drop their other work and focus on making things more reliable once you've burned 66% of your error budget for any given window. This naturally leads to the entire team focusing on reliability once you've exceeded the entire budget. Of course, this is just one example, and it might not make sense for your team or service; when deciding on your policy you'll want to take into account factors such as the reliability history at play and how mature your measurements and thresholds are.[8]

Another option is to use some calculus to calculate how quickly you're burning through your budget in order to determine when to take action.[9] If your burn rate exceeds a certain threshold, you could similarly assign a certain number of engineers—or the entire team—to "defend the error budget," and try to make sure you don't actually get to the point where you exceed it at all. This could involve an on-call engineer getting paged and immediately responding, an engineering team (or portions of it) taking on reliability and tech-debt tickets for their following sprint, or anything in between.

Bear in mind that error budget status is just the end result of a bunch of data (SLIs, SLOs, and their targets) that exists to help you make decisions. It's a great idea to document how you *think* you should respond when your error budget has been

---

8 If your thresholds and targets are very mature and representative of your users' experiences, you might not feel you need to take action until 100% of your error budget has been exhausted. This is discussed in more detail in the next section.

9 The math for how to do this and alert off of it will be covered in Chapter 8.

depleted by a certain amount, because this way you have a starting point for your conversation; at the same time, you should leave some room for interpretation, since you probably can't tell the future. Use words like *must, may, should,* and *required* in your written policies to help give people freedom to adapt certain parts of them. You're setting guidelines to help you make decisions, not hard-and-fast rules.

 When writing technical documentation that doesn't have strict rules, it's a good idea to take care to use the correct words to denote what should happen, what may happen, what is required, what is optional, etc. It is highly recommended that you read, and perhaps adopt, RFC 2119 (*https://tools.ietf.org/html/rfc2119*) for guidelines on how to do this effectively.

Additionally, it might be good to explicitly lay out what the contributing factors to your unreliability are when you observe these budget depletions. You'll likely react differently if your own team introduces a bug, or if your service suffers an incident purely due to another service becoming unavailable, and therefore the two circumstances should be classified differently in your policy. Another example could be situations where your service falls victim to a true black swan event, or in cases of planned load or stress testing. The next section discusses these situations further, but you should be keeping them in mind as you think about what kinds of qualifications to put in place in your error budget policies.

Error budget exceeded policies

Many of the same concepts apply to your error budget exceeded policies as your burn policies; it's just that your responsive actions will often have to happen quicker (with more people involved), will need to be communicated more broadly, and may result in more long-term fault-tolerance improvements.

One of the biggest differentiators between your error budget burn policies and your error budget exceeded policies is that you'll likely have fewer qualifiers here. A great example is that it's a good idea to mandate that an incident retrospective process be carried out and a post-failure report document produced any time you exceed your error budget. Even if the findings of this report are that you haven't been calculating your error budget correctly, or that you've chosen unreasonable targets, those are still great lessons to learn—which is the entire point of performing incident retrospectives in the first place.

Error budget exceeded policies might also include recommendations about communicating this status out to other people. If you're completely out of error budget, all the services that depend on yours might have had their own error budgets severely impacted, and the teams responsible for those services deserve to know about this. If the service you're responsible for comprises many services, or even an entire company's public-facing product, you should extend the extent to which you communicate this appropriately. For example, if you're out of error budget for your data processing pipeline, you need to make sure that the teams that rely on this know; however, it's one thing if the machine learning team is relying on this data for a long-term project, and a whole different thing if finance requires this in order to bill customers on time and remain in legal financial compliance.

It's a great idea to have mandatory *must* statements about some of these scenarios, especially for those that impact the bottom line of your business; however, you don't have to overuse them. Trust people to make the right decisions and use *should* and *may* statements where applicable.

In fact, trust people in general. There are many conceivable examples where two *must* scenarios could collide. For example, what do you do if your error budget policy says you *must* halt feature work, but your CEO says that you *must* ship a certain feature? I don't have an exact answer for you. Your situation will be unique, and you will have to use your own judgment. The important thing to remember is that SLOs and error budgets give you directly applicable datasets you can use to push back on these sorts of requests. They provide a starting point from which you can form an argument to disagree with other directives.

Justification and revisit schedule

Any good error budget policy should have some language that describes what the service in question actually is, and why these policies were decided upon. If you have policies that say no action needs to be taken until 80% of your error budget has been depleted, you need to explain to others how you arrived at that number. This section does not have to be incredibly verbose, but it can help keep stakeholders from wondering why you made that decision.

Finally, ensure you have a section describing when you will next evaluate these policies and decide if they're still set correctly for the current reality. You should include both a revisit date and a brief justification for why you have chosen that date. For example, you might explain that you're on a monthly revisit cycle because the policies are brand new and you're not yet sure if they're set correctly; or, if they've been in place for a long time and proven effective as currently written, you could say that you only plan to revisit your policies on a quarterly or yearly basis.

You're going to learn the most when you have discussions that surround changing things about your error budget numbers, from your SLI measurements to your SLO targets to your error budget windows.

Summary

Error budgets are the most difficult part of the Reliability Stack to get to, but they give you a huge amount of important data once you get there. Thinking about your services with SLIs is the first step; thinking about how you need to be reliable for your users with SLOs is the second; calculating how you've performed against your target over time is the third. Actually *using* your error budget status to have discussions and make decisions is the fourth and final step.

Error budgets give you ways to make decisions about your service, be it a single microservice or your company's entire customer-facing product. They also give you indicators that tell you when you can ship features, what your focus should be, when you can experiment, and what your biggest risk factors are.

Every step of the journey is an important one, and even just establishing a healthy culture of what SLIs for your services should be is a great start. But if you can build upon that and get to the point where your team, your organization, or your entire company uses error budgets as data to help them have better discussions, you can work out exactly when and where to focus your reliability efforts and when and where to experiment to learn how reliable and resilient you truly are.

SLO Implementation

CHAPTER 6

Getting Buy-In

David K. Rensin

SLIs, SLOs, and error budgets are really helpful mental tools to reason about the reliability needs of your systems. If you want them to be anything more than just interesting talking points, however, you will need to convince your company (or organization) to implement and live by them.

As an engineer, convincing your leaders to adopt SLOs is probably not first nature to you. That's where this chapter comes in. It will walk you through the steps you should take to get your company ready to live *la vida SLO*. This information was all learned the hard way by helping others on this journey, and I have compiled the most important bits here so you don't have to make the same mistakes I made along the way. There is additional discussion about how to get individual teams involved with this process in Chapter 13.

Engineering Is More than Code

We have a saying in SRE: *Our monitoring and logging do not decide our reliability; our users do.* As technical professionals, the code we write and the systems we design are all in the service of our users. After all, if we build something that nobody ever uses, then we would probably have been better off spending our time and effort doing something else.

Similarly, there is a very robust argument (*https://www.youtube.com/watch?v=oyJFxr4gYXc*) to be made that reliability is the most important requirement of any system, because it is the foundation of user trust. After all, if users don't trust the system, they won't use it, and pretty soon there will be no users. At that point, the effort spent was wasted (see the previous point). Even if new revenue-producing endeavors get more attention, they won't be trusted if they're not reliable.

All of this is to say that the real-world practice of engineering is somewhat different from what we may have learned in school. As engineers, we are called on to argue the merits of our choices in the context of what best serves the interests of our users. The theoretical optimality of some algorithm, for example, is only important insofar as it delivers meaningful value to our users (and by extension, to our organization).

As the person driving your team/organization/company toward the adoption of SLIs, SLOs, and error budgets, you will have to do a fair amount of convincing. For some people, the basic arguments for SLOs will run counter to the goals they have set for themselves and their teams. Others will want to prioritize feature velocity ahead of reliability work, and still others will doubt that the company is "mature enough" or "good enough" to really adopt these principles and techniques.

All those objections (and more) can be overcome, and I will show you how. It's important to realize now that the benefits of adopting an SLO-based approach will not be self-evident to everyone and that you will have to do a fair amount of patient explanation.

Key Stakeholders

Let's start by looking at the key stakeholders (the people you need to convince) and talk through their interests and motivations.

Engineering

The first people you have to persuade are your fellow engineers. Many engineers don't want to be concerned with the operational complexity of the systems they build. They want to focus on unique and interesting software problems and features. They (too often) think of operational details as "someone else's problem."

If that describes your current engineering culture, then your team is in serious trouble. That mindset *always* leads to ever-escalating levels of warfare between the people who carry pagers and the people who write code. Sometimes the arguing is obvious and direct. Most times, however, these silos wage a passive-aggressive cold war against one another. The end result is a stressed-out work environment with almost no feature velocity to speak of. Eventually your best people will quit.

When talking to engineers, it's important to stress some key points:

- SLOs (and error budgets) increase both reliability *and* feature velocity over time. They also make for a better work environment because they align incentives among previously warring factions.

- SLOs (over time) give engineers license to take more risks and to be subject to fewer launch constraints. There's less bureaucracy to get in the way of a cool new launch.

- The principled exercise of error budget policies makes people *better* software engineers because it creates a real and rapid feedback loop from the users.

I have never met an engineering team that didn't want more freedom to take risks or more control over their release velocity. SLOs give them both. As long as they are under their error budget, they are free to push pretty much anything they like into production with a lot less friction.

Product

The product team (or perhaps the product management team in your organization) is responsible for deciding which features go into the product and the relative priority among those features. Sometimes this is a different team from engineering, and sometimes it's part of the same organization. For this discussion, let's think of the product team as a separate functional area from the core engineering team.

These folks are most concerned about shipping the right features as quickly as possible. To get their buy-in, it's important to stress the following:

- Reliability is a first-class feature of the product. In fact, it's the most important feature. If the users get the idea that the product won't reliably meet their needs (because it's unavailable, serving errors, etc.), then they won't trust it. If they don't trust the product, then they will seek alternatives in the marketplace and you will lose your users. Nobody uses a system they can't trust for anything important (or for very long). Reliability (in the form of SLOs) should be part of the product requirements document (PRD) that this team writes.

- Modern PRDs include user journeys—specific use cases that are important to customers, and descriptions of how product managers would like users to experience them. There is a strong mapping between SLIs and user journeys. In fact, SLIs are an excellent way to measure and ensure that the user journeys in the PRD are being monitored and reacted to.

- SLOs will eventually increase the feature velocity of the product because they remove much of the friction from the release cycle.

- Suppose you have shipped a product where there are no formal reliability targets in the product definition, but your users seem pretty happy (i.e., they're not complaining much). That almost certainly means that you *overshot* your necessary reliability target.[1] You are wasting time and effort to hit a level of performance your users do not need. That effort would be better spent on feature

---

1 It could also be true that users are upset and you just don't know about it yet. This isn't an easily solved problem, and shouldn't discourage you from adopting an SLO-based approach to reliability. There are always things you cannot discover or know about.

development. SLOs give product managers the opportunity to turn that knob with data rather than luck.

Operations

For simplicity, let's define operators as *anyone who carries a pager for your system.* That could be a dedicated operations team, your customer support team, or even your engineers. If they go on call for the system, then they are operators for the purposes of this section.

If you have never had to carry a pager, then I can tell you with certainty that an operator's single biggest frustration is the idea that they will be paged (and possibly woken up) for a mistake that *someone else* made. To make matters worse, operators have very few options to share that frustration with the engineers who pushed the bad code. The whole setup feels unfair because it fundamentally is.

For operators, the important benefits of SLOs are as follows:

- SLOs and error budget policies put them on an even footing with the engineers. If engineering pushes too much bad code, then there are consequences—often in the form of a feature freeze. This gives the operators an equal voice.

- SLOs and error budgets also allow operators to remove some of the deployment friction accumulated over the years because they know that the engineers now have skin in the game as it relates to the stability of the system. This goes a long way toward deescalating the hostilities that often build between engineering and operations.

I have never met an operations team that wasn't immediately enthusiastic about the idea of SLOs and error budgets. (Many have been skeptical too, but we'll get to overcoming that objection a little later.)

QA

If you have a dedicated QA team in your company, this may be the most difficult conversation you have. Candidly speaking, QA teams tend to disappear as organizations adopt SLOs and error budgets.

Here's how this happens:

1. The engineers hear that they can do (pretty much) whatever they like as long as they don't blow their error budgets. They immediately decide to bypass the "onerous" process the QA team has put in place.

2. Free of their normal deployment friction (and certain that they always write rock-solid code), the engineers start deploying too quickly.

---

3. Almost immediately, they exhaust their error budget and the agreed-upon policy kicks in (usually a code freeze of some sort).

4. The engineers (at the behest of the operators) work during the freeze period on improvements that make future outages have less impact (better monitoring, automated rollbacks, slower rollouts, canaries, and so on).

5. Once the feature freeze is lifted, they start deploying again. They'll still probably exhaust their error budget, but it will take longer.

6. Eventually, the engineers get the idea that maybe they should add back some of the QA they threw away at the beginning, so they start adding things like presubmit tests, dry runs, and traffic replay. Slowly, they build a library of provably useful QA steps they will automate and follow for every release.

It's not that there's no role for QA in a world of SLOs, but in practice, the engineering team itself usually performs QA. In nearly every case where I've helped an organization adopt SRE practices (particularly SLOs), I have seen the dedicated QA team eventually get disbanded and redistributed into the core engineering team.

It's important to stress that *QA skills and people don't disappear*. Separate QA teams just usually get refactored into the various feature engineering groups. People with strong test engineering skills become more valuable and less stressed over time, as we'll see later in this chapter.

Legal

A company's legal team is responsible for minimizing risk. One of the ways they do so is by creating and publishing SLAs. SLAs are legal agreements between your company and your customers. They spell out the circumstances under which your customer may seek recompense (refunds, service credits, and so forth) if your service fails to perform at some previously agreed-upon level.

SLAs tend to be much looser than the actual performance of the product (otherwise, you'd be paying refunds all the time).

Your SLOs will be very valuable to your lawyers, for a few reasons:

- In the absence of tested SLOs, any SLAs your lawyers write will be correct only by luck. If you find that you almost never violate your SLAs, there's probably a good chance that they are too loose relative to your SLOs. That gap is a safety margin, but it's also a potential competitive advantage that you are wasting. Suppose that both you and your largest competitor offer a 99.9% availability SLA, but it turns out that your system routinely meets a 99.99% SLO. In that case, you have the opportunity to offer a better SLA (perhaps 99.95%) with almost no extra risk. That might be a very compelling selling point to your customers.

- In order to have effective SLOs, you will need high-quality SLIs and good monitoring. Your lawyers will come to appreciate the data you get from this. Until now, they only knew when a customer made an SLA claim. Now, however, they can be alerted *before* such a claim is made because the error budget is burning down too fast. The next best thing to eliminating risk is proactively alerting when risk starts to elevate. Then your lawyers can prepare and aren't caught flat-footed when a bad thing happens. (Lawyers really appreciate that!)

In my experience, legal teams quickly come to appreciate the value of both SLIs and error budgets because they help quantify and measure business risk.

If you happen to be in a regulated industry (financial services, healthcare, and others), then there may be a regulatory advantage to SLOs, too. Most regulators I have worked with understand that no company (or product) is perfect. What they want is to understand the risks, to know that *you* understand those same risks, and to know that you have good controls in place to manage the risks. SLOs are a great tool to demonstrate these things, and I have seen the sharing of this information create a lot of good will with regulators.

Tools that create confidence with your regulators make lawyers happy, too.

Executive Leadership

In theory it should be super easy to convince your executive leadership (CEO and other top managers) to adopt SLOs. After all, what leader *wouldn't* want better predictability, increased reliability, and faster feature velocity?

In practice, however, there are some hurdles. The biggest one is that senior leaders often think they should be driving their teams toward perfection (100% customer satisfaction, zero downtime, and so forth).

In my experience, this is the biggest mental hill to get senior management over. For any of this to work, you have to convince them that a goal of perfection is both impossible and counterproductive.

The (simplified) argument goes like this:

1. Our systems are not now nor ever have been 100% reliable. There is no reason to think they ever will be.

2. In fact, there is no human-made system that has *ever* exhibited 100% reliability over any reasonable length of time.

3. When we set goals of perfection, we eventually tell our employees to lie to us because we tie their career advancement to goals they cannot achieve. Our best employees will see this first and leave. Everyone else will just fudge the numbers to make it look like we're getting closer.

4. The other outcome is a rapid decrease in velocity because people are scared to make mistakes. Neither of these outcomes is good for our customers or our company.

5. We would be much better off as a company if we were to stop trying to make no mistakes and instead worry about noticing the mistakes faster and limiting the impact of each error. As we get better at those things, we will be able to take more risks—which will eventually turn into faster innovation and a better experience for our customers.

If you are interested in the more complete version of this argument, check out my talk "Less Risk Through Greater Humanity" (*https://www.youtube.com/watch?v=0zqBlRW_6jA*) at Cerner DevCon 2018.

The good news is that the overwhelming majority of CEOs, CTOs, CIOs, and VPs to whom I have presented these points wind up agreeing. (They have other concerns, but we'll get to those soon enough.)

Making It So

Now that we know who the key stakeholders are and their most important concerns, let's build a game plan to get everyone on board. Like most things in engineering, the order of operation is important.

Order of Operation

Based on experience, this is how I suggest you stage things:

1. Engineering and operations
    Your first step is to get both the engineering and operations teams on board with SLOs. This should be reasonably straightforward because SLIs, SLOs, and error budgets offer real benefits to each group. Their mutual agreement to the principles of SLOs is key to getting other teams on board. Note that I said *principles*. The implementation details (error budget policies, SLO targets, etc.) will be negotiated later.

2. Product
    Your next stop is probably your product managers (or whoever writes the PRDs). The key argument you are making to them is that this approach will give them better feature velocity over time. They will want to know that engineering and operations are on board, which is why they're in step 2.

3. Leadership

Once the engineering, operations, and product teams have bought in, it's time to talk to your senior leadership. The benefits of this change (greater release velocity, early insights into the user experience, a better work environment, etc.) are obvious, but they will want to know that "the big three" are in agreement.

4. Legal

Your next stop is the lawyers. You aren't likely to meet much resistance here if you've completed steps 1–3. They will be concerned (rightly so) about what this change will mean to the public SLAs (answer: if they aren't already fielding lots of SLA violations, then these changes will have almost zero effect and may present an opportunity to adopt more competitive SLAs; if they're fielding more than they'd like, that number will go down).

5. QA

This is your last stop. This is the group that will be most concerned about what these changes mean for them. The important part of this conversation is to keep the team focused on the skills they bring rather than the org they joined. Nobody is going to lose their job—far from it. You're not really there to *convince* the QA team. You're there to (gently) inform them that the company is moving to SLOs and that leadership, engineering, product, and operations all agree this is the right thing to do.

You will need to talk to other groups—sales, marketing, customer support, etc.—but they are consumers of this decision, not the implementers.

Common Objections and How to Overcome Them

Now that you know in which order you need to convince teams, let's talk about the most common objections you will hear from each.

Engineering

The most common objection/concern I hear from engineering teams is:

The ops team will never go for this. They will never give us free rein.

That's an easy enough objection to overcome:

I think they will be thrilled to make this change, but convincing them is up to me. I want to know that you are on board if I can bring them along. This is all upside for you, right? The only reason not to do this is because you don't think you can write reliable code. You don't think that, do you?

In my experience, the resistance pretty much ends right there.

Operations

The operations folks will have a similar concern:

> The engineers will never agree to a world where we have a say over how they spend their time. They think they can just throw code over the wall and dump it on us!

To which you reply:

> I've already talked to them. They are convinced they will write super-reliable code and have agreed that if you let them deploy whenever they want, they will obey the error budget policies we agree to. This is your chance to finally close the loop and have a real impact on how engineers spend their time. Where's the risk? If the engineers really aren't blowing their error budgets, then your pagers are never going off. In that world, who cares how fast they go? And if the engineers are constantly blowing their budgets, then you finally get to influence their work—which is strictly an improvement over the current state of affairs.

Once again, this pretty much ends the argument.

The next step is to get the engineering and operations teams (or managers) in a room. This is a 10-minute conversation where you say:

> I've talked to everyone here and I think we are all in agreement in principle. The engineers will have well-defined SLOs with error budgets and an error budget policy. By agreeing to follow these rules, the engineers get to deploy whenever (and however) they like until they exhaust their error budget.

> The operations folks agree to this with the understanding that if the error budget is exhausted, then the error budget policy will immediately kick in. We will negotiate the details after we get product and leadership on board, but we're all in agreement on the broad strokes, yes?

You may get a few questions (usually around the proposed policies). You should defer those questions because you can't discuss a meaningful policy without involving your business leaders and product folks.

Depending on the level of mistrust that has accumulated between engineering and operations over the years, it may take a few rounds of meetings to get everyone on board, but they will eventually get there. After all, this is a plan that is likely to make everyone's lives better with almost no risk of making anything worse for these two teams.

Product

As we saw earlier, product managers are mostly concerned with shipping features customers want into the marketplace as quickly as possible. For them, the key benefit of adopting (and sticking to) SLOs is that feature velocity will (eventually) get much faster. For them, the discussion goes something like:

How many releases are we doing in a month? A year? What if we could safely do 5 or 10 times that amount; would that be something you would want? The friction and fighting between the engineering and operations functions is costing us a lot of time and effort, and that translates into fewer features developed and shipped. Both engineering and operations are in agreement that by adopting SLOs we can move past that.

Also, when there is a problem in production (because there inevitably will be), our SLOs and error budgets indicate when we need to stop and focus on reliability, and precisely how long to do that for. The guesswork and arguing mostly go away.

All we need from you is to tell us what our users expect for reliability. What is our business requirement? (P.S. The lower the number we can live with, the faster we can go.)

Most product managers I've had this conversation with are concerned that they've never created SLOs before and don't know where to begin. That's what this book is for. Just assure them that they are not nearly the first people to have these concerns, and that this information is eminently learnable. What you need from them is their agreement to give this a try.

Leadership

Once you have an agreement in principle between the engineering, operations, and product functions, it's time to talk to the person or people at your company that can make this decision stick. In some firms this is the CEO or CTO. In other places, a senior-enough VP will suffice.

Here are the most common questions/objections you will hear, and how to answer them:

Q: There's no way you'll get engineering and operations to agree to this.

A: We already have. Everyone is in agreement that we can't continue in our current state and that we have to find a way to move faster while achieving (and keeping) the right level of reliability.

Q: In our firm, we strive for 100% customer satisfaction and 100% uptime! Our customers will tolerate no less!

A: Our customers already *do* tolerate less because we do not (and never have) delivered 100% of either to them. None of our competitors has, either. Nor has any software vendor our customers use.

Q: But I have reports that say *we do*!

A: Those reports are inaccurate. One of the consequences of holding ourselves to standards we can't achieve is that there is no incentive to give you accurate reporting. In fact, there is some incentive to do the opposite. In some sense we are flying blind and need to fix that.

Q: This sounds like a lot of work. We already have product commitments we have to meet.

A: You're right, it *is* a lot of work, but it's long overdue. And after we've done the work, we will have the ability to move much faster than we are now. This is a trend that's growing across the whole industry. Everyone is adopting practices like these, and if we don't make this change we are at a real risk of falling behind our competitors and not noticing until it's too late. Besides, if we try this and it doesn't work, then it's pretty cheap to go back. Also, once we have good SLIs, SLOs, and monitoring in place, we'll be able to know about customer pain *before* they call us to complain. We can be proactive with our most important customers—which should save you a bunch of unpleasant "surprise" phone calls.

In my experience, most senior leaders don't try to be experts in every facet of the business. There are just too many moving pieces. They rely on the judgment of their key functional leaders. Their primary concern is that their key managers are in agreement about an important change. That's the reason to line up engineering, operations, and product *before* you go see the CEO.

Legal

The most important thing the lawyers will want to know is what these changes will do to your existing SLAs or business risk. The simple answer is that there is no reason for the SLAs to change if customers aren't routinely claiming SLA violations. Your legal department is most concerned about noticing and minimizing risk.

The key thing to point out to legal is that when you're done you will have a better way to notify them about pending SLA risk (because your error budgets are burning too quickly), which will give them time to prepare. In the status quo, they don't know about a problem until *after* a customer complains.

As you develop your SLOs, it's important to regularly discuss them with your lawyers so that they can have an informed opinion about the state of your current (and potential future) SLAs.

QA

If you have a dedicated QA team/org, this is going to be your trickiest conversation. However, this group will likely be *consumers* of this decision, rather than part of the *deciding* chain. Your job isn't to seek their approval but rather to assuage their concerns.

The most important concern they will have is, "What happens to us?"

The important thing to stress is that the need for their skills and expertise in designing and instrumenting good testing is not going away. In fact, they will become key design partners whenever the error budget policy is triggered. This change *may* eventually lead to some reorganization, but there is a real upside for them, too.

QA teams are often seen by engineers as "no" teams or "roadblocks." They also tend to be caught in the middle of the friction between engineering and operations. This new regime elevates their skills from second-class roadblock to first-class partner—which makes for a happier work life for everyone involved.

Your First Error Budget Policy (and Your First Critical Test)

Once you have convinced everyone to go on this journey and have started to collect your first set of SLIs and design your first set of SLOs, the biggest negotiation you will have is over what the error budget policy should be (and whether you should have more than one).

Based on experience doing this with lots of groups, I strongly recommend the following:

- For the first year, have exactly *one* error budget policy.
- That policy should be a "no new features" policy.

No new features (feature freeze)

Some kind of new feature freeze is the easiest policy to start with and enforce. It looks something like this.

Suppose you have all agreed that your service should have an availability SLO of 99.9%. That means you have an error budget of 43.2 minutes every 30 days, following all the math described in Chapter 5. As long as you are not unavailable (as defined by your SLIs) for more than 43.2 minutes in any 30-day window, you are in good shape.

Now imagine that you push a change that causes a 60-minute outage. You have now spent 1.39x your error budget. You need to pay down that debt until you are even again. The way to do that is to ship no new features into production for 12 days. For those 12 days, you are in a feature freeze.

For that period of time, however, you are still making changes—you are just confining yourselves to improvements that will make whatever just went wrong less likely to happen again. For those 12 days, I *strongly* recommend that you let your operations team drive the development calendar. This is an important part of the new social contract.

Some (not nearly exhaustive) examples of things the operations team might say include:

- "If we had been able to notice the problem earlier, we could have mitigated sooner. Let's spend the next few days tightening up our monitoring."
- "We noticed the problem pretty quickly but didn't have a fast way to respond/roll back. Let's focus on that."

- "The problem spread too quickly. We should roll out into production more slowly. Let's go fix that."

Ideally, these items will come from the blameless incident retrospective you have all written together after this incident.

The most common question I hear when advocating for a feature freeze as a first policy is: "But what if a freeze is impossible? What if we absolutely have to ship by $DATE for $REASONs?"

That can happen. Maybe your big user conference is in the middle of your freeze period or you have an immovable regulatory requirement (like GDPR compliance). In those cases you have a couple of choices:

Silver bullets

A common way to address this is to give your head of products a small number of (usually three) "silver bullets" to use during the course of the year. At any point (and for any reason), they can exercise those options to break out of a feature freeze. If I'm being honest, I don't much care for this approach because it doesn't have any kind of feedback loop. (Also, what happens if you have more than three legitimate cases in a year?)

Thaw tax

If you are going to have a feature freeze error budget policy, then you should consider building a thaw tax into it. The basic idea is that for every day inside a freeze window that you have to "unfreeze," you pay a tax—say, 50%. Suppose you're in a 12-day feature freeze and decide you have to unfreeze for 2 days to ship some critical new feature. When you're done, you reenter the freeze and add another three days (1.5 * 2) to the freeze period. This approach encourages leaders to think very carefully about violating a current feature freeze. It's the option I prefer, because it's more flexible.

It's not important that you get your first error budget policy perfect. What matters most is that you *create it and stick to it.*

Your first test

When adopting SLOs, the most important moment is not when everyone agrees, or when you decide on your first targets and policy. The most important moment is the first time you exhaust your error budget and need to enforce your policy. That will be the moment that teaches everyone whether or not you are serious about this journey.

Unless you legitimately think that following through would risk putting your company out of business, the most vital thing you can do is follow your policy strictly the first time it is invoked. This will take some amount of corporate will and leadership. Your leaders will really need to step up and set a good example. If you can follow through this first time, then future events will get easier and your company will organically make the cultural changes needed to live a healthy SLO life.

On the other hand, if your leaders give in to the temptation to "make an exception this one time," you'll probably never really seriously adopt SLOs and get their full benefits.

Lessons Learned the Hard Way

Over the years I have seen teams learn some hard lessons about how to (or how *not* to) adopt SLOs. Here are some of the most common lessons that didn't quite fit into the preceding text:

Too much too soon
> When starting with SLOs, don't try to do everything at once. Start with one portion of one product. Better still, start with one *failure domain* (a discrete set of things that tightly depend on one another and fail together). That will limit the number of people you have to convince up front and make it much easier to get started and stick with it.

Less is more
> When getting started, try to restrict yourself to just a few SLIs informing just a few SLOs, and start off with just *one* error budget policy. You can add more later if you need to; the important thing is to begin with a set of measurements and policies that you can easily and quickly reason about.

Review early/review often
> In the beginning, I suggest you actively reevaluate your SLO targets every quarter, or even monthly. If your current SLO is for 99.9% availability, does that still seem like the right number? Are your customers complaining when you expect them to (i.e., when you don't hit your target)? As you mature and dial in your values, you can move your evaluation window to every six months, or even yearly.

Be completely transparent
> Set up dashboards and reporting that anyone in the company can easily find and see—including your executives (these topics are discussed in detail in Chapters 15 and 17). Make sure that these dashboards clearly explain (or link to explanations of) your SLIs, SLOs, error budget policy, and current performance. For bonus points, include a graph of your release velocity (releases per day). It may dip down during the first month or so as you find the right cadence, but eventually it will start moving up and to the right.

Summary

There are two final objections I often hear from teams when talking about adopting SLOs. Let's get those out of the way as we wrap things up:

Objection 1: But we're not Google!

> The SLO-based approach is not unique to Google, or any other large tech company. It can be applied in small teams and startups just as easily as in a large enterprise. The implementation of and adherence to SLOs doesn't have to be onerous, either. If that's the picture you have conjured in your mind, then you are making things too complicated. Stop it!

Objection 2: But we're not smart enough!

> I hear this all the time from teams/companies: "Oh...our people aren't smart/good enough to do something like that!" You wouldn't think people would talk that way about themselves (or their employees), but they sure do. Respectfully (and with love): this is a ridiculous thing to say.

None of this is rocket science (or even algebra). It's just basic arithmetic, maybe a little bit of statistics, and good ol' fashioned discipline. You can read. You can count. You can create and stick to a simple plan. You can do this.

CHAPTER 7

Measuring SLIs and SLOs

Ben Sigelman

It's one thing to understand the philosophy of what a good SLI for a service might be, but it's another thing entirely to actually understand how to implement and measure it. This chapter establishes clear design goals that can guide any SLO implementation and describes common machinery for SLO measurements that can be found within nearly any modern software organization. It then walks through the implementation of common-case SLIs and SLOs, followed with a broader discussion of the general case, and concludes with a few other considerations for anyone implementing SLOs in the real world.

Because SLIs and SLO measurements form the foundation of a healthy, well-managed, and reliable system, the infrastructure used to measure them ends up being sticky, for better or for worse. As such, this chapter goes into some detail about the trade-offs involved with common "brownfield" infrastructure components that are probably already in use at most software organizations today. Another chapter—or perhaps a book!—could be written about a "greenfield" environment where infrastructure availability and reuse are irrelevant.

Design Goals

Unsurprisingly, implementing SLOs is similar to most other software engineering projects: the quality of the results benefits greatly from some advance planning and a keen awareness of overarching design goals. That said, since SLOs and SLIs are often implemented on top of—or within—existing systems, and since they are often implemented incrementally and during spare cycles, we sometimes lose sight of the design goals for SLO measurement and waste time or sacrifice quality as a result.

The six goals outlined in this section can never be completely comprehensive, but if all have been considered and accounted for, your SLO implementation will be all the better for it! As you read through these six goals, remember that this is all just a model, and you'll have to do what works best for you, your systems, and your users.

Flexible Targets

Like the services they measure, SLOs must be able to evolve over time. Sometimes this is simply because we want to adjust an error budget to allow for more releases and faster product iteration. For instance, sometimes the actual structure of a consumer product changes, with implications for downstream services: if a cold boot of a smartphone app suddenly requests 25 user profiles instead of 3, the user profile service may need a tighter P99 latency SLO in order to maintain the same cold boot load time for the end user.

More generally, human operators should be able to adjust the heuristics embedded in the SLIs (for example, 25 ms to 30 ms), success thresholds ("95% of the time" to "97% of the time"), aggregation windows ("over the past 30 seconds" to "over the past 7 days"), and more, all without making code changes, redeploying software, or pushing new production configuration. The SLO performance history before and after the target revision should also be retained, and there should be some way to see how each SLO target has changed over time.

Testable Targets

When adding a new SLO, we need both an SLI and an objective, or target. As discussed at length in Part I, coming up with appropriate targets is often subtle and challenging. What's the right error budget given our reliability history? Should we measure P95 latency, P99 latency, or P99.9 latency? Regardless of the percentile we choose, what should the actual latency threshold be? What's more, per the previous design goal of *flexible* SLO targets, we may have to reconsider all of this any time there's a need to update an SLO.

In order to feel confident about our SLOs, it's immensely helpful to backtest possible targets against historical data. This becomes even more consequential when SLOs are involved in alerting (see Chapter 8)—nobody should ever have to set an alert threshold without a means to estimate alert frequency. As such, any good SLO implementation allows for some form of backtesting as an operator or system maintainer experiments with potential SLIs and target thresholds.

Freshness

Freshness is a measure of the time it takes for an SLO to reflect real-time data in production. Naturally, lower time deltas are always better as far as freshness is concerned, but the actual freshness requirements depend on the nature of the particular SLO.

For instance, certain SLOs may only be used for monthly managerial reports; with such coarse freshness requirements, it's immaterial whether the SLO incorporates data from the most recent 30 seconds or not. Yet in other situations, SLOs can be the first line of defense for business-critical production firefighting. In that context, freshness should be measured in seconds and data processing delays must be kept to a minimum.

Cost

It should go without saying, but cost must be a design consideration, too. Implementing flexible, testable, fresh SLOs is much easier with an infinite budget; but the data engineering requirements for effective organization-wide SLOs can be significant, especially for high-throughput or widely distributed applications. It's neither necessary nor realistic to estimate costs to multiple decimal places, but it *should* be possible to get within a factor of 10 by thinking ahead along three axes: *time series data, structured logging data,* and *opportunity cost.* We'll explore time series and structured logging data in more detail later in this chapter; the opportunity cost is really just the time that you and your colleagues will spend implementing your SLO measurements rather than implementing *something else.* Engineers notoriously undervalue their own time—don't make that mistake!

Reliability

You already know that SLOs are part and parcel of building a culture of reliability and delivering a trustworthy application to end users. Just as one must create SLOs for individual services, the SLO infrastructure must have SLOs of its own! This is usually accomplished by implementing SLOs on top of or within existing high-availability observability components. Sometimes, though, SLOs are implemented via rickety scripts or poorly monitored cron jobs, and clearly this introduces risk and unreliability. If there's a need to build net-new infrastructure in order to implement certain high-priority SLOs, so be it—but make sure to plan ahead and allocate time to make that net-new infrastructure highly available: SLO infrastructure must be among the most reliable software your organization runs in production.

 You should consider how to represent the state of an organization's many SLOs when the SLO infrastructure itself is unreliable or unavailable. If that state cannot be reconstructed after the fact, the ideal solution is to de-consider the period of unavailability entirely when examining longer-term SLO compliance. For instance, if SLO infrastructure is unavailable for 30 minutes in a given week, rather than considering individual monthly SLO compliance by dividing *compliant minutes* by 10,080 (7 * 24 * 60), divide by 10,050 (10,080 − 30).

Organizational Constraints

Finally, organizations often bring constraints beyond any technical or budgetary considerations. For instance, it's still common for organizations in certain highly regulated industries to require that all operational data stays on premises, in physical data centers or within the organization's virtual private cloud (VPC). In other cases, an organization will fight data silos by requiring that all durable time series data or all structured logging data reside within a particular database or with a particular vendor.

Especially with larger and older organizations, it's common to find the design space restricted considerably by what are essentially matters of organizational policy. These restrictions usually exist for good and necessary reasons, but they can be incredibly frustrating when discovered late in the game—do your homework early and be sure you understand the relevant organizational constraints before embarking on a net-new SLO implementation effort.

Common Machinery

Given our design goals of reliability and cost, we should make a best effort to reuse existing infrastructure in our efforts to implement SLOs. When it comes to monitoring and observability, there are many choices, and they are all adding features and capabilities all the time—in fact, some of the more progressive projects and vendors are even adding features specifically dedicated to SLO implementation and management!

To be clear, no part of this chapter is intended to serve as a comparison-shopping guide for monitoring and observability infrastructure. It *is* intended to establish common vocabulary and describe several important capabilities of that infrastructure; we will refer back to these terms and capabilities as we delve into the details of SLO implementation.

Centralized Time Series Statistics (Metrics)

Nearly every software organization has some sort of centralized, durable database of time series statistics about production systems. The exact name for this infrastructure varies from organization to organization, but it's most commonly referred to as a *metrics system*, an *infrastructure monitoring system*, or a *time series database* (TSDB). We use the term TSDB for its specificity and accuracy, but understand that these terms are mostly interchangeable in the context of an SLO implementation.

In some cases, this TSDB infrastructure is open source software (OSS); in others it is managed by a vendor (SaaS or otherwise), and occasionally it is a completely in-house system. In all of these cases, though, the central TSDB should satisfy certain basic requirements that we can leverage in our SLO implementation. The rest of this section lays these out.

TSDBs: The basics

Any general-purpose TSDB must make it easy to store and retrieve statistical data as a time series. Each time series is identified by some sort of unique identifier, and modern TSDBs support key:value tags to provide multidimensional analysis. There must be ways to easily and efficiently append new data points to the end of each time series, and there must also be ways to easily and efficiently query one or more time series, often combining the results to synthesize aggregate time series.

Multidimensional analysis

Every modern, popular TSDB supports some form of multidimensional analysis. This sounds complicated, but it doesn't need to be. The basic idea is simple: we want to be able to analyze our time series data in the aggregate, and we also want to be able to drill down into fine-grained time series data in order to understand variations in the aggregate data.

For example, we might be interested in the total HTTP request throughput for a horizontally scaled microservice. If that aggregate HTTP request rate spikes, an operator will naturally want to understand what's changed: is it just one particular client that's gone haywire? Is the change restricted to a single HTTP endpoint? Is the rate change uniform across all instances of the microservice in question? We can answer these questions within our TSDB if and only if the underlying time series data (often referred to as *metric data*) has been tagged with a client identifier, the HTTP endpoint, or the microservice container ID, respectively. And rather than forcing the operator to do all of the bookkeeping themselves, the TSDB accepts the finest-granularity time series data and manages the computation and storage of the aggregations.

Of course, multidimensional analysis is a rich topic unto itself, but for the purposes of production monitoring and/or SLOs, there's rarely a need to go beyond basic filtering and grouping by tags.

Statistical distribution support

Statistical distributions are incredibly important when implementing SLOs with a TSDB: per our design goals of *flexible targets* and *testable targets*, durably stored time series distributions allow us to measure P95 latency one day and P99 the next without changing code, changing configuration, or losing time series history. A high-quality distribution implementation will also be able to guarantee a maximum margin of error on percentile estimates while simultaneously guaranteeing fixed storage costs regardless of the number of observations included in the distribution.

Unfortunately, unlike multidimensional analysis (which is now ubiquitous), robust statistical distributions are not yet a built-in feature of all popular TSDBs. They can have many uses, but for SLOs they are most useful as a way to represent latency. Latency distributions are the most flexible way to represent the performance of distinct microservice endpoints, the delays added by message queues, or any other large collection of latency observations.

Some TSDBs can represent latency distributions via a histogram. These histograms rarely have linear bucket boundaries, as latency distributions are almost never uniformly distributed: typically the buckets in a latency histogram grow exponentially or geometrically, though there are also more sophisticated approaches, like high dynamic range (HDR) histograms. Other TSDBs represent latency distributions with "sketches" that may be difficult for a human to interpret directly but that can nevertheless be used to provide precise percentile estimates, often with impressively small durable storage requirements and, thus, with small cost. A prominent example is Dunning and Ertl's *t*-digest algorithm, used in some OSS and commercial TSDBs.[1]

For more detail about statistics and probability, see also Chapter 9, which goes into much depth about these approaches.

As mentioned, though, some TSDBs simply do not support statistical distributions as a built-in data type. This is unfortunate, but we can fall back on the key:value tags of multidimensional analysis to mimic a native distribution type.

For example, consider a latency SLI for a particular microservice endpoint, foo. The simplest form of latency distribution—in particular, a latency distribution that can only compute counts, totals, and averages—need only record the observation count and the sum of all observed latencies, as shown in Table 7-1.

Table 7-1. An example simple TSDB entry

TSDB entry	Description
foo_count	The *count* of all observed latencies for the foo endpoint
foo_total	The *sum* of all observed latencies for the foo endpoint

Both the counts and totals can be aggregated trivially (by summing) across microservice instances or other operator-defined tags. Reconstructing the average is simply a matter of dividing the sum of aggregated totals by the sum of aggregated counts.

Still, this is not much of a distribution—especially since we can't approximate high-percentile latencies, which are of outsize importance for SLIs and SLOs. To get closer to percentile estimates, we can populate a crude histogram using tags, as in Table 7-2.

---

[1] Dunning, Ted, and Otmar Ertl. 2019. "Computing Extremely Accurate Quantiles Using t-Digests." arXiv preprint arXiv:1902.04023. https://arxiv.org/abs/1902.04023.

Table 7-2. A simple way to start bucketing data

TSDB entry	Tags	Description
foo_count	none	The *count* of all observed latencies for the foo endpoint.
foo_total	none	The *sum* of all observed latencies for the foo endpoint.
foo_bucket_count	bucket_min	The *count* of all observed latencies for the foo endpoint that are ≥ bucket_min, and < the next-highest bucket_min. Typically these bucket thresholds are represented as milliseconds or microseconds.

It is not trivial to directly approximate P99 using the preceding schema with standard time series filtering and grouping aggregations. That said, it *is* trivial to directly approximate the percentile that corresponds to a given latency value: if we want to understand which fraction of observed foo latencies were less than a given threshold, k, we sum up the foo_bucket_counts for all buckets below k, interpolate the value for the bucket containing k, and divide that subtotal by the overall foo_count, yielding a fraction that we can convert to a percentile simply by multiplying by 100.

To make this more concrete, Table 7-3 shows a specific example.

Table 7-3. Implementing a real histogram

TSDB entry	Tags	Value
foo_count	none	2250
foo_total	none	2150
foo_bucket_count	bucket_min = 0	300
foo_bucket_count	bucket_min = 1	400
foo_bucket_count	bucket_min = 2	800
foo_bucket_count	bucket_min = 5	500
foo_bucket_count	bucket_min = 10	100
foo_bucket_count	bucket_min = 20	0
foo_bucket_count	bucket_min = 50	100
foo_bucket_count	bucket_min = 100	50

If the bucket_min values are specified in milliseconds, we can estimate the percentile corresponding to 75 ms by summing the foo_bucket_counts for bucket_mins 0 through 50, then assuming a uniform distribution within the bucket_min=50 value and dividing it by 2 to exclude samples between 75 ms and 100 ms. This yields a subtotal of:

$$\frac{30888}{7776} = 3.97$$

observations at or below 75 ms, which is 95.56% of the overall `foo_count`. In other words, 75 ms is approximately the P95.6 for the `foo` latency distribution.

If this is too daunting or expensive, there is always the standard deviation and/or the variance. To compute either, one can compute the sum of squares for all observed distribution values and store those values alongside the count and total. Note that there are numerical stability issues with sum of squares, especially for distributions with many observations and very high means relative to their variance. This was a material consideration at Google, for instance, and so a more cumbersome yet more stable online algorithm was used to compute the same standard deviation and variance. A discussion of these techniques is outside the scope of this book, though there's nothing mysterious about them: like the t-digest histograms mentioned earlier, they simply offer a trade-off between quality, cost, and the simplicity of the implementation.[2]

TSDBs and our design goals

Returning to our design goals for any SLO implementation, TSDBs have a lot to offer but are far from a silver bullet. Let's walk through the evaluation criteria:

Flexible targets
> Flexibility in a TSDB is accomplished through key:value tags and multidimensional analysis. If there is a native distribution data type, that also adds a great deal of flexibility for percentile estimates. All of this said, TSDB flexibility will always be limited by the fact that the raw event data is aggregated away immediately.

Testable targets
> In practice, testability for "standard" SLIs and SLOs—things like latency and error ratios—is good. Platform teams typically configure services to auto-report these statistics, so they should be available going back in time, even for net-new SLIs or SLOs. However, for nonstandard or bespoke SLOs, testability is a significant concern for TSDBs. The raw event data is inaccessible, so in many cases there is no way to backtest potential SLIs or SLOs.

Freshness
> Freshness guarantees vary from TSDB to TSDB, but typically are no longer than 60 seconds. In some cases, they can be quite good: seconds or less. That said, one must also consider the end-to-end length of the data pipeline connecting services to the TSDB itself. In some cases, this can involve cron jobs, batch processes, or worse.

---

2 This is not to say that the math itself is actually always simple, but luckily we have computers ready and available to perform this math for us. You can read more about this in Chapter 9.

Cost

Cost depends almost entirely on the need for high-cardinality tags. *Cardinality* refers to the number of *distinct combinations of values* for the keys associated with a given time series metric. Cost is proportional to cardinality, and incorporating unbounded sets like hostnames, customer IDs, or HTTP paths often leads to cardinality getting out of control. To make matters worse, it is often challenging to accurately forecast the cost of new tags before they're deployed to production. The "cost of the cost" can simply be the monthly spend on a TSDB or metrics vendor, or it can be the operational expense of babysitting an in-house TSDB that's struggling to perform under its own weight.

Reliability

TSDBs are almost invariably multitenant. This is both a good thing and a bad thing: it means that a single bad actor can potentially damage the shared resource for the other tenants, but it also means that TSDB reliability is closely scrutinized and an obvious organizational priority. TSDBs are often the first line of defense for incident response (whether formally using SLOs or not), and this also increases organizational motivation to keep the TSDB healthy and reliable.

Organizational constraints

Essentially, all organizations considering SLOs already rely on some sort of TSDB. There will likely be strong organizational gravity toward that TSDB, even in spite of missing features or shortcomings: the organizational cost of data siloization is high, and making the case for an $N+1$th TSDB will be challenging.

All in all, TSDBs are the single most popular place to durably store SLI and SLO data, and for good reason.

Structured Event Databases (Logging)

If TSDBs are the most popular place to store SLI and SLO data, a structured event (or "logging") database would be next in line.

First, regarding terminology: *logging* means many things to many people. Here, we use the term to refer to the collection, durable storage, and retrieval of *structured data about individual transactions, requests, or processes*—that is, *events*. These are in contrast to the *statistics* (often about these same transactions, requests, and processes) stored in a TSDB. Many people think of logging mainly in the context of `printf()`-style debug logs; these are indeed stored in structured event databases, though they are a questionable choice for SLIs and SLOs due to their informality and susceptibility to sudden changes at the whim of developers.

However, structured events representing distinct transactions, requests, or processes can be an excellent starting place for SLI and SLO assembly. The individual events themselves are too granular, but by performing simple aggregations we can estimate everything from throughput to latency percentiles to error ratios.

Aggregate analysis

Nearly all structured event databases allow for queries over time ranges and substrings. Some of these databases were originally designed for searches over human-readable debug logs; others were designed with richer structured data in mind. In either case, you should be able to easily compute all of the following:

- The count (and thus the rate) of matching events over a provided time range
- The sum of scalars (for example, latency values) embedded within log lines or corresponding to a given key within matching events
- The (percentile) rank of a given threshold value with respect to a larger population of scalars corresponding to a given key within matching events

Naturally there is variation in the specific query-time feature sets of the many structured event databases (and/or logging systems) in use today. For instance, some allow for the direct computation of user-defined percentiles, JOINs to external data sources, or time series anomaly detection. Others directly support SLOs as a named concept within the product built around the structured event database itself. This book is not meant to catalog the ever-changing feature matrices of the available options, but we strongly encourage you to research the SLO-oriented capabilities of your organization's chosen structured event database before making assumptions about what is supported and not.

Structured event databases and our design goals

Structured event databases are a compelling choice for SLI and SLO implementation. Here is how they stack up against our design goals:

Flexible targets
> Structured event databases are appealing primarily because of their flexibility at query time. As long as the actual structured events themselves include the fields needed to express an SLO—for example, things like HTTP endpoint names, error codes, or hostnames—then the event database's query language should be capable of expressing the filtering, grouping, and counting needed to implement most SLOs.

Testable targets
> Backtesting of SLOs is possible, as long as the events were recorded in the first place. Since aggregation happens at query time, even the most granular features of the underlying events can be extracted and used for arbitrary computations after the fact. One caveat is that, for cost or compliance reasons, many structured

event databases only retain the raw data for a fixed period of time—the *retention horizon*. In some cases that horizon can be less than a week, and that can be problematic when trying to estimate a baseline for an SLO.

Freshness

Freshness varies, but this is rarely a strength of structured event databases. In some cases, in fact, the freshness is downright disqualifying: for SLOs used for alerting, even seconds of detection delay can have a business impact, and some structured event databases can lag production by minutes, or tens of minutes. Be sure to not just look at the best-case freshness for your organization's structured event database; look back over the past several months (or even years) of monitoring data to get a sense of the variation in freshness over time. Structured event databases are typically multitenant, and freshness (and reliability, another of our goals) can be impacted by a single bad actor. This can be nearly catastrophic from a fiscal or infrastructure reliability standpoint, and is difficult to defend against. In contrast, with a TSDB raw event frequency has a near-zero effect on cost and reliability.

Cost

Traditional and historic structured event databases (again, often referred to as *logging systems*) can have cost and ROI scaling issues when faced with today's distributed architectures. This is not mysterious: if each service in a given architecture emits at least one event for each request or transaction processed, as we break monoliths down into hundreds or thousands of services the total volume of structured events grows proportionally. This is relevant because SLOs for individual services will rely on just this sort of *services* ✕ *transactions* event data, and if the CFO will eventually cry foul about the capital expenditure cost of the approach, it's better to preempt the problem and choose a different pattern. In practice, the cost of structured event databases can become problematic for SLOs in very high-throughput or very distributed applications. For low-throughput applications—or for monolithic applications—the cost of implementing SLOs in a structured event database should be reasonable.

Reliability

The reliability of structured event databases varies greatly from organization to organization and implementation to implementation (or vendor to vendor). In many cases, this comes back to cost: in order to keep costs under control, many structured event databases are underprovisioned for real-time applications like SLOs. But this is not a given, and the only way to find out is to ask around and get hard measurements for freshness, query latency, and raw up/down availability.

Organizational constraints

For the most part, these mirror the organizational constraints for TSDBs, described earlier. That said, compliance concerns about structured events will be even more stringent than for the largely statistical data in a TSDB, so it's more likely that structured event databases will be kept on premises or within the network confines of an organization's own VPCs. By consequence, the operational maintenance burden for structured event databases should be factored in, especially if there is a need to increase the reliability before relying on such a database for critical SLOs.

Common Cases

Of course there are a wide variety of SLOs worth implementing, but certain patterns come up more often than others. Here we present implementation suggestions for common-case SLOs. Note that these suggestions are just that: suggestions, which should be adopted where they seem appropriate and ignored where they do not. In all cases, we outline the implementations given a generic TSDB and a structured event database. Before choosing either implementation, carefully consider your organization's time series or structured event database in terms of our SLO implementation design goals, as sometimes basic criteria like freshness, reliability, or compliance are disqualifying.

Latency-Sensitive Request Processing

A wide class of systems and services implement the following basic pattern:

1. They accept requests, typically in the form of a network API call (whether REST, gRPC, SOAP, or manual input—it doesn't matter).

2. They do work, which may or may not involve system calls or the invocation of other services.

3. They return responses or errors.

SLIs and SLOs for latency-sensitive request processing typically focus on the *error ratio rate* (that is, the ratio of the raw error rate to the total request rate) and *latency* (that is, the distribution of request-processing durations, often measured as the P95 or P99). Our goal here is to be able to understand both the latency and error rate via one measurement. This is one of the advantages of an SLI-based approach to measurement—you can aggregate and combine many metrics into one understandable number.

Whether using a TSDB or a structured event database, you will need to record all of the following:

- The canonical name for the API call (such as the action name, endpoint name, or gRPC method name). Note that this canonical name should not include encoded query parameters: those have high cardinality and will defeat the aggregations required for SLO implementation.

- Request success or failure. This is harder than it sounds: if the service has a profound failure while processing a request, it may not be able to respond with an error code. For this reason, some organizations choose to implement an ingress proxy or service mesh which has a higher likelihood of surviving the request and accurately reporting about any errors.

- The response latency, ideally expressed in milliseconds or microseconds. Like errors, self-reported latency numbers are not always as reliable as one would hope due to queues in kernels and HTTP stacks that often precede the start time for application-level timers. Again, a service mesh or ingress proxy may have a more accurate picture of service latency, though it can also (ironically) introduce additional latency itself.

- Either implicitly or explicitly, an SLO implementation will likely rely on metadata like the service's cloud provider region, environment (e.g., staging or production), and software version. The metadata required here will likely be part of the boilerplate for any new service.

 From an instrumentation standpoint, all of this information should be encapsulated for generality's sake. This can be subtler than it sounds, as the response latency and error state are not determined until the end of request processing, so some basic bookkeeping may be required. Use of a common instrumentation API like OpenTelemetry can help here, as popular application-level frameworks may already be supported, corner cases and all.

For a TSDB, you will need counters for total requests and errors, possibly including a tag for error code where the error code is available and has well-understood cardinality. Error ratio rates can be implemented by simple division of an error rate query and a total throughput query, though sometimes it helps to include a minimum throughput value as well: otherwise, very low-throughput test clusters can create false positives with very high (apparent) error ratios. The treatment of latency in a TSDB is more implementation-dependent. Ideally, the TSDB directly supports globally aggregated latency distributions, and the individual latency measurements can be emitted as is. Where that is not possible, one can always fall back on the histogram-as-tags approach described in "Common Machinery" on page 114.

For a structured event database, try to emit a single structured event describing the entire request/response pair (in a distributed tracing system, the *span*). This should be sufficient to directly construct SLI and SLO queries for error rates and latency statistics.

Note that the cost of implementing a given SLO in a conventional structured event database will grow roughly linearly with request throughput, but will remain mostly constant with a TSDB. For this reason, conventional structured databases are rarely a good choice for error and latency SLOs in very high-throughput services; TSDBs are often the chosen alternative, though there are also more modern hybrid approaches that look like a structured event database for recent data and a TSDB for historical data.

Low-Lag, High-Throughput Batch Processing

Nested request processing (as described in the previous section) is not the only popular architectural pattern: more and more systems today are built around message queues (like Apache Kafka) or depend on the reliability of batch processing systems (like a MapReduce implementation, Apache Spark, or Apache Flink). Though the applications of these systems vary widely, the systems themselves are designed to support high throughput and data processing at acceptable cost via batching.

The batching and data shuffling can make observability and debugging of such systems extremely challenging, but thankfully the SLOs don't need to be. The single most important principle is to stay disciplined about measuring the health of these systems from the standpoint of their consumers (rather than their operators). In that respect, externally visible health is determined by two SLIs:

Data processing lag
> How long does it take a message inserted into a topic (or message queue) to be visible to consumers? How long does it take a new data point to be reflected by a model generated in batches?

Overall throughput
> How many messages or data points is the system processing per unit time?

The trouble with batch-processing systems is that lag will be fine—and constant—until it's not. Then, due to the cruel realities of queueing theory, it can back up incredibly quickly, and often catastrophically. This means we must measure not just the raw lag, but also the throughput, and we should proactively and assiduously ensure that throughput stays safely below fundamental maximum values supported by our infrastructure (and budgets).

The amount of data needed to measure SLOs for message queues and batch processing systems is typically small: it's constrained by the number of topics or data processing pipelines that should be assessed or guarded by SLOs. More details about how to do this are provided in Chapter 11 (in terms of thinking about the right approaches) and Chapter 9 (in terms of handling the sometimes complicated math of dealing with only a few data points).

Mobile and Web Clients

Part of the rationale for SLOs is to focus our operational attention on "the needs of the user." For a service in the middle of a deeply layered stack, that "user" may simply be another service; but if we keep on moving up the stack, the SLOs that matter most to most businesses apply directly to end users.

Measuring SLOs from the standpoint of an end user is challenging. Especially with the rise of mobile clients (whether web-based or native), the performance and reliability of an application is only as good as the cellular connection it's served over. Nevertheless, it is highly valuable to directly measure and strategize around end user–facing SLOs, as they can help inform the relative priority of potential optimizations and the costs and benefits of net-new product functionality from a performance and reliability standpoint.

The measurements themselves are conceptually similar to those described earlier, in the subsection about latency-sensitive request processing. In addition to the name of the API call, success or failure, and response latency, it is also helpful to capture mobile or web platform information (OS or browser version) and some sort of connection quality classification (the fidelity of which typically varies by platform).

Often these measurements are recorded as structured events (sometimes more specifically as distributed tracing spans) and sent to application backends in a side channel. For both power conservation and bandwidth conservation reasons, this side channel is often implemented as an optional telemetry field in an existing mobile-to-backend API call; upon receipt by the backend, the client telemetry data is then forwarded on to a TSDB and/or a structured event database, at which point it can be queried just like any other data in those systems.

In some cases, organizations work with SaaS monitoring or observability products that integrate into the web and mobile clients, then send the structured telemetry data directly and securely to the vendor's cloud services. This is an easier integration, but it is also less efficient from a bandwidth and power standpoint, and naturally furthers a dependency on a vendor.

When setting SLOs for mobile and web clients, outlier behavior will be dominated by network factors that are typically beyond the control of the application developer. While the performance and reliability of the network itself is not something we can directly control, we can still set goals around perceived application performance in spite of these network factors. These goals can help guide important engineering efforts, like edge computing, content delivery network configuration, and multiregion and replication strategies. For this reason, we suggest setting explicit SLOs for clients, perhaps broken down by platform and/or network connectivity class.

The General Case

Of course, not all SLOs fall into one of the common-case categories described in the previous section. When thinking through an implementation strategy, these are the main factors to consider:

- If the SLI pertains to a set of events, what is the event rate? If it's high (roughly ≥ 10,000 events per second), then a TSDB is probably more appropriate from an ROI standpoint. Otherwise, a structured event database will provide more flexibility as long as freshness and reliability are not disqualifying.

- If the SLI is a gauge—that is, if it is a nonmonotonic scalar value, like a queue length or a saturation percentage—then a TSDB is the natural implementation choice.

Any SLO must be a combination of an SLI and some objective or target. That said, there is flexibility in where the "indicator" stops and the "objective" begins. For instance, both of the following models represent the same SLO from a compliance standpoint:

1. SLI: The fraction, x, of requests that respond with 750 ms SLO: $x \geq 90\%$

2. SLI: The statistical distribution, d, of latency measurements for all requests SLO: $P90(d) \leq 750$ ms

The flexibility of structured event databases allows us to model the SLI and SLO in either of these ways, and even to change our model after the fact. For those who don't think about monitoring or observability all day long, the distinction between SLIs and SLOs will be either unimportant or (sadly) lost entirely—with this sort of flexibility, the SLO just boils down to a single computation, SLI and all.

With a TSDB, it's not as simple: we typically *cannot* reevaluate data from the past, especially on a per-event basis. For this reason, SLIs in TSDBs should be chosen to minimize coupling to particular heuristics (like the "750 ms" in the first of the preceding SLI models). In a TSDB, the most forward-compatible, flexible strategy is to move heuristics out of the SLI and into the SLO. For instance, the second of the preceding models places both the desired percentile (P90) and the latency threshold (750 ms) in the SLO.

Similarly, if we were setting an SLO about queue length where our objective is that it has at most 150 elements for at least 54 minutes (90%) out of every hour, we could use either of the following models:

1. SLI: A Boolean state representing whether the queue length is ≤ 150 elements

   SLO: The bool is true for ≥ 90% of samples in the past hour

2. SLI: The queue length, l

   SLO: A query measuring the percentage of the past hour where $l ≤ 150$

In a TSDB, the second model will yield greater flexibility and testability as heuristics are adjusted over time.

Other Considerations

We could easily devote an entire book to SLI and SLO implementation—but while that's more than is appropriate here, there are a few implementation topics that deserve additional attention. For other examples, you can find a plethora of defined SLIs and SLOs in Chapters 11 and 12.

Integration with Distributed Tracing

In this chapter we've talked quite a bit about *structured event databases*. Where SLOs are concerned, those structured "events" are usually parts of requests or transactions, and thus they usually have a duration. A structured event with a request or transaction identifier and a duration is semantically identical to a span from a distributed tracing system.[3]

Historically, distributed tracing was thought of as its own "product" with valuable but highly specialized use cases, mostly around performance analysis and distributed debugging. Really, though, distributed traces are just a data source that can be applied to a variety of problems, and SLIs and SLOs are well qualified to benefit from distributed tracing data and technology.

Some modern distributed tracing platforms allow for high-throughput collection of span (i.e., structured event) data, thus enabling flexible construction of SLIs and SLOs based on that distributed tracing data. The real value of the distributed tracing integration, though, is in what's done with the SLO: for instance, if an SLO violation constitutes a production emergency, a distributed tracing system can sometimes point toward the portion of the distributed system that's responsible for a change in latency, error ratios, or throughput.

---

3 For (much) more about spans, consider reading *Distributed Tracing in Practice* by Rebecca Isaacs et al. (O'Reilly), the 2010 Dapper paper (*https://research.google/pubs/pub36356/*) from Google, or even my more historically oriented blog post (*https://lightstep.com/blog/a-brief-history-of-the-span-hard-to-love-hard-to-kill/*) about the origins of "the span."

SLI and SLO Discoverability

As we describe in more detail throughout Part III of this book, adopting an SLO-based approach requires a cultural shift. As such, it's important that both SLIs and SLOs be discoverable and well documented. Due to growing recognition of their importance, SLOs are now formally incorporated into some OSS and proprietary monitoring and observability offerings. When they're not, though, it's important to plan for and create an organizational manifest of SLIs and SLOs, which should ideally be incorporated into an existing and well-used production service database. If SLIs and SLOs are implemented perfectly without being discoverable, they can have an additive effect within an organization, but miss out on the multiplicative effect of clearly describing and documenting service health to other engineers. We'll talk more about developing discoverable and understandable SLOs in Chapter 15.

Summary

At the end of the day, most useful SLIs and SLO measurements are complex, multi-stage computations, and like any such computations, their implementation involves trade-offs and conflicting goals that must be held in tension. Practically speaking, most organizations today will be able to implement common SLOs using some combination of a general-purpose TSDB (colloquially, a *metrics system*) and a general-purpose structured event database (colloquially, a *logging system*). That said, the latest generation of observability infrastructure can often provide more flexibility, testability, and freshness for equivalent cost—organizations capable of adopting new infrastructure would be wise to consider these more modern options. In this chapter, in addition to considering the current infrastructure options, we stepped through implementation for common-case SLIs and SLOs and learned where an SLI ends and an SLO begins. Finally, we explored the role of distributed tracing in SLO workflows and how to make SLIs and SLOs discoverable throughout an organization.

CHAPTER 8

SLO Monitoring and Alerting

Niall Murphy

Previous chapters have discussed how SLOs can help support thinking about the user, determine what work various teams do, and aid balancing between reliability and feature velocity. We've talked about setting SLOs and how to choose what to do with them, we've talked about error budgets and how your organization can react when the budget is burned, and we've talked about what you can do when there's budget to play with.

This chapter takes on the topic at the heart of implementing SLOs practically: monitoring, and especially alerting. It's a complicated topic, so I'll start off by explaining a few things that some advanced readers may feel they understand already—if this applies to you, it's perfectly okay to skip ahead to the "how to" section. There may, however, be some useful material in the motivational section that is relevant when you have to convince other people about SLO monitoring/alerting, so you may want to take a look at it anyway.

Despite it being a complicated topic, the good news is that SLO alerting really is one of the most promising developments in the management of production systems today. It promises to get rid of a lot of the chaos, the noise, and the sheer uselessness of conventional alerting that teams experience, and replace them with something significantly more maintainable. However, for this to be possible, you need to substantially change how you think about alerting.

Motivation: What Is SLO Alerting, and Why Should You Do It?

I could answer this question in a few different ways, depending on whether or not you've done monitoring before and whether or not you already have an existing monitoring "corpus" (set of monitors, rules, and so on).

For the purposes of this chapter, though, let's start off by doing precisely the thing they say you should never do: defining something by what it isn't, rather than what it is.

The Shortcomings of Simple Threshold Alerting

You're running a service. It doesn't matter what kind. It could be an image server, an ice-cream stock management service in an online gelateria, or a batch processor for credit card transactions. In all these cases you have a metric that you know you have to be concerned about, and it's usually related to the capacity of your system in some way. For the image server, let's say it's queries per second; you know (from bitter experience) that high CPU usage across your existing fleet adds about 500 ms of latency for each 100 qps added to the base load.

In addition to running the service, you are (of course) writing *alerts*—things that are supposed to bring a human, with their valuable skills and attention, into the picture in order to rectify problems.

For the purposes of this chapter let's say that the bulk of monitoring active at most organizations today, and likely also historically, takes the following approach to handling those problems:

1. Find relevant metrics (CPU usage, stock levels, queue lengths, and so on).

2. Make a guess (sometimes educated, sometimes not) as to a "bad" number you wouldn't want to see that metric hit.

3. Set up an alert for that metric hitting that value (a *threshold alert*).

4. (Optional) Occasionally tweak the number as you gain experience with the alert.

That, right there, is how "monitoring and alerting" (sic) is typically done. Its biggest virtue is that it is (comparatively) simple. Unfortunately, its biggest vice is that it doesn't actually work. Or perhaps more accurately, it *can* work, but it is very costly for what you get, is well defined only for very stable environments, and has many theoretical and implementation problems. Some of these are obvious, some subtle.

Let's look at these problems in more detail.

Thresholds don't stay relevant

It's a sad fact, but it's true: *absolute thresholds don't stay relevant*. The simplest way to understand this is to think about a small but consistently growing online business. If we say your business grows 4–10% a quarter—a figure far from unknown for success-ful operations—then in under a year it will have gone from 100% of what it's cur-rently doing to anywhere between 116% and 146%, as Figure 8-1 illustrates.

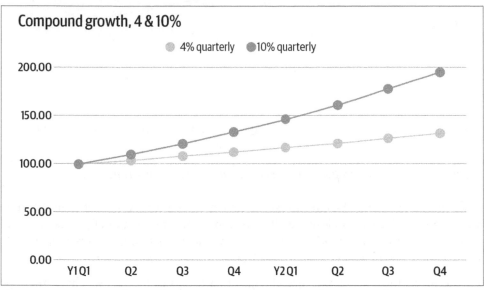

Figure 8-1. Compound growth over time, assuming 4% and 10% growth/quarter

Given that most online computing systems tend to operate with about 10–20% free capacity, a simple absolute threshold that you picked in January will be absolutely irrelevant within a year, and sometimes considerably more quickly.

As an example, let's say in January you are doing 100 qps, and you picked 90 qps as a significant threshold. In late December, given a 4% quarterly growth rate, you are now doing 116 qps, as illustrated in Figure 8-1. The problem is, your absolute thres-hold is still stuck at 90 qps! So your *effective* alerting threshold is now 90/116 = 77% of what it once was. In other words, a 90 qps threshold in January meant you were within 10% of peak when it triggered; in December, it's 23%. Figure 8-2 illustrates how thresholds decrease in relevance over time (assuming growth of 4% or 10% per quarter).

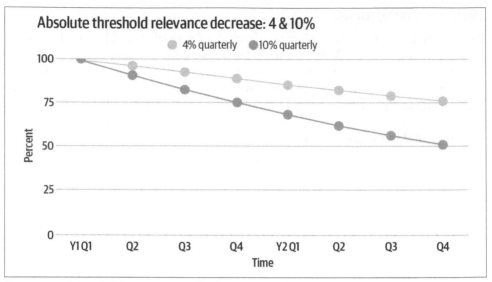

Figure 8-2. Thresholds proportionally decrease in relevance over time

Although the increase of irrelevance over time doesn't affect every metric in the same way, the overall effect is clear. You'll alert a lot more, proportionally speaking, and your alert-receiving teams will consequently be more tired, more distracted, and less able to effect meaningful change. (I'll talk about this effect more later.)

Furthermore, most businesses also change other things as they grow. There might be underlying hardware changes for cloud systems or on premises. New products are launched, requiring new code pathways to be executed: some are more CPU-expensive, some less. The business might buy another business, or shed a division to a competitor. Any threshold, well tuned for the conditions pertaining today, could be totally irrelevant tomorrow, and we don't even need an abstract reminder of how seismic events happen with astonishing regularity to know this.

Static threshold adherents will say, "That's fine—what you've just given is an argument for keeping the *idea* of thresholds, but regularly revising them so the signal to noise ratio stays about the same." Unfortunately, the reality is most organizations don't do this as often as they should, either for time/prioritization reasons or because everything becomes much harder to change when it gets into production. Instead, thresholds often only get changed as a result of an outage, which is inefficient.[1]

---

1 In some ways it's quite peculiar that we are so bad at this, because the issue of businesses growing slowly over time is widely and well understood and lots of processes take account of it—e.g., salary negotiations, inflation impacts on cost of goods sold, and so on.

SLIs and SLOs, of course, also have to change over time; it's a basic part of how they work. However, since they also work as reporting devices, it's much easier to spot when they should do so, and reporting is often better connected to the right place in a business to mandate change. This is discussed at great length in Chapters 14, 15, and 17.

Actually, though, the problem is worse than that, because it's really only the planned growth scenarios that are easily solved via regularly scheduled changes, while event-driven revisions are both more common and more disruptive. Even if you switch to an event-driven response mode for those cases—that is, changing thresholds after each potentially affecting event—you're still faced with the question of *which* events should motivate the change of thresholds, and in which direction.

But there's actually an even more fundamental problem than those.

Poor proxies for user experience

In our earlier examples, I noted that in an image server there is a "known bad" relationship between CPU usage and latency. We started off with the model that we needed to know about this CPU usage value so we could prevent it from getting too high. (The example was carefully chosen, but intended to be representative of a class of real-world systems and monitoring of those systems.)

So, there's one obvious problem here: we know that there's a correlation between CPU usage and latency, but we're not alerting on latency directly. In other words, CPU usage is being used as a *proxy* for latency, our real target. This is usually done because the true target is harder to measure, and the proxy is good enough for most purposes. Unfortunately, there are two issues with this approach:

- After a while you may forget that what actually matters is the target and end up organizationally fixated on the proxy.
- The proxy is sometimes not actually very good at representing the target, or might be good only under limited circumstances.

As you'll recall from the discussions in Chapter 3, the user experience is ultimately what is the most important, and this particular case is a good illustration of not paying attention to that. Here we are not monitoring latency directly, which means we're flying blind on a core contributor to user experience. What's more, CPU usage itself is a poor proxy for latency. Although we don't have enough time here to illustrate the underlying reasons for this with the full care they deserve, it's common to measure *server-side* CPU usage and expect that this is the primary determinant of latency. In fact, it's not—*client-side* latency, which is strongly impacted by network and device performance and reliability, can affect the user experience even more. But since server-side metrics are generally more easily available to an organization, that's what gets used.

Indeed, CPU usage isn't even necessarily the most important server-side determinant: disk I/O delays can be just as bad, and can add lots of avoidable latency to every transaction in a way that high CPU use might only do intermittently. We're really measuring the wrong thing in multiple ways here. So whereas ultimately it is the user experience that matters the most, these particular metrics leave us a long way off from being able to tell what that experience is.

 Although it is possible to argue that latency is itself just a proxy for the user experience, and therefore it is just as questionable as other metrics, client-side latency is certainly a more accurate one than server-side CPU usage. The map is not the territory, and therefore no metric is unquestionable. Your organization may settle upon and discard a variety of metrics and associated thresholds over the course of its existence, as it gets an increasingly accurate idea of what matters to the user. This is as it should be. Don't be afraid to change; do be afraid of paralysis and fixation on the wrong thing.

Context loss in static thresholds

Related to the discussion so far is the fact that using non-SLO alerting for user experience often means choosing arbitrary constants: for example, "10 users have experienced slow loading" or "the P95 latency has been above a certain threshold for too long." This is bad because static thresholds *lose context*: the P95 latency might be too sensitive to individual data points during times of low traffic, and a fixed quantity like the 10 worst user experiences might become noisy when you have tens of thousands of users at peak times.

Unclear correlation between threshold and behavior and nonrange alerting

As a partial refinement of our discussion, we also see scenarios where a metric can take a range of values (say, in this example, CPU usage from 0–100%), and we know that some of these values are definitely bad (say, 80%+). Other values might be bad too—say, 50–79%—but we can't say for sure. Unfortunately, in a world where you don't have anything other than threshold-crossing to trigger a new kind of behavior, the temptation is to set the threshold for when you last had an outage. So, inevitably, over time the threshold creeps down as more (and more complex) outages trigger at lower CPU values because of other contributing factors, even though, say, 63% is in fact a totally fine value for CPU usage (unless someone is running a batch job at the same time).

In this way, because we are using "triggering the humans earlier" as a mechanism to resolve our collective lack of understanding, the interactions that complex systems have end up driving alerting threshold values lower over time. Alas, what this really means, of course, is that we don't understand the system properly, and we end up making it worse by hastening alert fatigue.

 Chapter 17 offers advice on the relationship between SLOs, reporting, and outage life-cycle management. It may be useful to you in providing reverse pressure to offset the incentives that typically drive alerting toward being noisier.

Alert fatigue and fog of war

Human responses to alerts gradually decay in energy over time. The name for this psychological and physiological effect is *alert fatigue*. Intuitively, attention and the energy of response are sapped not just by real incidents, which of course happen regularly, but in particular by false positives. A long sequence of false positives in which true positives are interleaved leads to a decreasing ability to tell one from the other over time. (This is a noted effect (*https://www.healthcareitnews.com/news/how-one-hospital-tweaks-its-ehr-fight-alert-fatigue*) in, for example, medicine, and can have fatal consequences in that domain. It has even been observed in engineers maintaining the safety of nuclear power plants, in case you were finding sleeping at night too easy.)

A related effect is the so-called *fog of war*: with sufficiently large amounts of alerts going off during a large outage, the spurious alerts only serve to divert attention from the things that really matter.

Human beings can only pay fixed amounts of high-quality attention to things. Alerting on simple thresholds, not well correlated with user experience, does not spend that budget wisely. Instead, it makes it more likely you'll have outages, as ability to discriminate decreases; it also makes it harder to resolve said outages, as the sheer number of alerts increases. Even worse, most organizational alerting policies act over time to increase the number of noisy and spurious alerts, rather than decrease them.

If we develop that point, you'll see how pernicious that effect is. Organizations generally care about outages and want to have fewer of them and less severe ones, so there's all the incentive in the world to push thresholds lower "just in case." Furthermore, *perceived* negligence is almost always regarded poorly. "We could have spotted outage X by setting threshold Y lower? Why didn't we do that?" The counterargument that setting Y lower will lead to lots of false positives can be airily dismissed as you not doing your job. Alas, the paradox here is that attention and focus do not improve even if you are alerted about the same thing multiple times: in fact, the opposite is true. It's even worse if you are alerted for lots of things, and some of them are useful and some not.

We see over time, then, that there's an implicit process for making alerting "stricter" and "more aggressive," but no implicit process in the other direction. Ultimately, this is unsustainable. The best solution we have today is SLO alerting, which surfaces the trade-off and encodes it in the alerting logic. (Some organizations explicitly set aside time to revise thresholds *upwards*, or eliminate alerts entirely.)

Picking an SLO number is something a human should do

If none of the discussion so far resonates with you, perhaps this one will. Ultimately, simple threshold-based alerts are a numeric guessing game. You're trying to pick, from the context you have on hand, some number that will meet the goals of keeping your service going to an agreed standard, not burning people out too much, and not otherwise being too costly. In essence, you're trying to guess a number based on these priorities, and there's usually some range that definitely will not work, some range that definitely will, and some gray area in between. So, most teams start off by picking something arbitrary and then tuning it over time.

This isn't really a very good way of doing it, though. For one thing, picking an arbitrary starting point is better than not starting at all, but depending on the point you pick it will likely also result in an arbitrary number of outages. The stage up from that—using data to try to pick a good place to start, rather than guessing—is an improvement, but is usually done within a local team context rather than a full user-experience one. Since choosing an alerting target in the absence of an explicit, formal SLO essentially involves picking an implicit SLO, it is surely better to just do it as a formal SLO process, with full user experience trade-offs in mind. Being too geared to the local context is actually a mistake in this case.

Finally, simple absolute threshold alerting itself doesn't take into account all of the other problems discussed before: even an "AIOps"-style approach[2] where the simple thresholds are regenerated daily by some automated process will still be susceptible to oversensitivity effects, for example. If the process picks better numbers for a high CPU usage alert, in some sense that's an improvement, but you're still alerting on CPU usage when you should be alerting on latency. Finally, there are some strong reasons to believe using machine learning for picking better metrics will never work (*https://www.usenix.org/sites/default/files/conference/protected-files/srecon19emea_slides_underwood.pdf*).

---

2 Artificial intelligence operations (AIOps) is a growing field that attempts to use machine learning to help you perform operational tasks and monitor your systems. Serious questions can be asked about its general applicability.

Complexity and failure in distributed systems

Even though you might not know it, you're almost certainly running a complex distributed system. Even a simple web server and database combination qualifies: you know it's complex and distributed because your system is on more than one computer, it's connected to the internet, and it fails!

It sounds flippant, but it's true—even a *truism* these days—that today's system architectures fail *all the time*. This is by design. Rather than scaling up (for example, making more resilient individual machines), today's approaches are all about cheerfully accepting widespread failure in underlying components in order to make the reliability of the system as a whole improve. This approach is more complex than others, but you get a lot of flexibility and potentially a lot of reliability in return. More importantly, though, at a certain point, you can't really avoid getting on the complexity bus: the way today's underlying hardware, software, and cloud systems work basically mandates this approach.

But simple threshold alerting as it is is not aligned very well with this paradigm. This chapter has spent some time showing that across a "significant enough" number of subcomponents you'll get too much noise for threshold alerting to scale, and that's true, but there are additional consequences to distributed systems failures that simple threshold alerting doesn't work well for. Take, for example, the kind of emergent failure modes that flow from intercomponent interaction: those are almost always undermonitored precisely because of their nature. Similarly, simple threshold alerting on "common sense" metrics doesn't usually provide enough data to allow you to make sense of all possible incidents in advance; "CPU high" alerts on subcomponents 1 through 47 don't really allow you to effectively understand that Kafka is getting stuck on processing, because there generally isn't a single subcomponent that is suffering, and therefore no single smoking gun from which to reason backward.

This reality is what is driving the move to *observability*: the ability to ask novel questions of your systems without having to add new instrumentation. Observability allows you to debug from first principles. With rich telemetry you can start wide and then filter to reduce the search space. This is a requirement for responding to novel, emergent failure modes. The observability approach means that you scientifically take one step after another: ask one question and examine the result, then ask another. Instead of being limited by your existing alerts and dashboards, you can improvise and adapt solutions to any problem in your system. It goes hand-in-hand with SLO alerting.

In summary, there are many problems with the model of alerting on absolute thresholds. Even variants of it, such as using thresholds chosen as ratios of two primary indicators, still miss the main thing: a principled connection to the actual business goals we're trying to uphold. Only SLOs provide that connection.

This brings us back to our initial premise: SLO alerting completely changes the model, and the new model is not prone to the same issues as the old one in most circumstances, and not as prone in the others.

A Better Way

Our advice? Instead of alerting on internal system states (such as CPU usage), alert on what really matters: the user experience (for example, latency, errors, correctness, and other SLO-worthy concepts). Alerting on SLOs allows you to pay valuable and limited attention to the incidents that really matter, rather than noise, and automatically adapts to threshold changes caused by hardware, environmental concerns, etc. The incentive to create new alerts for every cause goes away because you are already alerting on the user experience, leading to improved maintenance of an alert corpus over time. This all goes hand-in-hand with observability-based approaches for understanding what's going on in your system, so that you can do better contributing factor analysis when something *does* go wrong.

In general, SLO-based alerting coupled with observability is a better conceptual framework for helping us to do alerting in a sustainable way. As per Rob Ewaschuk's "Philosophy of Alerting" (*https://docs.google.com/document/d/199PqyG3UsyXlwie HaqbGiWVa8eMWi8zzAn0YfcApr8Q/edit#heading=h.fs3knmjt7fjy*), and the refining follow-on "Reduce Toil Through Better Alerting" by Štěpán Davidovič and Betsy Beyer, the high-level precepts can be best expressed this way:

- Since human attention and energy are valuable and can easily be exhausted (*https://dave.cheney.net/2018/09/26/internets-of-interest-4-niall-murphys-polemic-against-on-call*), alerts should correspond to real and urgent problems.
- We should be able to actually do something about those alerts when we get them.
- It is possible for many different kinds of alerts to exist within an overall monitoring corpus and for them all to deliver value, but you have to be intentional and commit to refinement over time.

Okay, fine. Now, how do we actually usher in this brave new world?

How to Do SLO Alerting

Having beaten you over the head with why the old way doesn't work for many pages, let me explain the new way.

Choosing a Target

Let's start off with the simplest possible example: you have a request/response service of some kind. There is some fast/cheap way to distinguish successful requests from unsuccessful ones. (Note: in your *real* service, if you don't have a way to do that, this is a critical problem, and it needs to be fixed before any of this will be useful to you.) The image server example we discussed earlier is a useful illustration here: we have some sequence of successful requests—here, defined as 2xx-series HTTP response codes—and some sequence of unsuccessful requests. For the purposes of this discussion, we'll say 4xx and 5xx HTTP response codes are errors.

What we end up with is a way to count total requests and count requests that are to be considered errors—something like this:

$$\text{Current state} = \left(\frac{\text{Successful requests [/time period]}}{\text{Total requests [/time period]}} \right) \times 100 \, \%$$

Something that isn't necessarily clear from a static equation like this, but is crucially important, is that an SLO is defined *over a time period*. If you think of the current state as being a model where we have a stream of events, some of which are "good" and some of which aren't, the time period over which the SLO is defined—or, in other words, how much of the stream you have to look at—is the largest determining factor in how you have to act to defend an SLO.

It's intuitive, I suspect, that if you have an SLO defined over a year, you have much more freedom to act than if you have an SLO defined over five minutes. Let's assume our SLO will be defined over a month, and we want to set a three-nines (99.9%) availability target for our image server. This translates to 43.83 minutes of downtime, or a rate of no more than 1 in 1,000 events going wrong. Adjusting this target will affect the number of "bad" events that are allowed; six nines (99.9999%), for example, means only one in a million events can go wrong.

Table 8-1 illustrates the trade-offs, taking a time-oriented approach. This table shows, for each SLO value and measured SLO window, how long you can have a total service outage (in seconds) before the SLO is violated. (These tables build on those in Chapter 4, which discusses SLOs in detail.)

Table 8-1. A breakdown of SLO targets across time windows

| | | SLO window | | | | | | | |
		Second	Minute	Hour	Day	Week	30 days	90 days	Year
Informal name	Formal def.	1	60	3600	86400	604800	2592000	7776000	22896000
Six nines	99.9999	0.00	0.00	0.00	0.09	0.60	2.59	7.78	22.90
Five and a half nines	99.9995	0.00	0.00	0.02	0.43	3.02	12.96	38.88	114.48
Five nines	99.999	0.00	0.00	0.04	0.86	6.05	25.92	77.76	228.96
Four and a half nines	99.995	0.00	0.00	0.18	4.32	30.24	129.60	388.80	1,144.80
Four nines	99.99	0.00	0.01	0.36	8.64	60.48	259.20	777.60	2,289.60
Three and a half nines	99.95	0.00	0.03	1.80	43.20	302.40	1296	3888	11448
Three nines	99.9	0.00	0.06	3.60	86.40	604.80	2592	7776	22896
Two and a half nines	99.5	0.01	0.30	18.00	432.00	3024	12960	38880	114480
Two nines	99	0.01	0.60	36.00	864.00	6048	25920	77760	228960
One and a half nines	95	0.05	3.00	180.00	4320	30240	129600	388800	1144800
One nine	90	0.10	6.00	360.00	8640	60480	259200	777600	2289600

We shade the cells in the table gray if the total number of seconds is less than five minutes, which is an arbitrary but plausible threshold to indicate that human response is infeasible below this. (It might well be infeasible above it, too, but it's definitely infeasible below it!) Cells have been shaded light gray if they fall within a range above five minutes but still below the total error budget afforded by the target and the window.

We can learn two things from looking at Table 8-1:

- There is really a very limited array of practical options to choose from that allow for an effective human response (more on this in the next section). The table specifies impractical SLO durations (a second, a minute) for pedagogical reasons, but generally for time-based SLOs you're looking at some period between a week and a quarter, and a target of around 99.95% plus or minus a few categories.

- For events-based SLOs it's a little more flexible, because the SLO is amortized over the arrival rate of the events. In other words, if you get a million events a day spread very unevenly between day and night, you can still defend a six-nines SLO if you lose a few events going into nighttime with effectively zero traffic. Without other math applied to your low-traffic periods, a few misses overnight could cause you to report a failed SLO period, while an events-based target can allow you to more easily swallow these low-traffic bad events.

Error Budgets and Response Time

It's pretty clear that if we have an error budget, we have to alert before the budget is exhausted for this to mean anything. If we alert literally at the moment when it's exhausted, we can't act to preserve it. So logically speaking, we should alert after *some* error budget has gone, and before *all* error budget is gone, but not after *any* error budget is gone, because that's usually too sensitive.

What might help us to pick a good approach here? Chapter 5 has a more detailed discussion on this, but let's recap the high-level ideas here. Starting off, you need to give humans enough time to receive the page and start acting on it. Typically speaking, this puts a lower limit of at least five minutes on responses, allowing for transmission delays, device reception and processing, retrieving of laptops, etc.[3] It might not be five minutes precisely, and obviously different teams and different companies have potentially different response times for these things, but the key point remains: humans do have a minimum response time, and if you burn through your error budget even with the humans having "best-case" response protocols on receipt of a page, then you either need a new SLO, or you need auto-remediation.[4]

In the example we're working with, we have about 43 minutes of 100% downtime allowable before we blow the 30-day error budget: if we lose 5 or 10 minutes in signaling and getting ready, then we still have a comfortable half-hour to do remediation. That seems like it will work, especially considering many practical outages aren't all-or-nothing, and the further away from "everything completely down" they are, the more time you have. (Conversely, if you have a four-nines SLO, you have 4.38 minutes of allowable downtime a month, so by the time a human is able to respond to a page for a 100% outage, it's too late. Therefore, as mentioned previously, approaches where humans are in the paging path usually only work for SLO targets up to about 99.95%.)

If we pull back and think about the stream analogy used earlier, there are clearly two separate classes of problem that we need to concern ourselves with: a situation where the stream of events, or duration of uptime, is completely interrupted—100% outage,

---

3 I was once on call for a team with a three-minute SLO, which meant my laptop had to accompany me on every bathroom journey.

4 You may be wondering if it's useful to think about incidents as having a consistent upper bound on duration; the short answer is, sadly, that it isn't. Incidents should be considered as potentially being of indefinite length, especially for distributed systems—and even more upsettingly for some, measuring MTTX can sometimes be meaningless. See Chapter 17 for more on this.

or near to—or situations where the stream has enough intermittent errors in it that the budget will be blown, but it's not a 100% outage. The latter are known as *slow burn* problems.

Why two classes? Can't we just handle this with one approach? Well, it's complicated —while it is theoretically possible to express multiple conditions, thresholds, and the like via function composition, the practicalities of doing this today across the various monitoring systems that exist are very challenging. In particular, while the "100% outages" can be handled by simple threshold alerting, the slow burn is much harder to handle that way, and aggregating the two presents maintenance and motivational difficulties. There's no way to address that situation with simple thresholds on any kind of high-rate loss, given that slow burns can be arbitrarily slow, and thresholds to catch everything would be hopelessly noisy.

Another way of putting it is to say that simple threshold alerts are effectively stateless —catching a transition from one state to another when the justification for that transition is suitably large—but SLO alerts (slow-burn ones) have to be stateful in order to catch aggregations of failures, rather than simple transitions from "fine" to "full failure" states.

Error Budget Burn Rate

Here we take the first step that clearly distinguishes the SLO approach from the simple threshold alerting approach: we measure *the rate at which the error budget is being consumed.* In essence, this means forecasting the amount of error budget that your system *will have spent* by some future point. Then, in the simplest case, if the rate at which your error budget is being consumed means you'll violate your SLO, you alert.

In simple equation terms, this translates to the following:

Rate of error budget consumption =

$$\left(\frac{\text{observed errors per [time period or event count]}}{\text{allowable errors per [time period or event count]}} \right)$$

That will give you a real number. If it's > 1, you're consuming error budget faster than you are allowing for. If it's < 1, you're within budget. As per our previous discussions about alerting, triggering precisely when that number passes 1 will generate a potentially very large number of false alerts, so that's not recommended. Furthermore, calculating observed errors per time period or event count of course requires maintaining some history, which brings us back to the question of time periods over which we think of SLOs, and the time period over which we calculate alerts. They are not necessarily the same. Let's see why.

Rolling Windows

Chapter 5 discussed rolling windows in some detail, and laid out the argument for why it's better to think about SLO alerting on such a basis. So what are some good guidelines for thinking about window size?

First of all, we divide the problem into *baseline* and *lookahead*—how much data do we have at hand, and how far into the future are we trying to predict? These have to have an appropriate ratio: too much reasoning forward from too little history, and you'll get it wrong systematically. For example, if you use a baseline of 15 minutes to extrapolate out 3 days, then even a small blip will cause an alarm to go off.

In general, then, budget burn events can be treated as attempting to extrapolate where a line will cross the axis. In Figure 8-3, the y-axis at the top is 100% of budget; the thicker gray line at the bottom shows the moment when the budget is gone.

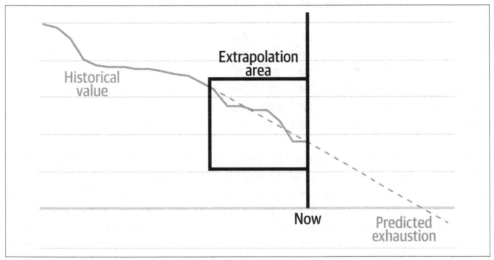

Figure 8-3. Extrapolating error budget burn rate

These "axis-crossing" situations are very common in engineering, mathematics, and the sciences generally, as well as (for example) burndown charts in project management, ticket rate completion in sprint planning, and so on.

While not immediately apparent from the figure, it's important to remember we are actually forecasting two possibly very different values: the rate at which we gain more error budget (for example, (1.0 − SLO) * *Successful Requests*), and the rate at which we lose it (for example, errors). Forecasting them independently, using different functions suited for the task, can lead to better results. This insight opens a path to more robust alerting. For example, your alerting can be aware that you're currently in a period of low traffic, such as nighttime, and consequently decrease sensitivity to errors.

The key question for these windows is really the duration over which they should be configured. The slow burns are generally configured over longer periods—say, over 48 hours. The fast burns are generally defined over short periods, < 48 hours. These splits are somewhat arbitrary, but for a practical alert you need to choose the window over which it considers data, and the sensitivity over that window. That will be what is ultimately encoded in your monitoring system. Table 8-2 explores some of the possibilities.

Table 8-2. Acceptable percentage of error budget loss

		10%	5%	2%	1%
Window size (hours)	1	0.42 (days)	0.83	2.08	4.17
	2	0.83	1.67	4.17	8.33
	4	1.67	3.33	8.33	16.67
	8	3.33	6.67	16.67	33.33
	12	5	10	25	50
	24	10	20	50	100
	48	20	40	100	200
Week	168	70	140	350	700
Fortnight	336	140	280	700	1,400
30-day month	720	300	600	1,500	3,000
90-day quarter	2160	900	1,800	4,500	9,000

Across the top we have the acceptable error budget loss, and down the side the window size; so, for example, if you lose 10% of your error budget in one hour, and therefore have 10 hours before you exhaust it completely, you can last 0.42 of a day (that self-same 10 hours). As another example, if you pick 2% loss and a window size of 24 hours, you have ~50 days before you run out of error budget. So, the main observation from the table is that you can't use such an alert to defend an error budget lasting just 30 days, because it will refresh before the budget is fully consumed.

In reality, though, there are many more contextual things to consider before picking the numbers. Since SLO alerting treats a consistently slightly bad experience and a single big event equivalently, your alerting probably can't distinguish between these events, but whether or not you need to treat them as separate from a *business* point of view is not a question we can answer here. For example, for some systems it's actually better to have a complete outage rather than a partial one, because constant low-key unreliability might drive away more customers than a brief unavailable window.

The *only* hard constraint is that you need to have an alert that will fire if you are failing to meet your SLO entirely. In this situation your burn rate doesn't matter at all. However, you should also have an alert that lets you know when you're exceeding your budget for any time window substantially shorter than your SLO evaluation window—in other words, if for that window:

$$\frac{\text{SUM(errors)}}{\text{SUM(all requests)}} > (1.0 - \text{SLO})$$

This allows you ample time to respond to slow-burn events.

If you are just looking for a place to start (beyond the hard requirement just mentioned), you can take a look at the following worked example below. Or, as a rule of thumb, *The Site Reliability Workbook* (*https://landing.google.com/sre/workbook/chapters/alerting-on-slos*) suggests 2% error budget burn in 1 hour as a good threshold for a paging alert, and 10% in 3 days for a ticketing (or otherwise low-severity) alert.

 Alas, one of the downsides of this approach is the possibility of dual alerting doing just that: alerting twice for the same situation— or sometimes worse, a long while after an event has happened and (typically) been resolved. How could this arise? It's mostly a function of the interpolation coming from different baselines. "Keep going at *<the rate for the last 30 minutes>*, and it will be a problem in 2 hours" and "Keep going at *<the rate for the last 2 hours>* and you'll be fine for the next 4 days." How to solve it? Well, most alerting systems offer some way to deduplicate or suppress alerts; alternatively, a number of teams say they value the extra signal provided by receiving both alerts, although we suspect this is not ultimately sustainable.

Putting It Together

Putting all this together, let's look at a worked example, keeping in mind the fast and slow alert structures and that we need to define them over separate windows, related to the SLO. We'll use the image server example from earlier: we have a 99.9% SLO, and we'll define its error budget over 30 days. That means a burn rate of 1 error per 1,000 requests over the month is precisely within our SLO, and anything more than that is out-of-SLO.

We decide to set the fast and slow alerting rates at 1% and 10%, respectively, across durations of one hour and one week.

Our reasoning goes something like this:

- A 30-day SLO of 99.9% availability is 2,592,000 total seconds (from Table 8-1).
- 100–99.9% of that is 2,592 seconds, or 43.2 minutes; i.e., 43.2 minutes of 100% outage is the SLO budget completely blown.
- We don't wait until the budget is completely blown to alert, so we'll alert on 1% loss across 1 hour and 10% across a week.

- Given that 1% of 2,592 seconds = 25.92 seconds and 10% = 259.2 seconds, we configure our alerting such that (by default) 25 seconds of complete outage will alert with the 1-hour window, and for the 1-week window a duration of 295.2 seconds will alert.

For real-world alerts and short durations, such as those less than a minute, you'd probably want to consider having the alert condition wait until this is sustained for some time before firing, to gain confidence that the event requires human interaction. Problems on the order of 30–60 seconds are common within standard internet infrastructures (for example, transit connectivity blips causing route recalculation and reconvergence, VM migrations, and so on) and often get resolved automatically.

You might think that in the case of a 100% outage, waiting for 60 seconds would effectively convert this alert to being a ~2% alert. However, recall that production outages are not always all-or-nothing situations. There is a large variety of partial outages that will, sustained over a sufficiently long period of time, violate this threshold; so (to ensure more alerts are actionable) it's reasonable to wait for the triggering loss rate to be sustained over a period of time. There is a meaningful difference between, say, a problem causing a 1.7% loss sustained over some time, and a problem causing a 2% loss; a 2% alert won't catch the 1.7% loss, no matter over how long it is sustained, and it will only be caught by the next alert in line with a larger time period.

How long should you wait for a problem to be sustained before alerting? There are no hard guidelines, but you might use as a rule of thumb what the *effective* loss percentage is as a result, and whether or not that ends up touching your other declared boundaries. For example, if a 1% alert would translate into a 10% alert if you were to wait for ~250 more seconds, then you should alert.

Another approach, somewhat more empirically oriented, is to look at the typical duration of events which turn out to be inactionable, and set your waiting time to accommodate those—for example, if 90% of your inactionable blip events last less than 30 seconds, you can clearly wait at least that long without significant error. Indeed, such analysis might even tell you that you need to modify your SLO, because you learn it might not be achievable within your practical constraints.

In this example, and throughout the chapter, astute observers may have noticed that very tight error budgets are hard to effectively respond to. At each stage you are balancing the requirement to defend a chosen SLO with the unreliability of the internet in general, and systems in particular, as well as the capabilities of human action to restore service. Generally speaking, tight SLOs (which for the purposes of this note we will define as 99.9% and above defined over a month or less) involve assuming so little time passes between the originating incident and invoking human protection that it is not realistic. Furthermore, although *numerically* defending one more nine is often interpreted as being 10 times harder, it is not a strict linear relationship: some constraints become impossible to fulfill given sufficient nines.

If you had a tighter SLO, how would that change the picture? Well, you could either tighten the time frame over which the fast-burn SLO alert was calculated, or decrease the amount of burn that you experience before alerting. But in general, following our earlier recommendations, the tighter the SLO, the more difficult it is to sensibly and sustainably react.

Troubleshooting with SLO Alerting

Okay, you've managed to implement SLO alerting, and now you're staring at your first alert saying, "10% error budget drop over last 3 days." What do you do now, given that you're not staring at a suggested place to begin your investigations?

Like in all the best detective stories, your job is to build a theory and compare it against reality (as described in Chapter 13 of *Site Reliability Engineering* (*https://land ing.google.com/sre/sre-book/chapters/effective-troubleshooting*) provides a great starting point). Even in the case where you don't have an observability system, you can still start off with the same high-level diagnostics that you typically would have relied on in the past.

But those coarse indicators are usually only of use (and sometimes marginal use) for fast-burn alerting. Slow-burn alerting, since it is necessarily predicated on something that isn't happening quickly, is a question of chasing high cardinalities: there is some exceptional event that is only getting triggered on certain code paths, and in order to track that down you need to do a breadth-first search across a number of top-level possibilities; an otherwise unguided depth-first search seems likely to waste a lot of time, on average. That's where, ideally, some kind of observability-oriented or tracing system comes in, allowing you to zoom in to explore the details of failing requests or events, find out what distinguishes them from succeeding requests or events, and then zoom out again to cross-compare across the whole set. To the extent that you can replicate this in your existing setup, perhaps by using labeled monitoring sets or the equivalent, you will have a much faster time troubleshooting.

Corner Cases

The mathematics of SLO alerting work well when you have enough events, duration of operation, or similar to make the sums come out cleanly, but not all systems that need monitoring actually have this property. For example, what if you have a system that only has 10 events per SLO-able period?

Very simply, if events are discrete or indivisible and you only have 10 events, you can't have 99% availability. Half a request doesn't work: a request either succeeds or it fails. Therefore, in order to preserve the concept of an error budget for any alertable/SLO-able period, whatever the size of your event base, you must permit at least one error. This means if you have 10 events per SLO-able period, you either make the deliberate decision that they all need to succeed (good luck and have fun), or you need to acknowledge your SLO cannot be better than 90% ((10 − 1) / 10).

However, there may be a way to recast the problem. For example, a batch system that takes input from disconnected offices two or three times a week over a month might have (say) 10 "events" over a month, but the actual underlying work involves unpacking uploaded sales and stock data and reconciling it with a central database; the underlying data itself is therefore probably what you want to define the SLO over. Not all systems will enable recasting the error budget like this (and that's what it is—recasting the budget rather than the alerting strategy), but for those that do, it can be pretty useful. For those systems that can't be recast in this light, perhaps the first question to ask yourself is what problem you are trying to solve with SLO alerting. If a system with a very low number of events is paging constantly, there may be an infrastructure deficit that needs to be tackled first. Another approach could be to inject false data in order to make the absolute numbers nicely divisible, but the details of this are highly system-specific.

On the other hand, systems with very high availability goals (say, five or six nines) and large numbers of events during every SLO period suffer the opposite problem: for six nines there's an allowed duration of 2.63 seconds of downtime *per year*, or 1 in 100,000 events failing. In those circumstances, a complete outage is not even necessarily within the domain of most automatic remediation, never mind human remediation. Although architecting your system or application to avoid complete outages is possible, and many cloud providers partition their systems to help with those situations, in most cases something being "almost impossible" is a strong signal that you shouldn't do it.

Having said that, the author personally once worked on a system that ended up with—after a very large rearchitecture, refactoring, and so on—six-nines availability for a quarter. Although in some sense a triumph, one could consider that the resources expended to achieve that could have been spent elsewhere to improve the availability of another system from (say) two nines to four nines. We encourage you to keep these trade-offs in mind.

SLO Alerting in a Brownfield Setup

Much of the preceding advice is entirely reasonable when you're starting from a clean sheet. However, there are two characteristics of starting with an existing system and set of alerts that complicate things: firstly, the (usually strong) attachment to the existing set of alerts that stakeholders have, and secondly, the set of incentives that lead to it typically being much easier to add alerts than remove them.

The first, which we call *alert attachment* (or if you're feeling unkind, a kind of Stockholm syndrome), can be particularly problematic. Earlier we talked about how there may be pressure to keep tightening alert thresholds, but no complementary pressure to loosen them. Attachment to alerts can come from a similar place. Stakeholders will generally not be eager to change an approach that might result in loss without hard data suggesting the new approach is strongly better. Chapter 16 has more details on SLO advocacy, but I'll mention a few techniques here that you can use to persuade stakeholders that an SLO alerting approach is worth trying.

Show the human impact of the current situation

There is a lot of evidence showing that human on-call performance suffers over time, particularly with an excessive signal to noise ratio (for more on this see Chapter 30 of *Seeking SRE* (O'Reilly), Niall Murphy). Circulating this information can help to establish that the current situation actually has problems, and can be improved, which is generally the first step in mounting an argument for change.

Review the existing outage footprint

Faced with this challenge in a team we previously worked with, the author went through the existing configuration and established for each of the 117 (!) defined alerts how often it had fired, what its total outage footprint was (that is, whether the alert had fired in the context of an outage, and if so how bad that outage was), its assigned severity and trailing six-month "real" severity as a function of the outage footprint, and some notion of how often it was changed, based on revision control. It took some doing, but this was a powerful, evidence-based way of persuading product development partners and others that not all alerts were equally useful. It followed logically that some of them could be changed.

Run the old and new in parallel

Observability and SLO monitoring go hand-in-hand. Stakeholders may view lack of observability in a system as a blocker to implementing full SLO monitoring, but it may be possible to manage this concern by maintaining an SLO alerting infrastructure in parallel with the existing one. In this case, of course, the existing system should decrease the severity of its alerts and stop paging directly, so human attention can be maintained at reasonable levels. If this is done, however, a sunset date for the infrastructure one needs to be committed to; otherwise, in the words of D. Tilbrook and Jamie Zawinski (*http://regex.info/blog/2006-09-15/247*), now you have two problems.

Parting Recommendations

I hope by this point you've learned something useful about how to implement SLO alerting in your organization, why it's good to do, what some of the drawbacks are, and how to get support for it in a brownfield situation.

There are, however, some other concerns to bear in mind on your SLO alerting journey, which are somewhat separate from what we've discussed here but still useful to consider:

What to do, in what order
> You should move away from alerting on internal attributes (CPU usage and so on). Simple threshold alerting on SLIs is better than alerting on internal attributes, and SLO alerting is better than that: it's the current gold standard. Although this chapter is about implementing SLO alerting, the most important thing is to stop alerting on internal attributes—it's completely okay to adopt an intermediate solution while building support for a full SLO transformation.

Capabilities of the alerting system
> We've done our best in this chapter and elsewhere to be technology-agnostic for obvious reasons, but at some point, you actually have to make sure your alerting system has the technical capability to count and display metrics, define different severities, alert on them in various flexible (maybe runtime-definable) ways, perform simple alert deduplication, and so on. If your alerting system can't do this—perhaps it's homegrown, or a commercial product without these capabilities—then you have a problem. In that case, hopefully this chapter will provide you with the necessary facts to argue for, and implement, the switch to another system that does have the required capabilities.

Observability
> A similar argument applies to implementing observability in your organization, and for your monitored application. As mentioned previously, alerting is often effectively used as a substitute for observability—you'll need a system that can help you actually do this, rather than being an inaccurate substitute. I'm pleased to note that there is a multiplicity of solutions in the marketplace for this.

Effort

Previous chapters have pointed out that implementing SLOs is ultimately a business decision, involving a trade-off on where to spend effort and resources. Alerting can provide a very useful way of surfacing these costs. An SLO that is too demanding compared to what the system can sustainably deliver will quickly manifest itself in the alerting, and therefore in operational load. In discussions with decision makers, it may be useful to make them aware that the choice of SLO has a real and meaningful effect on operational load. Figure 8-4 illustrates this; it is a simulation, generated from random data but representative, of how many alerts will be received by an operations team for different SLO targets. Each point represents an alert fired, paging a member of the operations team, requesting a response.

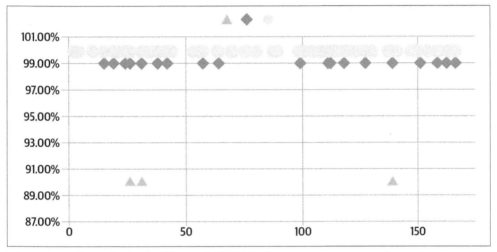

Figure 8-4. Alerts for 90%, 99%, and 99.9% SLO targets on an example service, generated empirically by simulating over historical data

As you can see, the main takeaway is the tighter the SLO, the larger the number of events. For your real situation, instead of relying on this simulation, you may be able to run a query across historical data and obtain the actual numbers. In either event, a picture resembling this can open the way for larger discussions: Is the tighter SLO worth it, given the operational load? Given a compelling business need for that SLO, perhaps we need a system redesign to support it? Conversely, if you examine the data, you might find that your system is sustainably reliable for the proposed SLO, or could even support a tighter one.

Summary

This chapter looked in detail at the drawbacks of simple threshold alerting, and how SLO alerting promises to address them. We went through the basics of working with nines, calculating SLOs across various periods, and setting realistic error budgets. We also took a closer look at how vital the concept of SLOs across windows is, and went through a worked example. We delved into some of the nuances of implementation and consequences of implementing SLO alerting, including how to do troubleshooting, how to handle some corner cases for low- or high-traffic systems, and techniques for handling brownfield versus greenfield setups. Finally, we provided some high-level recommendations for how to proceed, and what you might require from your management (or your alerting system) in order to be successful.

Good luck! You can do it!

CHAPTER 9

Probability and Statistics for SLIs and SLOs

Toby Burress and Jaime Woo

You've identified some meaningful SLIs, and brought together stakeholders to build thoughtful SLOs from them. Once you collect some data from your system to help you set those targets, that should be it, right? But as you've seen, when measuring SLIs, you need to ensure you have data that can allow for multiple analyses and interpretations. The data in and of itself does not tell a complete story: how you analyze it is key to its usefulness. What's more, systems change rapidly, so the SLOs you set could change as the systems themselves evolve. How do you determine the appropriate SLOs without being able to peer into the future?

This chapter is all about the interpretation of the data you're collecting. Reliability is expensive, and figuring out the amount of reliability you need is crucial for making the most of your resources. An incorrect analysis doesn't mean all your hard work has gone to waste, but it does mean you can't be sure that the results support what you want to accomplish. Misinterpreting the data can mean triggering alerts unnecessarily, or worse, remaining blissfully unaware of underlying problems that will violate your SLOs and lead to customer dissatisfaction.

This chapter is broadly concerned with two difficult problems that arise when implementing SLIs and SLOs:

- Figuring out what an SLO ought to be
- Calculating the value of an SLI

The former arises when, for example, a new service is launching and the service owners need to figure out the theoretical maximum SLO they can be expected to provide. You can't run a service with 99.9% availability if your critical runtime dependencies only provide 99% availability, unless you carefully architect around the deficiency.

Your service might also be a dependency itself. *What latency guarantees should it offer if another service depends on it to meet its latency SLOs, given its usage patterns? What will happen to your latency if you change your service from sequential database calls to parallel? Is it worth pursuing?*

The latter concern comes up when it comes time to act on the values of SLIs. Did I violate my SLOs this month? Am I violating my SLOs right now? What is my availability right now? What is my durability right now? Is my batch service receiving more traffic than I engineered for?

Answering these kinds of questions requires quantitative methods for dealing with uncertainty. The first set of questions, broadly speaking, are answered using techniques from *probability*, where we want to be able to discuss the likelihood of things that haven't happened yet.

The second set will be addressed using *statistics*, where we want to analyze events that have already happened to draw inferences about quantities we can't directly measure. Together, these techniques are a powerful tool for handling uncertainty and complexity.

For readers who aren't well versed in probability and statistics, you don't need to worry. We only scratch the surface here, but it will be enough for you to start your SLO journey, and will equip you to understand conversations around calculating SLOs happening outside the purview of this book. We'll take you through the math you need to know, how it's applied, and what the applications mean. (Alex introduced some of the concepts in Chapter 5, so if you haven't read that yet, we'd recommend giving it a look first.)

This chapter is meant to serve as an introduction to some basic concepts in probability and (to a lesser extent) statistics. It is not, possibly, the most *gentle* introduction. We do not intend for readers, especially readers new to the subject, to understand everything on the first go. We honestly don't expect most readers to read the whole chapter. Instead, let this chapter serve as a guide, pointing out interesting possibilities not explored elsewhere in this book. If it doesn't speak to you, that's fine. If it does, don't worry if it takes a while to get through it. If you are intrigued by what you read, please keep going. If you are not, that's fine too; you don't need any of this. It's just another tool in the bag.

Finally, there is some suggested further reading at the end, which we strongly recommend for anyone whose interest is piqued.

On Probability

The wonderful thing about computers is that whatever they can easily do once, they can easily do a couple of million times. The unfortunate thing about computers is that for any task of even mild sophistication it is unlikely that even a computer can perform it a couple of million times without fail.

As service owners who are also human, we don't have the capacity to treat several million discrete events individually: the successes here, the failures there. What we do instead is acknowledge the uncertainty around the execution of the task; we talk about the probability that a task will succeed, or finish in a timely manner, or contain the answer we desire. When we express our service in SLIs, we are implicitly acknowledging the uncertain nature of the things we are trying to measure.

Probability is a way to measure uncertainty. If we were never uncertain about how our service would act, we could have SLOs like "all requests succeed"—but we're actually uncertain about everything all the time, so instead we have SLOs like "99% of requests will succeed." In doing so, however, we're changing our focus from making statements about the events that occur to making statements about the processes that produce those events. The language of probability gives us a way to do this sensibly.

The Math

Unless you're already familiar with many of the concepts of probability, we recommend skipping all the math the first time you read this chapter. The important concepts are given in the text. Later, when you're familiar with the concepts, return to the math to see how they're treated formally.

Please don't worry that you need to memorize the math or know calculus to use these techniques. Most of the information derived here is available on Wikipedia, or codified in software libraries such as SciPy. However, we try to be explicit in this chapter about what is happening and to prove the assertions we make, so that if you are interested in seeing how it's done, you can.

That said, if you see value in these examples and want to learn more, it's going to be convenient to get used to the math and the formal treatment of these ideas. It is unfortunately very easy to try to perform an operation that appears to return a meaningful value (for example, averaging a set of percentile values) but which does not, and the only way to prove to yourself that the thing you're about to do is meaningful is by deriving it mathematically.

SLI Example: Availability

Let's say you are the newest member of the data storage team at Catz, the largest and most brightly colored cat picture service company in the world.

Your team owns Dewclaw, which serves the thumbnails attached to each post. Dewclaw has a single customer (for now), the web frontend, which has a nonnegotiable availability SLO of four nines, or 99.99%. Unfortunately, it cannot offer even partial service—say, falling back on cute little stock cartoon cat images—without the thumbnails.

Your service is therefore a critical dependency, and your first project is to establish the SLOs Dewclaw needs to offer to ensure that you are reliable enough for your customer.

Catz has three data centers in different metropolitan areas: DC1, DC2, and DC3. Dewclaw currently only runs out of DC1. You conclude, correctly, that for the frontend to meet its four-nines SLO, you also need to offer a four-nines SLO. But you're eyeing DC2 on the other coast.

If the frontend could first query DC1, and on failure automatically fail over to DC2, how much could you relax your SLO?

Sample spaces

To answer this question probabilistically we need to think about all the possible outcomes of a Dewclaw query. Since we are only considering availability, we can restrict ourselves to the cases where a response either is sufficient for the frontend (*success*), or is not (*failure*).

The set of these two states is called the *sample space*, and the sample space comprises all possible outcomes. Dewclaw has to respond with one of these (they are exhaustive), and every response is either one or the other (they are mutually exclusive). The queries that produce these responses are called *events* or *trials*.

Coin interlude

What we're describing sounds a lot like a coin toss, where pass or fail depends on the flip of a coin. This is where we go mentally whenever we are looking at something that can have only two outcomes. The technical term for this is a *Bernoulli trial*, after one of the *eight* mathematicians of that name.

A Bernoulli trial must be a random experiment that has exactly two possible outcomes. The experiments are independent and do not affect one another, so the probability of success must be the same each and every time the experiment is conducted.

The sample space for a coin flip is $\{H, T\}$, for heads or tails, whereas for Dewclaw it is $\{s, f\}$, with s for success and f for failure.

If you flipped a coin to decide some question, you'd probably expect the probability of heads or tails to be about 50%. Mathematically, we say that the coin has a *bias* of .5. But we could have gone to a specialty store for a weighted coin that lands on heads just slightly more often—say, 60% of the time. In this case the coin has a bias of 0.6.

A Bernoulli trial is *parameterized* by some value, p, which ranges from 0 to 1 and determines the outcome. A flipped coin will show heads with probability p, and tails with probability $(1 - p)$. p is the coin's bias.

Let's return to our example of queries. When we think about the response that a request will *probably* return, what we're doing is assigning numbers to the elements of the sample space. In other words, we're giving the probability of each response.

Table 9-1 shows what this looks like for a bias of .99.

Table 9-1. Probability of success and failure with a bias of .99

Outcome	Probability
Success	.99
Failure	.01

Figure 9-1 illustrates another way of showing this.

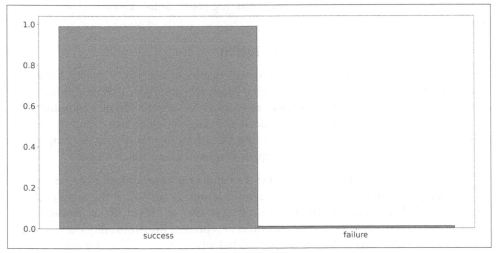

Figure 9-1. A histogram of the Bernoulli distribution with p = .99

This is a histogram. A histogram is a bar graph where each bar represents an element in the sample space and the height of each bar indicates the count of the number of events that resulted in that outcome. Note that for this example the order of the bars doesn't matter, so it could also look like Figure 9-2.

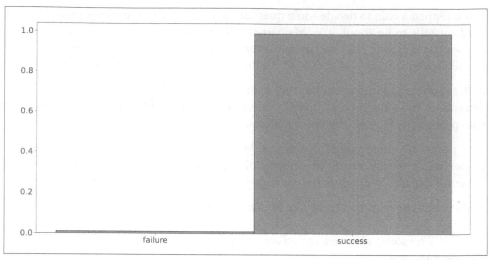

Figure 9-2. An alternative visualization of Figure 9-1

This is because the elements of this sample space have no intrinsic ordering: *success* does not come before or after *failure*. The data values in the sample space are said to be *categorical*, since events get mapped to categories. Later we will look at sample spaces that have different kinds of data, including continuous values.

Notation

In this chapter we will sometimes use notation that looks like $P(X = x)$, which can be somewhat confusing. In this context capital letters (for example, X, K) stand for *random variables*, which are the outputs of random processes; the flip of a coin, the roll of a die, etc. Lowercase letters (x, k) indicate standard variables, like count or length. So, the text $P(X = x) = ...$ means something like "the probability that the output of this random process, which we call X, equals any given value, which we call x."

Usually this gets shortened down to $P(x)$. Depending on the context x can be a specific value, or it can stand for every value in the sample space. When the sample space is discrete, $P(x)$ denotes the probability that $X = x$; when it is continuous, $P(X = x) = 0$, so instead we use this notation to represent the probability density at x. We'll explain probability density in more detail when we introduce the exponential distribution.

Dewclaw in a data center

In our example, when Dewclaw is only in DC1, a single query can only either succeed or fail. The sample space, which we'll call S, therefore contains only s and f. Because the frontend can only succeed if its query to Dewclaw succeeds, $P(s)$ needs to be at least .9999.

 In fact, it needs to be strictly greater; between Dewclaw and the frontend sits the network, which can fail, and we might not be the frontend's only critical runtime dependency. But for the sake of this example let's pretend that we are and that the network is, hubristically, perfect.

So, the only way for Dewclaw to meet the frontend's availability needs is to be at least as reliable as the frontend needs to be: $P(X = s) \geq .9999$.

Dewclaw in two data centers

If we add Dewclaw to DC2, now the frontend has a backup. It can send a query to the DC1 Dewclaw service (or, if the frontend is also running in DC2, to the DC2 Dewclaw), and after a failure it can attempt to query the other data center.

This expands the sample space. A trial, which corresponds to an RPC request, now has five potential outcomes, as shown in Table 9-2: success in DC1, success in DC2, failure in DC1 and success in DC2, failure in DC2 and success in DC1, or failure in both DC1 and DC2.

Table 9-2. The sample space of RPC outcomes

DC1	DC2
Success	N/A (never sent)
N/A (never sent)	Success
Failure	Success
Success	Failure
Failure	Failure

Or, $S = \{s_1, s_2, \{f_1, s_2\}, \{f_2, s_1\}, \{f_1, f_2\}\}$.

In order for the frontend to succeed, we can return any of the entries in this sample space that aren't the double failure.

Intuitively it might make sense that we have decreased the probability of a total failure: there are now four successful outcomes and still a single failure outcome. However, we don't know the probabilities of the individual outcomes. The single failure outcome could have a higher probability than all four of the successful outcomes combined.

We don't need to assign probabilities to every outcome in this space, though. Since we know that we want to avoid the double failure case, we just need to ensure that the probability of that outcome is less than 0.01%. Mathematically, $P(X = \{f_1, f_2\}) < .0001$.

The probability of this single event, $P(X = \{f_1, f_2\})$, is the same as that of two independent trials both getting failures, $P(X, Y = f)$. Because these trials are independent, the probability of both outcomes being true is the product of each outcome: $P(X = f)P(Y = f)$. Since the probability for each trial is the same, the probability is simply $P(f)^2$. So $P(X = \{f_1, f_2\}) < .0001$ requires $P(f)^2 < .0001$, which requires $P(f) < .01$.

This is remarkable! If Dewclaw is run in two data centers, each data center need only provide an SLO of 99% to ensure that the frontend can itself provide an SLO of 99.99%: Dewclaw can be less reliable than the services that depend on it by two orders of magnitude.

Independence

A lot of this analysis hinges on the assumption of *independence.* Trials are independent if the outcome of any one of them has no bearing on the outcome of any of the others.

In general, no trials are truly independent. Customers that receive errors tend to retry, services become overloaded, and bad software rollouts can have effects that violate our assumptions. We know of at least one durability event, in an otherwise extremely robust data storage system, that was caused by lightning.

But we have to start *somewhere,* and it may as well be here. No model you develop will be correct, and it's important to keep that in mind. But that doesn't mean it's useless, and it can give you insight you wouldn't otherwise have.

Why Not Retry? (Or, How Two 99%s Can Look Completely Different)

Although it will allow you to run Dewclaw at 99% availability, as opposed to 99.99%, you may find that standing up the service in another data center is the more expensive option.

You may be wondering, instead of routing the second request to a new data center, why not simply make the first request a second time? This is a good idea—sometimes! The answer is that it depends significantly on the gritty details of your particular service.

When you hear a phrase like "the service was at 99% for June," you likely interpret this as meaning that, at any given point in June, a request to the service had around a 99% probability of succeeding, as shown in Figure 9-3.

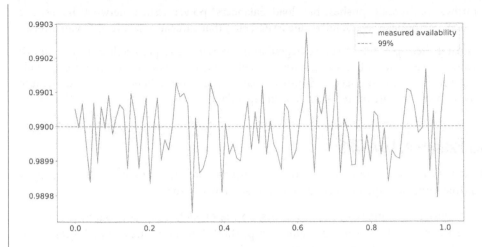

Figure 9-3. One way to achieve 99% availability—at any point in time the service has a measured availability of about 99%, with small variations around that number

In reality what tends to happen is that a service is more or less entirely available until it suddenly very much isn't, as shown in Figure 9-4.

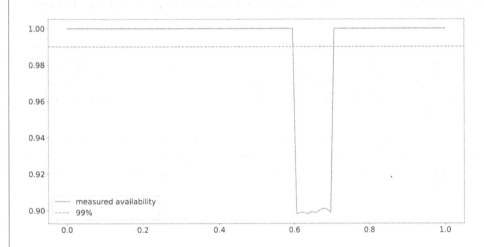

Figure 9-4. Another way to achieve 99% availability—the service mostly has a measured availability of much higher than 99%, except for a small period where it is significantly lower

That is, service failures can be catastrophic, not gradual (although they can certainly be either, or sometimes both). A service running on a single host is subject to all the kinds of failures that can remove that host from operation, and a service running in a single data center is still subject to a number of single points of failure (bad software pushes, bad config pushes, bad load balancers, power issues, network issues, fire issues, earthquake issues, hurricane issues, etc.) that can cause severe SLO violations.

During these periods of severe degradation, retrying a request will not help (and if your service is down because it is overloaded, retrying will be actively harmful). Sending a new request to a second failure domain is much more likely to succeed, because the two systems are more likely to be independent.

SLI Example: Low QPS

Back at Catz, you've been asked to help out with Batch, a new batch processing system that runs data query jobs on behalf of enterprise users.

Catz doesn't have many enterprise users, so the expected load on Batch is about one request per minute. But it is extremely important that the requests Batch gets are successful: the SLO, set before your arrival, is 99.9%.

The problem is this: the convention at Catz for measuring availability is to take all requests received in the last five minutes, and report the ratio of successful requests to the total. This works well for Dewclaw, with tens of thousands of requests per second, but Batch gets one request a minute. With only five requests in the calculation period, even a *single* failure will drop your measured availability to 80% and violate your SLO.

This alarms you—you don't want to cross your SLO by pure chance—but when you bring it up with your team, they assure you it's fine. Batch, they say, might have a 99.9% availability SLO, but its actual availability is closer to 99.99%. Since it never gets close to the SLO, you can be confident that SLO violations indicate real service issues. Right?

We'll start answering this by continuing with the coin toss analogy. Let's take a look at what happens when we flip a coin with some bias less skewed than our claimed availability: say, $p = 0.6$. If we toss this coin 10 times and plot the result, we might see Figure 9-5.

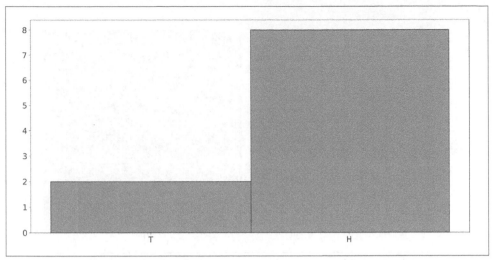

Figure 9-5. A histogram showing one possible outcome of flipping a coin 10 times

But we might perform the experiment and see the results in Figure 9-6 instead.

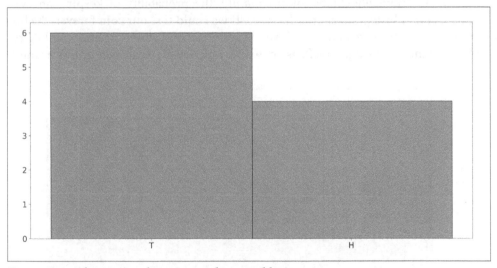

Figure 9-6. A histogram showing another possible outcome

Since a coin toss is an essentially random event, it is not impossible for us to get, by chance, a rare histogram. A third possibility could be what you see in Figure 9-7.

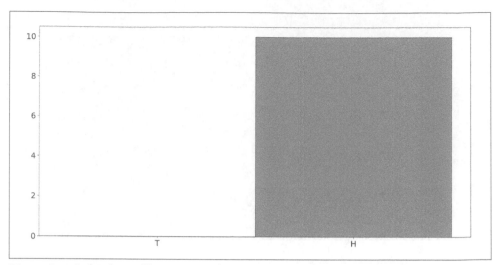

Figure 9-7. A third possible outcome: the coin came up heads every time

If we toss the coin more, eventually the skewed histograms will become *extremely* unlikely. As *eventually* climbs toward *infinity*, the probability of keeping an even slightly skewed histogram approaches zero. If we could toss our coin forever, the histograms we are likely to end up with would get closer and closer together until there's only one familiar histogram left, as shown in Figure 9-8 (recall that in this example $p = 0.6$).

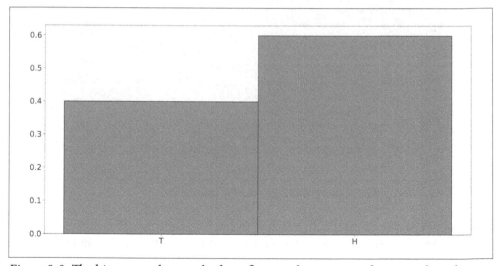

Figure 9-8. The histogram that results from flipping the coin an infinite number of times with p = 0.6

This histogram has been *normalized*; the values now add up to 1. Since we're dealing with an arbitrarily large number of coin flips, it becomes easier to work with histograms in this form. Now the height of each bar is also the probability of each outcome.

But this histogram doesn't tell us anything we didn't already know. It has heads at 60% and tails at 40%, but we knew that going in. What we're more interested in is this: how rare it is to see a histogram of 10 flips with 0 tails?

As you've no doubt already put together, answering this kind of question would be valuable to us in determining whether or not the SLO violations from Batch indicate real service issues. So, we want some measure of how likely each possible histogram is. The good news is that we have that in the *binomial distribution*.

Each time we toss a coin we get a result, heads or tails, from the sample space. Let's change our perspective slightly. Now, instead of working with a sample space of $\{H, T\}$, let's flip the coin 10 times and count the number of times we get heads.

We'll count each group of 10 flips as a single trial—a *binomial* trial—that yields a result from the sample space $\{0, 1, 2, 3, 4, 5, 6, 7, 8, 9, 10\}$. If we perform this experiment 10 times (flipping the coin 100 times), we might get a histogram like Figure 9-9.

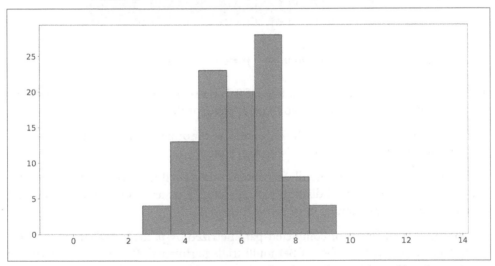

Figure 9-9. A histogram showing the outcome of counting the number of heads in 10 coin flips

Here, the height of bar 4 corresponds to the number of times we got 4 heads in 10 flips. (As a reminder, right now the coin we're flipping has a bias of 0.6.) In this trial we mostly got heads 5–7 times, and rarely more than 9 or fewer than 3.

We generated the histograms we were looking at before by flipping a coin 10 times, and the heights of the bars reflected the relative probability of getting heads or tails in a single flip. We then took those 10-flip trials and performed *those* successively many times. The histogram produced from that exercise now gives us the relative probability of getting any one of the original histograms.

If we keep going, eventually that histogram will converge to Figure 9-10.

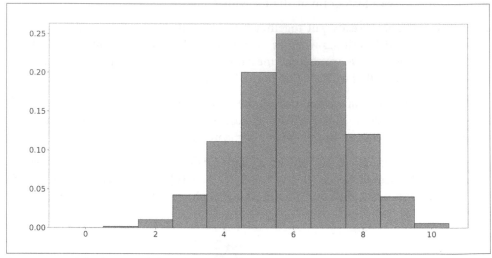

Figure 9-10. The binomial distribution with p = 0.6, n = 10

As expected with a coin that has a bias of 0.6, most of the time—but not all of the time!—flipping the coin 10 times, you'd get heads 6 of those times.

The histograms that the Bernoulli trials and the binomial trials ultimately converge to, when normalized to 1, are *probability distributions*.

In the same way that the Bernoulli distribution didn't tell us anything more than we knew going in, the binomial distribution doesn't give us any more information than the coin's bias and the number of times we flipped it.

The binomial distribution is completely parametrized by p, the parameter to the Bernoulli trial, and n, the number of Bernoulli trials performed. But because the sample space is now much larger, we can learn things from it that we might not have such a great intuition for. For example, we can see that even though $p = 0.6$, the chance of actually getting exactly 6 heads in 10 flips is only .25. Three-quarters of the time, we'll see some other value.

Since each bar in the binomial distribution assigns a probability to each element of the 11-element sample space {0, 1, 2, 3, 4, 5, 6, 7, 8, 9, 10}, now we have a way of saying that one histogram is fairly likely, but that another histogram is actually very unlikely.

Remember that coin flips are *independent*. The side the coin lands on in one flip doesn't affect the next flip. This is what lets us treat each individual flip as a Bernoulli trial with parameter p. When we generalize to other binary events, we need to make sure we are talking about events that are likewise independent; if a failed RPC causes a client to hammer the service with retries, then we probably don't have independent requests.

Often in modeling such problems you will have to assume that events are independent even when they really aren't—for example, users who receive an error from a request might immediately issue the request again, receiving another error. But for the most part this is a good assumption to start with.

Now let's try taking what we've learned to answer our original question: how often can you flip a coin of extreme bias before you land on tails?

Most of the named probability distributions you will encounter have mathematical formulae to map values from the sample space to probability distributions. When the sample space is discrete, these formulae—called *probability mass functions* (PMFs)—return the actual probability of each element of the sample space.

The PMF of the binomial distribution is as follows:

$$f(k; n, p) = \binom{n}{k} p^k (1 - p)^{n - k}$$

On the left side, $f(k; n, p)$ is the probability of observing k successes within n trials, where the probability for each trial is p. (Remember, a success case here is getting heads.) Now let's tackle the right side. This looks complicated, but it can be broken down into three main parts.

The first is $\binom{n}{k}$; this is the binomial coefficient, pronounced *n choose k*, and represents the number of ways to choose k items from a group of n total items.

The classic example of this is you're having a dinner party for yourself and three friends, Adora, Catra, and Scorpia. During dinner, how many different combinations of conversations could happen between exactly two friends?

The answer is six:

- Yourself and Adora
- Yourself and Catra
- Yourself and Scorpia
- Adora and Scorpia
- Catra and Scorpia

- Adora and Catra

That's easy to do for small numbers. The formula for the binomial coefficient is:

$$\binom{n}{k} = \frac{n!}{k!(n-k)!}$$

So:

$$\binom{4}{2} = \frac{4!}{2! \times (4-2)!} = \frac{24}{4} = 6$$

Any time $k = 0$ or $k = n$, the answer will be 1, because there is only one combination for using none or all of the items.

This corresponds to the number of combinations for which k successes can exist in n trials. Since we want to count all possible outcomes, we need to multiply by this factor.

The second part of the right side of the PMF of the binomial distribution is p^k, which is the probability of k successes. Since we assume all the trials are independent, the probability of k successes is the probability of a single success multiplied by itself k times.

Finally, the third part is $(1 - p)^{n-k}$, which is the probability that all $(n - k)$ of the rest of the trials failed, each with probability $(1 - p)$.

So, the PMF for the binomial distribution breaks down to:

$f(k; n, p) =$ [number of ways to have k successes] [probability of k successes][probability of (n-k) failures]

Figure 9-11 is a histogram of the PMF with $p = .9999$ and $n = 10$.

It's clear from this histogram that $k = 10$, getting 10 heads, is by far the most likely outcome. There is a tiny blip at $k = 9$, and smaller invisible blips down to zero. (If we do the math, we can see that for $k = 0$—that is, getting zero heads—the probability is 10^{-40}.) This gives us a good picture of how unlikely seeing a single tails is at $p = .9999$, but it still doesn't answer our question.

For starters, it doesn't give us a single number, which is what we're looking for. But beyond that, it's not clear how exactly to map our problem, which has two numbers (the probability p of a Bernoulli trial, which we know, and the total number of trials we expect to perform before failure, which we want to find out), to the binomial distribution, which has three (p, k, and n).

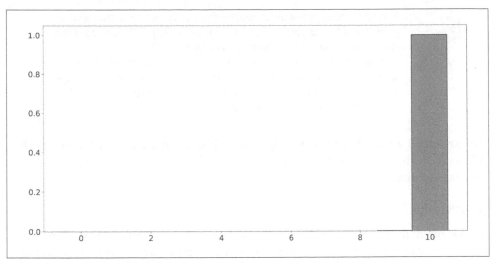

Figure 9-11. The binomial distribution with p = .9999, n = 10

What the binomial distribution tells us is, given a bag of n independent flips, what the chances are that k of them are heads. But we don't want a bag of n where *any one of them* can be tails. These requests are arriving in order, one after another. We want to know how many have to pass before the *first* instance of tails.

There's a distribution that's very closely related to the binomial distribution, called the *geometric distribution*, which stops the trial as soon as we get our first failure:

$$f(k, q) = (1 - q)^{k - 1}q$$

This is the PMF for the number of times we need to flip a coin (or perform any Bernoulli trial) of bias $q = 1 - p$ before we *succeed*. $(1 - p)$ represents a *failure*, and since out of k trials there are $k - 1$ of them, it is raised to that power. The kth trial being a success, it is multiplied by q. Finally, since the successful trial always happens at the end, we don't need to compensate for all possible orderings, so it is not multiplied by a binomial coefficient.

The sample space of this distribution is all possible values of k, from 1 to infinity. Each value of k represents a number of times we flip a coin before we land on heads, and this function assigns each of those values a probability.

Let's apply this to an example. If the chance of getting tails is 0.0001—that is, $q = .0001$—what is the probability of getting tails for the first time on the 20th flip?

The equation then is $.9999^{19} \times .0001$. The probability is a tiny 0.00009981017.

As you can see, we could do this for any number of flips.

Fun fact: For any geometric distribution, irrespective of the value of p, $p(1)$ will be the greatest, and $i > j$ implies $P(i) > P(j)$. Even if the chance of getting tails is .0001, you're more likely to get tails on the first flip than you are on any *individual* subsequent flip. This is related to the memorylessness of the process; once you're 100 flips in, if you haven't hit tails yet, you're basically starting from 0. This is also related to the gambler's fallacy.

We now need a way to turn that sample space into a single, representative number. Whoever in the back just shouted out, "Average them!" we like the way you think. Let's explore that.

Expected value

A fundamental aspect of a probability distribution is its expected value. This is also called the average, mean, or expectation, and it denotes an important central tendency of the distribution: if a process follows a random distribution, then it is the value that, absent any other information, is the best guess as to what the output of that process will be.

The expected value is denoted $E[X]$ and is given by the following equation (for discrete values in a sample space S; we'll look at a continuous example later):

$$E[X] = \sum_{k \in S} x_k P(x_k)$$

This is the sum of the values weighted by each value's probability. For example, in the roll of a six-sided die, the probability of getting each face is 1 in 6, so the expected value is just the average of all the faces on the die. That is, for a six-sided die, the expected value is $(1 + 2 + 3 + 4 + 5 + 6)/6 = 3.5$, although no face actually has that value.

If you average the output of a random process over many successive trials, the values you get will approach the expected value of the distribution that describes your process. This is called *the law of large numbers*. So when we say that we receive a request *on average* once a minute, the best way to interpret that is that we have collected data for long enough that the ratio of requests to total minutes is very close to 1.

It is possible to construct a process such that the sum in the preceding equation (or its continuous analogue, the integral, for continuous probability functions) does not converge to a finite value. These processes *have no expected value*. The Cauchy distribution is an example of a probability distribution with this property. If your process is described by a Cauchy distribution, you can expect to have extremely large outliers.

By the definition in our equation, the expected value of the geometric distribution is:

$$E[X] = \sum_{k=1}^{\infty} k(1-p)^{k-1}p$$

$$= p\sum_{k=1}^{\infty} k(1-p)^{k-1}$$

If you've studied calculus, you may recognize $k(1-p)^{k-1}$ as the derivative, with respect to $(1-p)$, of $(1-p)^k$. Because p is a probability we know that $(1-p) < 1$, and for any number $q < 1$ the following equation holds:

$$\sum_{r=0}^{\infty} q^r = \frac{1}{1-q}$$

Therefore, the sum of the derivatives equals the derivative of the sum (with $q = 1-p$):

$$\frac{d}{dq}\frac{1}{1-q} = \frac{1}{(1-q)^2}$$

$$= \frac{1}{(1-(1-p))^2}$$

$$= \frac{1}{(1-1+p)^2}$$

$$= \frac{1}{p^2}$$

The full expression for the expected value is then:

$$E[X] = p\frac{1}{p^2} = \frac{1}{p}$$

With $p = .0001$, the expected value for the number of requests before we are paged is 10,000—which maybe strikes you as obvious. If each request has a one ten-thousandth chance of failure, then it should take around 10,000 requests for us to see a failure.

Unfortunately, despite its name, the expected value of a distribution is not always a good description of the values that would come out of sampling from it. Or rather, it can sometimes fail to answer the question we're actually posing.

If we flip a coin of bias $p = .9999$, the expected value of 10,000 is calculated by multiplying each possible value of k by the probability of that value, $P(k)$. But the geometric distribution gives a value to every positive integer k. It's not *probable*, but it's *possible* to flip our coin a hundred thousand or a million times before we get tails, and this possibility is factored into the expected value of the distribution.

The values in a distribution that are extreme outliers make up what's known as the *tail* of the distribution. Some distributions (such as the Gaussian distribution, also called the *normal distribution*) have *light* tails; the probabilities of seeing values far from the center of the distribution are so remote that they may as well be zero.

Other distributions (for example, the log-normal distribution) have *heavy* tails. In these distributions, extreme values are still rare, but they happen often enough that they shouldn't be surprising. And some distributions, such as the Cauchy distribution, have such heavy tails that the expected value *does not exist*.

We're not saying that there are some distributions where the expected value is meaningful, and others where it is meaningless. The expected value, when it exists, is always meaningful—but it doesn't always mean what you might hope it does.

In the current case, a better estimator of what we want to know might be the median.

Median

The *median*, sometimes denoted $\tilde{X}$, is another central tendency of a distribution. It is defined as the value that separates one half of the distribution from the other. Let's consider if it would be a better answer to our question than the expected value.

Say we had a factory that produced bags of cookies, where each bag contains 10 cookies. However, a mechanical fault sometimes stops the bag line without stopping the cookie line, and as a result one out of every hundred bags ends up with a thousand cookies in it.

If you opened a random bag of cookies, how many would you anticipate seeing? Intuitively you'd probably see 10 cookies. Yes, some bags have a *lot* of cookies, but those are very rare. *Most* bags still have just 10 cookies.

The expected value of the number of cookies in a bag is:

$$E[x] = \sum_{k=0}^{\infty} kp(k)$$

Since the only nonzero probabilities are $p(10) = .99$ and $p(1000) = .01$:

$$E[x] = 10 \times p(10) + 1000 \times p(1000)$$
$$= 10 \times .99 + 1000 \times .01$$
$$= 9.9 + 10$$
$$= 19.9$$

So, the expected number of cookies in a bag is nearly 20! In this case, we would say that the expected value is not a good representation of the number of cookies in a random bag. This is because the expected value takes extreme outliers into account; the very rarity of those outliers is what makes the median (10 cookies) more attractive to us.

Jumping back to our coin example: the *median* of the geometric distribution is a more realistic value for how long it takes to get tails.

The equation for calculating the median of the geometric distribution is:

$$\tilde{X} = \left\lceil \frac{1}{-\log_2 1 - q} \right\rceil = 6932$$

where q is the probability. Half of the time, the coin will hit tails before even 7,000 flips, well short of the expected value of 10,000.

We break our SLO a lot, actually

For Batch, every query is a Bernoulli trial, and "99.99% availability" is conceptually the same as a coin with bias $p = .9999$.

The preceding analysis therefore shows that a service that is 99.99% available can expect to see a failure after about 7,000 queries. Since this service will violate its SLO whenever the failure/total ratio is above 1/1,000, and you only have around 5 data points to go on (there being, on average, 5 requests in a 5-minute interval), a single failure will push availability below the SLO. Seven thousand minutes is roughly 114 hours. Even with a *real* availability of 99.99%, Batch can expect to see a false positive roughly once every five days.

What can you do?

It's possible that a service with fewer than 1,500 calls in a day is not important enough to carry three nines. You could grab the SLO dial and twist it to the left. This is nice if you can get away with it, but if you could, you probably already would have. Batch's SLO is 99.9%, and (kind of unfairly, you think) you can't do anything about that here.

You could expand the window over which you calculate events. A 5-minute window only gets you 5 data points; a 2,000-minute window will give you space to have an occasional failure without going below the red line. But is this a good idea? That window is almost a day and a half long. If Batch collapses, how long will it take you to notice?

 You could write some probers. A prober is a piece of software that continually calls your service with known input and verifies the output. Probers provide much more benefit than simply increasing the number of calls, but you can use them to dial up the traffic as much as you care to. A problem with probers is that prober traffic is not always representative of customer traffic, and you risk drowning customer signals in prober noise. If your live traffic is failing because your customers are setting an RPC option that your probers don't, you risk never seeing it. You can get around this by switching to per-customer SLOs, but then you're back in the box you started in.

What you really want to do is somehow quantify the *confidence* you have in your measurement. If you have four successful requests and one failed request, you can't immediately know if that's because your service just took a hard stumble or if it's because the request (and the on-call engineer) are just unlucky.

For this, we need a new technique.

On Statistics

We can use the techniques covered earlier to find out what p means for our service. But how do we find p? We're rarely given these parameters, and when we are (for example, when a hardware vendor tells us the mean time to failure of some part) we often don't believe them.

If your SLOs are couched in terms of probability—which they usually are either directly, in terms of an availability ratio or some latency percentile, or indirectly, if for example your SLOs depend on traffic being *well behaved*, which you have defined in terms of some distribution or other—then statistical inference is a natural extension to measure the SLIs in the same language. Both sides fit together into the same model of (an aspect of) your service. But remember that it's only a model.

Maximum Likelihood Estimation

We want to measure p.

Well, really, we can't measure p. p is not an observable quantity. We can measure the *effects* of p, because sometimes requests will succeed, and sometimes they will fail, but we can only *infer* from these what p might or might not be.

One method of inference is called *maximum likelihood estimation* (MLE). Say in a given period we receive four successes and a failure. Then the *data* (or *evidence*) is $E = \{s, s, s, s, f\}$. In the section on probability—specifically on coin flips—we talked about the probability of getting some evidence given a specific value of p.

The way we write this in mathematical notation is $P(E \mid p)$, which is read as "the probability of E given p." If we know p, we can calculate this as we did before with the binomial distribution. Say, if $p = 0.9$:

$$f(k, n, p) = \binom{n}{k} p^k (1 - p)^{n-k}$$
$$= \binom{5}{4}(.9)^4(.1)^1$$
$$= 5 \cdot .6561 \cdot .1$$
$$\approx 33\%$$

So, the probability of getting this evidence of four successes and one failure, *given* $p = 0.9$, is about 33%. If we run the same calculation with $p = 0.8$, we get about 41%. That is, the data we got is *more likely* if $p = 0.8$ than if $p = 0.9$.

The goal of maximum likelihood estimation is to find the values of the parameters that maximize the likelihood of the data. To distinguish these, sometimes we give them little hats: $\hat{p}$.

First, we want a function that expresses the likelihood of the data. We have that already—it's just the binomial density function:

$$l(p) = \binom{n}{k} p^k (1 - p)^{n-k}$$
$$\hat{p} = \arg \max_p l(p)$$

If you took calculus, you may recall the method for maximizing functions: take the derivative and set it equal to zero.

Here is the derivative:

$$\frac{dl}{dp} = kp^{k-1}(1 - p)^{n-k} - (n - k)p^k(1 - p)^{(n-k)-1}$$

And setting the derivative of l to zero, we can solve for p:

$$kp^{k-1}(1-p)^{n-k} - (n-k)p^k(1-p)^{(n-k)-1} = 0$$
$$kp^{k-1}(1-p)^{n-k} = (n-k)p^k(1-p)^{(n-k)-1}$$
$$\frac{k}{p} = \frac{n-k}{1-p}$$
$$k(1-p) = p(n-k)$$
$$k - kp = np - kp$$
$$k = np$$
$$p = \frac{k}{n} = \hat{p}$$

Okay, this seems maybe a bit obvious. The value of p that maximizes the data we saw is, well, the number of successes divided by the number of requests; exactly what we were already doing. But what's valuable here is understanding how likely it is that that probability is the true probability. If our dataset is larger, this becomes clearer.

If, for example, we had a dataset with 500 data queries, then $\hat{p}$ would be a better estimator of the true value of p. Figure 9-12 is a graph of $l(p)$ for a service that gets 4 successes out of 5 (solid line), and 400 out of 500 (dashed line). Both graphs reach their maximum at $p = 0.8$, but the likelihood of seeing the data falls off much more sharply away from that value when we have more data in total.

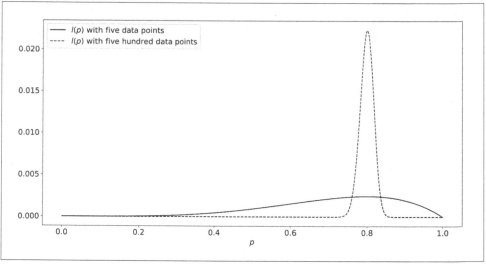

Figure 9-12. The likelihood functions $l(p)$—while the maximum value of each function occurs at $p = 0.8$, the function drops off much more sharply when it has more data

MLE doesn't necessarily involve actually doing the calculus by hand. Often we don't know the expression for the probability function, or it's too complicated, or we have more than one variable to optimize. In these cases we can turn to other optimization methods, such as gradient descent, but in all cases the goal is the same: to find the values of the parameters that maximize the likelihood function, given some data.

Maximum a Posteriori

It might make intuitive sense to you why the likelihood function with 500 data points is more certain about the value of p than the one with 5 data points. There's a pretty good chance that you'd get 4 successes and 1 failure at $p = 0.6$ or $p = 0.9$, but almost no chance you'd get 400 out of 500. It's possible, but extremely unlikely. The more data points we have, the more closely the realistic values will be concentrated around the MLE.

What can we do? Well, we could use more data points. Two (real-world) solutions to this problem that we've seen are to increase the window size over which samples are collected, and to simply include artificial *success* data points.

At first both of these approaches might sound a little bizarre. The first one allows for past performance to play a role; however, it will also heavily weight the analysis over that previous period of, say, several hours or even days. The second one just uses made-up data. How can that possibly be sound?

When we specified the likelihood function $l(p)$, we specified it as the probability of the evidence given p:

$$l(p) = p(E \mid p)$$

We then found the value $\hat{p}$ that maximized this probability.

An alternative method is to consider the probability of p given the evidence. This is called the *maximum a posteriori* (MAP) estimator. (*A posteriori* is a statistical—and philosophical—term that basically means knowledge augmented with evidence. It's contrasted with *a priori*, which means knowledge untainted by evidence. This is also why two of the terms in Bayes' theorem, which we explore in the next section, are called the *prior* and the *posterior*.)

Here we—in what is going to sound like a ridiculous tautology, but stick with us— maximize the probability of p given the evidence:

$$\hat{p} = \arg \max_{p} P(p \mid E)$$

What in the world, you sensibly ask, does this buy us? What is even *different*? To answer that we'll take a quick (we promise) detour through Bayes' theorem.

Bayes' theorem

When we talk about the probabilities of two events, A and B, we often want to talk about the probability that *both* events happen. This is denoted $P(A, B)$. Let's use an example here where A is the event of eating dumplings, and B is the event of ordering Chinese food. Now, what is the probability that you are eating dumplings and that you ordered Chinese food? Note that because both A and B have to be true, the order doesn't matter: $P(A, B) = P(B, A)$.

Now consider the probability of B by itself, $P(B)$. This represents an upper bound on $P(A, B)$, since A and B cannot *both* be true more often than B is true. So, $P(B) \geq P(A, B)$. It's the same story with $P(A)$. Therefore, the probability of you eating dumplings and ordering Chinese food cannot be higher than the probability of you ordering Chinese food.

Additionally, it's possible that A is true when B is not. You could be eating dumplings, but not ordering Chinese food: if you're eating *khinkali*, for instance, which are Georgian dumplings. So, we'll want to restrict our consideration of $P(A)$ to when B is already true, and then we have the two conditions that must both be true: $P(A|B)$ and $P(B)$.

This gives us the factorization law $P(A, B) = P(A|B)P(B)$. This is true irrespective of whether A and B are independent or how they are distributed.

But since $P(A, B) = P(B, A)$:

$$P(A, B) = P(B, A)$$

$$P(A|B)P(B) = P(B|A)P(A)$$

$$P(A|B) = \frac{P(B|A)P(A)}{P(B)}$$

What we can see here is that the probability of you eating dumplings given that you ordered Chinese food is equal to the probability that you're eating dumplings and you ordered Chinese food over the probability that you ordered Chinese food.

Besides making us hungry, the last equation, Bayes' theorem, will help us use MAP. There's a lot going on, but for the purposes of this section it tells us how to take a probability conditioned on one variable, $P(A|B)$, and cast it in terms of the other variable conditioned on the first, $P(B|A)$.

This is what we did previously:

$$P(p|E) = \frac{P(E|p)P(p)}{P(E)}$$

In this equation, we are already familiar with $P(E|p)$, the likelihood. $P(p)$ is called the *prior probability* (or just the *prior*), which represents the probability we assign to p. $P(E)$ is the *evidence*. $P(p|E)$ is the *posterior*, the probability of our hypothesis given the evidence.

Instead of maximizing the likelihood, $P(E|p)$, we now consider maximizing $P(E|p)P(p)$. (What about $P(E)$? We're going to ignore it. Why? One, it is famously difficult to calculate, and two, it doesn't depend on p at all, so we maximize the whole thing only by maximizing the numerator.)

In order to do this we need $P(p)$. Now we are treating p, the *parameter* of the binomial distribution, as a random number drawn from its own distribution. This means we don't have a single number to calculate with, but an entire sample space of possible values we need to calculate over.

If, however, we have good reason to think some values of p are more likely than others *before* we get any evidence, then this allows us to incorporate those prior beliefs into our calculations. If we do that, and do our calculations and maximize p, we will have calculated the MAP estimator.

The relationship between MLE and MAP

If we have no idea what probability we could possibly assign to $P(p)$, a natural prior distribution to assign would give every element of the sample space (here the sample space is all the real numbers between 0 and 1) the same probability, akin to the sides of a (many-faceted) fair die. This makes a kind of sense, in that as we have no information that would allow us to give more weight to any specific values, we end up giving them all the same weight.

If we do this and calculate the maximum a posteriori value, we will find that it is equal to maximum likelihood estimate. It turns out that MLE is a special case of MAP where the prior distribution is uniform. Such a prior distribution is called an *uninformative prior*. MAP allows us to bias our inference in a rigorous way.

Using MAP

We can use MAP to calculate an estimator for p that includes knowledge we might already have, such as "the last 600 requests were fine" and "it's actually pretty unlikely that the whole system is down." We've already discussed two ways to do this: extending the window and including artificial successes.

Adding artificial successes sounds ridiculous, but it's actually the more straightforward option. MAP is subjective, and it corresponds to a prior that gives high credence to success. Extending the calculation window to, say, 2,000 minutes corresponds to a prior that consists of the previous 1,995 minutes. This is actually *less* reliable than a completely artificial prior, since after recovering from an outage you have a high degree of belief that your service is up again (after, say, 20 successful queries), but the period that your service spent down will be part of the prior.

In the case of Batch, the team is *pretty sure* that the service is at least 99.9% reliable. One of the ways to encode this (there are many) is to pretend the previous data points were 999 successes and a single failure. This gives us a prior for $P(p)$ that looks like Figure 9-13.

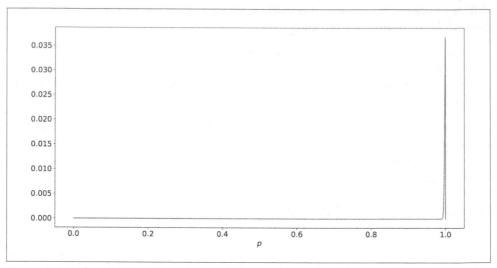

Figure 9-13. The likelihood function for 999 successes and 1 failure

This prior essentially only gives credence to a few values around .999. Figure 9-14 shows what it looks like if we zoom in on that space.

Most of the credible values for p are between .994 and very close to 1. This means that it will take a significant amount of evidence to move our estimate of p away from that region.

Using this prior, what is our MAP estimate for Batch's single failure? 0.998.

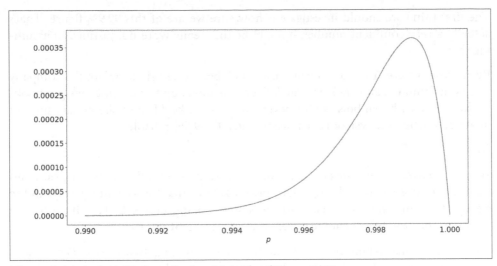

Figure 9-14. A closer look at the far right side of Figure 9-13

Because of our strong prior belief, a single failure only nudges us a little bit. In fact, our belief is *so* strong that even if we failed all five requests in a given window, our estimate would only go down to 99.4%! We definitely don't want that; the system could be completely down and we would never page. Our prior gives too little weight to values below the SLO, as shown in Figure 9-15.

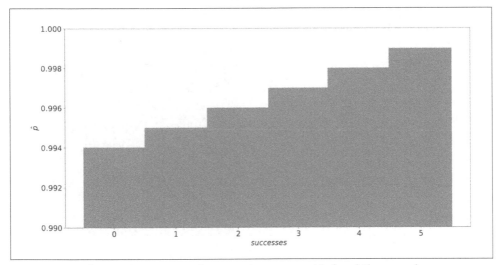

Figure 9-15. The MAP estimates of our service—even with five failures and no successes, our strong prior gives us an estimate of 99.4% availability.

The first thing we should investigate is how sure we are of this 99.9% figure. That's actually a *very* confident number. It might be that really we're not justified in assuming that.

But maybe we are. You have a teammate who's been there since before the company was even founded, and she's principal. Everyone looks up to her, and she's got books on her desk with symbols you've never even *seen*, like $\coprod$, and she swears up and down that, when the system is in a steady state, it's 99.9% reliable.

So.

When the system is in a steady state. We've baked an assumption into our prior, and we didn't notice we were doing it. Our prior assumes that the system is always in the steady state, and gives no weight to the system's being down. In fact, it gives *zero* weight to the possibility that the system is down (i.e., that $p = 0$).

We can add this assumption into our model by creating two priors, $P(p|u)$ and $P(p|d)$: the probability of p given the system is up, and given the system is down. Then $P(p) = aP(p|u) + bP(p|d)$, where a and b are the relative weights of how often we believe the system is up and down.

We don't have any data on that, and your teammate is doing the seven summits again so she's no help, so we'll give them equal weights, which is the same as saying "we don't know." As you can see in Figure 9-16, now $\hat{p}$ *flips* between the *up* and *down* models after three failures in a five-minute window.

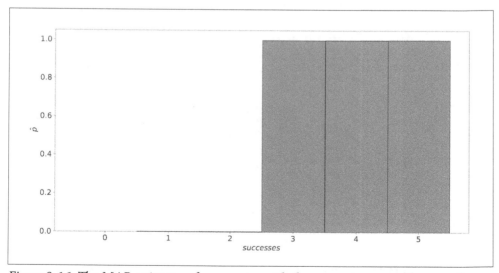

Figure 9-16. The MAP estimates of our service with the new prior—once there are fewer than three successes, the model places more likelihood on our availability being very close to zero

As we will explore in a later section, we may have more or fewer than five requests in a five-minute window. We can visualize the most likely request counts in a heatmap, as shown in Figure 9-17.

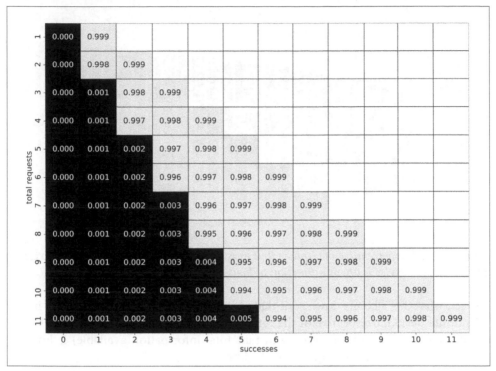

Figure 9-17. A heatmap showing the MAP estimates of our service over a range of success counts: the cells with light backgrounds are where the model estimates the service to be "up" and the cells with dark backgrounds are where it is "down"

Here, the total number of requests we see in a five-minute span is on the vertical axis, and the number of successes we see is on the horizontal access. The number in each box is the MAP estimator for p. The dark squares denote where the model has decided that the service is hard down; the light squares indicate that the model still thinks the service is up.

"Now wait a minute," you object, correctly. "This only pages when as many as *half* the sample requests fail?!" Well, yes. Again, this is an artifact of our frankly ridiculously confident prior. Choosing a good prior can be difficult. If you build a complicated model, you could end up in a situation where the result (the posterior) changes wildly depending on your choice of prior.

If we were implementing this in production, we would probably relax a little bit on that prior, and also extend the alerting window out to maybe 30 minutes. Figure 9-18 shows, under these conditions, the percentage of requests that must succeed, as a function of the total number of requests, in order for $\hat{p} \geq .99$.

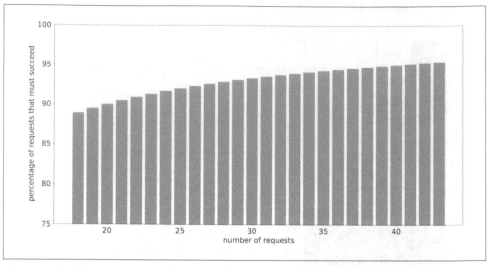

Figure 9-18. The percentage of requests that must succeed in order for the model to estimate that the service is up, as a function of the total number of requests

In fact, what this all boils down to is that we allow up to two missed requests in any 30-minute period, irrespective of the total request count. This gives us more leeway for error when the request count (and thus total information available) is low, but becomes more strict as the request count climbs.

This is a simple solution, and easy to implement, but it's grounded in analysis. Is it a *good* solution? That depends on how Batch actually behaves. You are probably wondering what the odds are that you'll end up regularly seeing failures but never tripping any alarms. The odds of seeing 3 failures in a 30-minute period when our reliability is above the SLO are quite small.

There are two important points here. The first is that we can make use of our expertise and our experience with a given system when interpreting measured quantities in a rigorous and mathematical way via a prior distribution. The second is that it can be fiendishly difficult to pick a good prior. If this were a real service, we would recommend hardcoding the alert threshold at two (or living with it at one) until you're able to collect more data about how the service acts in production.

Bayesian Inference

While MAP allows us to use a prior distribution to incorporate information we already know (or we think we know) into our inferences, MAP and MLE are still what we call *point estimators*. When we maximize $p(p|E)$ (in the case of MAP) or $p(E|p)$ (in the case of MLE), we're left with a single number, $\hat{p}$. This is the *most likely* value of p given the data we have. What we don't know is how certain we are about that value. The maximum likelihood estimate of p for 1 failure out of 10 is the same as for 100 failures out of 1,000.

If, instead of finding the value of p that maximizes the expression $P(p|E)$ as we do in MAP, we look at the entire distribution $P(p|E)$, then we'll have a complete picture of p.

For example, consider a 30-minute window during which we see exactly 30 requests. If we see no failures, what might we say about p? The maximum likelihood estimate would give us $\hat{p} = \frac{30}{30} = 1$. MAP might give us something else, but right now we'll use the uninformative prior $P(p) = 1$. Remember that this is a probability density; the probability density $P(p) = 1$ *for all real numbers between 0 and 1*. This assigns equal weight to all values.

But $\hat{p} = 1$ leaves out a lot of information. How much more likely is this value than any other value? Remember, with MAP we went from treating p as a parameter to a function to a random value in its own right. It has a distribution. What is that distribution?

We can calculate it analytically with Bayes' theorem:

$$P(p|E) = \frac{P(E|p)P(p)}{P(E)}$$

This is the same method we used for MAP, except now we need to know the denominator. In general, with Bayesian inference, this is the tricky bit. It is not necessary if you only want to establish *relative* likelihood between different values of p, but it is necessary if you want to calculate actual probabilities. The general form of $P(E)$ is:

$$P(E) = \int P(E|p)P(p)\mathrm{d}p$$

But this integral is often not directly computable. There are many techniques for numerical approximations, but we won't go over them here. For this example we are in the lucky position that we *can* compute this integral. Since we're using the binomial distribution to model E:

$$P(E|p) = \binom{n}{k}p^n(1-p)^{n-k}$$

$$= \binom{30}{30}p^{30}(1-p)^0$$

$$= p^{30}$$

Then, since $P(p) = 1$:

$$P(E) = \int_0^1 p^{30}dp$$

$$= \frac{p^{31}}{31}\bigg|_0^1$$

$$= \frac{1}{31}$$

If we think about this for a minute, it makes sense. There were 31 different numbers we could have gotten for *success* (0 through 30 inclusive), and we got one of them. Since we *explicitly* chose a prior to make them all equally likely, it makes sense that the probability of seeing what we saw is 1 in 31:

$$P(p|E) = \frac{P(E|p)P(p)}{P(E)}$$

$$= \frac{p^{30} \times 1}{\frac{1}{31}}$$

$$= 31p^{30}$$

So $P(p|E) = 31p^{30}$ for values of p between 0 and 1. This is illustrated in Figure 9-19.

This is the *posterior distribution*. Like with the MLE, the value of p that maximizes this function is 1, but now we can see how sharply that likelihood falls as p moves away from 1. We can see visually that while $p \approx .95$ is still reasonable, $p = 0.5$ is probably not. Can we put quantitative bounds on this?

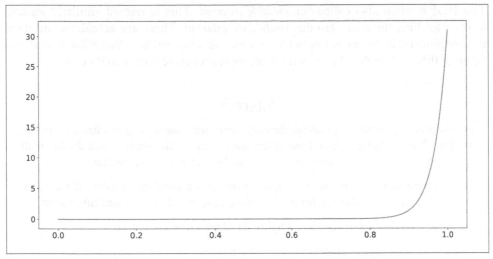

Figure 9-19. The posterior probability distribution for a service that saw no errors in 30 requests

The highest density interval

One thing we can do with this is calculate the *highest density interval* (HDI), the region of the state space that is the *most likely*. That is, as this is a graph of the probability density for *p*, we can highlight those values that *p* is most likely to be.

For example, the 95% HDI of the previous distribution is shown in Figure 9-20.

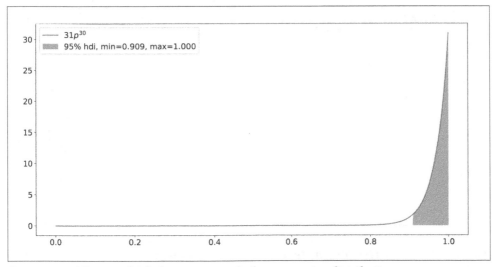

Figure 9-20. The 95% high density interval of our posterior distribution

The HDI is often also called the *credible interval*. This is named similarly to, and looks a lot like, the more famous *confidence interval*. There are actually some stark philosophical differences between the two, but we won't get into those; for now, if you think of this as "there's a 95% chance p comes from this region" you'll be okay.

Intervals

Philosophically, roughly speaking, the confidence interval says "p is a fixed value, and we don't know what it is, but if we collect data from its distribution and do this math on it, 95% of the time the interval we calculate by that math will contain it."

The credible interval, on the other hand, says "p is a random number. If we collect data and create a distribution for it, 95% of the time, it will come from this region."

People get into honest-to-goodness fights about which one is better.

HDIs can be a good way to quantify certain characteristics of a distribution. Specifically, the size of the interval denotes uncertainty in the inferred parameter.

Figure 9-20 is for 30 requests. If we had only 10, it would look like Figure 9-21. While the MLE and MAP estimates of these events are identical—$\hat{p} = 1$—the HDI reveals that our model is much more certain about p as we feed it more data. With only 10 requests there is a wider range of credible values for p. With 30 requests, that range is much smaller.

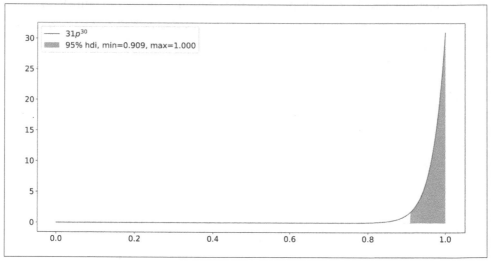

Figure 9-21. A 95% HDI for a posterior distribution with only 10 data points—the size of the interval (the number values along the x-axis that are within the interval) is much larger, reflecting the fact that we are less certain about the inferred value

Revisiting the Batch service, we can now calculate the posterior distributions for each of the likely numbers of requests, given one or two failed RPCs, as shown in Figure 9-22. We'll do this using a completely flat prior.

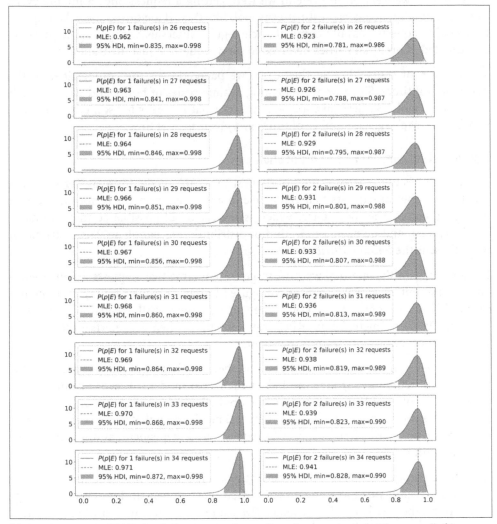

Figure 9-22. 95% HDIs for different numbers of total requests and either one (left) or two (right) failures: the HDIs get smaller as the total number of requests gets larger

This shows us that, even with a completely flat prior, the 95% HDI for a single failure still includes values of p as high as $p = .998$. But the HDI for two failures will only include our SLO if we have 33 or more samples; that's the 75th percentile of our sample count distribution.

SLI Example: Queueing Latency

When we introduced Batch, we said that it received a request *on average* about once a minute; then we went on to pretend we were getting a request once a minute every minute. But why should request patterns look like this? If anyone can send a request, how could requests possibly come at such regular intervals without some massive, coordinated effort by all parties involved to send requests at just the right time?

The answer, of course, is that they can't: we papered over the complexities of the query arrival times. Since we were looking at time scales of hours and days, this felt pretty reasonable. But let's take a closer look at what it means for something to happen "on average" a given number of times in a given span of time.

Modeling events with the Poisson distribution

When it comes to the arrival times of requests, we can't model those as Bernoulli trials. The number of requests that can arrive in any given moment is not limited to a binary outcome. The state space, which is the set of all possible configurations, is $S = \{0, 1, 2, ...\}$, and we need a new kind of distribution to handle it. The distribution we will use is the *Poisson distribution*.

For a service on the internet, we can't in general assume that requests are independent. For example, if an RPC client is configured to retry a request on failure (whether or not there's exponential backoff), then every failure will trigger a subsequent request. Or there might be an RPC argument that, when set, alerts other clients, which then causes activity from those clients.

Often, however, if we filter our data a bit and then step back and maybe squint a little, we can treat requests *as if* they are independent. No model will ever capture all the complexities of a system or offer perfect predictive power. But we only need the model to be *good enough*—while, of course, acknowledging that there is always a risk of model error. So, we often assume that requests are independent, and sometimes we get away with it.

If we have requests that arrive independently of one another, and we know the average timing even if we don't know exactly when they happen, and requests can't happen at once, then we have what's called a *Poisson process*. The number of requests that arrive in a given span of time follows a Poisson distribution.

The Poisson distribution for requests that arrive on average once a minute looks like Figure 9-23.

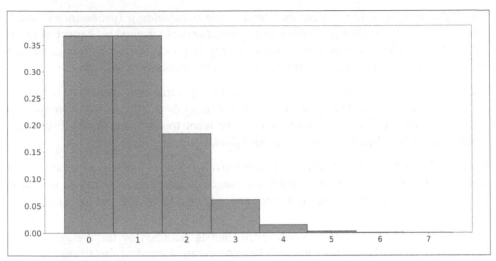

Figure 9-23. The Poisson distribution with $\mu = 1$

Let's break down how we got this graph. The PMF for a Poisson distribution is:

$$f(k; t, \mu) = \frac{\mu^k e^{-\mu t}}{k!}$$

where k is the number of events in an interval of time t, and the average number of events is μ. The specific probabilities are listed in Table 9-3.

Table 9-3. The probability of seeing x events in one minute, for a Poisson process with a mean arrival time of once per minute; note particularly that P(x = 0) = P(x = 1)

k	Probability
0	0.3678794412
1	0.3678794412
2	0.1839397206
3	0.0613132402
4	0.01532831005
5	0.00306566201
6	5.109436683E-4
7	7.299195261E-6
8	9.123994075E-6
9	1.01377712E-6
10	1.01377712E-7

The Poisson distribution is described by a single parameter, μ (pronounced "mu"), which is equal to the average number of requests (or other events) we expect to see in a minute (or other span of time). When we say requests arrive on average once a minute, we mean they arrive according to a Poisson distribution with $\mu = 1$.

In the PMF shown in Figure 9-23 we have a third parameter, t. When we're talking about a single unit of time (say, per minute) we can set $t = 1$ minute. But if we want to convert between different durations (say, if we want to compute the PMF on five-minute intervals), then t takes on different values.

Notice in Table 9-3 that a minute with zero arrivals is just as likely as a minute with a single arrival, but that there is a significant chance of seeing more than one arrival as well. This is why we stress that the arrivals are only *on average* one per minute.

 Sometimes the Poisson distribution is described by the average number of time intervals between events, instead of the average number of events per time interval. This is unfortunate and confusing and weird, but you get used to it. If you have a rate parameter μ in events per unit interval, and you want to express it in λ (lambda) unit intervals between events, then you can use the formula:

$$\mu = \frac{1}{\lambda}$$

The Poisson distribution is a good way to model any sort of count-based data that shares the characteristics of the requests we have been talking about. That is, if events have the following properties, the time-bucketed event counts will be Poisson-distributed:

- They occur zero, one, or more times per unit interval (the sample space is the nonnegative integers).
- They are independent, so that one event doesn't affect other events.
- They arrive at some average rate that we call μ.
- They arrive *randomly*.

The Poisson distribution can be used to model a large number of varied phenomena beyond RPC arrival times, including hardware failure, arrival times in a ticket queue, and SLO violations. Knowing this allows us to build systems that can anticipate these events, as well as to define SLOs around abnormal levels of events.

Variance, percentiles, and the cumulative distribution function

So, the number of requests Batch receives per hour is probably Poisson distributed. If you receive, on average, one request per hour, then often you will receive no requests within an hour, as we've seen, but sometimes you'll get two or three requests.

Batch queries are expensive, and you're trying to run lean, so you don't have a lot of room for sudden bursts of traffic. Thus, a question you might want to answer is: what's the highest number of requests we're likely to receive in an hour? This has to do not so much with the average value, which is μ, as it does with the tendency of the data to deviate from that value. The tendency of a random variable X to vary is called the variance, and it is defined as:

$$\text{Var}(X) = E\left[(X - \mu)^2\right]$$

 This formula is true generally, not just of the Poisson distribution. Here, μ denotes any distribution mean. For distributions where the mean doesn't exist, neither does the variance.

That is, the variance is the expected value of the square of the difference between the random variable and the mean. Unusually among distributions, the variance of the Poisson distribution is simply also μ. The larger the average number of events in a given time period grows, the greater the variation in that number also grows.

The variance is very closely related to another measure you may have heard of: the *standard deviation*, usually denoted σ (sigma). In fact, the standard deviation, which refers to the spread of a distribution from the mean, is simply the square root of the variance: $\sigma^2 = \text{Var}(x)$. So for the Poisson distribution, $\sigma^2 = \mu$ and $\sigma = \sqrt{\mu}$. This is what is meant when someone talks about *six sigmas*; they are referring to outliers that are six standard deviations away from the mean.

You might be most familiar with the idea of the standard deviation of a normal distribution, but it is a well-defined concept for any distribution that has a finite variance. It is simply the tendency of data to deviate from that distribution's expected value.

So, if you don't need to be too strict, you can pick a number of sigmas—three is nice—and rule out anything more than that. If you receive an average of $\mu = 100$ requests an hour, each hour you'll see between $\mu - 3\sqrt{\mu} = 70$ and $\mu + 3\sqrt{\mu} = 130$, and only extremely rarely will you see anything outside that range.

But this might still leave you with some questions. Why did we pick three? What do we mean by *extremely rarely*?

We can be more exact in our estimations by considering the *cumulative distribution function* (CDF), which is defined as follows: for any probability distribution function $f(x)$, which gives the probability that some random variable X is equal to the value x, the CDF $F(x)$ is the probability that some random variable X is equal to *or less than* the value x. Formally:

$$f(x) = P(X = x)$$

and:

$$F(x) = P(X \leq x)$$

Additionally, F is (in the discrete case) given by:

$$F(x) = \sum_{i = -\infty}^{x} f(x)$$

This is probably not intuitive or obviously useful the first time you see it, so it may be helpful to look at some graphs. If the PMF of the Poisson distribution for $\mu = 10$ looks like Figure 9-24, then the CDF of that distribution looks like Figure 9-25.

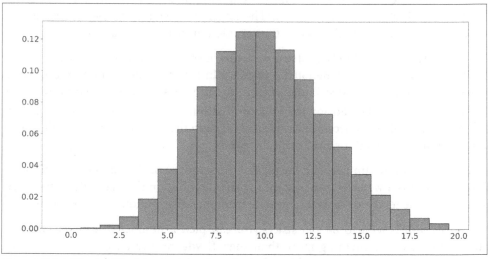

Figure 9-24. The PMF of the Poisson distribution with $\mu = 10$

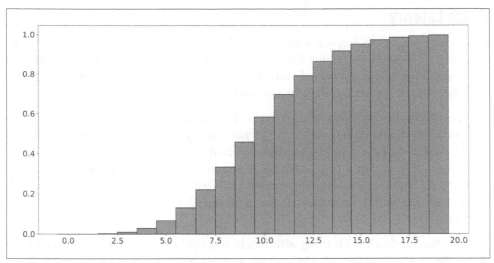

Figure 9-25. The CDF of the Poisson distribution with μ = 10

The height of each bar in the CDF for *x* is the sum of the heights for every bar in the PMF up to *x*. Notice that the CDF never decreases with *x*. This is universally true of every CDF and reflects the fact that as *x* increases, any random number we generate is increasingly likely to be smaller than it. Also, the smallest value the CDF attains is 0, and the greatest value is 1. This is true because all probability distributions must add up to 1, so the sum must as well.

The CDF is integral in defining the *quantile function*, which allows us to talk about percentiles. If you look at the CDF in Figure 9-25, you can see that the graph only starts showing significant values at 3, and essentially levels off by 17. If you follow the height of the bars over to the label on the y-axis (or calculate it yourself), you will see that $F(3) \approx .01$ and $F(17) \approx .99$. This is another way of saying that the 1st percentile of this distribution is 3, and the 99th percentile is 17.

The quantile function takes some value between 0 and 1 representing a probability, and tells us the value *x* that corresponds to the quantile at that probability. In fact, the quantile function is the inverse of the CDF.

Now we can say more accurately what we mean by "likely to receive." If the average number of requests per hour is 100, then the 95th percentile is 117.0. This means, in answer to the question of what the highest number of requests we're likely to receive in an hour is, that we would expect to receive 117 or more requests only in 5 out of every 100 hours.

Batch Latency

In addition to availability, you want to be able to establish an SLO around job completion rate. Both synchronous RPCs and batch jobs tend to have the same general structure: a request is submitted, and it's serviced by a worker if there is a worker available. If not, the request waits in a queue until a worker becomes available.

In the case of synchronous RPCs most of this happens on a scale too quick to be noticeable by humans until requests get *particularly* unlucky. The longest requests might stretch into the seconds, but the expected value of the request duration—the *average* amount of time a request takes—is usually too small for a human to notice or care about. This is one reason why latency SLOs tend only to bother themselves with some high percentile; it's only at these large durations that users become severely impacted.

It's tempting to do a similar thing with Batch: you could pick a large duration and call it the 99th percentile job completion rate. But for batch services, these "large durations" can be measured in hours. Instead, let's take a closer look at what contributes to execution time to see if we can identify some better SLIs.

Queueing systems

The study of how work wends its way through complex systems is called *queueing theory*, and it gets a bit involved, but we can look at some simplified examples.

The arrival rate of requests to Batch is about once a minute; let's call that μ_a. You've also been keeping tabs on the completion rate, which we'll call μ_c. You don't know what happens to the requests in between; you're still new, and you've been up to your neck in math and haven't had time to sit down and look at any of the code. You know that you need the arrival rate to be less than or equal to the completion rate, or else the system will fill up with work:

$$\mu_a \leq \mu_c$$

But you don't need that to be true *all the time*. It's fine if you accept six jobs in an hour and only complete four, as long as the long-run arrival rate is acceptable. But since you can't directly affect the arrival rate (and in fact you probably appreciate it when your service sees more use), this represents a lower bound on what you can provide. Only if μ_c drops below μ_a for long enough will you need to provision more capacity (we'll think more about what "long enough" means later in this section).

You can also measure the average amount of time a request spends in the system, w. Once the system is in a steady state, the total number of requests in the system, N, can be calculated via Little's law:

$$N = \mu_a w$$

This formula is correct regardless of the process by which requests arrive (whether it be Poisson or not) or how they are processed, as long as the system is in the steady state.

For now, let's think about the relationship between the arrival rate, the completion rate, and the amount of time before customers get their answers, which is what they really care about.

The exponential distribution

The relationship between the rate of a Poisson process, μ, and the duration between the events that comprise the process is described by the exponential distribution. It looks like Figure 9-26.

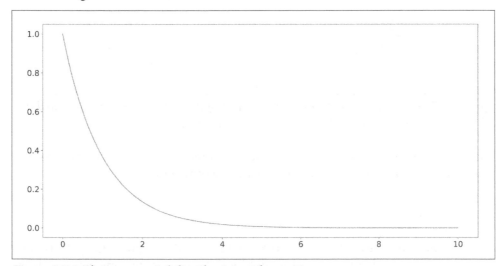

Figure 9-26. The exponential distribution with $\mu = 10$

The exponential distribution is our first example of a *continuous* probability distribution. Instead of a sample space consisting of a finite (or countably infinite) number of possibilities, now we have an (uncountably) infinite number of possibilities. When it describes a duration, it can produce a random result representing any positive length of time.

When the function representing the probability distribution is continuous, it is called a *probability density function* (PDF). Unlike in the probability mass function, $P(X = x)$ no longer represents the probability that a random value X is x. Instead, it denotes the probability density at x. Because the sample space is so large, we can't really talk anymore about what the probability is that a random number will *equal* an element of the sample space. Instead, we talk about the probability that a value will lie within a given range.

For example, in Figure 9-27, the shaded area represents the probability that a value will fall between 1 and 3.

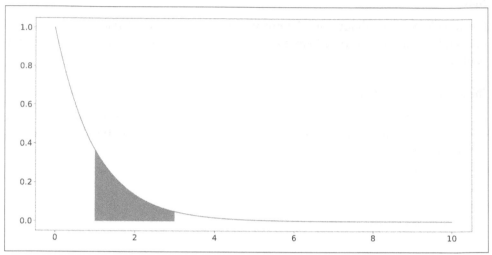

Figure 9-27. The exponential distribution: the area of the shaded region is the probability that a number drawn from this distribution will fall between 1 and 3

Like the Poisson distribution, the exponential distribution is described by the parameter μ, called the *rate*. The PDF for the exponential distribution is:

$$f(t; \mu) = \mu e^{-\mu t}$$

Here, t is time, but we could use x or represent some other exponentially distributed quantity. The semicolon indicates that while both t and μ are parameters, usually we pick a single μ when we're talking about all the possible ts.

The value for μ is the same for the exponential and Poisson distributions. A Poisson process with parameter μ will have interevent times described by an exponential distribution with the same value of μ.

We know the arrival rate into Batch is one request per minute, on average. So we'd expect the mean of the exponential PDF also to be about one minute, and it turns out that this is true.

An important thing to note is that while the *expected* value of the distribution is one minute, more than half the interarrival times will be less than one minute. We can see that by looking at the CDF, shown in Figure 9-28.

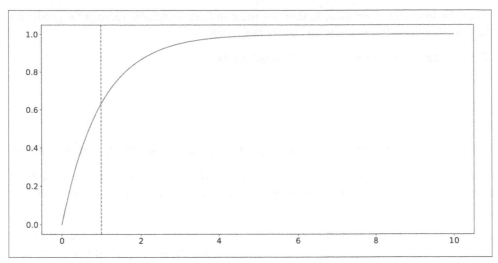

Figure 9-28. The CDF of the exponential distribution with $\mu = 1$

Here, the dashed vertical line occurs at $x = 1$. Note that the two do not cross at $y = .5$; they cross at $y \approx .63$.

Decreasing latency

After spending some time on the Batch team, you've become somewhat familiar with the inner workings of the service. Requests arrive at a load balancer and are placed in a queue. There is a worker service that watches the queue, pulls off tasks, and operates on them. Responses are written to a database, and clients can poll an RPC endpoint for the results.

This is what's known as an *M/M/1 queue*, or, somewhat more vividly, as a birth-death process. Requests arrive according to some Poisson process (here, $\mu = \mu_a = 1$) and are worked on according to some other Poisson process (say, $\mu = \mu_s$). Note that this is not μ_c; this is the distribution of completion times *once the request is being served*, and not the distribution of requests exiting the system, which depends heavily on μ_a. We'll call μ_a the mean arrival time, and μ_s the mean service time.

The first M in the name denotes that the arrival process is *Markovian*: its future states depend only on its current state, and not on any states prior to that. A Poisson process is a kind of Markov process. The second M denotes that the serving process is also Markovian. The 1 denotes the fact that there is a single server in this system.

So the first question we want to answer is, what is our expected latency? That is, we want to know the *average* latency (not the median or the 99th percentile). Of course, we could and should measure this, but we're not doing this simply to have an idea of what the latency is *right now*. Rather, *we want to have justifiable reasons for predicting how the latency will change as we change the system.*

The average latency of a request in this system is:

$$L = \frac{1}{\mu_s - \mu_a}$$

What does this look like? When $\mu_s \gg \mu_a$, the latency is essentially just $\frac{1}{\mu_s}$, and the requests are completed almost as soon as they arrive. If the mean service time for a request were one second, then most requests would exit the system almost as soon as they entered.

When $\mu_s \approx \mu_a$, then $\mu_s - \mu_a$ gets closer and closer to zero, and L becomes arbitrarily large. If the mean service time were 55 seconds, and the mean arrival time is 60 seconds, then $\mu_a = \frac{1}{60}$ arrivals per second, $\mu_s = \frac{1}{55}$ completions per second of service time, and the mean latency of a request is $\left(\frac{1}{55} - \frac{1}{60}\right)^{-1}$, or *11 minutes*.

Figure 9-29 shows a graph of mean latency as a function of $\frac{\mu_a}{\mu_s}$.

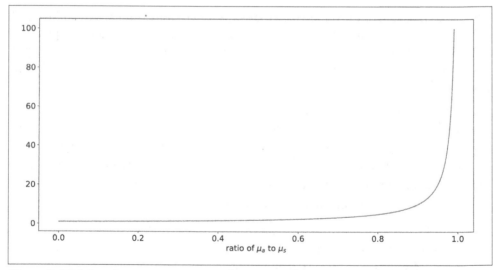

Figure 9-29. Mean latency as μ_a approaches μ_s—as the average arrival time comes closer to the average service time, the latency grows severely

The ratio between the arrival rate and the service rate is usually denoted ρ (rho). As Figure 9-29 shows, systems can be fairly insensitive to this quantity until they suddenly aren't. It makes sense, then, as latency or usage increases, to spend resources on reducing the processing time of each request.

So far we've been looking at the *mean* latency of the system. What does the median do, or the 90-something percentiles?

For an M/M/1 queue the full distribution function of response time depends on how the queue is implemented. A *last-in first-out* (LIFO) queue, in which the requests that have just been received are the ones that are served first, has an exponential distribution. Since the mean of the exponential is also its parameter, the distribution function is:

$$f(t) = Le^{-Lt}$$

$$= \frac{1}{\mu_s - \mu_a} e^{\frac{-t}{\mu_s - \mu_a}}$$

Here, again, as μ_a gets large (or μ_s gets small), the mean gets very large, but now we can see what happens to the tail of the function as ρ gets closer to 1. Let's look at a graph of the 95th percentile, shown in Figure 9-30.

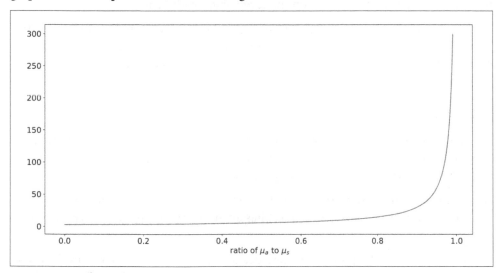

Figure 9-30. The 95th-percentile latency

This looks very similar to Figure 9-29. If we graph the two together, as in Figure 9-31, we can see that this function is strictly greater than the mean for all values of ρ.

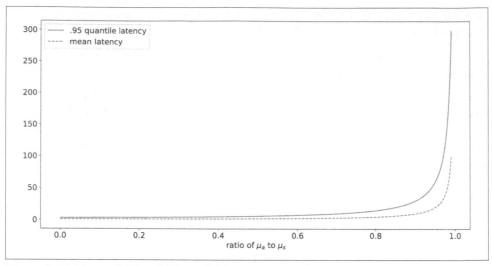

Figure 9-31. Figure 9-29 and Figure 9-30 superimposed

This shows one of the reasons that monitoring high percentiles is popular, even if they necessarily only affect a small portion of traffic: they are a good *leading indicator* that the system is moving away from its acceptable steady state.

But Batch probably won't get a ton of use out of the 99th, or even the 95th, percentile. The 95th percentile only has a meaningful value in the presence of 19 other data points, which would take (on average) 20 minutes to collect. You'd do better to measure μ_s or ρ.

Adding capacity

We've seen that reducing μ_s, the average time it takes to process a given request, can have a significant impact on service latency, especially as utilization increases. But what about just throwing more server processes at the problem?

A system with many workers is called an *M/M/c queue*; it's governed by the same arrival and service characteristics, but it has an arbitrary number of servers to handle requests.

The equations describing the characteristics of these queues are a lot more involved. Not only does the completion rate increase from μ_s to $c\mu_s$, but the probability that a new request will have to wait for service decreases.

With just two workers, the mean latency as a function of $\rho = \mu_a / c\mu_s$ becomes what you see in Figure 9-32.

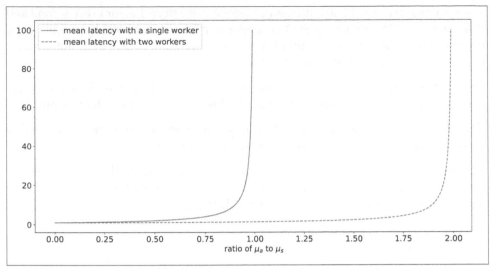

Figure 9-32. Mean latency as a function of utilization: with two workers we can (reasonably enough) absorb almost twice as much work before the latency increases wildly

Adding a second worker buys much more capacity! Of course, this is a somewhat idealized example. If both workers share resources (for example, if they both contend for network or disk access, or read from or write to the same database), then adding a second worker will *reduce* the service capacity μ_s for individual workers. But this kind of analysis can help you allocate resources when trying to determine the most beneficial places to spend them.

SLI Example: Durability

In this section we'll use the techniques described thus far in the chapter to define and analyze a durability SLI, and we'll look at how it changes as we change our replication model.

Availability and latency are probably the most common SLIs. They are convenient and (usually) easy to define and measure. *Durability* is not as easily understood, and possibly as a result is not as commonly measured. While availability for a storage service might be defined in terms of the ability of a client to receive data stored in the service at some moment, durability is the ability of the *service* to serve the data to the client at some point in the future.

Durability is tricky to measure. You can't simply watch traffic as it goes by and infer your service's durability from that. The events that comprise the durability SLI are not requests, or even successful data access events, but data *loss* events. And of course, in most systems *any* data loss event is considered unacceptable.

A service that receives 10,000 queries per second can return 1 error every second and still meet a 99.99% availability SLO. A service that loses 1 in 10,000 bytes will not be trusted again. This sets up a contradiction: we don't *want* to lose data, but we can't measure durability without seeing data loss.

To untangle this, first let's give a specific, mathematical definition of durability. We're going to start baking in assumptions as we do this, and we want to call those out.

There are many ways to define data durability, but we will use this one: the durability of the system is the expected value of the lifetime of a kilobyte of user data.

By defining durability in terms of the *expected value*, we get both an acknowledgement of its stochastic nature and an explicit formula (sort of) for calculating it. The definition of expected value for a continuous distribution is:

$$E[t] = \int t f(t) \mathrm{d}t$$

Where $f(t)$ is the probability density function for some yet unspecified distribution.

 There's another major benefit to using the expected value. $f(t)$ is going to be a complicated function to define; even if we assume ideal behavior and exponential distributions (large assumptions in themselves), finding $f(t)$ for even two disks is not the work of an afternoon. This is because combining these functions analytically gets intractable, and trying to simulate them with Monte Carlo methods, with the probabilities we're working with, is infeasible. However, expected values can *always* be added together to get the expected value of their sum, and if they are independent, they can be multiplied to get the expected value of their products. This lets us apply the techniques we'll use here. Unfortunately, we can lose a lot in the translation. Critically, the *variance* of our final distribution won't be available from this analysis, so we won't know how much deviation around the calculated mean we should expect. But what we *can* do is measure how our SLI changes as our system evolves. It will be very sensitive to the values we infer, and will change when those do.

Defining our SLI this way turns our problem into one of statistical inference. If we know $f(t)$ then we know $E[t]$, which by definition is our SLI. How can we measure $f(t)$? If we had millions of data points we could simply chuck them into a histogram, but of course we don't, so we'll make a second assumption: that data loss events such as hard drive failures follow a Poisson process.

Now, this isn't true. But it might be *close* to true. It's as good a place to start as any, until we get evidence to the contrary.

One of the reasons that the Poisson process is a good starting point is the sheer plethora of things that can cause data loss. Mechanical failure, software failure, *firmware failure*—the long-term survival of data is threatened by any one of these. But when there are multiple Poisson processes happening at once, their rate parameters can simply be added. If one hard drive class fails with rate μ_1, and a second class fails with rate μ_2, then hard drives will still fail in a Poisson process with rate $\mu = \mu_1 + \mu_2$.

This is particularly useful when modeling things like hard drives, which can be sensitive to manufacturing defects. It's possible to get a bad batch of drives that are more likely to fail than their neighbors. But because Poisson rates are additive, this doesn't invalidate the model.

Hard drives and other mechanical systems are also known to follow a so-called *bathtub curve*, where the failure rate for a unit starts out high but quickly falls (as those units prone to failure do fail and are removed), then rises again near the end of the unit's lifetime, as it starts to succumb to wear.

We tend to model this by using a *nonhomogeneous Poisson process*, in which the parameter μ is allowed to change over time. If you do any of the follow-up reading, you will almost certainly see this described as "in which μ becomes $\mu(t)$." This is shorthand for saying that μ, once a constant, is now a function of time and is allowed to vary. To avoid confusion, we will continue to just say μ, but understand that this quantity can now change over time.

We still have to measure μ somehow. Since it now varies with time, we can't accumulate data forever. Events we measured weeks or even days ago may no longer be valid. So, we need to measure enough relevant events in a recent window to have a good estimate of μ, all without suffering actual data loss. We almost certainly do have durability events that don't themselves result in data loss, but this depends heavily on the specific architecture of the system.

Let's look at Dewclaw, the thumbnail service at Catz. When last we left our heroes, Dewclaw had just transitioned to serving out of two data centers, DC1 and DC2. Internally, users upload a thumbnail, and it's replicated internally to three different machines.

Data replication is a subject that could and should fill a book all on its own, so for this example we'll treat an idealized version of it. We'll say that a new thumbnail lands on all three drives instantly, and that after a hard drive failure the thumbnail is replicated to a new drive after, on average, one hour.

These events—the hard drive failures—are what we need to measure to infer μ, and because the loss of a single drive doesn't cause data loss we can get measurements without impacting customers.

In fact, this nicely illustrates one of the paradoxes of engineering that SLOs highlight: if a service is *too* reliable, failures become too rare to anticipate. Here, the more often hard drives fail, the better estimate we can get of hard drive failure rate. But we can compensate for this by realizing that we don't need to measure μ itself; we only need an upper bound.

If we watch a population of a thousand hard drives for a month and see no failures, the maximum likelihood estimate for the failure rate is zero—but most people would intuitively push back on that. Using MAP or Bayesian inference, we could conclude that it is *at most* some value (depending on our prior), and let that be our estimate for μ.

With μ we can build $f(t)$. A single thumbnail lives on three hard drives, and whenever a thumbnail is in a degraded state (as in, is down to one or two hard drives), it is copied back to three drives after about an hour.

If images were only ever stored on one hard drive, $f(t)$ would simply be the PDF for the exponential distribution:

$$f(t) = \mu e^{-\mu t}$$

Remember that the Poisson process and the exponential distribution are buddies; the times between the events of a Poisson process with *rate* μ (in which a higher number means more events) are exponentially distributed with *rate* μ (in which a higher number means less time between events).

The mean of this distribution—and thus our SLI—is $\frac{1}{\mu}$. This is an estimate of the amount of time it takes to go from having a thumbnail on one hard drive to having a thumbnail on no hard drives.

If there are two hard drives, then in order to lose the thumbnail we have to lose either of those two drives, and then lose the second drive within an hour.

If our current estimate of drive failure is (say) 1,000,000 hours between failures, and our estimate of mean time to repair is 1 hour, then the probability we'll fail before a repair can be made is just about one in a million. Now we can view advancing from having lost one disk to losing two disks as a Bernoulli trial with probability p, and we know that the number of times we have to perform this trial before *success* is geometrically distributed with parameter p.

(If a million hours sounds high, consider that most hard drives don't actually fail. Remember, this is modeled as a Poisson process, and if the mean time to failure is a million hours, the *variance* on that is also a million hours. Most drives are fine, but this leaves plenty of room for drives to fail before anywhere near that amount of time has passed.)

The SLI for two disks as a function of the inferred value μ is:

$$E_2[t] = \frac{\mu + \lambda}{2\mu^2} + \frac{1}{\mu}$$

Here, lambda is the parameter for the process that governs recovery. We can use this to estimate the effect of any work we plan on the durability SLI. For example, increasing μ by 1% (thus increasing the mean time to drive failure by 1%) increases $E_2[t]$ by about 2%, while decreasing λ by 1% (thus decreasing the mean time to recovery by 1%) only increases $E_2[t]$ by 1% (when $\mu = 1/1,000,000$ and $\lambda = 1$).

If we finally take into account the third drive in our replication trio, the estimate of $E_3[t]$ becomes:

$$E_3[t] = \frac{(\mu + \lambda)(2\mu + \lambda)}{6\mu^3} + \frac{\mu + \lambda}{2\mu^2} + \frac{1}{\mu}$$

If we calculate these expressions given our candidate values for μ and λ, we find that with two drives our expected durability $E_2[t]$ is about 60,000 years. With three drives, it's about 1.9×10^{13} years. This is a significant improvement.

Of course, this can't and doesn't take into account all the other hugely complicated and important factors that are involved in safeguarding data. Numbers like 10^{13} are so fantastically big they approach meaninglessness.

You cannot and should not conclude from your analysis that you won't see any data loss until the universe ends. That is not what this is for. Rather, this analysis gives you a way of turning data gathered from your system into a single metric, an SLI, that can also be used as a baseline against which to engineer additional protections.

If you run a thumbnail service on disks with no replication, you will probably lose data due to hard drive failure. If you run a thumbnail service on disks with triple replication, you probably won't, but that doesn't mean your data is therefore safe. You will probably lose data for some other reason (our money is on a software bug) unless you take pains to anticipate and mitigate those as well. It's a lot of bases to cover, but that's the job.

Further Reading

If you're interested in learning more about the topics discussed in this chapter, here are a few recommendations for further exploration:

- *Data Analysis with Open Source Tools*, by Philipp Janert (O'Reilly)
- *Practical Statistics for Data Scientists*, by Peter Bruce and Andrew Bruce (O'Reilly)
- *Doing Bayesian Data Analysis*, by John Kruschke (Academic Press)
- *Artificial Intelligence, A Modern Approach*, by Stuart Russell and Peter Norvig (Pearson)—specifically, Part IV

Summary

This chapter gave a very brief, high-level overview of the ideas underlying probability and statistics and how they can be used to augment other approaches to defining and interpreting SLIs and SLOs. It is by no means comprehensive or complete.

The power of thinking in a probabilistic and statistical manner is that it allows verification of the gut feel that most team members will have developed around the behavior of the system. You can then try wielding the math and seeing what you can learn, even if you don't change anything. The ability to use these techniques to provide values that plug into your existing frameworks is very powerful, and gives you a place to start discussing your current situation with teammates *without* needing them to do a calculus refresher.

At the same time, while models are helpful, they cannot be completely correct. This is exactly why they are models. It is important that after understanding some of these techniques you also take some time to understand the risks around model error. This is naturally only the tip of the iceberg on this subject.

CHAPTER 10

Architecting for Reliability

Salim Virji

This chapter focuses on designing systems from the ground up with SLOs in mind. It explores the design and development of an example system through the lens of the system's architecture. Examining the system at a high level, we will look at the technical reasons behind various design choices made in order to meet potential SLOs.

From the perspective of system architects, we begin this design exercise with the problem statement, or *specification*. We gather requirements, including the SLOs for the expected interactions with the system's users. User journeys, which represent the same concept as SLIs (see Chapter 3), help us understand these interactions, as well as the implications for the user when the system does not meet its objectives. They help focus our attention on the path of a request from user to service, and back.

To illustrate the importance of thinking about user journeys, consider the difference between a single-serving website that plays a recording of a sad trombone (*https://sadtrombone.com/*) and a website for a multinational bank that provides access to funds and payment information in real time. A superficial distinction between these two lies in the implication that one is "serious," handling our money, whereas the other is entertainment. Although this is indeed true, the deeper distinction is that failures in the money-handling system may have immediate, grave, and irreversible effects on its users, while this particular entertainment site will not. This is why we talk about user journeys, and about the ramifications of system errors on users: we make decisions about system architecture based on the intent of the system with respect to its users. A system designed without input from users will result in broken expectations and more engineering effort down the road.

Whereas in previous chapters we've mostly been considering developing SLIs and SLOs for existing systems and services, this chapter takes an SLO-first approach and discusses how architectural decisions we make can reflect our SLO targets. Choices in hardware and software development patterns influence the style and shape of a system, and anticipating failure modes informs the overall system architecture and design. Identifying the types of requests that the system will respond to also guides architectural choices. This chapter explores reasonable, real-world strategies that architects can use to cope with the fact that nothing is reliable all the time—or, as Gordon Bell said, quoted by Jon Bentley in his book *Programming Pearls* (Addison-Wesley Professional), "The cheapest, fastest, and most reliable components are those that aren't there." The concepts presented here can guide system architects from various backgrounds, including technical designers and product designers.

As we iterate through increasingly sophisticated designs in order to build a system that is resilient against many failure modes, we must be sure to satisfy the intent of the user journey. System architects who understand the user's perspective will be able to incorporate principles of Site Reliability Engineering—anticipating failure, planning capacity, operating reliably—with a principled, metrics-driven approach to building a system that satisfies its users. This approach is consistent with the concepts of Non-Abstract Large System Design (*https://landing.google.com/sre/workbook/chapters/non-abstract-design*) (NALSD), as described in *The Site Reliability Workbook*. Driven by an examination of system requirements and an iterative design process, NALSD incorporates capacity planning, component isolation, and graceful system degradation to produce highly available production systems.

Systems engineering has a background in manufacturing processes. In his talk "Engineering and the Design and Operation of Manufacturing Systems" (*http://mim2016.utt.fr/gershwin-mim16-keynote.pdf*), Stanley B. Gershwin points out that designers of manufacturing systems (and by extension, software systems aiming to meet targets) can learn lessons from aerospace engineering:

> To design and operate manufacturing systems that deliver the best possible performance, we must use scientific tools for understanding variability, uncertainty, and randomness.

In our case, we are designing software systems to deliver performance according to an SLO, and we can accomplish this through building reliable systems that deliver mostly predictable results.

The analogy between factories—large, physical manufacturing plants—and online software services suggests that we can apply scientific tools in the same way Gershwin suggests to address the core manufacturing issues of "short lead times and impatient customers," in order to reduce variability, account for uncertainty, and adjust for randomness. For software systems, the SLO sets bounds on these factors, so that software engineers can describe the variability of a system as well as express its uncertainty. Just as manufacturing systems need to account for how physical material moves through the factory, a software system needs to account for the end-to-end latency of a request.

The SLO describes the overall movement of things through the system. The initial client request begins the SLO timer for a software system; this is the "short lead time" in a manufacturing system. The timer ticks on as the service processes the request, perhaps sending subrequests to other components within the system; the assembly lines in the factory produce goods, with several components being built in parallel for more complex products. Finally, as the service sends the response to the client, the timer completes. The analogy is not perfect: software systems can implement retry behavior that manufacturing systems often cannot, for example. Yet the comparison does offer some guidance on how system architects need to consider the system users in their design, and the interface for doing so is the SLO.

Over my time designing and evaluating systems of software, I have found that the metaphor of physical manufacturing extends beyond the creational patterns introduced by Erich Gamma et al. in *Design Patterns* (Addison-Wesley Professional), which describe software as being composed of many small, tightly scoped components. As software systems have evolved, the image of assembly lines has remained constant: receiving a request for some "product" and then assembling raw materials to deliver to the consumer. Again, the comparison is not exact: as we will see, a software system can respond to new requirements quickly, and engineers can develop massive systems that receive new software versions automatically—see, for example, the "Push on Green" model (*https://www.usenix.org/system/files/login/articles/login_1410_05_klein.pdf*). A factory cannot as readily retool. Even if the underlying infrastructure of the internet, data centers, and network cables is similarly in the physical realm, the software components can be easily extended and deployed.

Example System: Image-Serving Service

This chapter walks through the design of an example system, to demonstrate what it means to design with SLOs in mind. Our specification calls for us to build an image-serving service, to be launched to the world as *imaginit.app*. Based on the design, we figure we'll want to serve batches of thumbnails—10 or 25 to a page—as well as allow viewers to click on a thumbnail and see a detailed view, along with image metadata. The site does not offer any social features, other than URL sharing: this is purely about serving images at high volume. The volume suggests we will need a high-performance, highly available data store. The service does not yet offer an externally facing API, although the product managers (PMs) expect to offer that in a subsequent version.

The specification includes a few user-facing web pages, for displaying the thumbnails and the detail view. Users will discover the images by searching for a term or hashtag, resulting in a page of thumbnail images corresponding to a geotag ("4.2634° S, 15.2429° E"), a search term ("hummingbirds"), or a hashtag ("#photooftheday"). A user can click a thumbnail to see a full-size version of the image as well as the metadata associated with it, including geotags, descriptive terms, and hashtags.

Through discussions with potential users, the PMs examined the effects of system unreliability: they found that users who were unsatisfied with the service's reliability would turn away from imaginit.app in favor of other image-sharing platforms, which (once imaginit.app begins to sell API access) would lead to revenue loss. Recall that engineers are not the sole architects of a software system: PMs make a valuable contribution to the design, identifying SLOs and driving design decisions based on user research. The user interviews reveal the system behaviors that users will value: you are asking questions whose answers tell you *what the user wants the system to do*, such as "Given the choice between a free web-based image-serving system that is only available most of the time or an API-based image-serving system that provides strong availability in exchange for per-API-request fees, which are you more likely to use?" and "To what extent does your application rely on the availability of your image-serving platform?"

By considering SLIs in the design phase, the system architects receive guidance about the system they are building. These SLIs need to reflect users' expectations of the system and its APIs, and might include measurements like the number of requests that the API successfully fulfills within a latency window, such as 95% of requests within 250 ms. A future iteration might break out different API method types, so that thumbnail requests have a different measurement from full-size image requests, and both have measurements distinct from image upload requests. As the system itself evolves, thumbnails, full-size images, and metadata might each have their own API methods, their own SLIs, and their own SLOs.

An initial boxes-and-arrows diagram for this system looks like Figure 10-1.

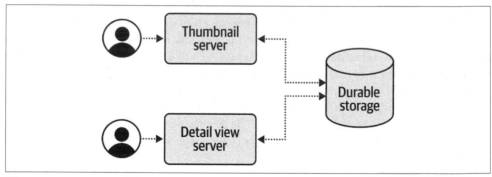

Figure 10-1. An initial boxes-and-arrows diagram for the image server

In contrast, consider a *nonexample*, the splendid site SadTrombone.com, which plays a distinctive four-note riff suggesting disappointment that participants in a meeting (for example) can use to share their feelings with the rest of the group. Should this site become unavailable, users may be briefly disappointed, but they'll probably either wait a moment and reload or find some other site offering the same or a similar sound clip. In either case, no significant repercussions result from the unavailability. The site does not offer any API; it is not (yet) STaaS (Sad Trombone as a Service). In contrast, the imaginit.app service will have a meaningful impact when it is not available. An initial SLI for the trombone site will be familiar: combining metrics on the number of requests made and the number of requests fulfilled yields a success metric. That's it: we don't need to measure the latency because we only care that the user is able to hear the clip, and the difference between waiting 250 ms and 500 ms for a response from the service is unlikely to matter to the user (at least, not to the extent that it's worth investing additional engineering effort to bring the system to that level of availability).

But for now, let's return to our image-serving service and discuss some of the architectural considerations at play.

Architectural Considerations: Hardware

Even as systems engineers tend toward microservices for NALSD, and the abstraction of software from hardware that this entails, it remains necessary to consider the hardware and its reliability when making architectural decisions. Lest we become embroiled in the discussion of size implied by the prefix *micro*, we can focus instead on a *service-oriented* architecture, in which system components share an RPC interface and can scale horizontally by adding instances of any particular task, as well as vertically by adjusting the resources assigned to a task or set of tasks.

Our user research has shown that users expect the initial results page of thumbnail images to appear quickly. The human mind begins to perceive latency at around 250 ms, so we'll want to deliver our image thumbnails to the user at least that quickly. Now we can dig into this specific metric and see how hardware choices affect it. Table 10-1 compares read latency and input/output operations per second (IOPS) for different storage options. It also provides input on the relevant cost of each option (total cost of ownership, including acquisition, development, operations, and depreciation). As this table shows, a significant portion of the response time for a request— up to 50 ms—will be taken up by retrieving data from a hard disk. The time it takes to retrieve 10 100 KB thumbnails will also be highly variable, as the disk seek and read times depend on disk hardware, on-disk layout, filesystem optimization, and caching. SSDs (flash drives) have more predictable and lower access times and can process many more transactions per second, but they're more expensive. Memory is a different story entirely—the lookup and retrieval times are much, much shorter—yet the cost involved in laying out and maintaining an entirely in-memory storage system for data like this would be considerable.

Table 10-1. Request processing hardware trade-offs

Choice	Latency for 1 MB read	IOPS	Impact on SLI	Cost
Hard disk	10 ms seek + 5–40 ms read	1	Baseline	$
Solid state disk (SSD)	1 ms	10,000	Reduces 10x: storage now more predictably within 5 ms	$$
RAM	.01 ms	100,000	Reduces 100x	$$$$

You can develop a similar table for an SLI in your system, and use it to make design choices. In this case a system architect could reasonably choose any of these options, knowing the baseline established by the hard disk choice. However, as the number of users and the number of images stored both grow, the variability in data retrieval times will become more evident. The hard disk solution shows a limitation, and suggests that the system will fall out of SLO once the service grows beyond a certain size.

Of course, latency is not the only concern. The example service we are building to serve images will require a considerable amount of storage. Given our service-oriented architecture, we are likely to use a cloud-based storage system—but what if we decide to have an on-premises storage solution, and use a room-sized array of hard drives managed by proprietary, vendor-provided software? This decision could be driven in part by legal or regulatory concerns. That would give us a very specific *failure domain*, and one that has a significant impact on our architecture and SLO.

On-premises storage is a single point of failure: it exists in a specific physical location and will at minimum require redundant network connections, both to the wide area network (WAN) and to interfaces for exchanging information with internal services such as the thumbnail server. It will also require redundant power supply units, ideally with connections to separate power distribution circuits and mains power supplies. We could further enumerate the physical parts needed, but this brief list drives home the point that many variables affect even this single critical component.

These variables all lead to an architectural element that constrains the system's SLO: without SLO-driven architecture, a software system will not be more reliable than, nor can it offer a stricter SLO than, the hardware it runs on.

A lack of redundancy or of resource isolation can bring down this single, critical component and thus all the upstream services that depend on it—the thumbnail server, the image server, and the repository for uploaded image data. You may get lucky and choose a managed SaaS that so thoroughly addresses the core reliability issue that you never need to change your architecture. However, as the scope of a system increases and more components enter it, you cannot rely on luck. A common SRE refrain is "Hope is not a strategy." End consumers of a system will see only its overall reliability, yet the architects will need to understand not just the overall availability number but also the reliability of key components within the system.

A different architectural choice would be to build this system with big iron—large, very reliable pieces of hardware such as dedicated database machines for storing images and metadata, and on-premises hardware for running the user-facing servers themselves. The system would benefit from the reliability of this hardware, with redundancy throughout the chassis. Multiple networking cards, power modules, and disks provide the level of redundancy that forms the foundation of a reliable system. However, this choice might not help with our overall reliability goals. Let's take a closer look at what happens when this system fails. As we have invested in very reliable hardware, the system is beholden to the hardware in order to function: we do not have multiple physical devices for the databases, nor is the database portable from one machine to another. This means that the mean time to repair (MTTR) depends on our ability to procure and install a new piece of hardware, as well as the time to configure, deploy, and verify the software and data. These variables can add up to a high MTTR, especially when we could have chosen to use services or another approach in which components are fungible across devices.

We can list the major factors involved in the MTTR for each approach, and then further break these factors down. For hardware, think of the time to provision a new physical server as the *hardware time*; in addition, the scenario with dedicated hardware will include software time for setting up the server and the services we need to run. For a hosted services–oriented solution, the number of variables is smaller.

Let's explore the variables involved in running dedicated hardware and in running services. For systems running on dedicated "bare metal" hardware, the MTTR equals the sum of hardware time and software time. Hardware time is itself the sum of several linear steps, *acquisition time + install time + setup time + verification*, and software time is the sum of *configuration time + deployment time + verification*. For systems running as services on cloud platforms, the MTTR equals the *rescheduling time* that the system takes to allocate and spin up a new instance.

The hardware time might be on the order of hours (or even days), so the MTTR for this scenario is much longer. Consider the difference in elapsed time between picking up a new database server, bringing it to the data center, installing it in the rack, and powering it up versus allowing the service's scheduler to reassign the task to an available Kubelet or equivalent. Suppose that it takes an hour to pick up a new server from the supplier and drive it out to the data center; getting it into the rack and powering on the server takes another hour, and installing and setting up the software takes another hour.

Now consider that the service has a three-nines availability SLO (99.9%), or fewer than three hours each quarter of user-facing downtime. If we use those three hours, or possibly more, to install a replacement piece of hardware, the system's error budget (see Chapter 5) is exhausted. We have no further room for error or unavailability of any kind for the rest of the quarter!

In contrast, the hosted solution using services needs only the rescheduling time, which is itself part of the SLO offered by the cloud provider's cluster management system. See, for example, the "Availability" section in the paper by A. Verma et al., "Large-Scale Cluster Management at Google with Borg" (*https://research.google/pubs/pub43438*) or the SLOs within the SLA offered by Amazon Web Services (*https://aws.amazon.com/compute/sla*).

This scenario is one of our first tangible examples of how an SLO can influence architectural decisions. During the process of designing the system, we may not have a specific SLO in mind. We may know that we expect the system to be globally available, and that users will interact with it throughout the day; we definitely know that we can make decisions about hardware that place upper bounds on how reliable the system can be, and thus how good our SLO is. When the failure of a single piece of hardware renders the SLO moot, we must either revise the SLO downward—changing the promise we made to users, either implicitly or explicitly—or modify the architecture.

Architectural Considerations: Monolith or Microservices

We already know that the system we are building will be *business-critical*, and it has an SLO that reflects this criticality to its users. With this foundation in mind, we can examine the question of whether to build a monolith—a system in which many or all of the services are coresident in a single binary—or microservices, in which services, or even subsets of services, exist as separate binaries. A single binary presents challenges for scaling: although the system architect may no longer be involved as the system scales, the system operators will need to take on the challenge. The *micro* part of *microservices* suggests small services, which can sometimes lead to different problems: a binary simply can't do what it needs to do! For this discussion we'll focus on a *service-oriented architecture*, where the services might be large or small, yet are all well-scoped and distinct. You'll note that the architect's choices have consequences long after the system has been deployed. The decision to go with a service-based system presents a pattern for rapid, flexible application development that suits building a system to an SLO; it also allows for easy subsequent iteration of the services when they need to change in order to continue to meet an SLO.

An open-ended system—one that allows for extension and change—is superior to a closed-ended system. Even though a closed-ended system will exactly match the specification, it inhibits behavioral changes in the system whose necessity may become apparent after the initial launch. Susan Fowler's book *Production-Ready Microservices* (O'Reilly) examines this topic in greater depth, and has a balanced discussion of the benefits of a service-oriented architecture. For the purposes of scalability, resource management, and ease of deployment we will use a microservices-based system in this chapter.

 User journeys can lead to preliminary SLOs. The development of a user journey provides a narrative that may help stakeholders understand the system's expected behavior. The user journey often correlates with KPIs or SLIs identified earlier in the product's development or ideation; other SLIs will become apparent during design discussions. Many organizations use a product manager to guide the product's entire development, with a focus on its marketability.

Architectural Considerations: Anticipating Failure Modes

When designing systems it's important to anticipate *failure modes*—that is, the problems that a system may realistically encounter and that it can respond to in order to maintain its SLOs. This type of planning can allow systems to continue to meet their SLOs in the face of adversity, and a thoughtfully architected system to degrade gracefully in order to maintain some parts of its SLOs even when real catastrophe looms.

Given congestion on the internal network between application servers and the storage component, a conscious architectural decision will, for example, allow our image-serving system to degrade such that thumbnail pages continue to serve within 250 ms, even though loading the detail view might take longer. This could be accomplished via something like a bandwidth manager that an operator can control remotely, prioritizing certain classes of inbound requests (e.g., for thumbnails) over others (for full-size images). To further balance bandwidth availability and system performance, the detail view could provide a lower-resolution image that is lazily replaced by a high-resolution image if the user remains on the page and available serving bandwidth permits. (This is an architectural choice similar to the control in YouTube that automatically provides the best available image for the user's device and available bandwidth, shown in Figure 10-2.) The architectural decision to allow this differentiated performance provides a release valve, so that the user's initial requests receive prompt responses.

Another architectural decision that allows for graceful degradation is the use of load balancing. Should a specific backend fail, such as one or more of the thumbnail servers, a load balancer can in real time reroute a user's request, sending it to another, healthy server. This rerouting is done internally and does not require a trip back to the client; it happens without the user ever knowing that the request initially failed.

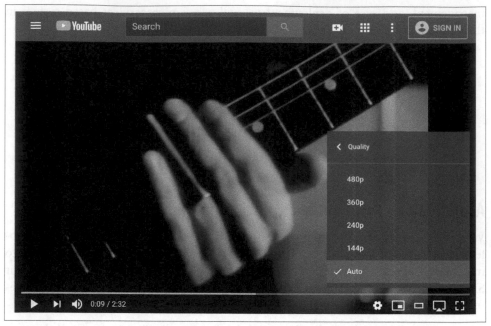

Figure 10-2. The "Auto" default selection for client bandwidth management in the You-Tube video player

Architectural Considerations: Three Types of Requests

Not all requests are equal, and system architects need to account for the different types of requests and their possible different paths as part of the system design. A contemporary service-based system such as the one being discussed in this chapter may include synchronous, asynchronous, and batch processes. Furthermore, some users of the system will require different treatment: these high-priority clients may be paying for access to the service, perhaps through an API, whereas other users may be casual, and you may want to service their requests after the paying clients' requests.

Synchronous requests

Synchronous requests usually represent the kind of interaction we expect with a website, app, or command-line program: the user issues a specific request, and the system responds. In the image-serving application, the detail view represents a synchronous request, as the user asks for and receives a full-size version of a specific image. In the usual and best case, the request comes from a properly configured client such as a standards-compliant web browser, uses correct formatting, and has no malicious intent. A bad request, however, might come from an incompletely implemented client and omit certain headers, or it might form part of an adversarial attack and include malicious characters in an attempt to exploit the server.

The system architecture should include a low-cost filter to identify and quickly dispose of these requests, without incurring the full cost of processing bad requests through the backend. Full processing of a bad request ties up valuable system resources such as memory and network bandwidth, as well as exposing the system to risk; a strong architecture provides a component in the serving path that examines header information and payload correctness, perhaps in a sandbox, before passing a request to the load balancer or application server. As an architectural decision, including this filtering step allows for efficient resource use and correctly prioritizes legitimate user traffic, preserving the SLO. In addition, requests that are dropped by the system before passing through the application server do not typically form part of the metrics used for composing the SLIs that inform the SLO.

Asynchronous requests

Asynchronous requests represent interactions that take place after some delay on the system side, while the user continues interacting with other parts of the system—or perhaps doing nothing at all. Candidates for asynchronous services include requests that are not in the response path, or requests for which the SLO does not include time as a dimension. For example, the SLO for the image server might specify that uploads succeed 99.9% of the time, without specifying a time boundary. Even if this SLO stipulated that the uploads succeed within 30 minutes 99.9% of the time, the upload request still makes a good asynchronous operation because it doesn't require immediate processing. A requirement to process uploads within 30 minutes will lead to different architectural decisions than a need for synchronous upload processing. So, in the image-serving application, the Upload view (or action) represents an asynchronous request, as the user submits a photo to the system and some amount of processing—metadata extraction, image analysis, etc.—takes place "in the background."

Similarly, a system architect could choose to implement the Thumbnail view as an asynchronous operation: the static assets of the page could load synchronously and provide a container for the application to deliver the thumbnails into as they become available.

Batch requests

Requests that both accumulate and are serviced asynchronously by the system are called *batch processes*. Despite their lower-priority status—the system knows that it can service these requests after synchronous requests, which themselves may have different tiers of service and isolation classes—these batch requests also need an SLO and accompanying measurement. Batch processing of requests typically happens because their results are not time-sensitive or in the critical path, yet SLIs still play an important role: they provide measurements for KPIs such as the duration of each batch process, meaning how long the process takes to execute, and the number of requests processed in each batch. Other metrics may be relevant for specific systems.

In the image-serving application, a pipeline that populates the index with image metadata might use a batch-processing approach: as the number of requests reaches a threshold, metadata is processed and added to the index.

Systems and Building Blocks

System architects should aim to build systems that use easily quantified representations of their resources. The trade-off for overall understanding is well worth a loss of accuracy: using 1 MB chunks for storing image data and estimating 10 such chunks for each image allows for easier storage system analysis than estimating the savings from image deduplication ("Which images are duplicates? Let's canonicalize these.") or from compression.

 Often, lower-level systems—the ones that your system relies on—work with more precision: at their scale, they gain much more through optimization for compressed data storage or from data canonicalization. Your system may eventually grow to the point where it, too, will benefit from properly accounting for compression. But not in the first version!

The first iteration of the system addresses one of our user journeys by building a landing page, which by default provides 10 random thumbnail images. On this page, the user can issue a query, such as a #hashtag or a search term, to refine and change the thumbnail view—perhaps to something such as #bumblebee or #lake. This page pulls data from storage and sends it to the client.

The specification calls out the user journey as arriving at a page of thumbnails selected for their relevance to a term or hashtag. But partway through the review of the design doc, we discover that we have omitted a user journey entirely: the *search page*. This omission is not catastrophic: the PM can identify it, sketch it out, and, together with the system's technical architects, drive the design. Finding new user journeys after an initial design is not uncommon, and indeed is part of an iterative design process!

While some might feel that this goes without saying, it helps to develop workflows to include in the design doc. You can see in Figure 10-3 that the user journeys for Upload, Search, and Detail view take distinct paths through the system, and therefore will have distinct SLOs.

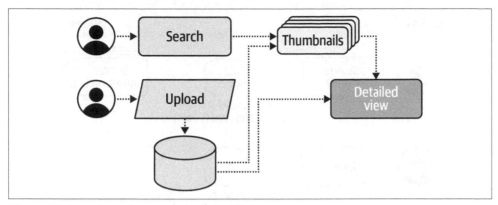

Figure 10-3. A view of user journeys for the image server

This workflow view elides some of the software components that make up the system. The search service, for example, does not appear explicitly; the diagram shows the search page, but not the components that index search data or respond to search requests.

The exercise of assembling the workflow also provides an opportunity to refine the system's architecture without spending error budget or affecting the SLO. For example, during an upload, the system will likely check the user's storage quota. As the system will have this information during the synchronous part of the upload, the upload page itself could provide quota information to the user: "Alice, you have used 79% of your 1 TB photo storage quota at imaginit.app." The system is less likely to have other information ready at hand, such as Alice's most frequently viewed images or most frequently occurring tags; that would be more expensive to display at this point so will likely be avoided unless we make a conscious design decision that we want to do so.

Another practical approach to visualizing the system architecture from an SLO perspective involves timelines. In Figure 10-4, we see the timing of a request passing through the system. By developing such views during the design phase, system architects are able to visually understand where the latency costs appear in the system; this view also aids engineers in understanding where in the system a request path offers wiggle room.

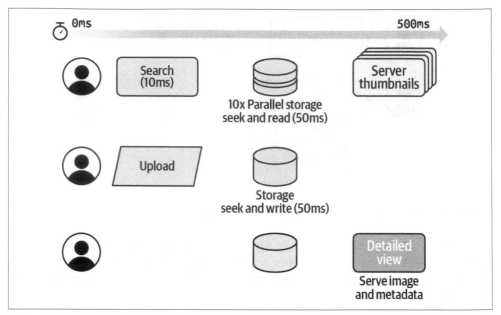

Figure 10-4. A timeline view of user requests in the image server

The timeline view provides a sense of how much time the various components in our system are taking, and also allows us to examine dependencies: for the image-serving system, we do not intend to build our own durable storage service, yet we depend on one for almost all of the system's operations.

Once the system's developers have deployed an initial version, they can examine aggregate tracing information (*https://static.googleusercontent.com/media/ research.google.com/en/archive/papers/dapper-2010-1.pdf*) to gain further insight into the timing of different operations in the system, and then refine the SLOs. Recall that system design is an iterative process, and that any architecture that leads to a closed-ended system precluding further iteration will wither and not yield to change.

Quantitative Analysis of Systems

As we saw with our image server, we may have dependencies that are in the critical path for our user journeys: we want to serve images, but we depend on a black-box storage system to serve these. This dependency directly affects the image-serving system's availability: a system cannot offer an SLO greater than any of its dependencies' SLOs (*https://queue.acm.org/detail.cfm?id=3096459*). The consideration of hardware earlier provides an illustration of this limitation.

Overall service availability can be expressed (*https://link.springer.com/content/pdf/ 10.1007/978-3-642-16132-2_12.pdf*) as a composition of the availability of its components, with several important variables such as price and quality of service (QoS) taken as additional factors. Even with a decade of cloud-based computing under our collective belt, we as architects of large-scale software systems sometimes do not see the math of software failures and worry instead about the more tangible, physical failures: a backhoe cutting through fiber is a more vivid nightmare than a incorrectly deployed canary rollout.[1] A strong, SLO-driven system design will account for both the expected hardware failures and the variety of possible software failures, allowing for risk when software provides cover for hardware (and vice versa).

Remember that we can also express the SLO of a system in terms of the human interactions necessary to identify and mitigate any outage:

$$1 - SLO \frac{MTTD+MTTM}{MTBF} \times IMPACT$$

Here is what those terms mean:

IMPACT
% of affected requests (or users)

MTTD
Mean time to detect

MTTM
Mean time to mitigate

MTBF
Mean time between failures

SLO
Service level objective, expressed as time per time period; for example, 99.99% availability at the 95th percentile would yield an error budget of 13.25 minutes per quarter

Instrumentation! The System Also Needs Instrumentation!

The times noted in the preceding section are each available as a mean of that metric over a time window, because the system has instrumentation that makes this possible (see Chapters 7 and 9). Instrumentation itself forms an essential part of system design, because without meaningful instrumentation and accompanying systems to collect, evaluate, and report on the data, a system is entirely opaque. Architects of software systems need to anticipate failure at every level, and instrumentation is the

---

1 Your mileage may vary in this scenario, and far be it from me to assume my SRE demons are anyone else's.

tool that allows architects and operators alike to identify abnormal events and to facilitate rapid analysis and response.

The instrumentation also offers the opportunity to evaluate the SLIs after launch, so that architects and product managers can understand the system's performance with respect to the user journeys. This permits iteration and optimizations to meet the SLOs. A sophisticated architecture includes instrumentation in the software components themselves, and a separate monitoring system to collect and analyze the data. In one system I worked on, we developed the primary (and most critically important!) piece of software to also have responsibility for collecting and reporting on the system's performance: this meant that when this software was running up against a resource limit or other performance obstacle, we could not see data in real time!

Architectural Considerations: Hardware, Revisited

Earlier, we looked at the limitations that hardware choices impose on a system's SLOs. Even with judicious choices made to manage risk (*https://landing.google.com/sre/sre-book/chapters/embracing-risk/*) with respect to opportunity, the system faces limitations in this fundamental layer of its architecture. As system designers, we can overcome such limitations through the use of software.

For example, to reduce the variability of the system, thus further increasing the certainty that it will deliver responses to the user within its SLO time frame, some software engineers will introduce caches. A *cache* is a component that stores some data locally in order to speed up subsequent accesses—usually reads—to that data. That is, a software cache can be used to reduce the latency of a user request through the system.

At this point, the architect of the system faces a choice: a capacity cache, or a latency cache? These will each help the system serve responses to user requests: the capacity cache reduces the amount of user traffic that passes through the entire system by serving precomputed results, while the latency cache improves overall performance by serving hot data from memory rather than from magnetic disks. However, their place in the critical path underscores a key difference between these two cache choices. When a capacity cache fails, the overall system performance will suffer, placing the SLO in jeopardy. When a latency cache fails, the effect is the same as a cache miss, which the system architect has already figured into the timing for the user journeys.

SLOs as a Result of System SLIs

The SLOs for a system follow from the SLIs we have identified, although not necessarily directly: *in order to have effective SLOs, we need to reflect the user experience, not only system performance.* Looking at the system performance numbers shows us unadorned metrics, without context. The *number of bytes transferred* or count of *requests per second* do not tell a story in the same way that *end-to-end image-retrieval latency* at the 95th percentile does. We don't just need SLI data; we want to have it in the context of our SLOs.

We can also approach the system design from the perspective of the minimum: what is the *minimum* availability and latency this system can provide to its users? To answer this effectively, we need to understand the system *and* its users, and recognize that the system will change through iteration as our understanding itself evolves. The users can be defined through some market research and user experience (UX) studies, where engineering and product partner with each other (the details of how this is done may vary by organization). The outcome should be a couple of clear user journeys, including mock-ups for the flow of information between the system and the user.

Actually developing SLO targets with the information you have available to you is covered in great depth in many other chapters in this book, but hopefully you now feel better equipped to consider them as you architect a new or growing service.

The Importance of Identifying and Understanding Dependencies

Once your product and engineering perspectives agree, you can develop SLOs, and we can turn back to "the system." Thus far we have designed a system that solves our problem as designed, without building any nonessential software.

As Figure 10-5 shows, we have some black boxes. These black boxes may be third-party or cloud-based systems; they are pieces of the system that are critical for us, yet outside the scope of our own instrumentation or SLIs. How can we meaningfully incorporate these into our understanding of the overall system's reliability? Figure 10-5 illustrates how understanding the boundaries of a system helps us design within limits. Referring back to the composition of availability, system architects will note that these black boxes provide inputs into the overall availability of the system we are building. Should we wish to improve our system beyond what the composed availability suggests, we can add caches to supplement the performance of the storage or network black boxes. These components will be part of the system we are building, and thus under our control: edge points of presence in a content distribution network to balance network issues within the black box; a cache of frequently or recently viewed items to offset tail latency or contention in storage systems.

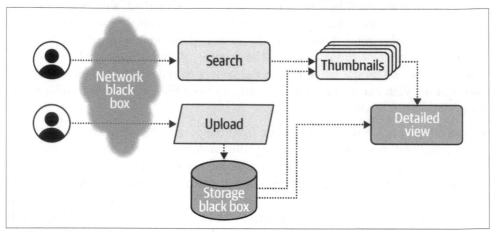

Figure 10-5. Understanding the boundaries of your system helps you design within limits

Summary

This chapter presented a structured approach to system architecture considering SLIs and SLOs. It examined how to incorporate SLIs and SLOs into the design phase, including these as key parts of the conversation in the initial design as well as in subsequent iterations, and discussed how user journeys inform these. By using the identified user journeys to inform design choices, the system architect will be able to build the components that best provide the services the user needs. These choices include when and how to isolate different classes of requests, where to add caches, and where to degrade gracefully. With well-designed systems built on these principles, it's easy for architects to extend them and operators to scale them as needed to serve more users.

CHAPTER 11

Data Reliability

Polina Giralt and Blake Bisset

The opening chapters of this book discuss how we live in a world of services. We also live in a world of data. Most services create, collect, process, or present data in some way. We're surrounded by data services! The goal of this chapter is to explore what makes SLOs for data services different from SLOs for other services.

First, we'll define data services and consider our data users. The heart of this chapter covers measuring service objectives via 13 data properties. For each property, we'll explore its measurement and its relationship to system design. We'll finish with a short explanation of how to ensure data quality via service level objectives, to keep users happy.

Data Services

Welcome to the world of data service reliability. We're bombarded with data each day. Financial data. Social data. Training data for algorithms. Data that is historical or near real time, structured or unstructured. Privately guarded corporate secrets as well as publicly available government datasets. Microservices consuming tiny amounts of JSON data from queues. Monolithic banking applications creating thousands of regulatory reports. And, of course, every other abstraction through which humanity has struggled to describe and make sense of the world since Grace Hopper plucked the first actual bug (*https://www.atlasobscura.com/places/grace-hoppers-bug*) out of a computer.

Data application owners need to ensure that their services are reliable—but the essentials of data reliability vary for each system. To examine data reliability, we have to consider the intersection of reliability precepts with the types of data and data systems we use. We need data-specific considerations like integrity, validity, and durability. Then we can balance them against each other and the service properties with which we are already familiar. Enter the SLO.

We can only optimize so many things about a service. Every measurable property for which we can optimize involves a potential trade-off with some other property. When architecting data applications, some of those trade-offs are irrevocable. SLOs help us evaluate these constraints for our applications, with measurable objectives.

Designing Data Applications

To deliver a good user experience, we'll need to align our points of view with our users' and establish clear shared expectations. In the immortal words of Obi-Wan Kenobi, another questionably qualified instructor, "You're going to find that many of the truths we cling to depend greatly on our own point of view."

For the typical case, reliability expectations are well understood. The most common signal of "reliability" is when systems are resilient enough to recover in ways that make degradation ephemeral to the user. Availability and latency describe a moment, and once restored, the utility of a service is as good for the user as it ever was.

 Data-related properties have a different calculus of risk. Properties like durability, consistency, and integrity must be considered in a unique light, because once lost they are difficult to regain. Recovering from a true durability failure can be impossible, and the effects of these failures will persist forward indefinitely into your users' future.

If you're running the streaming frontend for a popular cat-sharing platform, where both you and your clients make money from ads, at the end of the day nobody cares if you lose a few bits off the millionth stream of *Fluffy vs. Box XXVIII: The Boxening*. But if you make your living providing a safe place for people to store their wedding photos or their million-dollar empires of cat video master files (or their financial records that protect Fluffy from a stint in Club Fed for tax fraud), you don't get off so easy. Then your users' happiness depends on mastering a very different problem, at the heart of which is critical data. Financial, legal, creative, or sentimental data often cannot be replaced or reconstructed.

When the value of your service is the data itself, invest data engineering energy into mechanisms to prevent failures, or at least to keep them localized and temporary rather than systemic and sustained.

Like designing any software, architecting data applications requires us to understand what problems we're trying to solve. This is especially true because many data reliability properties exist in opposition to each other. For instance, the additional processing time needed to ensure completeness can be at odds with freshness or availability. It is important to determine the criticality of data and think about error budgets per application—or dataset—rather than just per failure type. SLOs can help us decide which errors or bottlenecks in the design are our best investment for mitigation.

What do we mean by "data applications"? A data application exists to create, gather, store, transform, and/or present data. This sounds like most services. For our purposes, a data application is a service for which data quality is the primary success metric and for which data-based SLOs will directly map to user experiences.

Users of Data Services

Who are data users? Everyone: services, humans, meshes of services, consumers, producers—anyone or anything that interacts with data. In complex applications, data is often used in several different ways. What are the integration points between services in a data pipeline? How does data move through the system? (We'll talk a little more about data lineage toward the end of the chapter.)

Defining SLOs requires determining what types of service degradations are meaningful to your users. The first step is understanding the entities that provide and consume your data.

Who will require the information you produce? Different users will have different service objectives (written down or not), and new users will have new SLO needs.

From the user's point of view, the service is reliable if it performs the function that they expect.

What mechanism(s) will data consumers use to receive your data (RESTful API, event stream, pull, push)? Some users expect durability, which will be at odds with retention policies—do you need different retention for different users? Think about what you aim to deliver (and how), and how you can control, protect, and enhance the value of data throughout its life cycle.

Don't forget that if your service has data providers, they are also users that hold expectations of your service. Metric forwarding clients are users of monitoring services, video channel owners are users of video platform services, and advertisers are users of ad platform services, just as much as the data consumers. What are their needs? Measure how you ingest data, and how it's internalized form remains true to the content they've entrusted to you.

Another question you'll need to think about is what level to set an SLO at. While thinking about the data properties, you'll make decisions about which elements are the most important for specific sets of data, for individual services, and for the organization as a whole.

Setting Measurable Data Objectives

This chapter lays out our personal ontology of data reliability (see Figure 11-1). The categories described here are just one of many possible sets of dimensions across which the reliability of data can be considered and measured. Some of them will sound familiar, because they apply to any system. What are they? Which are unique to data?

To observe data reliability with SLOs/SLIs, we need to consider measurable properties and the various kinds of data services. Many of these data properties are either tightly coupled, so it's hard to have one without the other, or can be in contention with one another, as mentioned previously. Figure 11-1 illustrates those messy relationships. And to further complicate matters, their meaning can be subjective!

 In our careers and in our research, we have come across many frameworks for categorizing data concerns. There are hundreds of terms in use describing attributes of data, with little consistency or consensus as to which terms are canonical or what each term means from author to author. We'll be narrow and opinionated in how we define these terms; we'll use them as tags for specific kinds of things we want to discuss. We apologize in advance for any offense to academic or professional sensibilities. Our definitions may not match your own; you are welcome to fight us on Twitter.

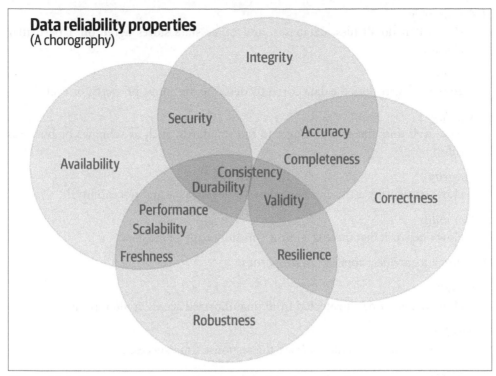

Data reliability properties
(A chorography)

Integrity

Security

Accuracy

Completeness

Availability

Consistency
Durability

Validity

Correctness

Performance
Scalability

Freshness

Resilience

Robustness

Figure 11-1. Data properties and their relationships to each other

Data and Data Application Reliability

live the heat death of the universe, despite all of the nines in the vast armada of servers its engineers construct for it, out in the black vastnesses between the stars. What, then, are realistic user expectations of data reliability, and how do we reason about them?

We can separate data reliability properties into two camps: data properties and data application properties. There are 13 properties that we've chosen to examine in detail for this chapter.

The first seven of these are data properties:

1. *Freshness*

   How out of date is the data compared to the most recent source inputs?

2. *Completeness*

   How comprehensive is the dataset? Does it include *all* data items that represent the entity or event?

3. Consistency

How often do all files, databases, and other state stores agree on a particular datum?

4. Accuracy

To what degree does the data correctly describe the entity, property, or event?

5. Validity

How well does the data conform to the standards, such as schemas or business rules?

6. Integrity

How trustworthy is the data (based on its governance and traceability)?

7. Durability

How likely is it that there is a known-healthy copy of the data?

The other six are data application properties:

1. Security

How well is the data protected from unauthorized access or alteration?

2. Availability

How is service continuity? What's the response time/success rate?

3. Scalability

How elastic is the data? How fast is the data volume expected to grow?

4. Performance

What is the latency, throughput, and efficiency of the data service?

5. Resilience

How quickly does the data recover after disruption?

6. Robustness

How well does the service handle invalid inputs or stressful conditions?

The remainder of this section explores each of these properties in turn. We start with data properties, and then cover data application properties. In addition to defining each property, we get into the details of how to measure them and discuss how to use these sorts of measurements to set meaningful SLO targets. The goal is to guide design decisions around them.

Data Properties

Data properties are those properties that are inherent to the data itself, mapping to data quality characteristics. Any definition of the term *data quality* is subjective and/or situationally dependent to the point of being useless, so we will use the SLO framework to set quantitative objectives. For any property, an SLO for that property that's aligned to the needs of our users and our business helps us assess the reliability of our data application.

Freshness

Freshness, sometimes called *timeliness*, is a measure of how out-of-date a particular piece or collection of data is. Does the data represent the actual situation, and is it published soon enough? This is not the same thing as the age of the data: week-old data can be fresh, and minute-old data can be stale. Freshness relates to the time difference between the *available* data and the latest update or additional processing input. That is, data is fresh until new information comes in that renders previous information less useful.

 Note that many data properties are strongly tied to the *availability* data application property, covered in the following section. Having data present in the system that is more fresh or complete or consistent doesn't matter if it isn't *what the user sees*.

Out-of-date information can cost companies time, money, or credibility. How *much* it costs is a function of the data's rate of change, the impact of staleness on the use case, and the periodicity of the use that relies on that data. To set an expectation on data freshness, ideally you can measure when and how often users access the data, and calculate the freshness level that keeps the impact within your service requirements.

Think of a weekly report that goes out every Monday morning to the board. In such a case, we might determine that the data it is drawn from can be incomplete or stale during the week, as long as the data is fresh and reliable by Monday morning.

> *Example SLO*: 99% of data for the previous week (Monday through Sunday) is available for reporting by 09:00 each Monday.

With this well-understood expectation, you might design the system as a weekly batch job to process the week's data and generate the report in time. Or you might decide that the potential business cost of a late failure in that single job would justify redundant jobs, or incremental processing through the week.

Contrast the preceding to a real-time dashboarding tool, which demands continuous freshness.

Example SLO: 97% of data is available in the dashboard tool within 15 minutes of an event occurring.

The expectations from this SLO make it clear that the system design will require a near-real-time event-based solution, such as streaming.

Note that both of these example SLOs also include reference to data *completeness*, covered in more detail later in this chapter.

Data with high freshness concerns is found in:

- High-frequency trading systems that need to respond to the market within milliseconds
- Any service where a user is making critical real-time decisions based on the data (military, air traffic controllers, etc.)
- Concurrent user systems, such as chat, multiplayer gaming, collaborative documents, or video streaming with real-time comments

Architectural considerations that may be guided by a freshness SLO include determining when to sync an event pipeline to disk; keeping copies up to date via streaming, microbatch processing, snapshotting, or replication; and determining when to use caching or materialized views/projections. Alternatively, query results can be calculated at the time they are requested. The more volatile the data, the more often it'll require refreshing.

 The data our users see—often an output of a data pipeline—is only as fresh as the time it takes to flow through the whole system. How do you identify which component service is the bottleneck? Record data interaction times, whether through data records, logging, or traces, for each component that touches it to provide visibility into system performance.

Completeness

Completeness, aka *comprehensiveness*, measures the degree to which a dataset includes all data items representing an entity or event. In a data pipeline, completeness is defined as the percentage of events available to a user after they are sent into the system. This property is correlated to durability and availability, since losing objects or access will result in incomplete datasets.

The importance of completeness is familiar to many of us: incomplete information might be unusable or misleading. Let's say you're notifying your customers of an important change. You need each customer's email address—without it, the user contact data is incomplete. Missing records of the users' notification preferences may result in the wrong messaging behavior.

In another case, you could be using a MapReduce or other distributed worker mechanism to build a dataset, and decide that waiting for 95% of records to return is a better balance than 99.999% because you're ultimately looking to query a statistically sufficient sampling of records, rather than laboring under a financial and/or regulatory requirement for every transaction in a system to be recorded.

For data that can be rebuilt from a persistent source, or has a predictable size and shape (e.g., a top-50 leaderboard), completeness may be straightforward to measure.

> *Example SLO*: 99.99% of data updates result in 50 data rows with all fields present.

This can be a useful measurement if this exact record count has significant impact; if leaderboard presence is a driving mechanism for user engagement, then any omissions will generate distrust. However, in many cases the expectations for consistency, accuracy, or freshness may be a more compelling representation of the user experience.

For the many provider-generated data sources that have no other source of truth, completeness can be much trickier to measure. One approach might be to audit the counts for all ingested data.

> *Example SLO*: 99.9% of events counted during ingestion will be successfully processed and stored within 15 minutes of ingestion.

Approaches to optimize completeness will depend on the size and scale of the data, as well as the use case. Are you processing financial data where there will be monetary implications to every discrepancy? Or is your application focused on big data for marketing impressions, where accurate aggregate counts are business-critical, but a thousand missed events out of several billion are a rounding error?

Remember that we can sacrifice this or any other property when it makes sense. When would ensuring a high level of completeness be a poor use of resources? For analytical data, completeness might not be a primary concern, as long as the data is directionally correct. Sampling can often give you enough data to make inferences, as long as you make sure that sampling bias doesn't affect the results.

> *Example SLO*: Each query will process 80% of its input set.

In this case, though, the real concern may be getting the data quickly so it's useful for analysis. If so, perhaps you could better measure the service quality with a performance or freshness SLO.

Data with high completeness concerns includes:

- Regulatory data, used for legal and regulatory reporting
- Financial records
- Customer data where you need a record for each customer, with required fields: name, contact info, product subscription tier, account balance, and so on

---

Operational Instrumentation for Completeness

Be careful with late-arriving data. Know if your system needs to be able to handle events that show up hours or even days after they happened. Is your percentage of late-arriving data enough to impact your SLO measurements? Do your completeness objectives anticipate replaying and backfilling data?

Increase telemetry (that is, record a timestamp) whenever a service handles the data. Audit data completeness and use the telemetry to track late-arriving-data faults.

Consistency

Consistency (an old stalwart of the CAP theorem (*https://en.wikipedia.org/wiki/CAP_theorem*)) can be a transaction property, a data property, or a data application property. It means that all copies of files, databases, and other state stores are synchronized and in agreement on the status of the system or a particular datum. For users, it means that all parties querying that state will receive the same results. After a "write" is acknowledged, any and all "reads" ought to result in the same response.

Does the data contain contradictions? We'll use an example from the healthcare field: if a patient's birthday is March 1, 1979, in one system but February 13, 1983, in another, the information is inconsistent and therefore unreliable.

 "Consistency" is not used here to discuss or measure in any way whether the data store is consistent with any actual real-world state or inventory, which would fall under accuracy, discussed next.

We might lack consistency when we choose storage techniques that store data in multiple independent locations, but for some reason do not ensure that all locations are storing the same data before marking the logical write as complete. Often this is done for reasons of performance or better failure isolation, and consequently better availability. Many use cases tolerate eventual consistency. How much delay is acceptable?

If both scalability and consistency are critical for your data application, you can distribute a number of first-class replicas. This service will have to handle some combination of distributed locking, deadlocks, quorums, consensus, and/or two-phased commits. Achieving strong consistency is complicated and costly. It requires atomicity and isolation and, over the long term, durability.

Multiple Datastores

Another important case for this property is a data application that relies on multiple related datastores. It's a common pattern to hold metadata in a smaller-scale structured datastore (for example, an SQL database.) and hold the data objects described by that metadata in a larger-scale unstructured datastore (for example, a blob store).[1]

For better performance, there's often a cache-like in-memory store in front of that metadata database as well. In such architectures, among other concerns, consistency problems—like widow and orphan records—tend to become common.

Measure consistency by quantifying the difference between two or more representations of an object. Data can be measured against itself, another dataset, or a different database. These representations can be the source upstream signal, redundant copies of the data, the downstream storage layer, or some higher-dependability authoritative source.

> *Example SLO:* 99.99999% of monthly financial data processed by the service will match the company's general ledger system (authoritative source) by the 5th of the following month (month close).

This kind of matching to measure consistency can be expensive, in both service resources and maintainer hours, since it generally requires a dedicated processing job that can iterate over all the data. The SLO can inform decisions about how rigorous this extra processing needs to be. Are incremental checks enough? Are there any filters or sampling that would make the problem more tractable, or the results more focused on the most critical data?

Following are some examples of data with high consistency concerns:

---

1 *Smaller* and *larger* are relative terms here—we have worked on exabyte-scale datastores that relied on multiple thousands of replicated SQL shards for the metadata portion of the service.

- When an authoritative source of data needs to match audits against derived or integrated systems. For example, a hedge fund balance sheet's gain/loss totals need to reconcile with the transactions in the credit risk management system.

- When user queries cannot tolerate out-of-date values. If a user performs aggregate queries where one target dataset has been updated and another hasn't, the results can contain errors.

Accuracy

Accuracy measures the conformity to facts. Data veracity or truthfulness is the degree to which data correctly describes the real-world entity, property, or event it represents. Accuracy implies precise and exact results acquired from the data collected. For example, in the realm of banking services, does a customer really have $21 in their bank account?

 Accuracy is often a crucial property. Relying on inaccurate information can have severe consequences. Continuing with the previous example, if there's an error in a customer's bank account balance, it could be because someone accessed it without their knowledge or because of a system failure. An amount that's off by a single dollar might be a big problem, but a bank's internal account system could set an accuracy threshold to be within a few thousand dollars. It's important to measure what's "accurate enough" for any use case.

When evaluating accuracy, we can measure and consider both granularity and precision:

Granularity
The level of detail at which data is recorded (periodicity, cardinality, sampling rate, etc.). Granularity helps us reason about whether a dataset has a degree of resolution appropriate for the purpose for which we intend to use it. This is heavily used during downsampling and bucketizing of data for time series monitoring and alerting, and so on.

Precision
The amount of context with which data is characterized, adding clarity of interpretation and preventing errors arising from accidental misuse of data. Are these actually apples and apples, or apples and oranges?

Precision is a measure of how well typed and characterized our data is—not how well it conforms to type (validity), but whether it's defined and described clearly enough to survive reuse in another context without generating erroneous conclusions or calculations. Consider a set of temperature readings where the temperature collection method varies, or where we measure temperature, then administer a medication, then measure temperature again. Without capturing context in the definition/labeling of either case, we could get errors in some uses of the data. With it, we expose additional avenues for normalization, correlation, extrapolation, or reuse.

When measuring accuracy, we typically need to talk about the ways to audit datasets for real-world accuracy. That is, it is perhaps reasonable to set an SLO that 99.99% of our records will be accurate; if we adhere to that target our system may well be fit enough for purpose, and our users may well be happy. But the interesting part is usually how we determine that real-world percentage. Data accuracy can be assessed by comparing it to the thing it represents, or to an authoritative reference dataset.

Is this a running tally as we reference records in the course of using them (for example, every time a cable technician goes to a customer site they check the records and note any inaccuracies, then we track the rate of corrections needed over a 30-day or 90-day rolling average)? Or do we pull some authoritative third-party source and benchmark to that? Or do we have a periodic real-world collection true-up, like with census data or a quartermaster taking inventory?

> *Example SLO*: 99.999% of records in the dataset are accurate.
> *Example SLO*: 99% of records are within two standard deviations of expected values.
> *Example SLO*: 90% of records have been verified against physical inventory within the last three months.

Accuracy is where our world of data can sometimes become the very real world surrounding us, and may require observing it independently of our normal data intake mechanisms and manipulations (whether through manual work, or RFID scanning, or national security means).

Data with high accuracy concerns includes:

- Personnel records, which must remain accurate for the company to operate smoothly
- Medical data used for diagnosis
- Bank account information, including the balance and transaction history for each customer

Validity

Also referred to as *data conformance*, *validity* concerns the question: does the data match the rules? Validity is a measure of how well data conforms to the defined system requirements, business rules, and syntax for format, type, range, and so forth. It describes the data's shape and contents, and its adherence to schemas; it includes validation logic and nullability. A measure of validity indicates the degree to which the data follows any accepted standards.

Quantifying validity involves measuring how well data conforms to the syntax (format, type, range, nullability, cardinality) of its definition. Compare the data to metadata or documentation, such as a data catalog or written business rules. Validity applies at the data item level and the object/record level.

For example, a nonnumeric value such as U78S4g in a monetary amount field is invalid at the item level. A six-digit zip code is invalid for US addresses but valid for Canadian customers, so the rest of the record needs to be considered in determining validity. Keep in mind that a zip code of 00000 can be valid, but inaccurate.

> *Example SLO:* In the dataset, 99% of values updated after Jan 1, 2018, are valid.

Data with high validity concerns includes:

- Any data that users depend on to be in a certain schema or format and that, if incorrect, will be deleted or cause errors in downstream systems
- Messages flowing through a schema-managed data pipeline, where any nonconforming message goes to a dead letter queue

---

Correctness

Correct data is data that is both valid and accurate. One does not necessarily guarantee the other. It is quite possible for data to be appropriately data-shaped (valid), but not reflective of real-world state (accurate). For example, suppose that for 10% of your patient entries the age listed is indeed "an integer greater than 0, but less than 200," but that integer varies by 1–10 years from the real-world subject's actual age.

Conversely, another subset of that same data pool can be accurate but not valid: we might find that for another, nonintersecting 10% of records the age is accurate, but is represented as a decimal value (e.g., 12.4 or 30.5 years). Either way, we have a dataset that is, at best, 80% correct, even though its accuracy and validity may be higher.

Some cases are even sneakier. Consider a birth date stored as 10/06/1985. The format looks correct, but the most common US date format, MM/DD/YYYY, is different from the standard European DD/MM/YYYY format. If the value isn't localized properly, it is incorrect, inaccurate, and invalid all because of the invalid localization, even though it will parse in the system.

Is it better to land bad data or no data? If you validate on the fly, any record that doesn't conform to a schema is rejected. If you want to be safe, send it to an error log and/or dead letter queue. Alternatively, land then validate. You can process and analyze a batch of data in a staging environment or isolated table(s). Maybe some of it is recoverable. This is a tricky trade-off because you don't want to encourage producers to provide you with bad data. By accepting malformed inputs, you're expanding your service's robustness (see "Robustness" on page 251), but taking on additional maintenance loads.

 Don't try to build services to clean up the data in the middle of a pipeline. This is an antipattern. Fix it at the source by convincing your upstream data producers to write a validity SLO.

Example: Balancing Properties

Let's look at a scenario that requires a trade-off between validity, accuracy, and completeness. Social Security numbers (SSNs) are nine digits long and can be critical to a system. Due to their unique nature, many systems rely on SSNs as primary keys (this is a bad practice). When a user submits a frontend form to input their SSN, you might validate that they input nine digits and make this field required.

What about a user who doesn't have an SSN, or doesn't want to provide it? A nontrivial number of your users might enter 111-11-1111 or 123-45-6789. Some might make up a real-looking random number like 543-67-3469. There *will* be bad data. How will you know which of your data is bad?

Maybe you should keep the validation, but make the field nullable and choose a better primary key. If the SSN field is optional, you'll know that some of your data will have a null value. Determine which is more important: accuracy or completeness.

Integrity

Data *integrity* involves maintaining data in a correct state by controlling or detecting the ways one can improperly modify it, either accidentally or maliciously. It includes data governance throughout the data life cycle: tracking data lineage, determining retention rules, and auditing data trustworthiness. *Integrity* is not a synonym for *security*. Data security encompasses the overall protection of data confidentiality, integrity, and availability, while data integrity itself refers only to the trustworthiness of data.

Data with low integrity concerns may be considered unimportant to precise operational functions or not necessary to vigorously check for errors. Information with high integrity concerns is considered critical and must be trustworthy.

In order to safeguard trust across that spectrum, integrity can deal just with local file data on our local system via a mechanism as simple as checking and/or updating the cryptographic hash of important files, or it can extend to secure boot mechanisms, TPMs,[2] and verification of the integrity of the runtime environment itself. File integrity checks are useful, but are also a lagging indicator. A more timely metric might be transaction integrity. Rather than measuring all transactions, we would likely focus on integrity when we process a transaction class that is particularly important, like the banking and digital rights management transactions that help make sure that we can continue to keep Fluffy in the Fancy Feast manner to which he has grown accustomed.

If, in addition to the checks of the transaction itself, we check the integrity of the attesting system before and after each transaction, and all the checks are successful, then we assume the transaction can be trusted, too.[3]

Combining all these, we can detect and measure the following:

- Files that don't match integrity checks during periodic scans
- Files that don't match integrity checks on periodic access
- Sensitive transactions that don't pass remote attestation runtime integrity checks

 Sometimes data integrity is maintained by locking down data or source code. If a system generates an immutable financial report, we need to be able to reproduce it exactly, even if our data application changed its logic to fix bugs. Regression testing, immutability, and limiting access to source code/databases are ways to help enforce integrity, whereas integrity checks help measure and monitor it.

There is no perfect mechanism for validating integrity—even less so in a distributed system, where getting every component to agree on something as "simple" as incrementing a counter can be a challenge. But scans, checks on access, and transaction/ attestation checks can work together to give a regular overall check, an as-we-go run-rate spot check, and an approaching-real-time check that the system isn't fooling us on the other checks.

---

2 Trusted Platform Modules (dedicated cryptoprocessor microcontrollers), not the folks who keep us honest about our post-incident reviews and action items, do backlog grooming, run our training programs, edit our handbooks, and generally handle the business of actually running things so that engineering managers have enough time to occasionally pretend like we're still engineers.

3 Mostly because at that point, anyone who is working hard enough to successfully mess with consensus reality in spite of all this arguably deserves to win one, and we personally don't want to have to contemplate the number of overtime hours necessary to detect, isolate, and unwind whatever shenanigans they've inflicted on our data. It may be genuinely better if we just accept that our flagship product is named Boaty McBoatface now.

Example SLO: 99.9999% of data has passed audit checks for data integrity.

Data with high integrity concerns includes:

- Billing application code, which must be unaltered in order to ensure proper application function and auditability for compliance
- Critical system logs, which must be unaltered in order to ensure proper detection of intrusions and system changes by security

Is the data required to remain uncorrupted? Can this data be modified only by certain people or under certain conditions? Must the data come from specific, trusted sources? If data integrity is a primary concern, make sure you have a comprehensive data management strategy. This includes procedures related to backups, access controls, logging, and data lineage, along with robust verification, validation, replay, and reconciliation processes.

Durability

Durability measures how likely it is that a known-healthy copy of your data will be in the system when you attempt to access it. This is *not* a measure of whether, in that moment, you will actually be *able* to access it, but rather whether the data exists to be accessed at all. Recovering from a true durability failure—where no copies exist and the data cannot be re-created—is usually impossible. Because of this, in cases where durability is important, we need to invest extensively in both robustness and resilience.

Azure claims between 11- and 16-nines durability (*https://docs.microsoft.com/en-us/azure/storage/common/storage-redundancy*), depending on the service that is used. Amazon S3 (*https://aws.amazon.com/s3/faqs*) and Google Cloud Platform (*https://cloud.google.com/storage/docs/storage-classes*) offer 11 nines, or 99.999999999% annual durability. This durability level corresponds to an average expected loss of 0.000000001% of objects per year. That means that if you store 1 million immutable objects, you can expect to lose a single object once every 100,000 years (*https://aws.amazon.com/s3/faqs*).

Example SLO: 99.999999999% annual durability

Examples of data with high durability concerns are:

- A general ledger accounting service, which is the authoritative source of a company's transactions
- Any system storing important data that cannot be re-created, such as sentimental data

Keep in mind that not all data is equally valuable to the user. Durability for legacy data might not be as critical as it is for current data. Also, certain datasets may be more useful for decision making, even if they're stored in the same tables as other data.

Operational Instrumentation for Nonrecoverable SLOs

How does an SLO like "11-nines durability" drive system behavior that will deliver user satisfaction? Consider a block data service where we replicate every block five times. Operationally, we could (and will) monitor what percentage of blocks are n-replica degraded. But this doesn't track with user experience or allow us to be forward-looking and allocate time and resources in light of expected user impact.

Is 100% of our fleet being 1-degraded actually a problem? Should we accelerate hard drive replacements or other repair measures at the expense of other work if 7% of our fleet is 2-degraded? It's hard to tell. We must measure resilience as well as robustness in order to predict the durability impact of any change.

Because cat videos are so crucial to the fabric of our society (and so justly lucrative!), we have millions of hard drives just for this service. So it's easy for small deltas in failure rate, replication speed, or anything else to outstrip repair capacity. Rather than just measuring the amount of failure that's already happened, it makes sense to measure the P90-something *time* blocks spend in a replica-degraded state, and manage that.

Very resilience! Much reliable! Wow! Now we have a better idea of the risk we're carrying, and an idea of where our failures outstrip our ability to recover from them. Pretty great, eh?

But not great enough when the value of our stock options is at stake. Such measures don't tell us quickly if we hit a tipping point or a correlated failure. We need to examine the *velocity* of change in our time- and percent-degraded metrics, so that we don't discover surprises too late to avoid permanent data loss in excess of our SLO budget.

Measuring velocity and change in an indirect metric like replica-degraded time lets us make decisions regarding long-lead-time allocation of resources and labor in a responsive way that is intelligently guided to deliver against the scary-nines SLO that actually represents our user experience.

Of course, not all data is created equal, and not all of it is irreplaceable. A service's durability SLO should reflect the inherent value of its data (whether intrinsic or sentimental) and the benefit derived from the preservation of the data.

Sometimes data can be reingested from the original source, or derived from related data. Where the reconstruction expense (in terms of processing, transit, and opportunity cost) is relatively low, a durability SLO can be more relaxed.

Example SLO: 99% monthly durability for all hourly summary reports.

Relaxed durability can also make sense in cases where the lifetime or relevance of data is brief. When the time or expense of enabling recovery would exceed the valuable life or the lifetime value of our data, we might reasonably decide that You Only Log Once and we're fine with the reasonably low chance something will happen to this ephemeral data between creating it and the point at which we will be done making use of it.

On the other hand, there's risk in dismissing critical data as "transient" or "metadata." Decryption keys, user-to-block indices, edge graphs for user notification preferences, or group editing rights and history are all distinct from user-provided data, but still critical. Consider carefully the importance of even automatically generated data to how your users interact with your services and your core data, and how much pain losing it would inflict upon them.

We've seen operators invest in globally distributed, highly replicated architectures for storing and reading data, only to relegate large swaths of "metadata" to cold start active-passive systems that meant days of recovery were needed to restore user access to all that carefully guarded primary data in the event the hot copies were lost.

That could be a perfectly acceptable recovery strategy—unless you make money when users are able to access their data in real time, and lose money when they can't. It doesn't do much good to tell them their groundbreaking O'Reilly manuscript is completely safe and they have nothing to worry about in spite of the fact that your entire West Coast data center just slid into the Pacific Ocean, if you have to turn around and tell them that you should be able to restore the "unimportant" metadata that will allow you to locate the "real" data they care about approximately two weeks after their print deadline.

When it comes to the intersection of durability and availability, the world usually doesn't care if the dog ate your data center. Regardless of the cause of data unavailability, your users only see the system as a whole, and are unlikely to be empathetic to the fine nuances of differences between "real data" and the data critical for that data to be operationally available.

Example SLO: 99.9999% of data will remain intact for the year.

Data Application Properties

Data application properties are system considerations about the ways data gets to and from users, or is transformed from one configuration to another. They are also the metaproperties that make the systems and data upon which we rely easier or harder to work with.

Putting these properties into SLOs encourages us to build systems with a greater reliability than the sum of their parts. They may look familiar because they apply to all services. Let's discuss their significance in defining data quality and measuring data reliability.

Security

Security focuses on protecting data from unauthorized access, use, or alteration, and in some contexts can be referred to as *privacy* as well to emphasize particular aspects and duties. It also covers *detection* of unauthorized use, for ensuring appropriate confidentiality, integrity, and availability. Not all data needs to be secure, but for some datasets, security is essential.

Confidentiality in particular is a data security aspect worth calling out because it shares with durability and integrity (and to a lesser extent, consistency) the characteristic that once lost, it can be very difficult, if not impossible, to regain for a given dataset. Plan and instrument accordingly.

> *Example SLO:* 99% of CVE/NVD[4] vulnerability hotfixes are applied to 99.9% of vulnerable systems within 30 days of release.
> *Example SLO:* 95% of administrator touches are performed through a secure system proxy, rather than direct access.
> *Example SLO:* 99.9% of employees have been subject to a phishing simulation test within the last 3 months.
> *Example SLO:* 99.9% of systems have been in scope for a penetration test within the last year.
> *Example SLO:* 90% of customer notices are delivered within 4 hours of breach detection.
> *Example SLO:* 99.99999% of processed data requests were from a known service with a valid SSL certificate.

 Security is too big of a topic to go into too much detail here. We mention it because we believe it is an important data application property.

---

4 Common Vulnerabilities and Exposures (CVE) and the National Vulnerabilities Database (NVD) are the two comprehensive databases that store information about necessary security fixes to software packages.

Data with high security concerns includes:

- Personnel data, such as employee salaries or Social Security numbers
- Mobile location tracking
- Personal health records that contain private information
- Trade secrets
- Government records (especially air-gapped classified data)

 How can you protect the confidentiality of data that's used for other purposes, shared between teams, or used for service testing? Mask the data by hashing or tokenizing values.

Design options to invest in security include vulnerability scanning and patching, rate limiting, firewalls, HTTPS, SSL/TLS certificates, multifactor authentication, tokenization, hashing, authorization policies, access logs, encryption, and data erasure.

Availability

Availability is currently the most common SLO. Is the service able to respond to a request? Can the data be accessed now and over time? Service availability measures service uptime, response latency, and response success rate.

Availability hinges on timeliness and continuity of information. Information with high availability concerns is considered critical and must be accessible in a timely fashion and without fail. Low availability concerns may be for data that's considered supplementary rather than necessary.

If having uninterrupted access to and availability of data is truly required, there needs to be engineering work to implement load balancing, system redundancy, data replication, and fractional release measures like blue/green or rolling deployments for minimizing any downtime. Recovery is a factor too. Ways to promote availability include automatic detection of and recovery from faults; quick, clear rollback paths; good backups; and the implementation of supervisor patterns.

> *Example SLO:* 95% of records are available for reporting each business day.
> *Example SLO:* 97% of query requests are successful each month.

Know when you *don't* need availability. If datasets have different availability concerns, look into tiered storage. Utilize cold storage for when low availability is acceptable, such as for backups kept only for legal reasons. Design the system based on the timing and frequency at which users need the data. If users only query data as a weekly report, don't spend time ensuring 24/7 high availability.

Data with high availability concerns includes:

- Customer-generated data, which might be key to a digital product, like cloud-based docs or customer relationship management database records

- Any data that's required to prevent downtime and user service disruption, such as in a credit card processing system

- Billing and account data, which must remain accessible to facilitate business continuity

Scalability

Scalability is about growth—the capacity to be changed in size or scale. How much is the data volume expected to grow, and over what period of time? Scalability refers to a system's ability to cope with increased load. Intentional architecture around scalability means rethinking design whenever load increases; managing demand without deteriorated performance. Options include vertical scaling (increasing the existing database's resources) and horizontal scaling (adding more databases). The choice of elastic or manual scaling depends on the rate of change, predictability, and budget.

Anticipating changes can be difficult with some systems. Load and performance testing are a good way to profile expected scale needs at a point in time. It's also important to understand fan-out in the pipeline. This can be accomplished by measuring load parameters such as cache hit rate or requests per second and determining which ones are the most important for the architecture of the system.

As Martin Kleppmann writes in *Designing Data-Intensive Applications* (O'Reilly), "The architecture of systems that operate at large scale is usually highly specific to the application—there is no such thing as a generic, one-size-fits-all scalable architecture (informally known as *magic scaling sauce*). The problem may be the volume of reads, the volume of writes, the volume of data to store, the complexity of the data, the response time requirements, the access patterns, or (usually) some mixture of all of these plus many more issues."

Understanding projected load and growth is important when determining the design of any service. With data applications, there are many tools to enable scaling: caching, implementing load balancers, adding more databases or database resources, database sharding, and using token authentication instead of server-based auth for stateless applications, to name a few.

> *Example SLO*: Service instance utilization will exhibit an upper bound of 90% and a lower bound of 70% for 99% of minutes with system loads between 1,000 and 100,000 queries per second.
> *Example SLO*: 99% of containers will deploy and join the active serving pool within 2 minutes.

Some examples of services with high scalability concerns are:

- A service that needs to handle millions of concurrent users, such as a popular social media platform
- Services that may experience surges or bursty traffic, such as a massive online retailer on Cyber Monday

Performance

Performance SLOs let us discover, profile, monitor, and reduce system bottlenecks. They help improve resource utilization and inform decisions as user needs evolve. There are two main categories:

Latency
> How long does the service take to respond to a request? Latency is the time it takes for data packets to be stored or retrieved. It can measure how much time it takes to get a fully formed response, which may come from a cache, be queried from a precalculated result, or be built dynamically from source dependencies.

Throughput

> How many requests can the service handle per minute? How many events can a data pipeline process in an hour? Throughput is a measure of how much work the data service can handle over a period of time.

> *Example SLO*: 99.9% of database writes will respond within 120 ms.
> *Example SLO*: 98% of query requests will complete in less than 10 ms.
> *Example SLO*: 99% of 2 MB chunks will be transcoded in less than 500 ms.

Services with high performance concerns include:

- Financial trading systems that need to process large volumes of transactions as quickly as possible
- Real-time systems, such as autonomous vehicle navigation and telemetry systems
- Facial recognition and identity matching services

Resilience

Fault tolerance is the key to any distributed system. Prefer tolerating errors and faults, rather than trying to prevent them. *Resilience*, sometimes referred to as *recoverability*, is the ability of a system to return to its original state or move to a new desirable state after disruption (*http://www.husdal.com/2008/04/28/robustness-flexibility-and-resilience-in-the-supply-chain*). It refers to the capacity of a system to maintain functionality in the face of some alteration within the system's environment. Resilient systems may endure environment changes without adapting or may need to change to handle those changes. The resilience of a data application can also impact its availability, completeness, and freshness.

Building resilient services requires rolling with the punches. Sustaining user functionality during/after a disruptive incident also improves other reliability dimensions, such as availability. When one or more parts of the system fail, the user needs to continue receiving an acceptable level of service. So how do we build services to withstand malicious attacks, human errors, unreliable dependencies, and other problems? Resilient services are designed with the understanding that failures are normal, degraded modes are available, and recovery is straightforward.

Measuring resilience (*https://www.it-cisq.org/pdf/How-Do-You-Measure-Software-Resilience-CISQ.pdf*) requires knowing which services or transactions are critical to sustain for users, the speed of recovery from disruptions, and the proportion of requests that can be lost during a disruptive incident. To measure resilient performance, we can conduct manual architecture inspections and create metrics for automatically measuring system behavior. We're limited by our creativity in simulating unexpected disruptive conditions, and therefore some organizations deploy chaos engineering for this purpose.

If resilience is a major concern for the users, optimize the system for quick and easy recovery from errors. Prioritize data recoverability with investment in tooling to backfill, recompute, reprocess, or replay data. Testing the recovery process needs to be a part of normal operations to detect vulnerability proactively.

> *Example SLO:* 99.9% of bad canary jobs will be detected by the Canary Analysis Service and rolled back within 10 minutes of deployment.
> *Example SLO:* 99.99% of failed MySQL promotions will be detected and restarted in less than 1 minute.

Example SLO: Privacy protection tools will detect and remove 97% of flagged records within 4 hours.

Data with high resilience concerns includes:

- Customer-generated data, which might be key to a digital product
- Any data that's required to prevent downtime and user service disruption
- Billing and account data, which must remain accessible to facilitate business continuity

Designing for resilience involves many of the same techniques we use to optimize for availability, durability, and performance: component redundancy, caching, load balancing, dynamic scaling, exponential backoff, timeouts, circuit breakers, input validation, stateless applications, and infrastructure as code.

Robustness

Complementary to resilience is *robustness*. The IEEE Standard Glossary of Software Engineering Terminology (*https://ieeexplore.ieee.org/document/159342*) defines robustness as "The degree to which a system or component can function correctly in the presence of invalid inputs or stressful environmental conditions." The lower the system's dependency upon its environment and the broader the range of input values that the system can operate within, the more robust it is.

In a distributed system your inputs are infinite and unknowable due to time/networks. The most robust systems need to evolve and adapt to new situations that may not exist at the time of development—probe with chaos engineering. Also important: input validation/sanitization and testing.

> *Example SLO:* 99% of code (including configuration changes and flag flips) is deployed via an incremental and verified process.
> *Example SLO:* 95% of changes successfully pass peer review before commit and push.
> *Example SLO:* 99.99% of all code in all repositories has been scanned for common date bugs within the last 30 days.

Robustness can provide excellent benefit to our users, but ultimately its guardrails can only protect us against threats that we have already anticipated. Sooner or later we will encounter a condition we cannot tolerate and the system will fail, which is why resilience—the ability to recover quickly from a bad state and return to normal operations—can provide more critical long-term benefit, even if robustness seems a more effective approach to many people at first.

Data with high robustness concerns includes:

- Customer-generated data, which might be key to a digital product
- Any data that's required to prevent downtime and user service disruption
- Billing and account data, which must remain accessible to facilitate business continuity

System Design Concerns

Once a data application has SLO/SLIs based on the properties described here, you can iterate its design based on the properties' relationships with system considerations, as shown in Table 11-1. There may be many possible designs for your application, but if a property that concerns you impacts it, you want to be intentional with that aspect of the system design.

Table 11-1. The intersection of data and service properties (left) with system design concerns (top)

	Time	Access	Redundancy	Sampling	Mutability	Distributed
Freshness	X	X		X	X	
Completeness	X		X	X		X
Consistency	X		X		X	X
Accuracy			X	X	X	
Validity					X	
Integrity		X			X	
Durability		X	X			X
Security		X	X		X	
Availability	X	X	X	X		X
Scalability				X		X
Performance	X			X	X	X
Resilience	X	X	X		X	X
Robustness		X				X

Data Application Failures

What else distinguishes data reliability from other types of reliability? The many types of data errors, and their persistence in our applications. Because of the persistence of their impact, investments in considerations and practices to minimize those errors quickly become reasonable, rather than excessive. SLOs can help quantitatively determine how much investment is reasonable in order to build systems more reliable than the sum of their unreliable parts.

As data gets bigger and more complicated, the systems that support data get more complicated too. The boundaries between different "types" of data services blend. Can Kafka be considered a database? How about Route 53?[5] Data services are optimized to store many types of data, either in flight or at rest: think databases, caches, search indexes, queues for stream processing, batch processing, and combination systems.

As discussed earlier, resilience and robustness characteristics will improve reliability. The failure of one component will not cause the entire system to fail. Fault tolerance is about designing systems that have faults that are deliberately triggered and tested.

Not all failure is created equal, nor handled the same. A fault is a condition that causes a failure—a deviation from spec. It may be correlated with other faults, but each fault is a discrete issue. An error is a failure wherein a single fault—or a collection of faults—results in a bad system state that is surfaced to the user or service calling our system. In an error, we have produced an outcome that cannot or should not be recovered to a known good state transparently.

Another way to think of this is that systems have errors, and components have faults, which can become errors if they are not remediated by the system. Errors can be handled gracefully (when we have anticipated the failure type and provided a means for the system to recover or continue) or ungracefully.

How should we handle a particular fault? Should we recover or retry transparently? Surface an error? Request client system or user action? Like everything else here, those decisions are rich with trade-offs.

Data systems are particularly prone to classes of fault that must be handled as errors, in that often bad data cannot be corrected without resorting to either user input or upstream data/processing/transformations that produced the data in the first place. Backfills, replays, or data munging to correct data takes time and effort.

Each data property has its own failure states, so we have to consider many types of data errors. How do you measure the impact of an outage? SLOs are a form of audit control for finding and fixing "bad data." SLOs will help you understand which faults to pay attention to.

Other Qualities

Let's briefly touch on some qualities of the system design concerns presented in Table 11-1, which we don't have time or room to get into in this chapter. They're all important aspects of data reliability you should keep in mind, but for the sake of not

---

5 Hi, Corey!

making this chapter an entire book, we'll be skipping in-depth conversations about them. We would merely be remiss if we didn't at least define their qualities:

Time

> Latency, throughput, bandwidth, efficiency, uptime. How fast can data be processed? How long does the service take to respond? Minimize response time via caching (local cache, distributed cache) and CDNs.

Access

> Access control, authorization, authentication, permissions. Covers both policy and accessibility.

Redundancy

> Backups, tiered storage, replication. Key to durability.

Sampling

> P95, full coverage, fully representative versus biased.

Mutability

> Write once, retention.

Distribution

> Transactions (not canceling transactions based on a single failure, but handling rollbacks/graceful retries), idempotence, ordering, localization, parallelism, concurrency, load balancing, partition workloads.

Data Lineage

Services store data in various ways, for different purposes. Data flows through every layer in a technology stack. This makes it important to understand the reliability of upstream data. Imagine a web application served by a single database. The web server depends on the database to render its content. If the only source of the data is unavailable, the site is down. To handle this, we set up objectives and contingencies around interface boundaries. SLO dependencies are dictated by the service dependencies. Downstream services must take the service objectives of upstream independent services into account.

Data can flow through an application like a river, which is probably why there are so many water-related metaphors in the space (streams, pools, data lakes). As the process goes from one step to the next, we're moving downstream. Where in the process is our application's data? Who are the upstream producers/publishers? Do these sources have SLOs? Who are the downstream consumers/subscribers of this data? How will they use the data?

A complex data reporting pipeline can consist of a dozen data services. Data lineage is the collected record of the data's movement during its life cycle, as it moves downstream. Keeping track of lineage in data applications is important for determining both data uses and the system integration points. Any data handoff point between services may benefit from SLOs/SLIs.

Summary

The definition of *reliable data* depends on what users need from our service. But with well-chosen SLOs, we can describe and quantify those needs to guide our designs and measure how well we're doing.

There are many sets of properties we can consider when setting data reliability SLOs. In addition to the properties common to any service, such as performance or availability, we've described several properties unique to data services. While a service property such as availability is usually ephemeral, the persistent nature of a data property raises the stakes for SLO misses. Any lapse in confidentiality, integrity, or durability may be an irrevocable loss.

In defining reliability SLOs, we must work with our users to establish quantifiable expectations. We can't just trust our own hard-earned or cleverly derived knowledge and perspective. The problem here is not that we as application owners don't know anything about our users' experience of our service, but that we know so much that our understanding isn't necessarily (or at least universally) true. Ask your users how they want to measure their service objectives. Agree with them on what "better" would look like across any set of data properties.

Modern organizations are often obsessed with "data quality." They hire tons of engineers to think about it. But quality is ultimately subjective unless you can define and measure it, and it's inextricably intertwined with the systems that collect, store, process, and produce our data. We must reframe these conversations, and use SLOs to provide a supporting framework of quantitative measurement to help define the mechanisms by which we provide users with reliable data.

CHAPTER 12

A Worked Example

Alex Hidalgo

At this point, you've learned a lot about SLO-based approaches to reliability. Assuming you've read all of Part I, you now have an understanding of how the entire process works and the various components of the Reliability Stack. If you've explored other parts of Part II, you've also potentially learned about getting buy-in, how to actually measure things and use them for alerting and monitoring, some of the statistics and probabilities you can use to pick good SLI measurements and SLO targets, how to architect your services with SLOs in mind from the start, and why data reliability is a special case that requires different conversations.

While the other chapters in this part of the book have given you lots of detailed insight into specific aspects of an SLO-based approach to reliability, and Part I outlined and defined all of the concepts you need to get started, what we really haven't talked about yet is how all this might actually work for a multicomponent service—or how it might apply to an entire company or organization. Consider this chapter as a way to put a lot of these concepts to work.

This chapter describes an example company and walks through defining SLIs and SLOs for various parts of its infrastructure. Looking at a concrete example can be useful when learning how to apply concepts that may have just been abstract in your reading so far. We'll be covering everything from a customer-facing web page to services that interact with vendors, internal applications, and independent services with few dependencies or dependees. But before we begin that journey, let's start with a story about a startup company, how it came to be, and how it grew into what it is today.

Dogs Deserve Clothes

A few years ago Jordan adopted a rescue Dachshund. Jordan immediately fell in love with their dog, and their dog fell in love with them as well. Dachshunds are also known as *wiener dogs* due to their shape—they look rather like sausages with legs, as you can see in Figure 12-1.

Figure 12-1. Wiener dog body shape (illustration by Denise Yu)

After a few months, as winter was approaching, Jordan started noticing their dog was starting to shiver a lot and was clearly cold on walks. So they did what any reasonable dog parent would do, and went online to try and find some clothing—a sweater, a jacket; anything that would help keep their dog warm on their long winter walks.

But no matter what Jordan ordered, none of it fit. If the coat was long enough, it was too large around; if it was the right fit around the body, it was too short. After trying several brands, Jordan gave up and decided to make their own jacket instead. After one long weekend, the prototype was ready, and Jordan's dog was comfy and warm on its subsequent walks (Figure 12-2).

Because of this experience, Jordan realized that other people must be in the same predicament—and not just with wiener dogs! There are pit bull mixes with chests too big for the rest of their bodies and mastiffs that exceed the size of clothing anyone makes and bulldogs whose dimensions can sometimes defy the laws of physics. Jordan knew what was needed: a dog clothing company that paid attention to all body shapes and sizes. So, The Wiener Shirt-zel Clothing Company was created.

Figure 12-2. Wiener dog all comfy and warm (illustration by Denise Yu)

How a Service Grows

The Wiener Shirt-zel Clothing Company was born on a single programmer's laptop. Jordan had an idea and just started working on it, and that laptop is where it lived for the first few iterations. It's how things grew from there that can be seen as fairly remarkable.

The next step was to add some sort of data storage service behind the prototype web service. Then the service itself was moved off the laptop and into a container, and from there to a rented server in a data center. With the prototype complete, as the service started to take real traffic, it needed to be scaled up. Now it was a distributed service, which meant some kind of load-balancing solution was needed, which required even more hardware running in the data center. As the distributed service took on more traffic, it turned out that the database did as well, so it was scaled out to be distributed as well.

The Wiener Shirt-zel Clothing Company is a web-facing product, so the next thing that had to happen was the introduction of a content delivery network. A CDN is a service that helps you route traffic and can hold cached assets for you in order to serve them to your users in a more efficient manner and protect you from attacks.

The company continued to grow, and as more engineers were hired, some of them pointed out that keeping all the logic in a single service isn't the best idea—so new features were added on as microservices instead of additions to the customer-facing application. And now that there were more services, those need their own databases. And now that the databases had more traffic, they needed a caching layer to help with performance. And then it was realized that handling transactions is a complicated business, so a new microservice was introduced that pulled this logic out of the customer-facing application. And then the business aspect of the company needed more data to make the marketing department more efficient, so a reporting pipeline was introduced. On and on it went. Services can become complex and deep very quickly. Let's take a look at what The Wiener Shirt-zel Clothing Company looks like after a year of growth.

The Design of a Service

The Wiener Shirt-zel Clothing Company has done well. It sells doggie shirts, coats, and more to people all over the planet. It's gone from a handful of customers to hundreds of thousands of visitors every day, resulting in thousands of sales. Figure 12-3 shows what the architecture now looks like.

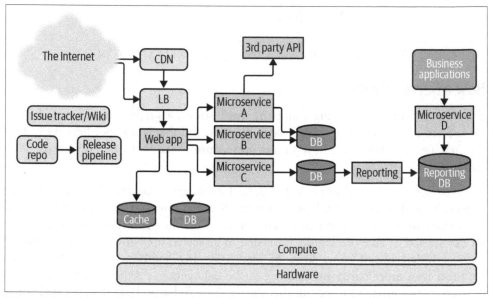

Figure 12-3. An example of a retail website architecture

Here you can see a whole ton of components in a reasonably architected service. It may not be perfectly architected, but as you'll remember, nothing ever is.

The primary flow of traffic starts with humans on the internet visiting the web app that powers the service. Most of this traffic goes through the CDN, but not everything does, since it's pretty difficult to capture every edge case. From here the traffic flows into the web app, where most of the important logic is performed.

Below this you'll see a DB that stores assets needed to serve the site. This includes things like the images and text descriptions of various items for sale on the site. Next to this you'll also find a cache—content that's served often and doesn't often change shouldn't require a full database lookup. This includes things like the currently featured clothing articles.

Next to the primary web app you'll see three microservices. These are smaller components of the overall service that serve very specific needs. Microservice A manages financial transactions involving customer payments. Microservice B, in the middle, is the inventory system. These two both rely on a database that contains data on product availability, quantity, price, etc. Microservice C tracks users' selections and where they spend the most time on the site. This data is sent to a database for further business trend analysis.

Data from this database is analyzed and converted into data that is more useful to humans in the marketing department via a data processing pipeline, which outputs the data into a new database. Finally, the processed data in this database is accessed via a business app that connects via Microservice D, which acts as a smarter API to the database. This data allows the marketing department at the company to make better decisions in terms of what kinds of new products should be developed.

Additionally, as The Wiener Shirt-zel Clothing Company grew, it needed places for employees to document things and keep track of priorities, so it now runs some open source issue tracking and wiki services to help with this. It has also implemented its own code repository and deployment pipeline.

Finally, at the bottom of the stack, you'll see that it has both a compute and a hardware layer. While perhaps a bit unconventional for a startup today, due to various concerns the company has decided to not live in the cloud, so it runs its own container platform setup on its own hardware in a data center.

SLIs and SLOs as User Journeys

As Chapter 3 discussed, different functions in your company may already have much more alignment about what users need than you initially realize. Good SLIs for engineering teams are often very similar to the user journeys product teams want to define, which are often very similar to what your business teams are looking to as KPIs. In the rest of this chapter we're going to explore various aspects of The Wiener Shirt-zel Clothing Company, primarily focused around three different groups of users: its external customers, services as users, and internal users (employees at the company).

We'll start our discussion about how you might define SLIs and SLOs for the various aspects of The Wiener Shirt-zel Clothing Company by considering what the *customers* actually need, and see how you can set SLOs keeping that in mind. Then we'll move on to what *internal users*, both humans and other services, might need and develop some example SLOs to cover that.

Customers: Finding and Browsing Products

The Wiener Shirt-zel Clothing Company is one that looks to make money, so it needs customers. And the needs of these customers (and their dogs) are its utmost priority.

Let's discuss an example of a user journey that customers of The Wiener Shirt-zel Clothing Company need to be reliable. We won't be covering every possible SLI or SLO that could be developed for the company's architecture, as that would get repetitive and take up too much space; rather, we'll look at a few representative examples of SLIs and SLOs for user interactions.

The primary focus of The Wiener Shirt-zel Clothing Company is to sell dog clothing to customers. In order for that to happen, customers will have to be able to browse and search through the products offered. The parts of the architecture involved here are emphasized in Figure 12-4.

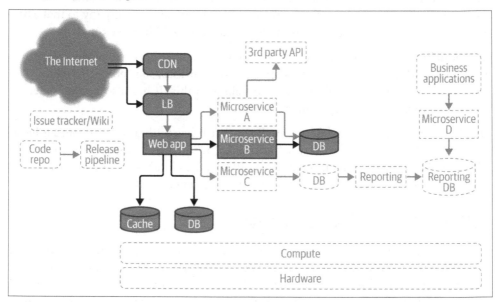

Figure 12-4. The components involved with finding and browsing products

The first thing you might notice is that a fair number of components are involved. This is a great example of the mantra from Chapter 3: you can measure many things by measuring only a few. By knowing whether a user can successfully search for a product, the company knows that the product catalog database and/or cache are operating well enough and that the inventory microservice is behaving. Additionally, it knows that its primary web app, the web asset database, and the network components at play are all performing reliably.

At The Wiener Shirt-zel Clothing Company, each component is owned by a different team, and they have defined SLOs for every one of those components. However, they *also* want to be sure that they're capturing the higher-level human interactions. This is because they need data not only to have discussions about how individual teams may prioritize their work, but also to have discussions about how the entire *organization* might prioritize its work. So, while each component has an SLO set, such as the web server being able to serve the front page in under 2 seconds, they also have SLOs set for multicomponent journeys like the user being able to successfully search for a product.

 We could imagine different teams being responsible for each of these services. In that case you'd certainly need SLOs defined at every step along the way, so you can set error budgets that can help each of these teams prioritize their own future work. The counter-example would be that one team is responsible for every component involved, in which case perhaps SLOs may only need to be set at the highest of levels. The point, as always, is that you're gathering data you can use to have discussions about what parts of your infrastructure require attention to keep your users happy.

Let's talk about the actual customers and what they as users of this service need. I've already mentioned that they need to be able to browse and search for products on the site, but that could actually mean many things. Let's drill down and talk about two very specific aspects of this user journey.

SLO: Front page loads and latency

The users of The Wiener Shirt-zel Clothing Company website are human customers. This means that they're actually fairly patient in a world of computer services where we often measure things on the order of milliseconds. As discussed in Chapter 3, humans are totally fine with a web page taking a few seconds to completely render in their browser.

A bit more important to people are error rates. If a website loads in 2 seconds 99% of the time, they're probably fine if it takes 5 seconds just 1% of the time. This is probably not a rate at which they'll abandon you for a competitor. But if a page fails to *load* a full 1% of the time, you're probably going to lose a certain number of customers. Despite this divergence, this doesn't mean you need to have two entirely separate SLOs. You can use the data you have about both of these aspects of reliability to power a single SLI and SLO.

In this case, a reasonable SLO might read like the following:

> 99.9% of responses to our website will return a 2xx, 3xx, or 4xx HTTP code within 2,000 ms.

You could absolutely get more detailed than this. For one example, we aren't accounting for a potential long tail with percentiles. For another example, you often want to count 4xx response codes as "good" responses, because you don't want to burn all of your error budget if someone with a large social media presence tweets out a link to a page that doesn't exist. However, an elevated rate of them could also mean that your own website has links that don't work. The difficulty comes from not knowing whether a request itself is "good" or not. Another example is that you'll generally consider 5xx response codes as "bad," but a 505 (while exceedingly rare in the real world) could be caused by a client when there is nothing wrong on your end. There are a lot of nuanced options at your disposal. Be as detailed (or simple!) as you need for your service and your realities—but no matter what your service looks like, it's best to start simple and get more complicated later.

Having 99.9% of responses completing within our parameters seems reasonable. Just convert this into a number of page views and ask yourself how you'd feel if faced with this as a reality. From an events-based perspective, if you were browsing a website for dog clothing and only 1 in 1,000 clicks resulted in a slow load or an error, you'd almost certainly be able to shrug this off. The Wiener Shirt-zel Clothing Company has been able to track that the average user clicks on approximately 25 links per browsing session. This means that only 1 in 40 customers is expected to experience even a single bad response during their time on the site. Trying to fix the database problems that lead to these errors would be a major project that could take several quarters, and it's been determined that users that experience an error rarely abandon their browsing, so the engineering, product, and business teams agree on 99.9%.

As you may recall from Chapter 4, that translates to about 43 minutes of downtime per month. From a time-based perspective, the company certainly might lose some sales if the site were down for a full 43 minutes in a row, but this target does account for it being able to endure blips in reliability. Everything has trade-offs, and the company feels good about this target for now.

SLO: Search results

Now that we have general page loads covered, we can talk about a special class of page load: search results. Here again you can make things easier on yourself when you put yourself in your users' shoes and think about what they expect.

Humans have come to expect computers to have to "think." In fact, it is not unheard of for UI designers to *purposely introduce delay* into a task because if things happen too quickly, the human user at the other end of things will assume nothing happened or that there was some kind of problem. Those spinny circles or bars that fill up are sometimes just there for effect. For this reason, you can relax your SLO for search result page loads versus just visiting the front page. The Wiener Shirt-zel Clothing Company did some research and determined it could make the following changes to its search results SLO when compared with the front page load SLO:

- Search results likely *will* take longer than a standard front page load, since the backend service is being asked to perform actual work instead of serving static assets that might already be cached.

- Humans are more accepting of failure, both in terms of error rate and latency, when a service is being asked to perform actual work.

- 4xx response codes can no longer be considered as "good" since this problem would be due to the company's own service and not to a user entering an incorrect URL. Even if there are no results to return, the service should be returning a 200 instead of a 4xx.

Acknowledging the findings of the research, the following SLO was defined:

99.8% of responses to product searches will return a 2xx or 3xx within 4,000 ms.

I could go on and on in this manner and define any number of SLOs for the website itself and how users interact with it, but that would get dry and boring. (For example, a lot of the lessons from Chapter 11 could be applied here—search results don't just need to return good HTTP response codes, they need to contain the correct data.) These two examples should put you well on your way in terms of thinking about what your own customer-facing website might need to do in order to be seen as reliable.

Other Services as Users: Buying Products

Now that we've discussed some aspects of what the external customers need from the company, let's talk a bit more about what services as users need in order to see The Wiener Shirt-zel Clothing Company architecture as reliable.

Response latencies for services that are relied upon by others have to be more strict. The humans loading your website are okay with a few seconds of response time—however, all of the services that are talking to each other in order to make that happen will have to respond to each other much faster. Since the company has SLOs that target end user experience in terms of latency, the latency of the services that back the web app need to be quicker and therefore have more stringent SLOs. A service cannot be faster than those it depends on for data.

For example, if you have a request and response service with an SLI target that requires responses within 2,000 ms, and that's talking to two other services that are vital to it being able to respond correctly, those both can't have a target of 1,000 ms at any percentage. Even if those services often respond much more quickly than 1,000 ms, the math just doesn't work out.

Going back to our architecture diagram, let's focus on microservice A, which acts as a payment gateway by communicating with a payment vendor. This will be a little more interesting than any of the other request and response services in the architecture since it relies on something that is itself an external paid service, instead of just another part of the internal architecture. Figure 12-5 shows the components involved.

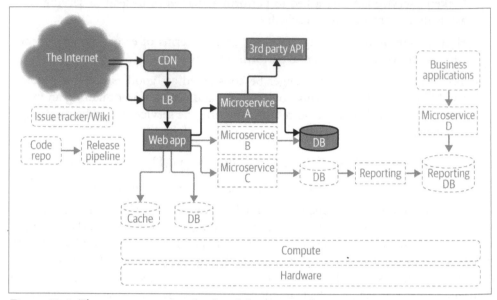

Figure 12-5. The components involved with buying products

The primary reason this service exists is to allow customers to actually check out and pay when they're done shopping. This is almost certainly the most important part of a retail business.

SLO: Checkout success

Checkout success rates for The Wiener Shirt-zel Clothing Company are directly tied to another company. Payment vendors have to be pretty good at successfully responding to their users, for a few reasons. Even if we account for retry logic that could cover some transient failures contained within the "humans are okay with a little extra latency when computers do work" bubble mentioned earlier, customers would quickly move on to another solution if they couldn't make money selling things to *their own customers*.

SLAs are business decisions, and I've mentioned why we don't talk about them much in this book. They require contract language and legal consultation and remuneration techniques and all sorts of other things that are simply out of scope for what this book is about. What is also generally true about them is that they're almost always much simpler than SLOs. Rarely do SLAs involve using percentiles or classifying various response types. They don't even always include any sort of threshold. In contrast to the SLO for the request and response service responsible for serving The Wiener Shirt-zel Clothing Company website's front page, the SLA provided by the vendor in a contract could be as simple as:

99.99% of transaction requests will succeed over any calendar month.

 A lot of vendor services actually define their SLAs depending on your volume of usage and/or how much you're paying. There is a reason many vendors don't have all (or any!) of their SLAs published: because they're often tied to each contract that is signed, with different thresholds and remunerations depending on the specific contract. This is another reason SLAs aren't discussed much in this book, despite being very closely related to SLOs.

This seems reasonably sufficient to account for with retry logic. Unless the vendor is down hard, having to retry 1 in every 10,000 requests should be workable without also severely impacting whatever SLO the clothing company has for checkout attempts. Even so, don't forget about how things can add up quickly. 99.99% is a difficult target to reach.

As always, this is a little easier to think about when using time-based language: 99.99% implies 4 minutes and 22 seconds of hard downtime per 30 days. Let's explore what that means in terms of the SLO that the payment processing microservice itself could have at 99.99%, 99.9%, and 99% percent (see Table 12-1).

Table 12-1. Comparing movable targets to the guaranteed SLA of a vendor

Vendor	Internal service	Result	Events failed	Time failed
99.99%	99.99%	99.98%	2/10,000	8m 45s
99.99%	99.9%	99.89%	21/10,000	48m 12s
99.99%	99%	98.99%	201/1,000	7h 22m 40s

And this goes in both directions, of course. Perhaps the vendor has a target that's lower than four nines. If the payment service can only promise a 99.9% reliability rate and the vendor does the same, you're now dealing with a guarantee of 99.80% reliability, which translates to 20/10,000 events potentially failing or 1h 27m 39s of downtime being considered acceptable every 30 days. From an events perspective, this might still be manageable when using retries—but when thinking about time, approximately an hour and a half when the site is unavailable and customers cannot purchase from the company is probably starting to be a bit much.

And it continues to escalate so quickly! Let's say the vendor can only promise 99% and the microservice can only aim for the same. Now we're at 98.01%, which equates to 299/10,000 requests and 14h 32m 11s of downtime per month. That's likely going to really start being a pain for customers, even with good retry logic.

And this doesn't even account for any other SLO targets, such as that of the database this microservice depends upon, or the front page SLO we defined earlier, or your networking setup, and so forth.

Clearly this is a service that not only needs to be very reliable, but has to set its own targets based on the contract the company signed with the vendor. You can use this kind of math to ensure that everyone knows up front what kind of service they're going to be maintaining and what kind of commitment they're going to have to make in terms of keeping it reliable into the future.

Let's return to our example where the vendor has promised you an SLA of 99.99%. If the company aims toward a goal of 99.99% reliability, and the database that is depended upon has an objective of 99.95%, you're left with an overall user journey percentage of 99.93%. This translates to 7/10,000 events failing, or just about 1 minute of unavailability per day per month. This seems like a number that can easily be accounted for via retries or other logic in other parts of the architecture. So, the SLO for the payment microservice itself reads:

> 99.99% of checkout requests will succeed on their first attempt.

And a further SLO is set for the entire payment workflow that reads:

> 99.93% of checkouts following the entire workflow will succeed on their first attempt.

That number can then be used to build the correct retry logic into the web app to ensure that actual customers of The Wiener Shirt-zel Clothing Company are happy with their day-to-day experience. It could also be used to draw attention to when the different teams responsible for this workflow need to work together to focus on the entire SLI-as-user-journey. Therefore, the following SLO is defined as well:

> 99.99% of checkouts following the entire workflow will succeed within 5 attempts.

You can apply this same sort of thinking in terms of setting SLOs for all your services that depend on other services, whether they be internal or external. Remember to do the math to determine how multiple target percentages impact each other, but also remember that you can use better math (see Chapter 9 to account for this) or retries and other methods to account for how multiple percentages impact each other.

Internal Users

Your internal users—be they other engineers, people on the business side, customer operations, or even your facilities staff—need things from you much in the way that your external, paying customers do. Here we're no longer thinking about other internal services that depend on each other, but the other humans that work at your company: your coworkers!

While it is often true that your coworkers can be more understanding about reliability problems than paying customers might be, this isn't always the case. Unreliable services aimed at internal users can be just as frustrating to people as those your customers rely upon, and it's not unheard of for people to leave their jobs entirely due to frustration with internal tooling not working well.

Let's examine two such services now: one that operates as a desktop application and one that is more of a standalone service. Figure 12-6 shows the components we're focusing on now.

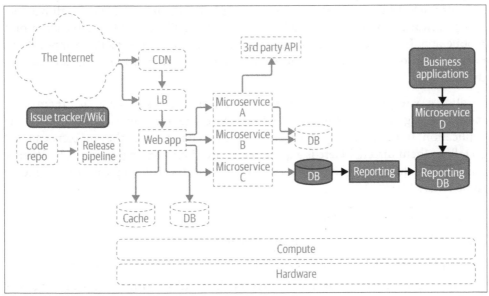

Figure 12-6. The components involved for some internal services

SLO: Business data analysis

One of the neat things The Wiener Shirt-zel Clothing Company does is provide its business and marketing departments with excellent data. Every single user interaction on the site is cataloged in some manner, from what is clicked, to how long is spent on a page, to what clothing options such as size or color are browsed most frequently. Of course, actual purchases are also cataloged, as well the number of "shares" to social media these items receive. This data is all sent from the web app to a database, where occasional batch jobs run to pass the data through a processing pipeline, with the resulting output data stored in a second database. A custom desktop application has been written allowing for various internal departments to interact with the analysis via a microservice that acts as an API in front of the results database.

This chapter won't be covering what an SLO for the processing pipeline itself might look like, since that's covered very well in Chapter 11. Instead, it would be more useful to talk about what SLOs for the application that lets humans interact with the resulting data might look like, since that's a rarely covered topic.

Almost without fail so far in this book (and elsewhere!), example services for SLO-based approaches revolve around response and request APIs. After that, you might see people discuss SLOs for things like databases and platforms, and even more rarely for data itself. What you essentially never see anyone discuss are SLOs for things that *aren't* network services, but instead act as something like a desktop application or a mobile app. Here, we're not concerned with the SLOs for the APIs these applications need to talk to in order to get their data (if they do that at all), but the applications themselves.

As always, you just need to put yourself into your users' shoes and ask them what they need. A good exercise in order to do this is to imagine yourself actually using the application. In this case the users are coworkers, so engineers at the company can just go talk to them directly! Here is a quick list of user journeys engineers at The Wiener Shirt-zel Clothing Company discovered via interviews that they can use to inform some SLIs:

1. Application needs to start

2. Application needs to not crash and remain running

3. Application needs to be able to deliver queries for customer interaction data

4. Application needs to be able to present the results of the queries in a manner human operators can understand

5. Application needs to be able to export this data for sharing or inclusion in documents and presentations

We could go much deeper, but that's a great start in terms of describing some things that the users of this internal application need it to do. Let's now dive a little more deeply into what #5 might look like to a user.

An internal user in the marketing department at The Wiener Shirt-zel Clothing Company is curious about what particular shirt patterns have recently been viewed often or for lengthy periods of time, but haven't actually been purchased very often. Familiar with the use of their internal application, they key in the appropriate query and wait for a result. Processing sometimes takes upwards of 20 seconds, but that's fine. That's how this system has always worked, and it's not really a detriment to the business. Not everything has to be lightning fast, and that should be remembered when you're thinking about SLOs.

But what *does* matter is whether the application is able to export the data once the user has it. Measuring this might seem a little tricky, but it's not all that different from how you'd measure any other sort of event-driven process. Let's say that the user should be able to click a button to save the results of their analysis to a file on local storage. Any reasonable piece of software that performs this sort of task likely has the capability to log about each step of the way. First the click is registered, then a routine is called to perform the export, and so on. You can collect metrics on each of these steps and use these metrics to inform an SLO.

If this feels pretty different from everything else we've talked about in this book, that's because it is. Log lines are not a great source for SLOs that help you understand high-performance web services. They are easily delayed, they are computationally expensive to parse, they require a lot of storage if you need to analyze them over lengthy periods of time, etc. However, that doesn't mean you *can't* use them in the right scenario. And using them to analyze the performance of a feature of an application that might only be used a few times per day (and not at all on some days!) seems like a totally reasonable choice.

 Remember, SLOs are about thinking about your users—and those users are not always millions of people on the internet. Sometimes they're three people in a marketing department. Maybe you can't gather enough data in this sort of scenario to ever properly develop alerting or even power an actual error budget, but you can use the *concepts* behind SLO-based approaches to reliability to tell you where and when you need to focus your work on improvements.

You might only have a few data points per day in this sort of situation, but you can still use that to drive discussions and decision making. You probably don't want to be alerting off of this data, and even a dashboard is likely overkill, but if you can identify an SLI that tells you whether things are working for customers or not, you can use it to pick an SLO target that tells you when you need to look at something. It's certainly an improvement over doing nothing, which could result in the marketing department having to constantly interrupt the engineering team to ask them why things aren't working.

For example, at The Wiener Shirt-zel Clothing Company, 95% of exports were working on the first attempt last month, but this month that dropped to 80%. Perhaps a bug introduced a regression into the code, or the users have changed their habits in a way that needs to be addressed; any number of things could be responsible. Even with just a few data points per day, the team responsible for this service is able to define the following SLO:

> 90% of data export attempts log a success over the course of a month.

This is simple, it's unambiguous, and it doesn't require anything more than a report produced once per month—but it forces the team to measure things and lets them think about their users and have better data about how to plan future work. Is the export feature still working, even if it's only used by one small marketing team? Suppose after a month the measurement says that 91% of exports completed correctly, but the marketing team is still upset. The target could be moved to 92% as a next step, since all SLOs need to be open to evolving—and it will continue to evolve with feedback from the users.

SLO-based approaches give you a way to find out whether users are happy or not, even if this example doesn't fit all of the traditional trappings of the general discussions about SLOs. Always remember that it's the philosophies behind these approaches that are the most important, not having the slickest technology to use to perform complicated math against statistically derived SLIs.

SLO: Internal wiki

Another great example of the kind of service that is often overlooked when discussing SLO-based approaches to reliability is pieces of third-party or open source software—especially those that stand alone and might be managed by IT teams that are unfortunately often left out of the discussions that surround software or systems engineering. They're services all the same, they have users, and those users need them to perform at certain levels!

It's always a great idea to try to ensure that your SLIs are as close to what your users need from you as possible—this is an idea that has been repeated over and over again. But we've also tried to be reasonable in terms of what data you have to work with. A service for which you don't control the codebase is a great example of where you might want to fall back on something simpler while still getting the job done well enough.

Well-known pieces of open source software are often fairly well written and tested. When problems arise, they sometimes have hundreds of developers involved and ready to respond to a bug or push out a fix. This sort of community is at the heart of what makes open source software beautiful. Some open source software is infinitely tunable and configurable. A lot of the more popular database options, for example, have so many layers of additional caching and tooling and replication orchestrators that surround them that you can have an entirely separate part of your architecture that's as complicated as the sum of the rest of your setup. This means you have many things to think about and measure, and therefore likely have many potential SLI candidates.

For the internal wiki documentation setup, the measurement options available to the team running it are a bit limited. And here is a great example of a place where something like "Is it up?" is probably sufficient for everyone! Not everything has to be complicated. An example SLO for the team responsible for the internal wiki in this case reads:

> The internal documentation wiki will be available to users 99.9% of the time during working hours.

Working hours at The Wiener Shirt-zel Clothing Company are defined as 08:00–18:00 ET. An SLO like this allows for the team responsible for it to experiment or perform upgrades or other work whenever they'd like outside of normal working hours.

Platforms as Services

The final part of The Wiener Shirt-zel Clothing Company architecture (shown in Figure 12-7) that we'll examine is one of the platforms everything else at the company relies upon. Because they're at the bottom of the dependency chain, these services need to be the absolute most reliable of all.

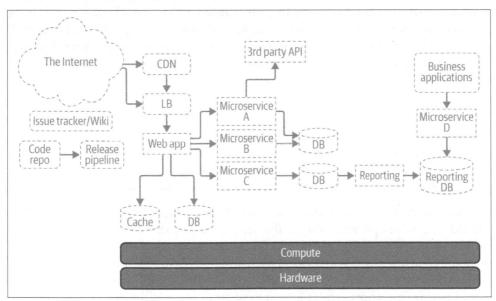

Figure 12-7. The components acting as platforms

Container platforms are a common way to make it easy[1] to manage, deploy, and scale services. Because The Wiener Shirt-zel Clothing Company is not entirely

---

1 Well, as easy as anything with computers ever turns out to be.

homogeneous, like most companies, some components (like the wiki and the release pipeline) run on VMs, but all of the microservices and the web app run on this platform. Because of this, the reliability of the container platform is incredibly important!

The way most container platforms are intended to work makes them a particularly interesting candidate for measuring via an SLO-based approach. I'll very briefly outline at a very high level how everything works in order to explain why this is.

The primary working unit is known as a *pod*, which is a grouping of containers (or sometimes just one) that is managed as a single object and guaranteed to run on the same host. The reason this is important to call out is because if you have a replicated service, you'll have more than one pod—in some cases, hundreds. These individual pods, while all being part of the same service, can run on many different hosts. This helps with the reliability of a service, because if there is a problem on a single host and the pod (or pods) running there subsequently experience problems, your service as a whole shouldn't go down, and will hopefully only be degraded at worst.

But the real twist is that pods are *intended to be ephemeral*; that is to say, they're not all guaranteed to exist at any point in time. When building services on top of container platforms, you should be building them in a manner that can afford for pods to be restarted and moved from host to host as needed so the entire platform cluster itself can ensure load is distributed, so that *it* can *also* remain reliable. Here you might start to pick up why it can be an interesting challenge to develop user journey–based SLIs for the users of such a platform.

SLO: Container platform

For example, since pods are intended to sometimes not be available, measuring total pod uptime doesn't give the company a great data point, even if at first glance that would seem like a thing users would care about. When something is a platform, you can't just measure the health of the platform itself; you need to keep users in mind.

A better SLI might be something that talks about having a certain percentage of an individual service's pods running at the same time, but that can run into additional problems. If you say that 90% of pods for a certain service should be available, how do you handle the fact that you can't have partial pods? You can't round up, since, for example, 90% of 7 is 6.3, which rounded up would just be 7 again. So instead you round down. This works, but it's just an example of some of the extra calculation you have to do in this situation.

However, this also now means that you are aiming for all services with fewer than 20 pods to never have more than a single pod unavailable at a time. This probably makes sense for services that have, say, 10 or fewer pods, but it may be stricter than necessary for services with closer to 20 pods. For example, The Wiener Shirt-zel Clothing Company has 200 pods running the primary web app, but only 19 handling communication to the payments vendors. Perhaps those smaller services should never have more than one missing pod at a time. But it could also seem reasonable that a service with 19 pods should be able to handle only 17 being available at a time. This is a great example where the company decided it needed multiple SLOs powered by a single SLI measurement, as follows:

> For services with 20 or more pods, at least 90% of their pods will be available 99.9% of the time.

> For services with 10–19 pods, no fewer than 2 of their configured number will be unavailable 99.9% of the time.

> For services with fewer than 10 pods, no fewer than 1 of their configured number will be unavailable 99.9% of the time.

As you can see, this allows you to set a reasonable SLO target percentage like 99.9% while allowing the services that are dependent on yours to set even higher targets. Introducing multiple constraints to your target can make your SLOs much more meaningful without you having to resort to a ridiculous number of nines in a row.

Other great ideas for something that acts as a platform include thinking about things like pod startup time or eviction rate.

Summary

A lot of this book has been abstract, since SLO-based approaches are mostly philosophical. You might use a lot of math and numbers to help you gather data, but it's ultimately about using this data to engage humans to make decisions. Have we been reliable enough? Are our users happy? Are our engineers happy? Are our measurements correct?

A lot of this book has also been very technical, since you need the most correct numbers you can get in order to provide you with the best data. How can we measure this better? What does probability tell us about whether this makes sense or not? What math can we use to ensure we're only alerting on a problem when we really need to?

In this chapter, I've tried to be as practical as possible. By examining an example company with an example architecture, I've hoped to bring some of these concepts into a new light. I didn't cover every facet possible, but doing so would be infeasible. Complex systems are unique, and if I'd tried to address every single component that our example company should be measuring and setting targets for, you'd have just ended up with an endless and dry chapter.

But hopefully between the examples in chapters elsewhere in this book and this one, you've been able to spot one that at least *kind of* looks like your service. Hopefully there is a bit of a template there. And if not, remember that it's really the philosophies that matter most, and not the exact implementation. I'm sure you'll do great at finding your own approaches to figuring out how to turn your user journeys into SLIs and SLOs.

SLO Culture

CHAPTER 13

Building an SLO Culture

Harold Treen

This book so far has explained the importance of SLOs, how to implement them, and even how to get various departments on board with them. If you're an engineering team of one, that might be enough for you to go and start making the world a more reliable place. For the rest of us, there's more work to be done.

It's one thing to understand and live by these principles yourself, but it's another to spread these ideas throughout your organization and get others working alongside you. That means having a team interested in using error budgets and having discussions about implementing feature freezes, and it means being able to rely on the systems managed by external teams. SLOs are most powerful when everyone is following the process and invested in building reliable systems. It will be easier to iterate on your systems and improve their reliability if the systems they depend on are doing the same. If you are working alone, it's going to be a continual battle of priorities.

This can be one of the most difficult challenges in getting SLOs off the ground. Adding measurements, monitoring, and alerts can sometimes be done in a couple of days, but changing how your organization works takes more than a package install and configuration files. Luckily, you're not the first to venture out on this journey.

While Chapter 6 discussed how to convince your organization to adopt an SLO-based approach, this chapter aims to guide you through the actual motions and steps of building an SLO culture within your team and beyond.

A Culture of No SLOs

Alerts are going off. Something about a job failing? You stop working to look into it, but it seems like the job retried and succeeded. Back to work. Another alert fires for a different job. Probably just a flaky database connection. You ignore it. Two hours later a customer is complaining that your service isn't returning any data. Hasn't been for a while. They've been asking around to figure out why and finally found your team. You look into it, and find that a job failed and never got restarted. You run it again and tell your customer to check back in an hour. They confirm the problem is fixed. You go back to cranking out your feature work.

We often don't know when our services are working or broken. Alerts are in place, but it's unclear if they are firing unnecessarily or catching major issues. Responsiveness is a function of how quickly customers complain. Our systems can't be trusted and we instead expend our energy trying to make sense of them all. The time used not fighting fires is spent building unreliable features as quickly as possible, which inevitably just furthers our users' frustrations.

Or, maybe a different scenario: our system works great. Test coverage is maintained at 100% and all changes are rigorously tested by QA teams over the course of multiple days. An engineer is on call and available at all times: middle of the night, weekends, holidays. All alerts are triaged and resolved within minutes. Extra time is taken to ensure changes are made with zero downtime. It's an expensive operation to maintain —but users have never complained about outages. However, they do wonder why simple tweaks and changes take weeks to get out the door. We pour energy into keeping our systems perfect. We delay features until they are flawless. Failure is not an option, and we pay heavily to live by that standard.

There is a balance at play between shipping new features and supporting existing features. The two preceding examples are extreme, but they highlight the issue with investing all your energy into one or the other. If we don't invest in reliability, our systems break down and we lose our users. If we overinvest in reliability, we never make progress in developing the features our users need. SLOs are a gauge for balancing these opposing priorities. A culture of SLOs helps us become more intentional in how we strike that balance.

Maybe you aren't at either extreme, but no matter where you are, SLOs are essential to finding that balance. Creating a culture of SLOs will help you pinpoint where you are on the spectrum and be more intentional about where you end up. SLOs are data to help your team set more meaningful goals.

So, where do we start?

Strategies for Shifting Culture

It might be tempting to think that getting your teams to adopt SLOs will simply involve showing up at a team meeting and saying, "Let's develop SLOs!" At which point everyone will return to their desks and perfectly instrument their services in a day. If that approach works for you—congrats!

More likely, however, it will involve tons of conversations and pushing through friction as you rewire your team to take an SLO-based approach. Here are some things to keep in mind as you are going through this process:

Start small

> If this is new for your team, it doesn't make sense to try and change everything overnight. Success isn't measuring every corner of your system, achieving 99.99% availability, and having weekly outage simulations. Generally it's best to bring these practices to your team gradually. Start with a single SLO set to whatever your current level of reliability is, and work your way up to multiple SLOs trending toward the desired level of reliability.

Be patient

> It may take a while for SLOs to catch on. Don't be discouraged if change doesn't happen overnight. Continue discussing these tools and concepts with your team, experimenting with ideas, and trending toward better monitoring and reliability agreements. Look for small wins as you go through this process. Those might be verbal commitments to prioritize SLOs, receiving time to work on SLOs, a colleague asking a question about SLIs, a month of SLI data getting collected, or a meeting with stakeholders to agree on reliability standards. There are lots of small steps that will happen along the way. Use those steps as motivation to carry on as opposed to getting discouraged by how much there is left to go. This book has *a lot* of information in it, and it might feel like you aren't succeeding until it's all been implemented. That isn't the case.

Engage with your team

> At the end of the day, SLOs are there to help your team—engaging with them throughout the process is how you'll be able to ensure you're creating a process that everyone is on board with. It might not be intuitive at first how these practices will help your team ("We won't be able to ship anything when we exceed our error budget?!"), but go back to the agreed principles and work from there. At the end of the day, this is about making users and developers happy—so keep working together to get to that place.

Reflect as you go

> The whole reason to adopt an SLO-based approach is to get you to a place where you and your users are happy with the reliability of your application. So, continually reflect on where you are and what you can do to get to that final state. Think about whether the changes you're making are getting you closer to that goal. Don't have any monitoring? Add some so you can see how your system is behaving. Notice that a feature is frequently broken but nobody cares? Maybe that's a sign it's no longer needed.

With that aside, let's break down what paving the way to a culture of SLOs looks like.

Path to a Culture of SLOs

Maybe you'll bring these principles to your team and everyone will be on board right away. More likely, these ideas are going to seem counterintuitive to some, or people will agree in principle but push back when it comes time to actually prioritize the work. Here's a high-level overview of the work required to move your team toward an SLO approach:

1. *Get buy-in.*
   Communicate how SLOs work and get everyone in agreement that they provide value.

2. *Prioritize SLO work.*
   Get the work on your roadmap, assign it to one or more people, and make it a priority.

3. *Implement your SLOs.*
   Decide what SLIs to track, how to monitor them, and what level of reliability you want to provide, and learn how you're performing against those targets.

4. *Use your SLOs.*
   Decide as a team how to alert on your SLOs, how to use your error budget, and how to inform work using your SLOs.

5. *Iterate on your SLOs.*
   Discuss what is and isn't working, add/remove/adjust your SLIs/SLOs, and continually revisit your SLOs to check that they reflect your stakeholders' needs.

6. *Advocate for others to use SLOs.*
   Use what you've learned to educate others about the benefits of SLOs.

Let's talk about each of these steps in a little more detail, and how they move you toward making SLOs a part of your culture.

Getting Buy-in

Before anything can happen, people need to be in agreement about the value of SLOs. If your team doesn't value reliability, it's going to be hard for you to justify creating SLOs. Sure, you can go rogue and start trying to change things on the side, but what's the point if people aren't going to want it?

How much buy-in you need to get will depend on your situation. If you're on a pretty autonomous team that gets to pick and choose its priorities, maybe just getting your team on board will be enough. If you're working on a project with more stakeholders and dependencies, there are likely going to be more people to convince before everyone is in agreement about the importance of SLO-based approaches (QA, engineers, executives, and so on).

Note that getting buy-in doesn't mean everyone is now brainstorming SLIs and signing up to do the work—it just means they agree SLOs should be a priority and would be happy to see someone do that work. Chapter 6 is all about getting buy-in, so if you're feeling uncertain about who the stakeholders might be and how to convey the importance of SLOs to them, go take a look there for an in-depth explanation. For the purposes of this chapter, I'll just mention it as a critical step in the SLO culture–building process.

Prioritizing SLO Work

You've achieved consensus that reliability is your most important feature and that SLOs will help you build reliable systems. People seem to be on board, but when you arrive at your next planning meeting the feature work is once again at center stage and nobody is talking about reliability.

This brings us to the next stage of the process: prioritization. Many will agree that SLOs sound like a good idea, but when faced with what to work on next they'll revert back to whatever the previous priorities were. Shifting the culture means catching these moments of relapse and getting in the practice of reasserting the importance of SLOs.

Once you have buy-in, look for an opportunity to make the work a priority. If you have a major launch in a week maybe that won't be *today*, but eventually it needs to happen. It's also important to decide who will be responsible for this work. Without accountability it can be easy for people to go back to whatever work was previously their priority. When it comes to *who* does the work, there are generally two scenarios.

Do it yourself

The easiest way to make something a priority is to make it *your* priority. Offer to do the work necessary to get an SLO defined for your service. Explain to your team why it is important to you:

- Our customers are complaining, and I think it's important we show progress toward making the system more reliable. SLOs will help ensure we do that.
- I've wasted three hours this week responding to false alarms. I want to work on SLOs so I can be confident in our alerts and respond to issues more efficiently.

It's difficult to argue what's right for every member of the team, but if you're able to frame the importance of SLOs in terms of your own values it becomes a lot harder to brush your argument aside:

> **Team member:** I agree SLOs are important, but don't we want to get these bug fixes out?
>
> **You:** Do we know how often these bugs cause issues? I haven't heard any complaints about them. It's not clear to me that these issues are important because we don't have any data on how they impact our users. I think it makes more sense to have an SLO for the feature so we can learn about the bugs that are having the biggest impact on our users and address those.

Figure out how SLOs will be a benefit compared to your team's competing interests, and communicate that. Unless there's a hard deadline for something else approaching, you should be able to make the case that SLOs are overdue.

Having read this book, you will likely be the most knowledgeable on the subject and the most driven to make the move to an SLO culture. Leading by example and making the work your priority will signal to others that you're committed to making this change. Working on the initial SLOs will also create a baseline for others to refer to when taking on SLO work in the future. Going through the process yourself will help you understand more of the intricacies of SLOs and make you a better advocate for SLO culture down the road.

Assign it

Maybe you're not involved with day-to-day development, and implementing SLOs is not aligned with your responsibilities. In that case, you'll need to assign the work.

Ideally, your buy-in conversations will have helped you identify a person who might be a good fit for this job. If people have bought in they've agreed this is important work, so it shouldn't be a big jump to convince them it's important enough for them to work on. Communicate the importance of this work and how it's going to improve things for the both of you.

Document the work that needs to get done and make someone responsible for completing it. Depending on your process, that might mean any number of things: creating tickets with detailed descriptions of the work that needs to get done, pulling the tasks into your sprint, adding SLOs to your OKRs or roadmap. Whatever it may be, make this work visible as part of your process, and find someone to be responsible for it.

Once someone has agreed to do the work, be available to coach them and support them along the way. If someone is new to SLO work, they may get stuck or confused and be tempted to switch back to picking up feature work. Make sure the SLO work is encouraged and supported. Creating an environment where people feel motivated and equipped to work on SLOs is the goal. That is a much bigger step toward creating a culture of SLOs than any single SLO being completed.

Implementing Your SLO

Your team is excited about SLOs, and the time has been set aside to define one. It's time to get it done.

This book is full of information on how to implement SLOs, but for the purposes of this chapter I'll just mention what I consider to be an ideal start for an initial SLO. Your first SLO is going to be important in a few respects. First, it demonstrates to your team the benefits of SLOs: improved prioritization, clearer agreements on feature versus reliability work, time to work on system stability, etc. Second, it materializes what an SLO is and provides a concrete example of how to implement them. As mentioned before, it's usually a good idea to start with something simple so you have something digestible to point to as an example for others.

The cost of those benefits is additional work to reach consensus on what you should be aiming for. Your initial SLO will likely involve the following:

- Create an SLO document.
- Debate on what is most important to measure.
- Debate on the best SLIs to measure with.
- Implementing monitoring and tracking SLIs.
- Debate on your SLO target.

Start with a document

Chapter 15 talks about the concept of an SLO document. This is a great place to start your SLO implementation process. A document will allow you to identify stakeholders and reviewers for your SLO and get everyone referring to a single source of truth.

This document will formally specify a list of approvers and stakeholders who will sign off when they are satisfied with your SLO. You will find a template for the SLO document in Appendix A.

What is important to measure?

As described throughout Part I of this book, your users decide what "reliable" means for your service. When deciding what to measure, think about what your users care about most and where your service is failing to meet those expectations. Focusing on these areas will strengthen your SLO—it's hard to debate the importance of something that your users are currently complaining about.

- Is your service too slow? Does it produce incorrect data? Does it frequently crash? Is it inconsistently available?
- What parts of their experience are your users the least satisfied with?

Based on the answers to those questions, you might choose an SLO around latency, or data quality, or error rates, or availability.

Or maybe you're on the flip side—your service works great, but you want more room to experiment and experience failure.

Where does it feel like you are exerting excess effort? Are you trying to launch all features with zero downtime? Are you feeling pressured to respond to and resolve all errors with no delay? Are you trying to avoid bugs at all costs by having all features go through a rigorous manual verification process?

Where would it be nice to have more flexibility?

Based on those answers you might choose an SLO around availability or error rates.

Put yourself in the shoes of your users and come up with a proposal for your team based on your findings.

What Will Your SLIs Be?

Knowing that most of your user complaints are around latency or error rates is great, but it's time to get more specific.

Is there a certain feature that has a lot of errors? How do you detect an error? What does "slow" mean to your users?

Narrowing down on these things will help you understand what parts of your service need to be instrumented to measure the error rate or latency. Maybe you add a middleware to your API that increments a counter every time there's a 500 response. Maybe you add timers to your code that measure the time certain functionality takes. Maybe you query your database to see how long jobs for the past week took and continually report that statistic.

Whatever it is, you need to think of a way to develop meaningful SLIs that capture the problem. If you don't have much infrastructure in place for monitoring, the task of tracking this data and making it easily exposed might seem like a burden. It doesn't need to be fancy, though—start with command-line tools and manual querying if that will get things off the ground. Build a little application that uses your business-critical APIs and measures the time they take. Get creative.

Once you've determined the data you can expose and how to combine it into an SLI, add that to your document. At this point it can be good to check with your team and your users to see if your plans for the SLO and SLI are correct.

What Will Your SLOs Be?

It might be tempting to get into a philosophical debate about the true needs of your users and the ideal SLO. The problem with that is that you may be setting your sights too high and end up failing in the end. If your team hasn't thought too much about reliability until now, a simple solution is to just measure your service for a couple of weeks and determine your SLO based on whatever you see as the current level of reliability. Sometimes maintaining a consistent level of reliability can be a challenge, so starting with some realistic baseline and sticking to that can be your first step.

You can also think of tiered SLOs. Maybe your application is only needed during the work week, and won't be used on the weekends. That could allow you to say that you only want to be 10% available on the weekends, but 95% reliable during the week. The world is your oyster.

It can also be helpful to think of your unavailability in the context of a time range. A day of downtime each week is very different from a day of downtime each month. That time also feels very different when considered as a single incident as opposed to 24 hour-long incidents.

Whatever you choose, make sure it's something your team is willing to stick to. Commit to it. Monitor how your SLO performs, ship features when you have excess error budget, and seek out needed reliability work when your error budget is exhausted. If you select an SLO and then everyone shrugs when it's violated, that could be an indication that your team hasn't fully bought into the process or your SLO is wrong. If alerts are going off and being ignored, it might mean that people don't really care. When you are interested in having your team adopt SLOs, it might be tempting to think that alerts being ignored is a sign of them not being bought-in enough. In reality, it probably means that your SLO is more stringent than they care about.

Using Your SLO

You've outlined your SLO, had it approved, and implemented all the technical details. It's time to put it to use!

Now that you've agreed on what the reliability target is, there are a few more things to agree upon with your team:

- How should the SLO tie into alerting?
- What do you want to do when you run out of error budget?
- What will you do with your additional error budget?

All of these things will need to be decided on through a conversation with your team, but there are many best practices described in this book that you can bring to the table. Be willing to advocate for the best practices while also being open minded about the concerns of your team. It's better to have everyone following a less-than-optimal strategy than to be following the "best practices" all on your own.

Alerting

Given that you now have a metric that correlates to the happiness of your users, it makes sense to raise alerts based on that. In the beginning, you may want to be conservative with your alerting. Many find alerts distracting and lose trust when alerts fire when they shouldn't. Since you're in the middle of experimenting and have limited goodwill to spare, alert when things seem legitimately concerning. If this ever results in issues being detected too late, use that as justification to adjust your alerts to better catch rapid burn-through of your error budget.

Because your SLIs map to a user's experience, you should find these alerts to be better at detecting real issues than other alerts you had in place in the past. Eventually you may be able to disable those other alerts and get a better pulse on the health of your system.

Give alerts time and attention. If alerts are going off when they shouldn't, debug the issue. Figure out ways to make metrics less noisy and systems more stable. SLOs should protect you from being bombarded by alerts, not create more noise.

There's lots more that can be said about SLO monitoring and alerting. Chapter 8 covers this topic in depth.

Exhausting your error budget

If you've developed your SLO correctly, you've defined clearly what is expected by your users. Breaking those expectations too often will wear on your users' trust, so exhausting your error budget warrants a response. Ideally this will be a team effort, and all engineers will be accountable for keeping services up and running. If only one person is in charge of maintenance, it doesn't incentivize others to take reliability seriously.

What happens when you exhaust your error budget right before a feature deadline? Talk about such situations and how to make the necessary trade-offs. Perhaps you have a "thaw tax" that requires additional time be spent on reliability after the launch, as discussed in Chapter 6. Perhaps the response will vary based on the severity of the issue. Maybe small error budget overages can be overlooked, but severe outages require work on reliability to be completed before any further feature work can happen. Remember that it's always the discussions that matter most.

That being said, exhausting your well-defined error budget should usually trigger some type of shift to reliability work. Use those moments to start a discussion about what is wrong and what can be done to address it. You should take as much time as needed to fix issues and improve the system until your error budget surplus returns. If you have multiple services it might also make sense to refrain from feature work across all of them until things return to a level of reliability the team is comfortable with.

If you find your applications are breaking SLOs and there's a lack of urgency to repair the situation, it might be a sign that you need to make some adjustments. Perhaps you aren't measuring the right things, and your SLIs need to change. Perhaps there needs to be a conversation with the team about how the SLO process is working to ensure people are still on board. Perhaps your SLO is higher than users really care about. For whatever reason, that level of reliability isn't important to the team or to your users, so it's best to adjust to remain more realistic about what you want to maintain.

Using surplus error budget

Your team is amazing, and you never break your SLOs—great! What do you want to do with that excess budget?

Maybe there's a large migration that would be much easier if all systems went down. Maybe you want to do chaos testing and introduce random errors to see what happens. Maybe you want to try a new implementation of an algorithm. There are all sorts of options!

Using up your excess error budget is the fun part of SLOs. It's a rare thing to have permission to fail. Lots of things become easier when you're able to accept a certain level of failure. That big risky change that might break everything? Ship it! You can learn so much from pushing things straight to production.

If the thought of doing this scares you, that might be another opportunity to use your error budget. Spend it developing infrastructure to quickly roll back broken changes, or experiment with shipping bugs to see how well you're protecting against failure. Practice recovering from controlled failures so you are better prepared for real outages.

Iterating on Your SLO

Chapter 14 covers how to iterate on your SLO in great detail, but here are some starting points.

SLOs are a process, not a project. As such, your first SLO is likely not going to be great. It will be way too ambitious, not ambitious enough, or not what customers want. You'll realize your SLIs are poorly implemented and incorrect. Your monitoring hasn't been correctly configured, and you aren't collecting the data you thought you would. A dependency goes down all the time, and you aren't in control.

All sorts of things can go wrong. But that's okay! We're allowed to fail.

Decide with your team a cadence for reevaluating your SLO. Take turns reexamining it so that everyone gets exposure to working with the SLO. At the start this should be done at least once a month, with longer gaps as you gain more confidence in your SLO.

When reevaluating your SLO, look at things holistically:

- Are your SLIs correctly identifying issues?
- Is your monitoring correctly reporting the state of your system?
- Is your SLO actually aligned to what your customers care about?
- Is the SLO giving your team more confidence in the system or becoming a distraction?

There are all sorts of things to think about.

Iterate on your practices, too. Are people happy with the alerts? Does it feel like reliability is being worked on when it's needed? Is this process helping you or becoming dogmatic? Are you finding you can ship features faster? Are these metrics useful?

Your goal is to build a culture of SLOs, not build out SLOs. If something is not working, it's worth taking a pause to figure out why. Steamrolling concerns will go nowhere in getting people on board with SLOs.

Don't think that you'll be able to book off a week, knock out some SLOs, and call it a day. Solid SLOs are built from continual iteration and evolution with the service you're building. As such, don't get hung up on making things perfect. At the start, cut some corners and make risky bets if need be. You can always patch things up down the road if they aren't working.

Determining When Your SLOs Are Good Enough

At what point do you stop? What is good enough?

As we've said before, your SLOs are not a project, so they'll never be "good enough." That being said, SLOs should eventually get you to the point where your service is just reliable enough to make your users happy. You should be able to detect issues before floods of users come complaining to you. You should have enough error budget that features can be deployed without overthinking every potential consequence. You should be able to do fun and interesting experiments with your error budget. You should be able to develop systems that expect and manage failure. You should have systems that self-heal and are easy to roll back. You should end up with a system that is reliable.

Chapter 14 is a deep dive on SLO evolution and will cover these topics in more depth.

Advocating for Others to Use SLOs

After you've established an SLO for one service, you'll have more solid footing for applying these concepts elsewhere.

Maybe your SLO will help identify poor reliability of a downstream dependency that's impacting your ability to meet your goals. Advocate for that service to implement an SLO so that you can provide better service to your users.

Maybe your SLO will reduce the number of alerts your team needs to respond to. Look at your other projects generating endless alerts and see where these learnings could be applied there.

Maybe your SLO has helped you realize you can ship much faster than you have been. Look at which projects you're nervous to deploy and see if SLOs can help increase your velocity.

Maybe your SLO has increased team satisfaction—people are happier not getting paged for every issue. See if any other projects despised by the team could use a more realistic set of expectations.

Or maybe the effects will be something else entirely. Whatever the results might be, look for ways to communicate that value and get others on board.

Some of these things can seem like bold statements to make. Who are you to say that everybody on your team is better off after implementing SLOs? In those cases, talk about your own experience. Do you feel more confident in your projects and happier with what you're working on? Do you think there are better things to be done?

A great way to keep SLOs top of mind is to build the conversation into your team dynamics. Schedule some time in your weekly meetings to discuss the state of various SLOs. Ask others how their services are striving to be more reliable and hold them accountable for making reliability a first-class citizen in their applications.

Making the shift to SLOs starts on your team, but there's no need to stop there. Chapter 16 talks more deeply about how to shift this conversation from your team to your organization at large.

Summary

In this chapter we discussed the importance of building a culture of reliability. Reliability is the number-one feature of your service and not worth leaving to chance. Creating a culture of reliability is about being intentional about what reliability means for your team and efficiently delivering that to your users.

The math and theory behind SLOs are thoroughly discussed in the rest of this book; here we focused on the conversations required to get SLOs prioritized and make them part of your team's process. We discussed getting buy-in from the team, assigning the work to implement SLIs, deciding on targets for SLOs, using your SLOs, iterating on your SLOs, and finally spreading the SLO culture beyond a single team/project. Hopefully this has made clearer the challenges you'll need to overcome as you shift to an SLO process and the ways to respond to roadblocks as they arise. Although SLIs and monitoring can be added to a service with a bit of code, reprogramming how your team thinks about reliability will likely be a larger endeavor.

This chapter should also remind you that at the end of the day, SLOs are about people. Creating a culture of SLOs is about making your users and your team happier. The process has been validated; your job is to figure out how to make this process fit in with your existing team dynamics. Should you encounter resistance, listen to your stakeholders until you can figure out a way forward that works for everyone.

SLOs are a process, not a project. They won't stick overnight, but hopefully the content in this chapter has given you a better sense of how to circle back and iterate on these approaches until things begin to click.

SLO Evolution

Alex Hidalgo

Service level objectives work best when you're willing to let them change and grow as your service does. The reality is that your service will change over time, be it in terms of increased or decreased use, changes in the performance of your dependencies, the retirement of old hardware/introduction of new hardware, or shifting expectations of behavior from your users. When these things change, your SLOs should change with them.

Additionally, even if there are no drastic shifts, you're not always going to be able to pick the correct targets—especially when you're first starting out. Until you've been analyzing your measurements for some time, you can't be entirely certain that the targets you've set for yourself are reasonable.

Finally, you can use aspirational SLOs when you know that your service is in a bad state and that your users are unhappy. Use SLOs to drive change! In these cases, you should be using the immediate error budget burn as a signal to your team and others that reliability work needs to be a focus. As you improve the reliability of your systems, you can make these targets more stringent in an iterative manner.

Revisiting your SLO definitions may sound like a simple process, but there is quite a lot to consider in order to do so in the most effective manner. There are many reasons why SLOs might have to change, and some of those reasons can't be predicted. The discussions that surround the process of changing your SLO targets are some of the most important aspects of how the entire philosophy works—don't shy away from these. This chapter attempts to outline some of the most common situations you'll run into, and that should allow you to better anticipate having to revisit your SLOs.

Throughout this chapter we'll mostly be discussing how and when to update or change your SLOs. Please note that I mean this in the holistic and general sense that encompasses all parts of an SLO-based approach. You should be thinking about how and when to change your SLI measurements, your SLO targets, *and* the time windows for your error budgets throughout the chapter.

SLO Genesis

If you're just starting your SLO journey, you're not always going to get things right on the first try. In fact, it's quite rare that you'll pick the exact right target the first time around. This is often because you don't have enough historical data to know that your decision is the right one, but also just because in many modern complex computer systems changes are constantly being made. What is true on day one may not be true on day two—or even hour to hour, or minute to minute.

The First Pass

While it's recommended to establish an SLI measurement and collect that data for a while so you can analyze things before picking your first SLO, there is no reason you can't just take a stab in the dark and rely on your intuition or some basic math to get started. SLOs are not SLAs, so by definition there is no legal impediment to change: they can change when they need to. This is not to say they *should* always be in a state of change, but that they *can* change without breaking a contract if they have reason to.

If you've just developed and implemented your SLI measurement and want to immediately start off with a first-pass SLO target, go for it. Just know that this kind of first-attempt SLO is one that will likely have to be updated once you've actually been measuring things for a while. Get ready to monitor your SLO status closely when choosing a target without a lengthy measurement history, and be prepared to make changes to it on short order and frequently.

Listening to Users

The most important thing you can do if you want to measure things from your users' perspective is to listen to them. This is often easier said than done. Not everyone has the tooling or knowledge to do this in the best possible way.

This is not a domain where we can stand on a stage like Steve Jobs and declare that we know what's best for the users, irrespective of what they say. (For one thing, an SLO often operates in the context of a continuous economic interaction between a service and a customer set, not a one-time transaction.) It is of course perfectly possible that your users will tell you unhelpful things like "This needs to be available all the time," but there are techniques for peeking behind the more superficial response there and figuring out what is actually going on.

Customer Research

by Matt LeMay, author of Product Management in Practice (O'Reilly)

Customer research is one of the safest and soundest investments any company can make. The worst-case scenario for doing *too much* customer research is that you have devoted extensive time and resources to continuously validating an approach that remains largely unchanged. By contrast, the worst-case scenario for doing *not enough* customer research is ruinous. Assumptions are dangerous in any part of a business, but assumptions about the specific needs and goals of customers are *particularly* dangerous for service providers of any kind.

In nearly all cases, discovery-level research into customers' fast-changing needs simply does not take place unless it is directly encouraged and incentivized. This is particularly important for organizations whose customer-facing employees (such as sales representatives and account managers) are compensated for meeting sales or satisfaction-related goals. While high-level customer trends and insights can be purchased from vendors, there is no substitute for building a customer-centric culture within your own organization.

One important step we've seen successful service providers take is to create regular opportunities for customer-facing employees to share insights with their colleagues in product management, marketing, and engineering. Any insight from a customer-facing employee that leads to a meaningful change in the service itself, the way that the service is marketed, or the SLA or SLOs is directly incentivized with a spot bonus. This helps align individual incentives with the overall health of the company by encouraging people to seek out opportunities for customer-driven change, rather than avoiding or resisting such opportunities.

Periodic Revisits

When starting off with your first SLO targets, it's a good idea to schedule frequent revisits. These can be anything from meetings involving your entire team and all stakeholders, all the way down to tickets assigned to a single team member. "Revisit Schedules" on page 308 covers how to think about revisits, but it's important to know that these can sometimes end up having to be frequent when you're first starting off.

Usage Changes

Services are introduced, adopted, abandoned, and retired all the time. As a service progresses through its life cycle, it will almost certainly see changes in how it is used. How reliable that service can be—or should be—will likely change too.

Increased Utilization Changes

As a service grows and matures, you're probably hoping that it will attract more users, and this will mean an increased utilization of that service. As utilization increases, your SLOs will likely have to change as well. As a service becomes busier, there are a few things you need to keep in mind about how reliably it is performing.

The first is that a service may become overwhelmed by the increase in requests, causing it to either fail more often or respond more slowly. As this happens, you need to continue to determine how this is actually impacting your user experience, since these degradations in performance could range anywhere from being catastrophic to unnoticeable to the users. Use this data to figure out how you should scale, and if you need to set new objectives.

Another is that as a service sees an increase in use, it is often scaled up. This could involve anything from adding more VMs or Kubernetes pods to making the distribution span more regions. When you have more places to measure, you have to make sure that your SLO targets still make sense. With more data you can be more precise in the targets you use, and this is true whether your data is entirely aggregated or measured separately for every machine, VM, or pod. As your service scales up, you might find that your measurements now tell you that you can have a more stringent SLO, or a more precise one. Remember that just using the number nine (and sometimes the number five) isn't always the best idea. As you get better insight into how your service operates at scale, you can choose better targets that diverge from the generic targets you see most often. Recall that there is nothing wrong with a reliability target like 98.3% if that's the one that best represents your service's capabilities and what your users need from it.

Dealing with Low-Frequency Metrics

When you have a system that handles a low number of requests per second, individual observed failures can have an outsized impact on the total percentage of good observations. For example, if you only have 10 API calls per hour, just one of them resulting in a bad result will put you at 90% good results. However, this kind of behavior is not always indicative that a full 10% of your responses would actually result in errors or other bad results if you had a higher level of traffic. As traffic to your service ramps up, you'll often find that this one bad observation per hour persists while the number of good observations grows, quickly dwarfing the previous

---

percentage of good events over total events. In situations like this, it can be the case that as your service takes on more traffic, you can actually provide a more stringent SLO target.

Traffic growth does not need to imply that your service operates less reliably; in fact, not only can the math work better in your favor, but if you add components like caching layers those can make your service more responsive even with an increase in requests.

Dealing with low-frequency metrics is covered in greater detail in Chapter 9.

Services can scale vertically as well as horizontally—that is to say, you can give individual instances of your service more resources instead of just providing more instances of said service. When this happens, your SLO might need to change as well. For example, if a request takes 2 seconds to complete due to processing or dependency constraints, it won't matter if you have a single instance in one data center or 5,000 of them distributed across multiple regions—the calculations needed to provide the response in this situation will still take 2 seconds. However, if this service is provided with more processing power, perhaps these requests can now be responded to in just fractions of a second. This would allow you to set a stricter SLO.

It is important to point out that scaling up does not always mean that things become more performant. As you expand your footprint, you will often require more complicated routing and load-balancing solutions, and you might have to introduce entirely new layers to your processing stack to handle this. These implementations can slow things down even more. However, on the other hand, as we just discussed, perhaps you have also added a caching layer in your scaling efforts. If you have more traffic, your caching layer can do a better job of determining what to store, which could actually mean that higher service utilization results in better reliability performance.

Finally, you may also have to change your targets or error budgets when you know about and expect temporary changes in behavior. We'll discuss concepts like retail websites preparing for Black Friday and more in "Intuition-Based Changes" on page 306.

How complex services grow is way too broad a topic to cover in entirety in this book, but always keep these considerations in mind and adjust your SLOs to be reasonable for both you and your users as you go.

Decreased Utilization Changes

If your service sees a decrease in utilization and requests, many of the same things that apply to increases also apply, just in the inverse. However, there are some specific situations you can find yourself in as a service is slowly becoming used less frequently or being retired that you need to keep in mind.

As your service is ending its life cycle and getting less traffic, remember that it will likely also have a lower fidelity and resolution in terms of metrics that it can report. If you were previously able to set incredibly precise SLO target percentages due to your high level of traffic, you might now have to loosen those somewhat. With fewer data points, your analysis will always be less precise.

In fact, if your service is coming to the end of its life and you know that it will soon be deprecated or disappear, perhaps you don't need any defined SLOs at all. It's not the case that every service is helped by having these sorts of measurements.

Additionally, as services are retired they often experience lengthy periods of being overprovisioned. If you once needed 50 instances running across multiple regions in order to handle peak traffic or other utilization, it is very common for this level of provisioning to remain in place for longer than it strictly needs to. This could cause your service to be much more performant than it was previously for a period of time. As utilization decreases, you may not have scaled things down yet. Remember this as you revisit your SLOs for a service seeing a steady decline in use. You don't want to be caught off guard by breaking your SLOs when your total provisioning is suddenly cut down by 90%, even if that is a very reasonable provisioning decision to make.

Functional Utilization Changes

Usage changes are not always just about the number of users interacting with your service or how often they're doing so. Sometimes these changes are brought about by changing existing functionality or adding new functionality that is more or less performant. Even if the mean number of incoming requests remains approximately the same, changes in how your service responds to those requests can have a huge impact on its performance, and therefore its reliability.

A good example of this can be tied directly back to the entire SLO process itself. If your service has been burning through all of its well-defined error budget on a consistent basis, you should have switched priorities to working on reliability. Let's imagine you did, and after a few weeks some new fixes were rolled out to production. Now you find that your service is way more reliable than it had been in the past. This reliability could be in terms of better latency, better data quality, fewer errors, or many other things—but whatever it looks like, you now find yourself with a huge surplus of your error budget. You could choose to spend this error budget (some ideas on how to do this were mentioned in Chapter 5), but it also could be the case that your users weren't really happy with your old targets, so this is a great time to improve upon them to take account of these feature changes.

On the other hand, sometimes feature changes will degrade things. Perhaps more transactional math is now required, or more data sources need to be spoken to in order to complete a request. This could slow things down or otherwise adversely impact reliability. These kinds of changes could lead to several different situations.

The first and most obvious is that these changes might degrade your performance enough that you are now no longer able to meet your SLO targets. When this happens, you have two choices: change your SLO or make things more reliable in different ways. Both of these options are sound and potentially a good outcome.

The second example I'll give is a little less obvious. A good SLO allows you to overcome the failures and outages that come with feature changes and absorb them into your error budget without making your users unhappy. If a service's features change, and its performance is now slightly worse, you might still meet your SLOs; however, due to this change in reliability, you may now find yourself so close to error budget exhaustion that you don't have room to account for other incidents. If your service's overall performance and reliability change, you need to revisit your SLO targets and determine if they are still set at the correct level. This can alert you to make decisions before your users are upset with you.

 You shouldn't just revisit SLOs when they're greatly exceeding or missing their targets—you sometimes need to revisit them even if reliability is changed by only a small amount.

Dependency Changes

Even if nothing has changed about your service, things will constantly be changing about the things your service depends on. Here, I don't only mean changes in the APIs of the other microservices your service might talk to—I also mean things like changes to your support platform, changes in the database layer, changes to the ISPs that route traffic into your data centers, or changes in terms of which cloud provider you're using. These are all dependencies, even if they don't show up on a dependency chart of your product.

Service Dependency Changes

The most common type of dependency change you'll run into is a change in another service that your service needs to communicate with in some way. If you have a microservice that is dependent upon five other services, any change in the reliability of those services will bubble up to yours unless you have robust mitigation techniques in place.

The simplest example to talk about here is transactional APIs, where your service gets one request, which results in additional requests from your service to several others. In situations like this—assuming an unreliable dependency response results in your service being unreliable—you can never be more reliable than that service. It might be tempting to try to mitigate this by spinning up more backends, but as discussed in

Chapter 9, unless you are also distributed, this isn't actually how the math works. If your hard dependencies can only promise you a correct response 99% of the time, that 99% chance remains the same no matter how many backends you deploy.

If these dependencies don't have their own SLOs defined, you can just measure the reliability of your own service and go from there. However, things change a little when the services you depend upon have their own reliability objectives. Remember that you're generally encouraged to run only slightly better than what your target is, up to and including purposefully burning your error budget. You should assume that your dependencies will operate in the same manner, even if they've appeared more reliable than their defined SLOs in the past.

How to take these numbers into account depends on the circumstances. For example, suppose your service dependency is publishing and defining its SLO for the first time. As we've discussed, first attempts at targets are often not the right numbers, so that SLO might change in short order. In this situation you can either choose to just ignore things for a bit, since a well-chosen SLO of your own means you can weather some error budget burn, or decide to work in unison and update your SLO every time your dependency updates its target. Either approach is fine, and you can use your own service's error budget status to determine whether you can handle unexpected dependency changes.

If you have a well-defined SLO that your users trust, you might need to use changes in the reliability of your dependencies as reasons to change your own architecture. For example, say you've been hitting a target of 99.98% on a consistent basis—and your users have been happy with this—but then you find out that a service you depend on has set its own target of 99.95%. Even if this service has been operating at a more reliable percentage in the past, if the newly defined target has been set at a different level, you need to assume that this service will only operate at that level of reliability moving forward.

There are two potential outcomes here. The first is that you might find out that your users are actually totally fine with your SLO only aiming for the 99.93% that a 99.98% service running on a 99.95% service implies. The other is that your users still need your original 99.98% SLO, in which case you'll have to make improvements in how your service runs or is distributed to make up for the underlying change in the defined SLO of your dependency.

You can find much more information about how to use the SLO targets of your dependencies to determine your own objectives in Chapters 4 and 12.

Platform Changes

When people talk about SLOs, discussing the reliability of dependencies is common. However, focusing only on the reliability of the services your system might communicate with directly tells only part of the story. You need to make sure that you're thinking about all the infrastructure and platform services you rely upon, as well. Luckily for your targets, if there are any services that both should and can aim for a long string of nines, these are the ones. But you need to make sure you're watching for changes in their reliability or defined SLOs.

The most common example here is your data platforms. These can be anything from databases to storage systems to messaging queues to caches. Just as you generally cannot be more reliable than any of the microservices you have a hard dependency on, you also cannot be more reliable than the data platforms you need.

For example, if the Postgres database your service relies upon only promises to be reliable—whether this is tied to availability, performance, or error rates—99.99% of the time, you are going to have a hard time being 99.99% reliable yourself. And just as your service will inevitably change over time, things like databases change over time as well. Even if the primary codebase is open source and hasn't been forked by your database team, these are complex systems and they will evolve. As a result, their SLOs might change (say, from 99.99% to 99.98%), and you need to keep this in mind when revisiting your own SLOs.

You also need to ensure that you're considering the reliability of even deeper infrastructure, such as the platforms that your binaries actually run on. This could be an in-house VMware or Kubernetes stack, a cloud provider, or physical hardware running in a data center. The reliability of your network comes into play here, as well. If the teams managing these services have published SLOs, watch for how those are defined and how they change. Measuring hardware and network reliability is not something everyone does, but Chapter 12 covers how to do so.

Dependency Introduction or Retirement

Another situation in which you will need to revisit your SLO is when your dependency list changes. This could be for a variety of reasons, from the introduction of a new service to the retirement of an older storage system. Nothing is really different about the approaches you need to apply in this case, but scheduling a revisit and carefully monitoring your SLO status when these kinds of changes occur is essential. It could be that you shouldn't change anything about your objectives because you've finely tuned them and know that they're set properly in terms of your users. However, the introduction or retirement of a dependency service could impact the reliability of your own service—either positively or negatively—so this is a great indicator of when you should revisit your numbers and ensure they still make sense.

Failure-Induced Changes

Failures are a great way to learn more about your complex systems. By investigating how and why things break—especially when viewed from the perspective that incidents are generally unique and always present new opportunities for learning—you can better understand the actual reliability of your service. Any time you have an incident that causes you to burn through your error budget, given this new data, you should be asking yourself if your SLO target still makes sense. If you have a very mature and well-defined SLO, maybe you don't need to change anything at all; however, all SLOs are in some state of evolution, and perhaps this incident has shown you that your previous target was unrealistic all along. Use this data to determine if you should change your SLO target. For example, if you exhaust your entire error budget, but through discussions decide you don't need to take action, it could mean that your targets can be made more lenient; alternatively, you may be happy with the amount of error budget you have during reliable periods of time and now know you can more readily spend any excess on experimentation.

Not every incident or failure you encounter requires a change, and it's not the case that every time you burn through your error budget you have to change things or even focus on reliability work at all. Some incidents are completely out of your control in every conceivable way, and the work needed to ensure you can survive one could vastly outweigh the chances of this kind of event occurring again. Great examples include large-scale cloud provider outages or widespread internet backbone connectivity problems. These are things that happen, but even if these events cause you to run out of error budget, that doesn't imply you need to change anything about your measurements or your targets. What you should do is take these opportunities to evaluate whether your SLIs and SLOs are as accurate as you think they are. Have these discussions. They're how you ensure you're thinking about reliability in the correct manner, and that's one of the most important aspects of SLO-based-approaches—not necessarily exactly what the numbers say at any point in time.

User Expectation and Requirement Changes

Another reason you should revisit your SLOs periodically is because your users' expectations will change over time.

 As a quick reminder, when you read the term *user* in this book, it means anything or anyone that uses your service, from a paying customer to another service and everything in between.

User Expectation Changes

The users that depend on your service may experience changes in their expectations over time. This could be for many different reasons, and we'll outline just a few of them here. The actual reasons expectations could change are highly dependent on the details of your systems. Often this will require becoming more stringent; however, while a bit rarer, it's also possible that your users no longer need you to be as reliable as you were in the past. A situation where a service is slowly being retired is the most common example of this. In these cases you can either lower your target, or perhaps stop measuring it from these perspectives in the first place. Not everything has to have a formal defined and measured SLO.

Running too well

The first reason that expectations might change is because you've been running too high above your SLO target for too long. If you haven't been burning your error budget on purpose, and have been running at closer to four nines than three nines, your users will come to expect you to continue to run at close to four nines in the future. This is an incredibly common scenario, and not one you should feel bad about running into. Purposely burning error budget can be difficult, for many reasons. To name a few, it can be hard to get buy-in from leadership, it's not always easy to actually do and might require building entire new systems to perform the degradation for you, and it's not very often at the top of anyone's priority list.

Note when you've been outperforming your objectives over time, and revisit your SLO definitions appropriately. If you've had a target of 99.9% but have been running at 99.99% reliability for extended periods of time, perhaps you need to just accept that you're a 99.99% service now—or, at the very least, define an SLO that's stricter than three nines. This could happen at the expense of velocity, as you'll now have to be more careful with your changes; therefore, this should also be a lesson for why you should be burning error budget where possible.

Market changes

Another reason expectations can change is that competing products might now routinely offer a better level of service. Those products could be internal offerings or from competing companies in the same space, and could be new services or just improved ones. We've mentioned before that one of the ways you can assess whether you're setting your SLO correctly is if you're both retaining and growing your user base. If a new or improved service shows up that provides most or all of the same features yours does, but users consider it more reliable, you'll almost certainly start losing those users in short order. In these situations you need to update your SLO target to better match that of your competitor, even if it means you immediately burn through your error budget. This just gives you the data you need to say that reliability improvements need to be your new focus.

User Requirement Changes

In addition to users changing their expectations, their actual requirements for the reliability they need can change as well. While this book isn't about service level agreements, which is where strict requirements often first come into play, service level objectives are often the first step in defending an SLA. If your SLO has a corresponding (and hopefully less strict) SLA, your SLO will have to change when your SLA does.

One example of this is when the business makes changes to what it promises. This isn't always done hand-in-hand with engineering teams, so you might suddenly find yourself in a situation where the contracts with your paying customers now promise a higher level of reliability than they did before. While this might not be ideal if the new promised SLAs don't actually line up with user expectations, there isn't much you can do in this scenario but bolster your SLO target and focus on hitting it to the best of your ability. If you're not able to over time, you have a great data point to bring to the business side of your organization to show them why the promised SLAs may not be reasonable. On the other hand, you could find that these new targets are absolutely reachable. In either case, your SLO will need to change.

Another example is when different tiers of service are introduced. For example, if you're an ISP that offers different bandwidth packages, you don't have to always provide that exact level of bandwidth in order for your users to be happy. Like with almost everything, you just need to provide it often enough. However, users that are paying for higher-bandwidth packages are more likely to care about their bandwidth limits, or they wouldn't be paying extra for them. You'll have to make sure you're targeting a higher percentage for your higher-paying users than you might for your lower-paying users in order to keep both groups appropriately happy.

Tooling Changes

Another situation that will require you to revisit and perhaps update your SLOs is when the tooling you use to measure and/or calculate them changes. These kinds of changes could include the introduction of new systems, configuration changes, or changes in resolution or retention period.

Measurement Changes

The first way that tooling changes could impact your SLO measurements and calculations is when changes happen to how you can observe or measure things in the first place.

The most obvious example is when a new metrics system is introduced. This new system could be a replacement for a previous system, or it could be a totally new one. Either way, you'll need to rethink how to best approach your SLOs when provided with a new way to look at your systems. Even if you believe that your metrics will look the same with a new system, that isn't actually always the case. Regardless of how confident you are that your data will be similar to what it was in the past, you need to at the very least revisit your measurements and data to ensure that everything still makes sense with the new system in place.

Another way that measurement changes could take place is when new configuration options are put into place. If you're using Prometheus to scrape your metrics endpoint for new data every 30 seconds, you'll have to revisit how you're calculating things if you change this to every 10 seconds or every 3 seconds. In a similar vein, perhaps the team responsible for maintaining your Prometheus instances introduces the ability for you to store your data for a longer period of time. A change like this will also necessitate a revisit of your SLO, even if no updates ultimately need to be made. With more data, either via greater resolution or longer retention, you have better insight into how your service is actually behaving, allowing you to set more accurate objectives. As always, use these changes as an opportunity to have discussions that allow people to think about reliability for your users in the best possible way.

Calculation Changes

Most metrics collection systems cannot perform all of the calculations you need in order to have meaningful SLIs and good SLOs, so it is very common that you'll need to build additional tooling to help you accomplish this. This could be anything from a black box metrics collection system to one that performs math on the data and then exports it to another system. Especially in terms of error budget calculation, many organizations will need to roll their own solution. When one of these systems changes, or a new one is introduced, you have another reason to revalidate your defined SLO.

The ways that your calculation systems could change are too numerous to attempt to cover here, but whenever anything changes in the pipeline that starts with metrics collection and ends with how much time or how many events you have remaining in your error budget, you should revalidate your SLO and all components of it and make sure everything is still reasonable.

Intuition-Based Changes

Another reason why you might decide to update your SLO is because you just feel like you need to. While we have provided you with some common examples and situations that call for revisiting your targets, the truth is that such a list can never be entirely comprehensive. If you have any reason to suspect that your current definitions aren't working for you in the way they need to, change them.

Additionally, you might have to change things during particularly important times for your business. Perhaps the best example of this is when you're responsible for a retail website during Black Friday and the rest of the Thanksgiving shopping season. For some businesses this period can account for a huge percentage of their total yearly revenue, in which case you might want to temporarily implement more stringent targets that necessitate having more people ready and able to defend the error budget. This could be true both during the event and in the time leading up to it; the former can help you monitor the reliability of your service during a high-volume event, while the latter can help you discover reliability problems you might not have noticed with a more lax SLO ahead of such an event.

Finally, you never know what could change about the world. Natural disasters, pandemics, and all sorts of other long-running emergencies could drastically change how your service is depended on or how your team is able to work—in these situations, too, you should examine your numbers and determine if they're still appropriate.

Setting Aspirational SLOs

You can also use SLOs to drive change. If you already know that your service isn't being reliable enough, you can set an objective that you know you can't hit to help bring this into focus. It doesn't have to be an objective your users are actually happy with, just one that you can use as a starting point to gather data that proves you need to improve the reliability of your service. However, as you make these improvements, you'll want to ensure that you iterate over everything and that your eventual target promises user happiness.

For example, suppose you have a service that's depended upon by many other teams. It has been running incredibly flaky for a very long time, and while people are still consistently annoyed by this, users have stopped complaining at all because they have no evidence that things will ever get any better. Your team, being responsible for this service, is well aware that it often runs unreliably, but they too see the situation as hopeless; attempts to fix things have fallen to the wayside long ago.

In situations such as these, you might set an aspirational target that is better than what you're currently offering, if still lower than what your users would ultimately be happy with. Perhaps you can start with a target of 99% reliability, and use the immediately depleted error budget as motivation and a source of data for your team to use to finally get to work on fixing things. Once you've shored things up and your service has been running at 99% for a period of time, you could bump up your target to 99.5%, and use your newly depleted error budget to once again provide motivation and data to make things better. You can perform this work iteratively until you finally hit a target that your users and your team are actually happy with.

Identifying Incorrect SLOs

It's one thing to be able to identify events that indicate when you should consider changing your SLO, and another thing to determine that your SLO is defined incorrectly in the first place. While the various situations described so far in this chapter are a great starting point in ensuring you are revisiting things on a sensible schedule and having the right conversations, they cannot encompass the entirety of what it looks like to have a process of meaningful SLO evolution.

Listening to Users (Redux)

When evaluating your SLOs, the single most important thing you can do is to continue to listen to your users. You've seen that to develop meaningful SLIs, you have to take your users into account. Similarly, to develop meaningful SLOs, you have to listen to your users. But this isn't something you should do only when you're starting on your journey; it's something you need to do for all time.

SLO-based approaches to reliability are all about ensuring that your users are happy. In the case of your customers, you need to know how they feel about your reliability, since it is their perception of it that is most important—not your own. Just because you took a step back and took your users into consideration when you were first defining your SLIs and SLOs doesn't mean that those definitions will hold true for all time. Listening to your users and thinking about things from their perspective is an ongoing part of the process—one that never ends. No matter how mature or appropriate you feel your SLIs and SLOs are, they can never tell the true story if your users don't agree.

You should be interviewing your users and looking at things like KPIs when you first define these, and you should continue interviewing your users and looking at things like KPIs throughout the lifetime of your service. Talking to users ensures you're keeping them in mind, and looking at KPIs ensures you're aligned with the business and product side. Remember that SLO-based approaches to reliability are exactly that: they're approaches, ways of thinking, a philosophy—not a thing you can ever complete.

If you're always out of error budget, but your users aren't unhappy, you don't have properly defined SLOs. Conversely, if you always have error budget remaining, but your users are unhappy, you also don't have properly defined SLOs.

Paying Attention to Failures

Another way you can determine you aren't measuring things correctly, or don't have accurate SLO targets, is when you have failures and incidents that don't move your data enough—or at all. If you know that you've had a full outage from your users' perspective, but you didn't burn any of your error budget, you now also know that you're either not measuring things in the correct manner or not calculating those measurements properly. Failures, incidents, and outages need to be reflected in the status of your SLOs. If they *aren't*, you need to take a look at your SLIs, your SLOs, and your error budget definitions to make sure they *are* moving into the future.

How to Change SLOs

We've discussed a lot of different indicators for when you should revisit your SLOs, as well as how to identify if they're set incorrectly. But once you determine that you need to make a change, how do you actually do so without just guessing?

Your first stop when determining what a new SLO might look like should be your SLIs. If they've been properly set up to capture the experience of your users in a meaningful way, they should be able to help you unearth what your SLO targets should be.

First, look at your SLIs and figure out if they're measuring the things they should be. Next, look at your SLOs and figure out if they're the right objectives for user happiness. Finally, look at your error budget windows and figure out if they cover the right amount of data.

You can do this using the techniques covered in many of the chapters in this book. There is very little different about how to best choose a new SLO versus how to best choose your first one. Almost everything will be a moving target you need to adjust to, both when you're first getting started and when you've been around the SLO block a few times.

Revisit Schedules

In addition to all of what we've covered so far, you also need to have scheduled revisits of your SLOs. Exactly what these revisits should look like will depend a lot on your service, how many stakeholders it has, and how it has performed over time. But no matter what, you need some kind of scheduled revisit, even if it only takes two minutes and all stakeholders agree that no change needs to be made. Without ensuring you have something scheduled, it can be too easy to let your SLOs and error budgets be forgotten until things are in a terrible state.

Additionally, a schedule can help you push back and retain focus. If a dependent team or group of users wants an update, that doesn't mean this *has* to happen immediately. As long as you're not losing users, customers, or revenue, or breaking a contract, you can absolutely wait until your next scheduled revisit instead of dropping everything to address these concerns. Always remember that all of these measurements are sets of data you can use to think about the reliability of your service, and not hard and fast rules.

Summary

Service level objectives are exactly what they sound like—they're objectives, not agreements. They *should* be malleable, and they *should* change over time. While it is sometimes important to hold fast and try to defend your error budget, you should also feel free to change your SLOs when it makes sense to do so.

As you progress in your journey to adopting an SLO-based approach to reliability, you should be identifying situations, incidents, and other signifiers that tell you you should rethink your SLO. This doesn't mean you actually have to change anything at all—often a revisit and a discussion about the state of the world can lead you to determining that everything is actually just fine as it currently is. But you need to make sure you're taking the time to have these discussions in the first place. Talking about changing SLOs is one of the most important tools that this approach gives you.

Schedule revisits on a regular basis, but also ensure they take place after incidents and outages. When your dependencies change their SLOs, make sure you look at yours as well. When your users expect or need different levels of reliability from you, make sure you're still operating in line with their wishes. As long as your SLOs remain easy to understand and discoverable, and meet the needs of your users, change them to whatever they need to be to suit the current reality.

Services evolve over time, which means your SLOs should, too. Use the data they provide you to have better conversations and make better decisions.

CHAPTER 15

Discoverable and Understandable SLOs

Alex Hidalgo

An SLO-based approach to reliability works best when everyone is on the same page. You need to ensure that everyone involved within your organization buys into the process in much the same way. Each team should feel free to adapt the system to how they work, what their services are like, and what kinds of data and measurements they have available to them. However, they still need to ensure they're using terminology and definitions that are consistent with everyone else, so that members of other teams can easily understand them. This is important because when things become too divergent, you lose one of the primary benefits of SLOs: the ability for others to quickly and intuitively discover how you're defining the reliability of your service, as well as its current state.

In addition to making sure that your SLO definitions are consistent, you need to make sure that others can discover them in the first place. A beautifully crafted, detailed overview of the definitions and statuses of your systems' SLOs means nothing to others if they can't find it.

This chapter focuses on best practices and other tips for ensuring your SLOs are as discoverable and understandable as possible.

Understandability

When defining SLOs, you need to make sure they are understandable by anyone who might be involved. This starts with your own team. The SLIs, SLOs, and error budget policies you define need to be agreed upon by everyone responsible for managing your service, and you can't have proper agreement if they don't all understand exactly what is being said.

Additionally, you need your SLOs to be understood by engineers on other teams, who might either be direct human users of your service or be operating services that depend on yours. They need to know how your service is performing, and that isn't possible if they don't understand how you're choosing to measure things (how to spread this kind of understanding is covered in depth in Chapters 13 and 16).

The data about your service's reliability needs to be usable by people well beyond engineering teams, too. This isn't always easy—in some organizations these sorts of measurements are considered guarded data that doesn't warrant being shared. However, if you can push for a culture change, everyone will get along better.

For example, product teams need to know:

- That operational teams are trying to understand things from a user perspective
- How reliable a service is aiming to be
- How reliable a service has recently been, or currently is

The leadership chain needs to understand these same things, or it won't be able to allocate resources to the places that need them most. Your customer support teams likewise must be able to internalize SLO-related definitions and data so that they can properly communicate reliability status to paying customers. These same teams will likely be the first to know if your SLO is out of alignment with what your customers expect, so they also need to have a way to communicate this back to engineering teams.

Consistency is invaluable to ensuring that your SLOs are understandable by everyone. This is where templatized SLO definition documents come into play. You can find an example SLO definition template in Appendix A.

SLO Definition Documents

SLO definition documents are incredibly important to having discoverable and understandable SLOs. Even though (as discussed in Chapter 14) SLOs can and should change over time, they also need to be formalized at any specific point in time. An SLO definition document is the clearest and easiest way of accomplishing this: you need to make sure that your SLOs are formalized in writing somewhere, and by using templates you ensure that they're written down *in the same way*. This makes it easy for everyone to follow them. Let's outline some of the most important parts of what such a document needs to contain.

Ownership

The first thing people should be able to understand about your SLO definition is who is responsible for it, and who calls the shots when it comes to determining future work based upon error budget status. Ownership of an SLO is an important part of how the entire process works, since someone needs to be in charge of making the decisions that SLOs give you the data to make. For services owned by a single engineering team, the owner should likely be the entire team, since individual people might transfer teams or even leave the company entirely. However, there is nothing necessarily wrong with choosing a single primary stakeholder. In fact, this is the recommended process to follow for services that encompass many other services, because there isn't often a single team responsible in these situations.

In such cases, you might have to bring in ownership at higher levels. For services that represent many aspects of an organization, or perhaps even your entire customer-facing product, the correct owner should be a director, a vice president of engineering, or even the CTO or CEO themselves. Whoever the owner is needs to be able to mandate change. If the SLO in question is for your entire customer-facing product, that has to be someone near the top of your org chart.

At the end of the day, someone has to be responsible for how things are being measured, how decisions are made, and how resources are allocated—but this doesn't have to be a single person, or even a single team. Ownership of SLO definitions should be assigned to the most appropriate people, even if they aren't directly working on the operations or contributing code to the service at all. Leadership should not be excluded from these conversations.

 SLOs are about having better data to help you make better decisions. If you're establishing targets for your entire company to follow, there is nothing wrong with identifying leadership to be responsible for reacting to this data. Just make sure they're aware of that role and on board with the concept. If you need to shift an entire engineering organization's aims for some period of time, you need an owner who has the power to make this happen. But, of course, you can't just sign someone up without them understanding what this all entails. Chapter 6 covers how to have those conversations and get buy-in.

By establishing formal ownership, you are not just communicating who is responsible for making decisions about the reliability of a service; you're also letting people know who to reach out to in case they have qualms or disagreements about the SLO. If the owner of the SLO is not the author of the definition document or the team responsible for the service, that should be made clear. You should also provide some indication of how to contact the owner. This could be anything from an individual's email address or a team mailing list to a ticket queue or a chat channel. Use whatever communication channels are most commonly used at your organization.

Approvers

All SLOs should have a number of approvers, and these should be sourced from across all stakeholders. A single person or a single team's take on measuring reliability is, from the perspective of the service's users, often insufficient. Having a diversity of voices involved in setting objectives and determining how to measure them is vital—what might seem important about a service will often differ greatly from the engineering team, to the operational team, to the product team, to customer support, and so on.

An *approver* is different from an *owner* in a few important ways.[1] An approver is someone who has reason to care about how an SLI/SLO/error budget is defined, but is not someone who can mandate a change in focus if the error budget is being exceeded by too much. Additionally, they're often a stakeholder, but are likely not in the direct management chain of the team at the base of the service in question. This doesn't always have to be true, of course—sometimes you're setting SLOs for an entire company's product.

Although the exact details of who needs to be involved with the approval process of an SLO definition should vary depending on the nature and size of the service itself, here are some best practices to follow:

- No SLO definition should ever be approved by just a single person or team. Keep in mind other teams, such as product and customer support.
- You should always ensure that at the very least you have a senior engineer or two from outside of the responsible team involved with the process. Individual teams can become blind to how others depend on them.
- If your service is depended upon by many services and teams, you should have representatives from a reasonable number of those teams. For example, if three other services depend on yours directly, it makes sense to find approvers from the teams responsible for those three services; however, if you are in charge of the database platform that every microservice at your company relies upon, you probably don't need to find approvers from every single team.

---

1 A good way to think about these sorts of differences is by using a responsibility matrix. I personally like RACI, which is a methodology that helps you define who is Responsible, Accountable, Consulted, and Informed about any particular project. As always, use what works for you, but it can be useful to have a defined system in place to assign and define these sorts of responsibilities.

Finally, ensure that a certain number of members of the team responsible for this service have approved the definition as well. This might seem obvious, but you need to make sure that your list of stakeholders includes the people that directly take care of the system on a daily basis, through operational and code contributions alike.

Your definition document should include a list of all the approvers and an indication of whether and when they have signed off on the current version of the SLO definition.

Definition status

An important aspect of your definition to communicate is its status—not the status of your SLO or error budget, but of the definition itself. For everything to be as understandable as possible, you should have a number of dates documented.

The first date you may want to include is the original proposal date. This lets people know how long this service has been managed with an SLO-based approach and provides an indication of the maturity of your SLO.

A very important date to provide is the last-updated date. As we've discussed at great length throughout this book, SLOs are always evolving and changing, and it's important that stakeholders know when you last revisited the various aspects of your SLO definition—this date should be incremented every time a revisit occurs, even if no changes to the definition document are made. This allows people to discover not only the last time things may have changed, but the last time they were reviewed.

 Ensure that previous versions of your definitions are still available to people as well, either through explicit mentions of older versions and changes made in your rationale section or, at the least, via a code repository history.

In addition to or instead of the original proposal date, you may want to provide an approval or implementation date. This tells people when the ideas behind the objectives were actually put into practice and allows them to understand how long the measurements have been taking place (bearing in mind that this may have begun some time after the initial proposal date).

Finally, you should mention the next revisit date. All SLOs should be revisited at some interval; as well as when the last review of the various aspects of your SLO definition was held, stakeholders need to know when the next one will be conducted.

Service overview

A simple summary of what your service actually does is an important part of your definition document. You shouldn't assume that everyone interested in your SLO definition or status necessarily knows exactly what it is that your service does or how it is architected. This section does not have to be lengthy, but it should be comprehensive enough to allow anyone from any department of your company to understand the basics of the purpose and functionality of the service being described. A paragraph or two with accompanying links to more in-depth documentation is recommended here.

An example summary could be something as simple as: "This microservice provides an interface for processing user logins. It is used by all customer-facing services and validates login information stored in an encrypted database." If you're responsible for the database behind this service as well, you should expound on this and add some additional details. For example: "This database additionally stores login history and metadata of customer transactions. Due to GDPR laws we are careful about our retention period and only hold data for 28 days."

Be detailed enough to ensure you're not overlooking any important service features (especially those related to compliance or security), but succinct enough that any visitor can quickly understand the functionality and purpose of the service in question.

SLO definitions and status

It probably comes as no surprise that SLO definition documents have to contain the definitions of the SLOs themselves. In this section, you need to describe in the simplest fashion exactly what your SLIs are, what your SLOs are, what your target percentages are, and so forth. While you should focus on using simple language so that people not familiar with your service can understand what you're measuring and how, it is also often useful to have a second definition that is more technical.

For example, for each SLO, you might have one section written in easy-to-understand language, and then a second one that outlines the exact query or math you're using to measure the results. The former allows people to understand *what* you're measuring, and the latter allows people to understand *how* you're measuring it. People who just care about what your definition is can focus on the text description, whereas people interested in the exact mechanics involved can focus on the second part. An example of the sentence-based definition could be something like, "We will serve 200 HTTP responses within 500 ms to 99.9% of incoming requests," while the query-based definition might say something like `sum(http_requests{status="200"})` / `sum(http_requests)`.

You should also provide a link in this section that allows people to discover the current status of your SLO and your error budget. In the best possible scenario this information should be presented in a dashboard, or something similar (we'll discuss building SLO dashboards and how to discover SLO and error budget status in more detail in "Dashboards" on page 321). The important part for building your template is that this should be a link to a dynamic data source, unless you can embed dynamic data directly in your document system. Avoid relying on a human trying to keep this information up to date in the document itself.

Rationale

Your SLO definition should also include an explanation of why you've chosen the SLIs and SLOs that you have. This is a very important data point for people on other teams that the owners of an SLO definition may never think about. You can stave off many questions by documenting your decision-making process for others. Ensure that people not only know what your definitions look like today, but have some idea of how they came to be.

Revisit schedule

You should lay out clearly what your revisit schedule is, and explain why you've chosen the schedule you have. Is this a new definition that will require frequent review? Is it an established measurement that is trusted and only needs to be revisited quarterly, or even yearly? Make sure your justification is sound and your rationale is clear.

Error budget policy

As we discussed in detail in Chapter 5, having an error budget policy can help jump-start the conversation that examining SLO and error budget status necessarily implies. This section is likely going to be much more free-form than other sections of your document, because it's going to be much more unique to your exact service and team. You don't need to try to plan out every possible scenario here, but this is a great place to lay some foundations. For example, you might say things like:

- If 50% of the error budget has been depleted, the team will have a meeting to determine how to proceed.
- If the error budget has been entirely exhausted, the team will dedicate its next sprint to the reliability backlog.

Remember that you don't *have* to adhere to whatever you define here; the idea is just to have some suggestions to look to when having discussions about project priority. When issues come up, it can be tremendously helpful to have some sort of starting point mapped out.

This doesn't mean that you *can't* have strict rules, of course. Perhaps your SLO is tied very directly to an SLA, in which case you might not have a choice but to pivot people to defending the error budget. Or perhaps you've been at this for a very long time and trust your numbers very much, and you have evidence that having two engineers spend their next sprint focused on reliability issues makes sense when you've exceeded your error budget. Strict rules are fine if they work for you, but they're not mandatory to implement the philosophies at play.

External links

Finally, you'll want to have a consolidated section providing external links to things like more in-depth documentation about your service, dashboards or other places where people can discover the current status of your SLO and your remaining error budget, and perhaps the source code repositories where your SLI and SLO calculations are formalized. Even if you mention these elsewhere in your document, you should have a single, clearly marked section that contains all the relevant links. This way, visitors to your definition document can go straight there to find, for example, your dashboard without having to wade through the rest of your document.

Phraseology

Phraseology is important to creating understandable service level objectives. The basic idea behind phraseology is that words have different meanings when they're used next to other words, or when they're used in the same way often enough, and knowing these things can help you communicate ideas better to certain populations. Using the concepts behind phraseology, you can make your SLO definitions more understandable.

Using a definition template is the first step. If every SLO someone encounters is defined in the same manner, they'll be more easily understood the more of them that person reads. But you can go a step further by also ensuring that people use the same terms and phrases to indicate the same things. For example, "SLO" or "service level objective" is generally understood to mean the entire defined system, from SLI to error budget window, while "SLO target percentage" is understood to be just the actual number that represents what kind of reliability you're aiming for.

Whether you develop a glossary for people in your organization to refer to is entirely up to you. In my experience those kinds of lists end up being ignored as time passes, so the effort is not always enduring. The main thing is to be aware of how humans think about words, phrases, and acronyms, and build your templates in a way that promotes a unified language.

Discoverability

Once you can trust that your SLO definitions are as understandable as possible, you also need to make sure that they're discoverable. No matter how well written your document is, it's no help to anyone if they don't know that it exists, or can't find it. Additionally, interested parties need to be able to discover the status of your SLOs, not just their documentation.

Document Repositories

The best way to ensure SLO definitions are easily discoverable is to ensure they all live in the same place. Having a centralized repository for all SLO documents at your company or organization is the most painless way to do this. How to set this repository up will depend a lot on how you handle the rest of your internal documentation, but we'll outline a few good options here.

The simplest way to handle this is to just create a folder or a tree of folders in a documentation system like Google Docs or Office 365. If you have a lot of SLOs, you might want to organize them by department, product, or team; however, unless you trust the search functionality available to you, you should also have a single document somewhere that lists every single definition. While this might seem unwieldy, there is a benefit to allowing someone to search for a text string in a single location to find what they're looking for. You shouldn't always assume that everyone will know who owns every service; in fact, one of the biggest problems at tech companies in general is that no one knows exactly who owns what. Additionally, team and organization names are prone to change, while service names often stay the same over their life cycle.[2]

A slightly better option is something like a wiki system. Whether you choose to use the wiki as a repository that links to documents that live elsewhere or actually make the definition documents available there is up to you. In either case, wikis have been built from the ground up to facilitate discoverability by having the built-in concept of spaces to contain related material. As we discuss in further detail in Chapter 16, you're going to want a lot of documentation about how SLOs work for your organization, and a wiki-like system is great for ensuring your document repository is available right next to all of your other SLO-specific documentation.

Documentation-as-code is another great option, especially if you use it to feed into a wiki-like system. Templates can be a little more difficult to use with markup languages like Markdown, but the history you get from storing your documentation in a

---

2 Of course, service names sometimes do change, and sometimes multiple services are combined into a new one. The point is just that you need to be aware of these sorts of changes and try to be proactive in preventing them from confusing people down the road.

code repository can be excellent. Additionally, assuming your actual SLO configs, metrics definitions, and monitoring queries also live in a repository, you can ensure the two are linked in a way that guarantees your documentation does not drift from what your tooling is actually measuring and calculating.

Do be aware, however, that not everyone at your company or in your organization may be comfortable with things like code repositories or Markdown as a text formatting language. Try to have a low barrier to entry for everything instead of relying on the state-of-the-art engineering solutions.

Discoverability Tooling

Even better than using something like a wiki system by itself, you could develop custom tooling to keep your repository up to date. Today, almost any documentation system you might use has an API you can interact with. You can use this to build tools to automatically scan through your documents and populate the repository landing page itself. Writing some software is often the best way to ensure there's no drift between reality and what has been documented.[3]

In addition to making sure that your SLO measurements are in sync with your documentation, and ensuring that all of your SLO documents are discoverable by programmatically aggregating them in the same location, this kind of tooling can provide you with other benefits. If you have a system that already scans through your SLO definitions, you can have it analyze the data contained within them as well.

For example, you could have your tooling autopopulate your repository with dates like when an SLO definition was last updated, or when the next revisit date is. This can allow stakeholders to quickly glean this information at a glance. You could also use this to automatically mark documents as past due or even open a ticket in a team's queue if they've missed their revisit date. You can set SLOs for the freshness of your SLO definitions!

SLO Reports

Creating a centralized repository for your SLO definitions will help with discoverability, but you can also proactively take steps to increase awareness of SLOs, their definitions, and their status. It's a great idea to regularly report on the definitions and statuses of the most important SLOs in your organization. This could take the form of anything from a weekly or monthly email to a scheduled visit to a repository or dashboard during meetings. Chapter 17 discusses how to report on SLOs in much greater detail, but don't forget that reporting on them is a way to make them discoverable in the first place.

---

3 You can even define an SLO for this tooling!

Dashboards

In addition to reports, you should have dashboards that help people discover various aspects of your SLOs. In a way, you should view these dashboards as a second repository, since they should also be grouped together in some way.

SLO dashboards don't have to be complicated, and they really only have to consist of a few items in order to be effective. Before we look at a visual example with real data, let's talk about the components that should exist on dashboards such as these.

The first thing your dashboards need to show is the current status—that is to say, "Is this service at this moment meeting its objectives or not?" This is most often best represented by a binary value or string, and not a graph. People should be able to glance at the dashboard and immediately know what the current state of the world is. Most large SaaS or cloud platform companies, like Google, Amazon, and Microsoft, have these sorts of status pages for their external customers to discover, and many different vendors exist that will host status pages for you.

 A status page is a prime candidate to be handled by a vendor, because if your own infrastructure is having problems you want to ensure you can still publicly post your service status somewhere. It can be pretty embarrassing if you're down so badly that you can't even let anyone know that you're experiencing problems.

Next, you should have an SLI violations graph. This allows people to discover the exact moments when your measurements determined that your service was unreliable versus when it was reliable. Having this kind of data presented over time can make it easier to correlate SLI violations with other events.

Another key feature of a useful SLO dashboard is a "burndown" graph. This shows how reliable you've been in terms of percentage over time. Closely related is your error budget status. A panel showing how much error budget you have remaining— whether positive or negative—allows stakeholders to quickly ascertain the state of your service. I personally think it's a great idea to represent both of these values as a line graph as well as with a single numeric value showing where you stand at this exact moment in time.

Finally, these dashboards need to include links to the SLO definition documents in question. People should be able to discover the specifics of what is being presented on the graphs and panels in front of them without having to do much research.

Now that we've outlined what sorts of items you might have on an SLO dashboard, let's look at an actual visual example in Figure 15-1.

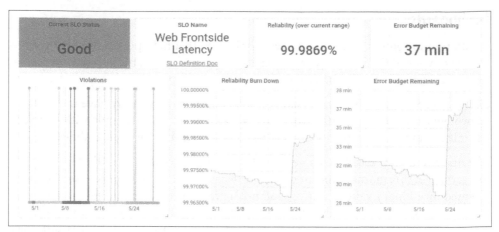

Figure 15-1. An example SLO dashboard for a healthy service

This screenshot shows some example output measuring the latency of responses to human-generated requests to a website. The target SLO percentage for this service is 99.9%, so you'll notice that it has been operating reliably for some time. The service uses a 30-day error budget window, which means you get around 43 minutes of error budget per month. Knowing that you're sitting at 37 minutes remaining is a good indication that you probably don't need to allocate any new resources to improving the latency of this service. You could quickly use this kind of dashboard in a weekly sync or something similar to make that case.

Figure 15-2 shows what such a dashboard might look like for an unreliable service.

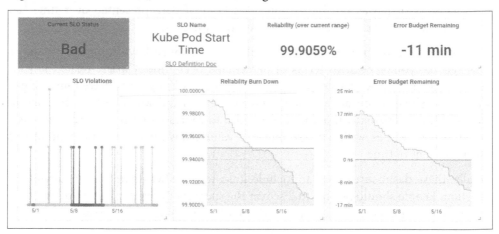

Figure 15-2. An SLO dashboard showing an unreliable service

Instead of measuring response latency, this SLO is concerned with the start time associated with Kubernetes pods. In this case the target is 99.95%, and it looks like things haven't been going so great recently. The measurements are currently in violation of their targets, and the error budget (just shy of 22 minutes per 30 days in this case) has been completely depleted and looks to be continuing to drop. With an 11-minute deficit incurred over the course of almost two entire weeks, this probably isn't a complete emergency, but it's likely that one of two things needs to happen:

1. Assign engineers to figure out what can be done about improving startup time.
2. Reassess whether your SLI measurements and SLO target are reasonable.

Humans are often great at spotting trends in a visual manner, which is why dashboards are so popular for many uses across the industry. You should make sure that all of your data is discoverable via nonvisual means as well, of course—you should always be thinking about accessibility—but the benefits of having SLO status dashboards are innumerable for many organizations. If SLOs are about providing you with better data to make better decisions, then you need to ensure that this data is presented in a format that the humans involved can use to make those decisions.

Summary

Reliability requires people to know what's going on, and SLOs provide a clear, customer-centric picture that speaks a thousand words. This is true whether these people are on the team responsible for a service or at the highest levels of the leadership chain, and everything in between. You can simplify all of this by doing just a few things: creating intuitive and informative SLO definition templates; ensuring that these filled-out templates are discoverable; using tooling to validate the status of various SLOs; and creating reports and dashboards that make it easy for stakeholders to discover not just how things are defined, but also the current and historical reliability status of a service.

CHAPTER 16

SLO Advocacy

Daria Barteneva and Eva Parish

They always say time changes things, but you actually have to change them yourself.
—Andy Warhol

Previous chapters have explored how to get buy-in from your organization when adopting SLOs, and the importance of building an SLO culture. By now, you understand why your organization needs SLOs and how much they will impact your engineering processes and your users. You can't wait to start advocating for SLOs across your organization!

But wait—there are three questions you need to answer before beginning:

- Do you have *leadership buy-in* on implementing SLOs in your organization? It can be helpful to have an executive sponsor with a vested interest in SLO implementation who will be able to support you and unblock you in the case of conflicts of interest.

- Does your management chain *agree on expectations and the time investment* required to drive SLO adoption? Being an SLO Advocate will probably be a full-time job for you for the first few months (or even longer if you're in a large organization).

- Are you ready to have a *horizontal role* that impacts an entire organization? Such a role will require skills in multiple domains, from communicating with senior leadership and stakeholders, to writing documentation, to analyzing data and building reporting, to reviewing monitoring implementation, to delivering training, and more.

If you answered yes to all three questions, congratulations: you're ready to be an SLO Advocate. But what does that mean?

Your role is to help your organization successfully implement SLOs by doing all of the following:

- Cultivating a deep understanding of SLO implementation for different types of services (see Chapter 4)

- Understanding your monitoring platform, statistics in general, and your organization's data visualization platform (to do instrumentation and produce dashboards and other outputs for your metric signals)

- Most importantly, motivating and inspiring people to reach beyond their current role and scope

Your people and leadership skills will be critical during this journey: you will need to convince others of your vision, teach them what they need to know, and generate positive energy to inspire them and drive successful SLO adoption.

It will help a lot if you have experience designing training materials and delivering technical training. If you don't, you might want to team up with someone who does. If teaming up isn't an option, however, don't worry: this chapter gives you some tips on how to do all of this successfully. It focuses on activities, artifacts, and processes for SLO adoption that have worked in other organizations.

 In sum, becoming an SLO Advocate is an opportunity to improve your leadership, engineering, and project management skills, while creating positive change in your organization.

As with many things in life, and especially engineering projects, it's best to start small and iterate as you go. We can break this journey into three phases: *Crawl*, *Walk*, and *Run*.

Throughout each phase, make sure you are soliciting feedback to understand whether what you're doing is working or you need to change your approach. You'll face some challenges (we'll talk about those in more detail in "Learn How to Handle Challenges" on page 334), and at times you may even think you have failed. But remember: you learn more from failure than you do from success.

First People, Then Processes, Then Technology

Your organization's most valuable asset is its *people*. When you start implementing SLOs across your organization, remember: you won't be able to do this without working with people across your organization and without having their support and commitment to make it work. Your people skills will be critical on this journey. Being a good listener and having a growth mindset will allow you to create effective feedback loops that will ensure the success of SLO adoption.

Don't forget that you will want to scale and inspire others to become SLO Advocates as well. In large organizations with geographically distributed teams, scaling is the *only* way to succeed.

One challenge you might experience in the people phase is encountering teams with extensive backlogs and no time to focus on new projects—SLO creation being one of those. These teams might agree that writing SLOs is important, but other work they have in the backlog is important too. Leadership buy-in will be crucial to prioritizing SLO work.

Once you have a group of SLO supporters, it's time to review your engineering *processes* and work with process owners to incorporate SLOs into them. How do you use SLOs for alerting, for troubleshooting, for retrospectives? How do you do problem management and project prioritization using SLOs? Identify which processes your team or organization have in place, and work with process owners to see how SLOs can bring value to those processes.

And finally, *technology*. As you move forward with SLO implementation, your platforms may need to adapt and improve. You may find out your monitoring platform is not SLO-ready, or that your alerting mechanisms don't support SLOs. Work with your engineering peers to find solutions that will better support your new SLO culture.

Crawl

The *Crawl* phase of your SLO advocacy journey is where you'll build the foundation of your program. You'll educate yourself, create artifacts to help you spread your message, start to connect with leaders and teams in your organization, and run your first few training sessions.

Do Your Research

First, you need to become an SLO expert yourself. The fact that you're reading this book shows that you're on the right path! You should also read the chapters on SLOs in *Site Reliability Engineering* (*https://landing.google.com/sre/sre-book/toc*) and *The Site Reliability Workbook* (*https://landing.google.com/sre/workbook/toc*).

There are many online resources you can use to deepen your knowledge, from technical conferences to written works to online courses. Choose what works best for you. Define your learning process in advance and track it as you would any other activity. Learning without a timeline and without clear outcomes may become demotivating.

We also recommend creating a working example of a service with SLOs while you're learning. Having a concrete, small example to apply each new piece of knowledge to will keep you focused and help you retain what you learn.

Prepare Your Sales Pitch

> It usually takes me more than three weeks to prepare a good impromptu speech.
>
> —Mark Twain

Imagine you meet the CEO of your company in the elevator, and they ask you what you do. With only a few seconds of their attention, what would you say?

Spend some time preparing your SLO "elevator pitch," and remember to adapt it to different audiences. You should be able to articulate the value of SLOs and why others should care about them, and you should be able to do this when speaking to people with all different perspectives.

What do your engineers care about?

Engineers usually appreciate understanding if their service is working well enough, so shape your conversations with this goal in mind. You could talk about real-time measures of service reliability and the ability to get insights into the health of service dependencies; about correlating different signals and using that data to detect service degradations; and about embedding SLI metrics into your CI/CD pipeline to detect regressions and perform automatic rollbacks. Don't forget to mention how SLOs and error budgets help with assigning the best priorities to service incidents and improve alerting efficiency, both of which are especially critical to on-call engineers.

What do your company executives and business partners care about?

Here you can talk about real-time measures of user experience and satisfaction, or about a data-driven approach to service reliability and the ability to prioritize efforts that will improve user satisfaction in the areas where it really matters. Mention that SLOs will allow them to identify the right investment opportunities, because "reliability is the most important feature of any system" (*https://landing.google.com/sre/work book/chapters/reaching-beyond/*) and the only way to gain your users' trust is to provide reliable and secure systems.

Feel free to pull from this book in your sales pitch. Identify the language that will resonate with your organization, and borrow it. A strong message that works for both audiences is this quote by Peter Drucker: "If you can't measure it, you can't improve it." Above all, SLOs are new and better measurements of your service from your users' point of view.

Create Your Supporting Artifacts

Having done your research, you have a good understanding of SLOs and are confident about defining them for a simple service. You're also prepared to talk about the value of SLOs with anyone you encounter. Next, you can focus on creating artifacts to support your engineering organization as it adopts SLOs. These artifacts fall into two main categories: *documentation* and *training materials*.

Don't forget to define where all your artifacts will live—for example, a wiki paired with a code repository—and make sure they're discoverable and easy to navigate to. The biggest mistakes we see across engineering organizations are not taking the time to create well-structured and discoverable technical documentation, and not demanding that documentation undergo the same quality review process as code. Don't underestimate the power of documentation to support you and your organization during SLO implementation.

You might be tempted to use this book as your documentation, and just ask everyone to read it. Some people in your organization may do that, but many will not. Even among those who do read it, people will take away different things from the book. It's more effective to create your own documentation, tailored to your organization's needs, than to expect everyone to read an entire book. See the next section to learn what types of documentation you need to increase your chances of successful SLO adoption.

Documentation

Your goal is to break down SLO creation into three phases: *define the SLO*, *collect SLIs*, and, later, *use the SLO*. Here is a list of the documentation we recommend at this stage:

One-page strategy document
  The one-page strategy document will be the most important document in the Crawl phase. What are you trying to accomplish? Why? How will you do it? This will be the very first document you share with people when they ask, "What is this effort all about?" You should make it short enough for anyone to read in less than 10 minutes. It's critical that you get this document right. Use this book as a resource to help you articulate *why* your organization needs SLOs: what it will get

out of creating SLOs, and how SLOs will improve service reliability for your users and help your engineering teams. Make sure you review this document with your leadership and have their sign-off and total support for the strategy you plan to communicate across your organization.

Two pages defining SLOs (high level)

Next, you'll need a more detailed (but still brief) document that explains what an SLO is, gives examples of good SLOs, and tells the reader how they can get started. You don't want to scare your readers by asking them to read an entire book about SLOs just to understand what an SLO *is*. Make it easy for engineers to get an idea of how to implement SLO-based approaches and try to build their interest.

FAQ

Collect a list of the questions you expect people to ask as they begin their own SLO journeys, and compile them into an FAQ document. To start with, you might include questions like:

- What if my "user" is another service? Do I still need to care about SLOs?
- What if my service's dependencies don't have SLOs?
- How many SLOs should a service have? How many SLIs?

Defining SLOs for your service, step by step

You'll need a document that explains, step by step, how someone in your organization can define an SLO (the first phase of the SLO creation process). Don't talk about instrumentation and metrics collection here; focus on the high-level process. You might want to share an SLO definition template that teams can use.

Instrumenting your service to collect SLIs

As a follow-on to the previous document, this document will give step-by-step guidance, with examples, on how to instrument a service to collect SLIs (phase two). You can be very specific here and look at the monitoring platform your organization uses to give examples of SLI instrumentation for different types of services. For example, how would you collect latency data and translate your metrics into SLIs using percentiles? How would you instrument a pipeline service to collect SLIs? Give as many examples as you can and provide ready-to-use code snippets, making it easy for engineers to move forward with the monitoring instrumentation step of the journey.

Use case

If you've already implemented SLOs for any of your services (or for the example service you developed while doing research), write up the details in a use case document to give your SLO early adopters a concrete example of how this is done.

Training

To supplement your documentation, we recommend developing a few training programs creating the following trainings that you can run at this stage. Here are some ideas:

30-minute overview of what SLOs are
> Capture the interest of the audience, and use this time to inspire and motivate them to want to learn more. You can also record this training session and distribute it across the organization so that people can watch it on their own time as a first step of SLO onboarding. The overview should mostly focus on defining concepts and outlining the value of implementing SLOs.

Hands-on workshop on defining SLOs for an example service
> Choose one service that will be familiar to all attendees, such as a common dependency, or construct a hypothetical system or service that's easy to understand, like a mobile game or an online store. Provide your students with the high-level service architecture and data flow diagrams, describe the service's main functions, and give examples of usage patterns for that service. Organize sessions where small groups of four to five people define SLOs for the service and then explain their approach to the other groups. This type of workshop is more suited to being held in person (or at least live over video chat) as a collaborative learning experience, rather than recorded.

Hands-on workshop on instrumenting a service to collect SLIs
> As a follow-on, walk your audience through your sample service and the instrumentation you implemented to collect SLIs. Building a hands-on lab for your audience may be time-consuming, but depending on the complexity of your platform, building it now may save you time in the future by establishing consistency in how to instrument SLIs.

 Make sure to give your attendees a break between hands-on workshops.

Collaboration-based training

People enjoy (and get more out of) real-time, collaboration-based training than watching recordings. In a large enough organization, you may be able to train a few other teachers to help with this. Adding new teachers also provides advantages such as being able to cover more time zones, if a company is distributed, and helping your colleagues in their career growth. But even with multiple teachers, if you need to reach thousands of people it won't be feasible to train everyone in person, so you'll need to scale your training by leveraging recordings and online collaboration.

Usually, if the training is lecture-based (that is, for sharing definitions and concepts), a recorded session works great. But if you need to teach people how to think in a specific way and to solve a problem, a collaborative environment will give you a much faster outcome. The 3 hours of collaborative SLO workshops that we attended at a technical conference gave us the same amount of (or even more) experience defining SLOs as 40 hours of watching recordings and reading on our own. In person or online, you can build a collaborative environment by organizing your students in small groups of five or six people, assigning a mentor to each group, and defining the rules of engagement and the desired discussion outcomes. If you are doing this online, consider using a digital whiteboard and video chat to encourage more effective collaboration between group members.

Run Your First Training and Workshop

Tell me and I forget. Teach me and I remember. Involve me and I learn.

—Benjamin Franklin

Most likely, your first training and workshop will not be perfect. This is to be expected: remember that one of the foundations of an SLO-based approach is acknowledging that nothing is ever perfect, and this extends to your SLO advocacy efforts as well.

Make sure you create a survey to collect feedback from attendees and learn how you can improve the training. It's also a good idea to deliver your first couple of training sessions to a friendly group of people who already have an idea of what SLOs are, and who can give you candid feedback on what's missing from your training. As with everything in life, you may get it wrong at first. Listen to your attendees, iterate, and improve. Either online or in person, ensure that you create a collaborative environment among your students so they can practice discussing SLO-based approaches with each other while going through the exercises.

 In the first SLO workshop w ran, the hands-on exercise was to define meaningful SLOs for a simple request and response service. After a few workshop sessions, we got clear feedback: the service type we were looking at was too easy. Attendees wanted exercises on working with more complex types of services—storage services, pipelines, continuous compute services, network services, serverless services, and so on. They also asked for a hands-on lab on instrumentation for SLIs, with examples of each service type for them to pick from. We took this feedback on board and added more and more service examples to the workshop over time.

Implement an SLO Pilot with a Single Service

To bring SLO adoption to the next level, you need an example of a real service that has implemented SLOs and can show how much those SLOs have impacted service reliability.

Choose one of the smaller services in your organization and develop SLOs for it. Request and response services without many dependencies are a good option. Define an SLO for the service, instrument it to collect SLIs, and build visualizations for the SLIs that demonstrate the value of SLIs and SLOs in improving service reliability. Work with the engineering team that owns the service to gather their feedback, make any necessary adjustments, and help them start to use SLIs and SLOs in their engineering practices. Then, crucially, document the pilot as a case study and add it to your documentation, so that other teams can read about the experience.

Spread Your Message

> The single biggest problem in communication is the illusion that it has taken place.
>
> —George Bernard Shaw

Your next goal is to ensure that your organization is aware of the work you're doing, the push toward SLO implementation, and any new content you're building.

Talk at internal meetups or conferences. Organize engineering review sessions to deep-dive into SLO implementation examples. Use every opportunity to talk about SLOs at your internal community events. You need to make sure people know what your role is as SLO Advocate, and how they can find you.

Publish the schedule for your next training sessions, outline who the experts available to help are, and share how people across your organization can get in touch. *Understand what channels your organization uses to share information.* Make sure you have an SLO landing page with an easy-to-read shortlink and share it over and over, until everyone knows where to find information on SLOs.

Here are some ideas for what information to publish on the landing page:

- Your training schedule
- An email distribution list that can be used to ask SLO experts questions
- A list of Slack or Teams channels dedicated to SLOs
- An SLO newsletter, and a distribution list people can subscribe to
- Your office hours schedule

Learn How to Handle Challenges

As an SLO Advocate, you are the agent of change. You may encounter some challenges in this journey, and facing them with an open mind and positivity is critical to your program's success. Remember, we learn more from failures than from successes! Here are a few of the issues you may run into, and our suggestions for dealing with them.

First of all, your role may be misunderstood. Some teams will expect you to do SLO implementation *for them*. You can overcome this obstacle by setting the right expectations, up front and clearly, when you engage with teams. You might also encounter people who simply don't know what you're doing at all. You can add clarity to your role by making sure you have a clear backlog and you are tracking SLO advocacy work in the same way you would track your engineering work, breaking it down by artifacts, activities, and other deliverables. Tracking your work will also help you do retrospectives for this program and communicate your deliverables and timeline clearly.

Second, you may encounter some resistance while trying to implement changes to the processes and practices used by your partner teams. People are naturally resistant to change, and you should be prepared for pushback as a result of this. Breaking the changes into smaller iterations and making them easy to implement will help you to overcome change aversion. Try to use your earliest successes to build confidence in what you are doing and turn those teams into SLO evangelists—it may help their career growth and will help your organization to adopt an SLO-based approach faster.

Helping by Showing

by Daria Bartaneva

One team I worked with in the past agreed that SLOs were very important, but they felt that they never had time to define their SLOs and add missing monitoring instrumentation.

To convince them it was worth the effort, I reviewed the existing metrics the team were already collecting for their service, and determined which ones would be suitable to use as SLIs. Then I transformed those metrics into SLIs by calculating the ratio of successful events to total events, and used this data to analyze how the service had performed over the last two months. This was two days of work for me, including getting a deeper understanding of the service's architecture and existing metrics, performing data analysis, and building reports.

Then, I proposed an SLO target for these SLIs and built a report with some time series visualizations. I proposed multiple visualizations, including distribution of the

---

minutes below the SLO, 24-hour rolling windows, and correlation of the SLI time series with user-impacting incidents.

When I showed the reports to the team and explained how they could use them to inform discussions around service reliability, they were excited and decided to give it a try. After a few weeks, they decided they wanted to define additional SLIs, and then reviewed their proposed SLO targets with stakeholders—my experiment had successfully led to implementation. They even asked me for additional training, and asked if someone with SLO experience could participate in their discussions with stakeholders.

Looking back, my engagement with this team was successful because I made it so easy for them to get started. Having the first SLO done for them gave them the opportunity to see the benefits with very light process change, which later led to full adoption.

Third, as we mentioned before, you may encounter teams that are overloaded with work or that have well-defined priorities that are *not SLOs*. In these situations, you can work with leadership to see about prioritizing SLO work against the team's other responsibilities.

Walk

In the Crawl phase of your SLO advocacy journey, you laid the foundation for SLO implementation in your engineering organization and had some initial success. Now, in the *Walk* phase, you'll expand your work to other teams and continue building a library of examples. You'll also make sure your feedback loops and internal communication methods are working well, expand your training program, and revisit how much time you spend working with each team.

Work with Early Adopters to Implement SLOs for More Services

By now, you already have one or two services piloting SLO implementation and working on incorporating SLOs into their engineering practices, aiming to improve service reliability. You need to move further, but you can't tackle all the services in your organization at once. (I'm assuming you have more than three services in your organization; if you don't, congratulations, you may be very close to completion!)

Choose a number of services to implement SLOs next that you can give white-glove assistance to. It's a good idea to pick a few services of *different types* (request/response, pipeline, continuous compute, etc.). It may be tempting to keep looking at request and response services, but you need to build a body of real-life SLO implementation examples for different service types.

Variety is not the only criterion you should use when choosing to which services you will give white-glove assistance. Other things to consider are:

- Level of complexity (look for variation here too)
- Amenability of the teams
- Criticality of the service to the system
- Closeness to human users

Schedule weekly meetings with the owners of each service to assist them on their SLO implementation journey. Define a timeline for completing the different SLO implementation phases, and keep each team accountable to ensure that this work doesn't get deprioritized.

Celebrate Achievements and Build Confidence

We can't stress this enough: celebrating achievements will bring positive energy to your mission and accelerate SLO adoption. If teams are not moving forward fast enough (or not moving at all), try to understand what challenges they are facing. It's not always aversion to change or conflicting priorities; teams may find that in order to implement SLOs, they first need to make fundamental changes to the way their service is built.

To help build confidence about SLO implementation for those services, you could try some of the following:

- Start with something as simple as possible, even if that means the SLO isn't as useful as intended—for example, a single, easy endpoint or a subset of the user flow.
- Try something like measuring through synthetics or a dedicated client instead of the service itself.
- If the issue is with some other piece of knowledge that is missing from the team, try to get someone knowledgeable in that area to pair with the team. Gaps in knowledge could be in middleware patterns, particular frameworks or tooling, and so forth.

Create a Library of Case Studies

By now, you hopefully have multiple teams interested in implementing SLOs that are trying to get your assistance with that work. While continuing to work with your handful of early adopters, you need to make sure all these other teams have a good level of support, without overloading yourself. Your best friends in this phase will be well-structured documentation and a set of internal case studies teams can use to learn more. Being able to follow the example of your early adopters will help other engineering teams with their own SLO implementation, making it easier for you to scale this program.

If you find yourself receiving a lot of requests from teams to meet with you to ask questions about SLOs, define your boundaries. You can't meet with every team individually; ask them to read the documentation and attend your office hours. Often, these teams will have one or two questions that can be answered in a few minutes in office hours, and there's no need to schedule a separate meeting with them. The most frequent question will likely be, "My service looks like this; do you have any examples of SLO implementation for this service type?" Having case studies for different service types from your early adopters will help many other teams.

Scale Your Training Program by Adding More Trainers

By now, if your organization is small, you might have trained everyone. But if you're dealing with a medium or large enterprise, with teams distributed around the country or globe, it's time to scale your training program. Train other people to deliver the training sessions and workshops you've created. If your organization has an internal training team, they might be able to support you in scaling your training. You might even consider handing off training to that team completely, and focusing on other aspects of SLO advocacy. Otherwise, seek out passionate individuals in the organizations you've been working with who understand SLOs well, and engage them to scale your training program. Handing off your training work to others will allow you to focus on the other important tasks in this phase.

Scaling SLO Training

We've always prioritized in-person training and workshop options, but after receiving feedback that we needed to offer training opportunities to more people and that the current approach wouldn't scale, we decided to try creating an online version. We teamed up with a few engineers passionate about professional training and video editing, and we started by recording the theoretical parts, broken down into 10-minute sessions. The practical parts of the workshop were distributed separately, and there was a communication channel open for any questions and discussion while people worked through these parts.

The feedback we got confirmed our intuition: participants tended to feel that the recordings weren't enough, and that workshops where engineers can work in groups with experienced mentors are more productive and useful. While it wasn't a practical option in this case (especially in the midst of a global pandemic), attendees seem to strongly prefer collaborative workshops, where they can ask questions in real time, work in groups, and brainstorm together. Currently, we're testing a hybrid approach: we're running an online version of the workshop where, after the theoretical part, we divide students into smaller groups and let them brainstorm the SLO definition process. Tutors join each group discussion and help to answer questions. At the end, each group shares its results with other groups.

It's important that students drive their discussion to a logical conclusion and have an opportunity to share it with the larger group. Walking away from the training with a completed exercise gives students more confidence in the content and results in higher satisfaction with the training experience, as measured by our surveys.

Scale Your Communications

Earlier, we mentioned that as your advocacy work ramps up you will no longer be able to spend as much time working with every single team. You need to scale how you engage and communicate with teams. Some activities and artifacts you might consider at this stage include:

Office hours

If you haven't already, schedule a periodic meeting (say once a week, for one hour) where you and a group of SLO experts from your early adopter teams will be available for anyone to pop by to ask questions. Make sure the meeting invite is broadly distributed, that people can join remotely, and that everyone knows the purpose of the meeting.

FAQ document

Capture all the questions you're getting from teams and consolidate them in a frequently asked questions document. Then, when a repeat question comes up, you can simply send teams the link to that document.

Not everything can be scaled, unfortunately, so there will be exceptions when you may need to provide 1:1 consultancy to a team with in-person engagement. We recommend limiting this to large or core services that carry significant complexity, with multiple upstream dependencies.

To deal with time zone challenges and maintain your work/life balance, make sure you have at least one SLO expert per region who can provide support in local time. Leverage your early adopter teams to support other teams working on SLO implementation, too.

Communicate, communicate, communicate. Keep yourself accountable, and keep teams implementing SLOs accountable as well. These teams should capture their SLO work in the same work-tracking platform that they use for engineering work (Jira, Bugzilla). Build dashboards reporting on SLO adoption progress. Communicate as much as you can!

Run

When you get to the *Run* phase, SLO implementation is going viral and everyone is at some stage of SLO maturity. (If this isn't the case, you might want to consider going back to the Crawl or Walk phases and continue iterating on them until you achieve enough momentum to move to the Run phase.)

In the Run phase, your role is to use what you've learned so far and keep improving, by sharing your library of case studies, creating a community of SLO experts, driving platform improvements, and improving your advocacy process. *Remember that defining and implementing SLOs is just a first step toward improving reliability.* The game changer is actually using SLOs as part of your engineering practices to drive service quality and operational excellence.

Share Your Library of SLO Case Studies

Continue the work you began in the Walk phase, adding more case studies to your library. Pick the most successful services. Having concrete examples of success will help convince those who still don't fully believe in SLOs that they, too, should care about them.

Don't focus only on documenting the use case. Make sure you also reference code and give specific examples of reliability improvements that the team saw over time. Some improvements may be purely operational: for example, noise reduction or toil reduction. Other improvements may be less data-driven; for example, "Before SLOs, we didn't know how users perceived service reliability, but now we do" or "Before SLOs, we didn't have enough data to prioritize work that will have a greater impact on service reliability, but now we do." (Other chapters of this book will help you determine what to focus on when writing these case studies.)

Create a Community of SLO Experts

Build an internal community of SLO experts, pulling from your early adopters, your other trainers, and anyone else who is passionate about SLOs. SLO experts can support engineering teams across your organization by answering questions and helping with hands-on SLO implementation. Create an email distribution list for these SLO experts, or use other internal communication channels (for example, chat) to give teams an easy way to reach them.

Continuously Improve

As you go on, continue to improve your platform, review your SLOs, and update your documentation.

Based on what you've learned so far, you may have discovered that you need to make some changes at the platform level, or that you need to rethink your observability strategy or reporting toolset. Work with your internal partners on defining those platform improvements.

Even if you've had some initial success implementing SLOs for a service, you should review them again a month or two later. Remember, SLOs are a process, not a project. Services evolve and platforms change. What worked well before may no longer be relevant. Use your SLO maturity framework to review SLOs for specific services periodically.

Other ways you can keep improving include:

SLO reviews
Pick a service and review its SLOs. Suggest improvements, and document the team's implementation efforts as a case study.

Quality of service reviews
Assuming your team has periodic service health reviews, make sure SLOs are one of the discussion topics.

SLO deep dives
Periodically do a deep dive into a team's SLO implementation process, inviting other teams to observe.

SLOs driving discussions
Review how SLOs are being used to drive critical discussions to improve service reliability.

Lastly, review your existing documentation periodically to make sure it's up to date. You might even try defining a "freshness" SLO for your documentation and making sure you maintain it above a certain level!

Summary

> Progress is impossible without change, and those who cannot change their minds cannot change anything.
>
> —George Bernard Shaw

This chapter looked at the different phases of the SLO advocacy journey, and the recommended goals and tasks for each one. Your role as an agent of change, seeking not just to implement SLOs in your organization but also to build an SLO culture, is one of the most challenging roles. To help ensure your success, make sure you have executive support and surround yourself with people who believe in your mission and who will keep you accountable. Iterate on everything, overcommunicate, and don't forget to celebrate successes, no matter how small.

CHAPTER 17

Reliability Reporting

Alex Hidalgo

At their absolute core, SLOs are a means of providing you with data you can use to have better discussions and therefore (hopefully!) make better decisions. The entire process is fundamentally about thinking about the data you have in ways that you might not have before. The data you collect via an SLO-based approach should be meaningful in terms of being representative of what your users and customers feel and experience every day using your service. Because of this, your SLO data becomes a prime candidate for reporting on your service status to other people.

Who these "other people" are will depend heavily upon your exact service and who its users and stakeholders are, but reporting doesn't have to just be about presenting quarterly status updates to management and shareholders. Using SLOs to report on the general health of a service to the team or teams that support it is also an incredibly powerful communication method.

Reporting on SLOs is valuable for you, your team, your organization, the teams you depend on, the teams you're dependent on, external customers, external businesses, and even more. By measuring the performance and reliability of your service from the perspective of your users, you're also compiling data that can be meaningful directly to those users. And remember: when we say *user*, we mean literally anyone— or anything—that depends on your service. If your SLIs and SLOs capture their experience and requirements well, then you also immediately have data you can use to have conversations with those users about how reliable you've been, how reliable you currently are, and how reliable you're aiming to be in the future.

This chapter explains the ways that service reliability is often reported on today; how SLO-based approaches are different, and why these approaches are much more meaningful than alternative systems; how to use these new numbers to make your project decisions clear to others; and the most valuable SLO-based metrics you can use to build useful dashboards and other tracking mechanisms.

Basic Reporting

Your service will have many stakeholders, including some or all of the following:

- Software engineers who work on the service
- Operational engineers who keep it running
- Product teams who plot the purpose of it
- Customer operations teams who have to answer questions about it
- Leadership and business people who need it to operate well so that your organization or company can perform well

It is also often the case that your service has stakeholders who don't even realize they are stakeholders. The stakeholders in a high-level service are stakeholders in all of the services that it depends on, whether they are aware of this or not. Just because the owners of the frontend of a website don't often think about the reliability of the network hardware that delivers data to their service doesn't mean that they aren't also stakeholders.

The stakeholders will likely expect to get regular updates on how your service is doing, and/or to have a discoverable way of checking on its status in the event of a problem. When things go bad, people need to know how badly. If you are able to get buy-in across the company about an SLO-based approach to reliability, stakeholders will especially want to know how the service is performing against its SLO.

Luckily, SLOs are basically built to be self-reporting. They are directly based on metrics related to the service behaviors that the users—and therefore the business, and therefore also the stakeholders—care about. Monitoring performance against SLOs is therefore much more straightforward than trying to extract signals users or stakeholders care about out of low-level signals not tailored to match user experience.

Without SLOs, it is not easy to report on the reliability of a service. You could try to count pages fired or tickets opened, but these are prone to being inaccurate due to false positives or the whims of the people opening the tickets. You could try to report on something like uptime, availability, or error rates, but as we've discussed, those things rarely tell the whole story.

Because meaningful SLIs give you better insight into what users need, SLOs give you an easy way to say something along the lines of: "We have been reliable 99.76% of the time this quarter" or "We exceeded our error budget by 1 hour and 6 minutes this month." These are simple sentences that can be digested quickly. Not only will they give your engineering teams a better idea of how users were impacted by any incidents that occurred, but leadership will be better able to infer potential revenue or customer confidence loss. You can use these numbers to build dashboards or populate documents that can then be discovered by anyone that wants to know how your service is performing.

But before delving into how you can meaningfully report on service and team health via SLOs, let's discuss how organizations today do this in an ineffective manner.

Counting Incidents

The most common way I've seen people try to quantify the reliability of their services is to count how many incidents have occurred over time. This is a completely reasonable starting point: it's not difficult to follow the logic that says that, since incidents cause moments of unreliability, many incidents implies more unreliability, while few incidents implies better reliability. However, once we start to look at the math surrounding this sort of approach, things unravel quickly.

The Importance of CVEs

by Isobel Redelmeier

There's a special type of incident that's worth calling out separately: the security incident. Besides letting the public and our customers know about attacks on our systems that may have affected their data, it's important to also let them know about vulnerabilities as they are discovered (and, hopefully, patched). This data lets them determine the appropriate mitigations, such as updating once a fix is available or monitoring for active exploitation.

As with other types of incidents, traditional metrics for tracking common vulnerabilities and exposures (CVEs) within a company may mislead or even lead to perverse incentives. We want our systems to both *be* secure and *seem* secure—and being and seeming secure are not always the same!

Consider counting CVEs with the goal of reducing their number in the future. On the surface, this is sensible. Alas, the easiest way to reduce the number of CVEs is not to stop having them in our systems, but instead to stop *finding* them; and attackers, unlike customers affected by outages, don't generally let us know first before exploiting whatever weaknesses they may discover.

There are other ways to better align the reality and appearance of your security posture. Publicly reporting a larger number of CVEs may, perhaps unintuitively, actually signal that you take security seriously and are therefore actively trying to detect vulnerabilities before they get abused. Especially when coupled with a proven commitment to patching them quickly, this sort of transparency is invaluable for protecting your users.

The first problem is that it's difficult to define what an *incident* even is. Is it any time a team is paged based on metric thresholds? In that case, you have to be sure that your alerting is incredibly accurate, that false positives never trigger, and that you're constantly updating your thresholds as various aspects of your system change. Chapter 8 discusses the problems surrounding threshold-based alerts in greater detail.

Alternatively, you might say that an event only qualifies as an incident when things are severe enough that you have to post a public status page update to your paying customers. Or perhaps you wait until customers are filing tickets and calling your support queue—except now your approach is entirely subjective and plenty of real problems could be hidden. Not everyone is going to make the same decision about when something needs to be communicated externally, just like not every customer that notices a problem is going to have the same threshold for when they decide to complain.

Due to the ambiguity surrounding exactly what an incident is, people often try to resolve the problem by introducing the concept of *severity levels*.

Severity Levels

The basic premise behind severity levels is to establish some number of buckets with strict definitions that allow you to categorize your incidents. Most often these levels follow some kind of numbering system, where the lowest number equals the most severe type of incident. Table 17-1 shows an example of a traditional set of severity levels.

Table 17-1. An example severity level list

Severity	Description
S5	A feature is less convenient to use or there is a minor cosmetic problem. Unnoticed by most users.
S4	A minor feature is not operating correctly, but there are obvious workarounds available. Likely unnoticed by most users.
S3	A major feature is experiencing sporadic unreliability, but there are workarounds and many users won't notice.
S2	A major feature has significant problems. If there are workarounds, they are difficult to discover. Most users will be aware.
S1	A major feature is completely down. There are no workarounds. All users are aware.
S0	The entire service is down. All users are aware.

The intended outcome of defining such a list of severities is that you can now classify any incident or outage that may occur within one of these severity levels. With this data, you can better report on the reliability of your service! Except you probably can't.

The problem with severity levels is that, while they provide you with some guidance in determining exactly what a reliability incident is, and they're certainly better than just having a binary "Was this an incident or not?" dichotomy, there is still far too much ambiguity at play. No matter how extensive you make your descriptions for each level, you're never going to be able to completely accurately classify every problem you encounter.

For example, when trying to classify a problem you're encountering as S3 or S2, how do you determine where the dividing line is between *sporadic unreliability* and *significant problems*? You could develop a strong rubric for this by adding more qualifying criteria. But how would you classify a problem that's flapping between the two? It's not often the case that incidents remain in the same state as things evolve.

Suppose that for the last hour 5% of requests have been failing, but every 10 minutes the failure rate increases to 95% for 30 seconds or so. Is this incident an S3 (sporadic unavailability) or S2 (significant problems)? You may have decided that S3 corresponds to availability between 50% and 99% and S2 to availability between 0% and 50% for a particular feature, but the service is alternating between the two.

Additionally, we could easily imagine a problem that starts by exhibiting *sporadic unreliability*, moves on to exhibit *significant problems*, and finally is just *completely down*. How do you classify such an incident?

You could say something like, "The most severe level reached during an incident is how that incident should be classified." This seems fairly reasonable in some ways, but again I can come up with some very simple counterexamples that muddy this view very quickly. For example, do you really want to have to classify an incident that *at one point* and *for 15 seconds* was entirely down as an S1 incident when it spent a full hour being sporadically unreliable before and after that brief moment of complete unavailability?

We can go even deeper. What does it mean if you're down at 03:00, when you basically don't have any traffic, versus during your normal daily peak, versus on your most important business day of the year? How do you accommodate these differences with severity levels?

Despite these ambiguities, I normally see organizations just kind of accept them as necessary.

A much better way to measure things is to use error budgets. If you have a meaningful SLI and a reasonable SLO, the data an error budget gives you will be much more representative of your reliability from a user's point of view than severity levels/buckets.

The next step most organizations that are using severity levels take to try to measure reliability is introducing some math in order to figure out how often they experience incidents of a certain severity level. This is when *mean time to X* is introduced.

The Problem with Mean Time to X

Once organizations have established their severity levels, they often realize that they still don't have a way of thinking about reliability over time. This is when the *MTTX* acronyms tend to be introduced. MTTX stands for *mean time to <something>*, with the *X* taking many possible values. I've seen all of the following used out in the real world:

- Mean time to acknowledgment
- Mean time to detection
- Mean time to engagement
- Mean time to escalation
- Mean time to failure
- Mean time to first action
- Mean time to fix
- Mean time to know
- Mean time to mitigation
- Mean time to notification
- Mean time to recovery
- Mean time to remediation
- Mean time to repair
- Mean time to resolution
- Mean time to response

There are probably more examples of this concept out there. We all might be better served by tracking *mean time to new mean time measurement*. This list alone should be enough to start sowing some seeds of doubt about the entire concept.

The idea behind measuring any type of average (or mean) time is that these numbers can help you understand incidents of level S0 or S1 that impact the reliability of your service. That is, if you measure the mean time to failure in the event of S0 and S1 (and S2? or even S3?) incidents, you can better understand how often a particular service fails to work as intended. Furthermore, if you're measuring the mean time to resolution, you have a data point about how long it takes, on average, for your team to fix problems of a certain severity.

This chapter is about reliability reporting, and the arguments here against using MTTX methods must be viewed via that lens. The argument is not that MTTX is always misleading (in fact, we demonstrate some useful applications of these measurements in Chapter 9!) but that they become very nebulous for anything involving incidents. Measuring the time-to-failure of hardware components, for example, is useful information and these sorts of measurements are used by engineers of all disciplines; however as soon as there is a direct human element involved, things change a bit. A major focus of this book is that you need math, but also that you need to use that math in the most meaningful manner.

These sorts of measurements are very common in reporting on the health of a service, and making decisions about allocating resources. Has your *mean time to X* been too high for the previous quarter? Better allocate resources to bring that number down!

The problem here is threefold:

1. Incidents are unique.

2. Using averages for your math is fallible.

3. As with counting incidents or defining severity levels, defining what any of this even means in the first place can be very subjective.

Let's dive into why incidents are unique and why means aren't always meaningful.

Incidents are unique

Complex systems generally fail in ways that are unique and have different contributing causes and factors each time. When you want to measure the mean of the time it took for something to happen or be resolved or acknowledged, you're gathering dirty data. MTTX measurements can only work if you have strict severity buckets to ensure you're not comparing apples to oranges. We don't have the space here to go into the details of exploring and learning from complex system failures, but the core idea is that due to the many factors at play—including, not least, the humans involved—you can't reliably categorize system failures into the same bucket over and over again. (John Allspaw (*https://www.adaptivecapacitylabs.com/blog/2018/03/23/moving-past-shallow-incident-data/*) has written a great article on this.)

For example, let's talk about an incident type almost any web-facing service will have to endure at some point or another: a distributed denial of service (DDoS) attack. Even if the same type of attack is aimed at the same website more than once, there are still going to be differences. For example, the attackers will likely have different motivations and use different techniques, targeting different endpoints, sending different traffic patterns, and so on. These factors alone make these sorts of incidents unique.

Even if you're willing to bite those bullets, DDoS incidents can manifest in countless ways, making data you've collected about previous DDoS attacks you've endured murky in terms of being able to predict anything at all. You might think a DDoS is just a DDoS, but in reality there are a vast number of techniques and approaches that can be used to bring a system down due to load.

The most common type of DDoS attack is known as a *volumetric attack*. Attacks of this nature seek primarily to overwhelm the network bandwidth available to a service, making it difficult or impossible to respond to legitimate requests for data. One of the most common types of volumetric attack is the SYN flood, where tons and tons of incoming requests are sent to a single service. However, even this one type of attack can be split into many categories.

For example, you can have flood attacks that originate from a single source with lots of bandwidth, or you might be dealing with one operating from a botnet with thousands or even millions of source IPs. Additionally, spoofing the source IP is easier than most people realize, so chances are many of the source IPs involved in the attack aren't even the actual originating addresses.

And volumetric attacks are just one example. Some attacks seek to starve the resources of your network equipment and services instead of overwhelming them; others try to "bust the cache" by introducing request parameters that are just slightly unique each time, exhausting the space you have in your cache and preventing you from responding quickly enough to legitimate requests; still others target known weaknesses in applications rather than the server itself.

We've barely scratched the surface here, but it should be clear it doesn't make a lot of sense to consider all DDoS attacks as a single incident type. Even if you're willing to start counting these sorts of incidents into different buckets, though, how do you deal with an attack that switches tactics? Since DDoS attacks are orchestrated by humans, they'll often change up or diversify their strategy as time goes on. If they see your teams successfully mitigate one approach, they might switch to another. Or several others. Or distract you with several others while also turning the first approach back on.

It goes on and on. We could conduct this same thought experiment with almost any sort of incident. All incidents are unique, regardless of how homogeneous they might appear at a high level.

And even if you want to believe that the incident vectors you face are similar enough that you can throw them all into the same buckets in order to perform some sort of MTTX analysis, you need to consider that the humans responding will be in different states. This could be anything from a different engineer being the primary on-call to the same human being busy with a different thing when they get paged. There is a very real difference between your most experienced veteran engineer responding to an incident, and one that has just joined the rotation. Additionally, there is a very real difference in response time if your on-call engineer is sitting at their desk during working hours, or out on their lunch break, or being paged at 03:00 on a Sunday. Even if all of the other details of the attack are similar, the human factors will always be unique.

These might seem like nit-picky details, but they're important to consider when attempting to establish equivalence between incidents. Equivalence requires all factors to be the same, but they never truly are. This almost immediately throws the validity of an MTTX approach out the window. If you're not convinced yet, though, there are also purely mathematical reasons for why these aren't good approaches to measuring reliability.

Means aren't always meaningful

The other problem with using a means- or average-based approach to analyzing your unreliability incidents is that they can cover up how your users actually feel about your service. This is most provable by using a simple counterexample.

Let's say your organization uses mean time to resolution (MTTR) or something similar to measure how well teams are able to respond to incidents of unreliability. Let's also imagine that you have an objective for the quarter to improve your MTTR by lowering it. The idea here is that lowering your MTTR will result in your users having a better experience interacting with your service. This isn't the most absurd thought: if you are able to bring your system back into the correct operational parameters when it experiences a failure faster in this quarter than you did in the last one, users should be happier about your reliability, right?

This isn't how the math actually works, however. We can use an extreme counterexample to prove this, although more minor versions will result in the same outcome.

Imagine that the first quarter of the year has just ended. During this time your service had 20 total incidents. Even though they each directly impacted the reliability of your service from your users' point of view, they were all relatively minor. You were able to detect them quickly, and in most instances you simply had to roll back to a previous release to get the system running again. In this example your organization has been able to provision a strong CI/CD pipeline with an easy rollback system. The average time it took for you to resolve these sorts of problems (your mean time to resolution, or recovery, or remediation) was about 20 minutes.

During this quarter, your team has learned a lot about the failure modes and reliability of your service, and you'd like to improve on your MTTR for the next quarter. So, you set an OKR that aims for the team to improve its MTTR to 10 minutes. This all seems very reasonable from a high level.

But then math happens in ways you might not expect.

The following quarter your service is much more reliable. You learned a lot from the 20 incidents you had in the first quarter, and you've been able to fix a lot of the problems your system experienced previously. Things run smoothly for almost the full quarter—until you have a disastrous outage. It isn't even directly your service's fault: the underlying database you depend upon was down for three hours when a human accidentally dropped the primary tables and a restore had to take place. (This isn't just a dramatic device; this sort of thing happens all the time!)

When it comes time to perform your end-of-quarter math, you look at your MTTR. It now reads 3 hours, while in the previous quarter it was 20 minutes. This very much goes against your goal of improving your MTTR from 20 to 10 minutes! And more importantly, it obfuscates how much your users actually suffered.

Twenty incidents at a length of 20 minutes each equals 400 minutes, or 6 hours and 40 minutes of time that you were unreliable for your users during the first quarter. The single 3-hour incident you endured in the second quarter is well under half of that amount of time, yet a means-based approach to measuring things would tell you that you had been less reliable in that quarter than the one before.

This is, of course, an extreme example, but it acts as a good starting point for how to think about these sorts of quandaries. You don't need to be comparing 20 short incidents versus 1 long one to understand that perhaps your more frequent and short-lived reliability issues are actually more of a problem for your users than isolated longer periods of downtime are.

It turns out that neither counting incidents nor measuring mean timings around them really answers the questions your users need you to answer. The questions you need to be asking are "During which of these two quarters did our users experience more unreliability?" and "How can we quantify this better?"

The answer, as you should suspect, is SLOs.

SLOs for Basic Reporting

In contrast to counting a number of incidents or MTTX approaches to measuring the performance of your systems over time, SLOs can provide you with a much more holistic sense of your reliability. Not only can they ensure you don't fall into the math-based traps described in the previous section, but they can also give you more concrete goals to work toward.

Let's start with a reexamination of the situation we just looked at, where two quarters were being reported on: one with a single large period of unreliability and the other with many smaller periods.

An SLO-based approach to reliability using error budgets would have correctly told you that your users experienced 6 hours and 40 minutes of unreliability in the quarter with 20 incidents of 20 minutes each—far worse than the quarter with the single 3-hour incident. Purely from a math standpoint, error budgets do a better job of exposing what your users experienced than any kind of MTTX calculation ever could.

Additionally, SLO-based approaches can help you address the concerns we identified about using severity levels and counting incidents. Think back to our discussion about how severity levels are inherently flawed because it's impossible to fit all incidents into strict buckets. Remember the example of the incident that was flapping between the definitions outlined for S3 and S2, and even briefly entered S1 territory? Using severity levels and thinking about incidents in terms of the number of times they happen, we run into a problem of definition. Ambiguity and subjectivity abound. If you have well-defined and meaningful SLIs, using SLOs can help you avoid this.

Let's tie all the examples laid out so far into one cohesive story.

A worked reporting example

Imagine that you're responsible for some kind of web-facing service. For our purposes here it doesn't have to be something incredibly out there or complicated; let's say your primary function is to serve journalistic and opinion-based content about the New York City restaurant scene. You cover things like new openings and changes in dining trends, and have a forum where people can express their opinions—and you need to be able to report to people about how your services function in terms of those user journeys.

One day, one of your restaurant critics writes a post that is particularly scathing about a restaurant that has been considered sacred by NYC foodies for years. Some people agree with the review; perhaps this once-esteemed restaurant really has been going downhill of late. But it also has legions of fans, and one of them is so upset with this new review that they decide they want to take you down. They launch a DDoS attack.

At first, their attack is primitive and doesn't accomplish much. Your traffic is routed through a CDN that offers automated DDoS protection. However, it does take a few minutes for this protection to kick in, and during this time your site serves errors to some people requesting content due to the load. Of the approximately 9,000 requests you normally serve per hour, you end up serving about 630 errors because of this attack, consolidated within a 6-minute period where 50% of your responses were errors.

If you're counting incidents, would that have even been one? Does that six-minute period of partial unavailability count as an incident? Perhaps it does. Perhaps it goes on your incident register as an S1 incident with an MTTR of six minutes.

The upset restaurant fan gave up when they realized their attempt to bring your site down had failed, but they return an hour later with a more sophisticated attack. They've scoured the web and found a botnet they can lease for some amount of bitcoin, so they try again with a more complex approach. This time they're hitting you from hundreds of thousands of IPs, and your CDN cannot comprehend this as an attack at all. Suddenly it's all hands on deck on your end, as you have to figure out how to block this traffic. This time around, your entire site goes down for a full 30 minutes until you're able to resolve things.

Are these the same incident? Are they separate ones? How do you quantify the impact of 50% of responses being errors versus 100% of them timing out? Does an error count differently than timing out? What severity level do you apply if this is all treated as one incident?

These are all important questions in terms of learning from the incident and improving your resilience to these sorts of attacks in the future—but they tell you almost nothing about how your users perceived the reliability of your service during the incident. This is especially true if you're just counting incidents or applying MTTX math.

When did the incident start? Was it when you first got an alert? When the attack was first triggered? When the first user received an error response? When the first person complained on Twitter?

How can you resolve all of this?

If you have a meaningful SLI measuring your users' interactions with your website, you don't have to worry about things like what severity level to lump things into or if this situation counts as two incidents or one. You have an error budget, and that budget tells you how bad things have actually been.

During the first part of the attack, where 50% of responses resulted in errors over 6 minutes, you will have burned 3 minutes of your error budget. During the second wave of the attack, you will have burned 30. This equals 33 minutes of total unreliability. Since you've picked a reasonable and well-studied target of 99.9% reliability every 30 days, this means you have 13 minutes of error budget remaining before the bulk of your users are likely to decide your site is too unreliable and go elsewhere.

We could extend this example infinitely in terms of how hard you're hit at any one point in time. Perhaps you had 2 minutes of 90% errors and then 7 minutes of 10% errors followed by 4 minutes of 40% errors—an SLO-based approach would allow you to actually capture how users experienced interacting with your service during this time, whereas a counting incidents/severity level approach or one relying on MTTX would have left you with extremely incomplete data.

However, SLOs provide you with much more than just a better alternative to the basic reliability reporting you might be used to.

Advanced Reporting

As we've discussed relentlessly throughout this book, SLO-based approaches to reliability are at their base almost entirely about providing you with new telemetry that's better than what you may have had before. It doesn't matter if you're dealing with metrics that only report in once per minute or using an advanced observability vendor that allows you to analyze every single real event that occurs within your system: SLOs allow for you to think about your service in better ways than raw data ever will. Because of this, you can also report on the state of your services in new and better ways.

The first and hopefully most obvious difference is that SLO-based approaches are entirely focused on your users or customers. If you've taken the time to ensure that your SLI is as close to your users' experience as possible, you no longer have to worry about things like whether the errors in your logs or metrics actually correlate to your users' experience. You might recall that Chapter 3 made the case that developing meaningful SLIs is the most important part of this entire story. At the end of this book, that still holds true. Measure the things your users actually care about, and you're already in a much better position than you were before.

However, beyond SLIs, we've also discovered together how SLO targets and error budgets can help you better understand your users' experiences. Let's talk now about how to use those to better report on the reliability of your service.

SLO Status

One of the most confusing parts about moving to an SLO-based approach to reliability is talking about your current status. You can say things like "Our service is currently meeting SLO" or "Our service is currently not meeting SLO," but what does that actually mean? If your service is expected and allowed to fail a certain amount of the time, what does it mean to say that it's *currently* doing so?

The short answer is that it's an indicator to yourself and others that something is currently wrong. This can be incredibly powerful and useful data, even if you aren't exceeding your error budget.

A major focus of this book has been to communicate that you're allowed to fail, so long as you're still meeting your users' availability expectations. Therefore, it can be tempting to not care about anything until you've exceeded your error budget, which is what should be representing how much failure your users can absorb. However, you should also be paying attention to your current and recent status in terms of your target. The goal is not to only react when your users are extremely unhappy with you—it's to have better data to discuss where work regarding your service should be moving next.

One of the easiest ways to do this is to report on your *reliability burndown*. Burndown is a number that is very closely related to your error budget status, but focuses more closely upon the percentage of recent events that have reported a good versus bad status. While an error budget is necessarily tied to a specific time window, your reliability burndown can be used to look at how you've performed over any window of time. The math is no different than what we explored in Chapter 5, just with a flexible number in terms of the total time units you care about at any point in time. Remember our discussion about building dashboards for discoverability and understandability in Chapter 12? Figure 17-1 shows an example dashboard of a service that has burned through its budget and is continuing to do so.

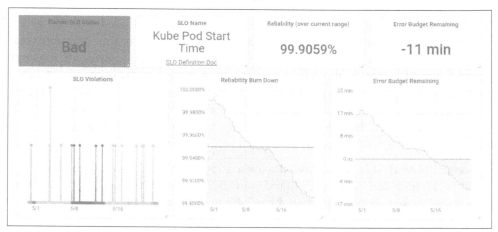

Figure 17-1. A dashboard showing the burndown of a service operating unreliably

Reliability burndown is also closely related to alerting on burn rates, as discussed in Chapter 8. It's not uncommon for people to declare that dashboards are obsolete if you have the best, near-perfect observability tooling—but in practical terms very few of us do. Therefore, dashboards that include things like graphs showing reliability burndown rate can be instrumental in allowing humans to spot times where they should take action before computers can. Humans are exceptionally good at spotting patterns in visual data.

Build dashboards like the ones discussed in Chapter 12, but use them as a reporting feature and not necessarily as a thing your engineers should be actively monitoring. Burndown graphs are a great thing to review during daily or weekly syncs, not something someone should have to have their eye on at all times. They should be flexible in a way error budgets aren't—that is to say, their time windows should always be malleable and not defined and fixed. Always trust your humans to spot important changes before a computer can. An SLO burndown graph is a great way to enable this.

Another important aspect of dashboards is that they can provide a simple indicator that reports on whether your service is currently meeting its targets or not. This can be a purely Boolean "yes or no" kind of indicator. It can help inform users of the status of your service, and is especially useful to other internal teams that might depend on your service. If their own service is currently experiencing problems and they suspect it is due to a dependency, having a Boolean yes or no, good or bad status that is discoverable on a dashboard or something similar can help them determine what action to take, if any.

Error Budget Status

Error budgets are meant to be the ultimate informer of how a service has performed over time. It should be no surprise that accurately reporting on them is one of the most important aspects of using SLOs to report on your services. We've already discussed at length how you can use error budgets to drive discussions, but let's now talk about how they can also drive communications and reporting.

Error budget status is a bit more complex than SLO status is. Error budgets have to have a defined window of time, making their reporting more absolute, regardless of whether you've chosen a rolling or fixed window. Whereas you can use an SLO burndown chart to figure out how you've performed over the last hour, six hours, or day, error budgets have a defined window that cannot change from a reporting perspective.[1]

Error budgets can be tied to individual events or time-based events, and there is a reason why I prefer the latter. You already have SLO burndown charts to help you calculate and visualize what things look like in totality; I love time-based error budgets because they communicate to other humans in a way that humans immediately understand. A sentence like "We have 17 minutes of error budget remaining" is immediately understandable and actionable by another human.

 An argument could be made that it's actually more accurate to say something like "We project to be able to have 17 more minutes of unreliability before we start losing users" instead of talking about your remaining budget. This is a bit of a semantic argument, but it's worth calling out here. Choices about the language you use are important and worthy of thought! Use the terms that best help you have the discussions you need to have.

---

1 This is not to say that error budgets cannot change over time, and they absolutely should when needed, but they cannot be static values in terms of reporting.

In addition to providing point-in-time information, the error budget remaining is a great metric to plot on a time series graph. It's one thing for people to see that you're "negative 2h and 35m" and an entirely different thing for people to see a time-based chart showing how you got there.

Reporting on error budget lets you do many things that you can't otherwise. The first is that you can report to leadership how you've actually performed against your users' expectations. As we discussed earlier, counting incidents, using severity levels, or doing any kind of MTTX calculation doesn't really cover the user experience. SLOs, however, do cover those bases. By having meaningful SLIs that fuel proper SLO targets that inform error budgets, you'll be well equipped to let leadership know how component services—or your entire product—have looked over time. This can be a watershed moment for your organization or company.

Summary

An SLO-based approach to reliability gives you many benefits. One of the most important of these is how you can report on the status of your services to others, whether that be via better dashboards, better reports, or just better numbers.

SLOs are all about providing you and your business with data that is more suited to having discussions about the future of the focus of your work. You can use them for many things. You can use them to have better discussions within your own team, and you can use them to have better conversations with other teams. You can use them to set SLAs and have better conversations with your paying customers.

SLOs are about learning and making the best decisions you can. You can do many things with them, but all of them revolve around the idea that you can have better discussions in order to ensure the humans involved—be they external customers or your internal coworkers—are happier. That's the entire point of all of this. Measure things from your users' perspective in a way that can also make your coworkers happier. Being able to report properly on your status is perhaps the single most important part of being able to have these discussions.

Remember the lessons Molly taught us in the Preface. You can't be perfect, no one needs you to be perfect anyway, it's too expensive to try to be perfect, and everyone is happier at the end of the day if you embrace this. You have all the tools you need; you're going to be amazing.

SLO Definition Template

As mentioned earlier, consistency is invaluable to ensuring that your SLOs are understandable to everyone. This is where templatized SLO definition documents come into play.

SLO Definition: *Service Name*

SLO Dashboard: *Link*

Primary Author(s): *Who owns this document and should be contacted about it?*

Team: *Who owns this service and should be contacted about it?*

Collaborators: *Anyone who contributed but isn't a primary author?*

Original Proposal Date: *Date*

Last Updated Date: *Date*

Approval Date: *Date*

Next Revisit Date: *Date*

Approver(s):

Approver	Status	Date
Name	*Yes/No/Pending*	*YYYY-MM-DD*
Insert as many rows as you need.		

Service Overview

Briefly describe the service in question here. Keep things to about a paragraph. You can provide links to additional documentation about the service if you would like. Focus on the service from the viewpoint of its users (whether those are humans or other services).

SLIs and SLOs

Dashboard: *Link to where people can get a visual representation of your performance.*

Category	SLI	SLO
Part[a]		
Category[b]	Description[c]	SLO1[d]
	Query[e]	SLO2[f]
Part		
Category	Description	SLO1
	Query	SLO2

Insert or remove as many rows as you need.

[a] The part or component of your service that is being addressed by a certain SLI. For example, this could be an API, a public-facing HTTP server, a data processing pipeline, or something else. Your service might have only one or many components that warrant an SLI.

[b] The type of SLI being measured. For example, this could be availability, latency, data correctness, data freshness, and so on.

[c] A human-readable description of what is being measured. For example, "The proportion of successful HTTP requests from external sources."

[d] The SLO that is being informed by the SLI in question. For example, "95% of requests < 200 ms."

[e] The actual query from your systems that deliver the SLI.

[f] A single SLI might drive multiple SLOs. For example, while "95% of requests < 200 ms" might be your first SLO, you might also want to ensure that "98% of requests < 400 ms."

Rationale

Provide a short rationale for why these SLIs and SLOs were chosen. Try to keep this to a paragraph or so. You can link to additional documentation here if you would like.

Revision	Date	Details
Revision #	YYYY-MM-DD	Summary of the changes

Insert as many more rows as you need.

Revisit Schedule

Describe here how often you plan to revisit the defined values in this document and send it back out for approval. When first establishing your SLIs and SLOs, this should be frequent (once a month is a good starting point), but as your values become more in line with reality, you can scale this back to every quarter or even every year.

Error Budget Policy

Error budget	Threshold	Actions
SLO	X	Action to be taken

Insert as many more rows as you need.

External Links

This section is optional and just here to prime you to think about any other documentation or other data that might be useful to link to for people to understand this document in the best way possible.

Proofs for Chapter 9

Theorem 1

Let $X \sim$ Pois (λ) and $Y \sim$ Pois (μ). If $Z = X + Y$ and $\tau = \lambda + \mu$, then $Z \sim$ Pois (τ).

Proof

The definition of the Poisson process is:

$$P(X = k) = \frac{\lambda^k e^{-\lambda}}{k!}$$

Consider $P(X + Y = k)$. This could happen if $X = 0$ and $Y = k$, or $X = 1$ and $Y = k - 1$, etc. So:

$$
\begin{aligned}
P(X + Y = k) &= P(X = 0, Y = k) + P(X = 1, Y = k - 1) + \ldots + P(X = k, Y = 0) \\
&= \frac{\lambda^0 e^{-\lambda}}{0!} \frac{\mu^k e^{-\mu}}{k!} + \frac{\lambda^1 e^{-\lambda}}{1!} \frac{\mu^{k-1} e^{-\mu}}{(k-1)!} + \ldots + \frac{\lambda^k e^{-\lambda}}{k!} \frac{\mu^0 e^{-\mu}}{0!} \\
&= \sum_{i=0}^{k} \frac{\lambda^i e^{-\lambda}}{i!} \frac{\mu^{k-i} e^{-\mu}}{(k-i)!}
\end{aligned}
$$

We can pull out $e^{-\lambda}$ and $e^{-\mu}$:

$$P(X + Y = k) = e^{-\lambda} e^{-\mu} \sum_{i=0}^{k} \frac{1}{i!(k-i)!} \lambda^i \mu^{k-i}$$

But $\frac{1}{i!(k-i)!} = \binom{k}{i}\frac{1}{k!}$, and we can pull the $\frac{1}{k!}$ out of the sum, too, so:

$$P(X + Y = k) = \frac{e^{-\lambda}e^{-\mu}}{k!} \sum_{i=0}^{k} \binom{k}{i}\lambda^i\mu^{k-i}$$

Now, since exponents are additive:

$$e^{-\lambda}e^{-\mu} = e^{-\lambda-\mu}$$
$$= e^{-(\lambda+\mu)}$$
$$= e^{-\tau}$$

Finally, the binomial theorem states:

$$\sum_{k=0}^{n} \binom{n}{k}a^k b^{n-k} = (a+b)^n$$

So:

$$P(X + Y = k) = \frac{e^{-\lambda}e^{-\mu}}{k!} \sum_{i=0}^{k} \binom{k}{i}\lambda^i\mu^{k-i}$$
$$= \frac{e^{-(\lambda+\mu)}}{k!}(\lambda+\mu)^k$$
$$= \frac{\tau^k e^{-\tau}}{k!} = \text{Pois}(\tau)$$

Theorem 2

If $X \sim$ Expon (λ) and $Y \sim$ Expon (μ) then $P(X < Y) = \frac{\lambda}{\mu + \lambda}$.

Proof

By the law of total probability:

$$P(X < Y) = \int_0^\infty P(X < Y \mid Y = y)P(Y = y)dy$$

So:

$$
\begin{aligned}
P(X < Y) &= \int_0^\infty P(X < Y \mid Y = y)P(Y = y)dy \\
&= \int_0^\infty P(X < y)P(Y = y)dy \\
&= \int_0^\infty \left[1 - e^{-\lambda y}\right]\left[\mu e^{-\mu y}\right]dy \\
&= \int_0^\infty \left(\mu e^{-\mu y} - \mu e^{-\mu y}e^{-\lambda y}\right)dy \\
&= \mu \int_0^\infty e^{-\mu y}dy - \mu \int_0^\infty e^{-(\mu + \lambda)y}dy \\
&= \frac{\mu}{\lambda + \mu}e^{-(\lambda + \mu)y}\Big|_0^\infty - e^{-\mu y}\Big|_0^\infty \\
&= \left(0 - \frac{\mu}{\lambda + \mu}\right) - (0 - 1) \\
&= 1 - \frac{\mu}{\lambda + \mu} \\
&= \frac{\lambda + \mu}{\lambda + \mu} - \frac{\mu}{\lambda + \mu} \\
&= \frac{\lambda}{\lambda + \mu}
\end{aligned}
$$

Theorem 3

If $X \sim$ Expon (λ) and $Y \sim$ Expon (μ), then $E[X|X < Y] = \frac{1}{\lambda + \mu}$. That is, if you draw from X and from Y and only keep values from X if they are less than the value from Y, then the mean of the values you keep will be $\frac{1}{\lambda + \mu}$.

Proof

The law of conditional probability is $P(A, B) = P(A|B)P(B)$, so $P(X < Y, X = x) = P(X < Y|X = x)P(X = x)$. I am being slightly handwavy, but here $P(\cdot)$ is a density function, not a probability (which would be zero).

By the definition of the exponential distribution:

$$P(X = x) = \lambda e^{-\lambda x}$$

For the other factor:

$$
\begin{aligned}
P(X < Y|X = x) &= P(x < Y) \\
&= 1 - P(Y < x) \\
&= 1 - \left(1 - e^{-\mu x}\right)
\end{aligned}
$$

This follows since the cumulative distribution function of the exponential distribution $F(x; \mu) = 1 - e^{-\mu x}$. So:

$$P(X < Y|X = x) = e^{-\mu x}$$

Therefore:

$$
\begin{aligned}
P(X < Y, X = x) &= P(X < Y|X = x)P(X = x) \\
&= e^{-\mu x}\lambda e^{-\lambda x} \\
&= \lambda e^{-(\lambda + \mu)x}
\end{aligned}
$$

Again, by the law of conditional probability:

$$P(X = x|X < Y) = \frac{P(X = x, X < Y)}{P(X < Y)}$$

But from theorem 2, we know $P(X < Y) = \frac{\lambda}{\lambda + \mu}$.

So:

$$P(X = x | X < Y) = \frac{P(X = x, X < Y)}{P(X < Y)}$$

$$= \lambda e^{-(\lambda + \mu)x} \frac{\lambda + \mu}{\lambda}$$

$$= (\lambda + \mu) e^{-(\lambda + \mu)x}$$

This is an exponential distribution with parameter $(\lambda + \mu)$, so its mean is $\frac{1}{\lambda + \mu}$.

Fun corollary! This proof is symmetrical in X and Y, so $E[X | X < Y] = E[Y | Y < X]$, irrespective of how different X and Y are.

Theorem 4

If X and Y are independent, then $E[X \times Y] = E[X] \times E[Y]$.

Proof

$$E[XY] = \int_y \int_x xy P(x, y) \, \mathrm{d}x \, \mathrm{d}y$$

This is the definition of the expected value of $X \times Y$. It requires integrating over the whole joint distribution of $P(x, y)$. Think of a joint distribution as a multidimensional probability distribution with an X and a Y axis.

If $P(x)$ and $P(y)$ are independent, then the joint distribution is simply the product of the individual distributions: $P(x, y) = P(x)P(y)$. We can use this to rewrite the expected value:

$$E[XY] = \int_y \int_x xy P(x) P(y) \, \mathrm{d}x \, \mathrm{d}y$$

We can pull y and $P(y)$ out of the inner integral:

$$E[XY] = \int_y y P(y) \int_x x P(x) \, \mathrm{d}x \, \mathrm{d}y$$

But $\int_x x P(x) \mathrm{d}x = E[X]$:

$$E[XY] = \int_y yP(y) \int_x xP(x)\mathrm{d}x\,\mathrm{d}y$$

$$= \int_y yP(y)E[X]\mathrm{d}y$$

$$= E[X] \int_y yP(y)\mathrm{d}y$$

$$= E[X]E[Y]$$

Theorem 5

$$E[X + Y] = E[X] + E[Y]$$

Proof

$$E[X + Y] = \int_y \int_x (x + y)P(x, y)\mathrm{d}x\,\mathrm{d}y$$

$$= \int_y \int_x xP(x, y) + yP(x, y)\mathrm{d}x\,\mathrm{d}y$$

$$= \int_y \int_x xP(x, y)\mathrm{d}x\,\mathrm{d}y + \int_y \int_x yP(x, y)\mathrm{d}x\,\mathrm{d}y$$

$$= \int_x x \int_y P(x, y)\mathrm{d}y\,\mathrm{d}x + \int_y y \int_x P(x, y)\mathrm{d}x\,\mathrm{d}y$$

$$= \int_x xP(x)\mathrm{d}x + \int_y yP(y)\mathrm{d}y$$

$$= E[X] + E[Y]$$

Theorem 6

$$E_2[t] = \frac{\mu + \lambda}{2\mu^2} + \frac{1}{\mu}$$

Proof

When we have two disks, either of which can fail at rate μ, the total failure rate for both disks is 2μ (see theorem 1). Once one disk has failed, either the second disk fails (at rate μ) or the system is repaired (at rate λ). This is a Bernoulli trial with "success" as the loss of the second disk, which means that the number of times we have to experience the loss of one disk before we experience the loss of *both* disks is geometrically distributed, with probability $p = \frac{\mu}{\mu + \lambda}$ (see theorem 2).

The expected value of the geometric distribution is $E[n] = \frac{1}{p} = \frac{\mu + \lambda}{\mu}$, which is the mean number of times we lose one disk before we lose two.

The mean time between each disk loss event is $E[l] = \frac{1}{2\mu}$. Additionally, every time but the final time we lose a disk, we wait for the repair event. The mean time to repair is $\frac{1}{\lambda}$ but since we know this happens *before* we lose another disk, it's actually $E[r] = \frac{1}{\mu + \lambda}$ (see theorem 3).

Finally, we spend time waiting to lose the final disk. The mean time to losing that disk would be $\frac{1}{\mu}$, but again, it happens before the repair, so it's also $E[f] = \frac{1}{\mu + \lambda}$. Putting this all together, we have:

$$E_2[t] = E[n](E[l] + E[r]) - E[r] + E[f]$$

We subtract $E[r]$ since it doesn't count (we don't experience the final repair event). But since $E[r] = E[f]$, we can simplify this:

$$
\begin{aligned}
E_2[t] &= E[n](E[l] + E[r]) \\
&= \frac{\mu + \lambda}{\mu}\left(\frac{1}{2\mu} + \frac{1}{\mu + \lambda}\right) \\
&= \frac{\mu + \lambda}{2\mu^2} + \frac{1}{\mu}
\end{aligned}
$$

Theorem 7

$$E_3[t] = \frac{(\mu + \lambda)(2\mu + \lambda)}{6\mu^3} + \frac{\mu + \lambda}{2\mu^2} + \frac{1}{\mu}$$

Proof

The argument is the same as Theorem 6, except now we have to lose one, two, and finally three disks to experience data loss, so we start out with a mean time to losing one disk at $\frac{1}{3\mu}$. We'll assume the repair time is the same, and that repairs take us back to full health (i.e., we don't go from two disks down, to one disk down, to all disks fine; we just go from missing two disks to being fully replicated).

The expected number of times we lose one disk before we lose two is now $E[n] = \frac{2\mu + \lambda}{2\mu}$, and the time we spend in that cycle is $E[l] + E[r] = \frac{1}{3\mu} + \frac{1}{2\mu + m}$.

So, the time it takes to lose two disks (call it D_2) is:

$$D_2 = \frac{2\mu + \lambda}{2\mu}\left(\frac{1}{3\mu} + \frac{1}{2\mu + \lambda}\right)$$

$$= \frac{2\mu + \lambda}{6\mu^2} + \frac{1}{2\mu}$$

Which is akin to what we got in theorem 6, except now *this* is just the amount of time we spend getting to the penultimate disk. We need to apply this argument again to get the mean time to lose the final disk:

$$E_3[t] = \frac{\mu + \lambda}{\mu}\left(D_2 + \frac{1}{\mu + \lambda}\right)$$

$$= \frac{(\mu + \lambda)(2\mu + \lambda)}{6\mu^3} + \frac{\mu + \lambda}{2\mu^2} + \frac{1}{\mu}$$

Index

S

SaaS, 114, 125, 214
sample, 58
sample space, 156
sampling, 254
scalability, 248-249
scalars, 120
scale, 198
Search as a Service (SaaS), 1
security, 246-247
Security as a Service (SaaS), 1
Seeking SRE, 149
Serra, James, 229
service
    sorts of, 54-54
        (see also hosted services, open source
            services)
    truths, 2
service components, 52-53
    (see also multiple-team component services,
        single-team component services)
service dependency, 49-52
    (see also hard dependency, soft dependency)
service failure, 43
service level agreements (SLAs)
    business changes and, 304
    definition of, 4-5, 99
    legal team and, 99, 102, 105, 266
service level indicators (SLIs)
    approaches, 28, 126
    benefits of, 27-30, 100
    complications with, 10, 11, 13
    definition of, 3-6
    determiners, 124
    durability, 203-207
    meaningful, 28-34
    measuring, 33, 57, 286, 308
service level objectives (SLOs)
    adoption lessons, 108
    alerting, 288 (see alert, threshold alert)
    approaches, 12-13, 16-17, 18, 30, 40, 88, 281,
        351, 353
    benefits of, 96-100, 103, 253
    buy-in for, 95-102, 283-284, 328
    changes to, 308-309
    culture of, 282-291
    definition of, 3-7, 223
    definition templates, 357-359
    document, 285, 312-318, 319

example services and, 9-12
goals, 111-114
implementation strategies, 122-127,
    284-289, 294-295
    (see also latency-sensitive request pro-
        cessing; low-lag, high throughput
        processing; mobile and web clients)
measuring, 286-286
objections to, 102-105, 109
problems with, 48
reports, 320
targets, 55, 56, 61, 112
    (see also flexible targets, testable targets)
silver bullets, 107
single-team component services, 53
Site Reliability Engineering (book), 75, 327
Site Reliability Engineering (SRE), 12, 15, 53,
    210
Site Reliability Workbook, The, 145, 210, 327
SLO Advocate
    about role, 326-327
    Crawl phase, 327-335
    Run phase, 339-340
    Walk phase, 335-338
slow burn problem, 141-142
soft dependency, 49-51
Software as a Service (SaaS), 1
span, 123
specification, 209
standard deviation, 193
statistical approaches, 57-61
statistics, 58, 154
Stockholm syndrome, 149
Storage as a Service (SaaS), 1
stress test, 73, 90
structured event database, 119-122
structured logging data, 113
    (see also structured events database)
SYN flood attack, 348
    (see also flood attack)
synchronous request, 218-219
system failures, 43
systems architect, 210, 220
systems engineering, 210

T

telemetry, 1, 53, 125, 137, 236
testable targets, 112, 115, 118, 120
thaw tax, 107

threshold alert
    about, 131-133
    definition of, 130
    problems and, 136, 137
    problems with, 344
        (see also reporting incidents)
    slow burn problem and, 142
throughput
    data application properties and, 249
    high, 113, 121, 124
    low, 121, 123
    use of, 41
Tilbrook, D., 150
time, 254
time series data, 113, 114-119
time series database (TSDB), 114-119
time windows, 83-86
    (see also calendar-bound window, rolling
        window)
timeliness (see freshness)
tooling, 304-305, 320
training, 331-335, 337
transactional API, 299
trials, definition of, 156, 160
Trusted Platform Modules (TPM), 241

U

understandability, 311-318

uninformative prior, 179
uptime, 2, 15, 31, 247, 254
user
    definition of, 2, 8
    expectations, 302-304
    happiness, 44
    internal, 268
    service expectations and, 27-28

V

validity, 239-241
variance, 60
virtual private cloud (VPC), 114, 122
volumetric attack, 348
    (see also SYN flood attack)
VPC (see virtual private cloud (VPC))

W

web services, 9
Wiener Shirt-zel Clothing Company, The,
    258-263
Wright, Hyrum, 19

Z

Zawinski, Jamie, 150

About the Author

Alex Hidalgo is a site reliability engineer and expert at all things related to service level objectives. He developed an interest in computers at a young age, started writing his first BASIC programs at around the age of nine, and remembers the Internet when it was all still text. He eventually turned his hobby into a career, working in various capacities as a network engineer, security engineer, and systems administrator and in many roles within the world of IT support. After moving to New York, he joined Admeld as a Technical Operations Engineer, only to find himself employed by Google a few months later due to acquisition.

At Google, Alex was first introduced to the discipline of Site Reliability Engineering, which connected so closely with him that he wonders how he ever did anything else. Eventually, he found his other calling as an educator, writer, and speaker, traveling all over the world training other site reliability engineers, becoming one of the primary developers of the Coursera Google IT Professional Certification, and contributing to multiple chapters of *The Site Reliability Workbook*; most notably "Implementing SLOs" and "SLO Engineering Case Studies."

Recently, he has joined Squarespace, where his focus is now on spreading the concepts of SLO-based approaches to service reliability—both internally and across the entire industry. When not sharing his passion for error budgets with others, you can find him scuba diving or watching college basketball. He lives in Park Slope, Brooklyn, with his partner Jen and a rescue dog named Taco. He thinks about SLOs so much he once had a dream about defining some for Taco. Twitter handle: @ahidalgosre

About the Contributors

Daria Barteneva is currently a senior software engineer on the Observability Platform team at Azure. With a background in applied mathematics, artificial intelligence, and music, Daria is passionate about data mining and diversity in tech and opera. In her current role, she is focused on changing organizational culture, processes, and platforms to improve service reliability and on-call experience. Daria is originally from Moscow, Russia, spent 20 years in Portugal, and now lives in Dublin, Ireland.

Blake Bisset, Azure SRE, Microsoft, got his first legal tech job at 16—so long ago he's allowed to shakeyfist while shouting "Get off my LAN!" A startup with a bunch of kids wondering why they couldn't watch movies on the internet led him to Google, where he broke enough things to win the go/bestpostmortem link. Then, as Head of Reliability Engineering at Dropbox, he lost a bet with Niall Murphy and is now stacking turtles in the reliability mines at Microsoft Azure.

Toby Burress is a site reliability engineer at Dropbox, where he spends all day shoveling bytes into little byte-sized holes. He lives on an island with some people and some dogs. He spends most of his free time shipping cartoon characters.

Polina Giralt, staff engineer, Squarespace, studied information technology and informatics and psychology at college. She's also a Recurse Center alum. Now Polina leads a streaming data team, focused on architecting and scaling reliable data pipelines. She lives in Brooklyn and prefers deleting code to writing code, but understands that the latter is necessary.

Niall Murphy is currently director of Site Reliability Engineering for Microsoft Azure. He is probably best known as the author/instigator of the first SRE book(s), but is secretly more interesting than that would suggest. He lives in Dublin, Ireland, with his wife and two children, who are openly more interesting than he is.

Eva Parish, senior technical writer at Squarespace, has worked as a technical writer for the past eight years, creating documentation for a variety of audiences including developers, system administrators, and nontechnical end users. Besides writing the docs herself, Eva is passionate about creating a culture of documentation within and across technology organizations, and loves mentoring others on their writing. Outside of her daily work, Eva is an accomplished conference speaker. She also enjoys learning languages and has been studying Russian for the last five years.

David K. Rensin is the senior director of Engineering in the Office of the CFO at Google, where he serves on a small team of technical advisers to Alphabet's CFO. He provides guidance on the appropriate allocation of Google's capital to its various businesses and long-term technical investments. Prior to that, Dave founded Customer Reliability Engineering (CRE) and also ran Google's global network capacity planning. He has more than 25 years' experience designing and delivering planet-scale cloud and mobile products. Prior to joining Google, Dave worked at Amazon on its classified (now declassified) C2S project. As an entrepreneur, he has cofounded and sold several businesses, including one (Riverbed Technologies) for more than $1 billion, and has served as an officer in two publicly traded companies (Omnisky and Aether). He is also a bestselling author and editor with 16 US patents to his name. Dave earned a degree in statistics from the University of Maryland, and is married with three children.

Ben Sigelman is a cofounder and the CEO at LightStep, a cocreator of Dapper (Google's distributed tracing system), and a cocreator of the OpenTracing and OpenTelemetry projects (both part of the CNCF). Ben's work and interests gravitate toward observability, especially where microservices, high transaction volumes, and large engineering organizations are involved.

Harold Treen, senior software engineer at Squarespace, started his career working in test engineering at Xtreme Labs (now Pivotal) and Microsoft. The experience led to a fascination with software failure and the tools available to mitigate it. Ever since, he's been focused on strategies for building reliable software and helping others to improve their development process.

Salim Virji works in Google's SRE group and currently focuses on developing reliable engineering practices and processes. Salim's interests include fairness in machine learning and distributed storage.

Jaime Woo began his career as a molecular biologist before working at DigitalOcean, Riot Games, and Shopify—where he launched the engineering communications function. He cofounded Incident Labs, focusing on providing teams with improved SRE tooling to return more time for planned work. He is also an avid lover of dumplings.

Colophon

The animal on the cover of *Implementing Service Level Objectives* is the breed of dog known as the Spanish Water Dog.

The Spanish Water Dog is bred for herding and retrieving ducks and other waterfowl. They are known as a good family dog and watchdog, and are intelligent and energetic. Medium-sized and curly-coated, these dogs can be black, brown, or beige and white.

This breed had ancestors in the northernmost and southernmost parts of Spain. Dogs from the regions of Asturias, Cantabria, and Andalusia contributed different qualities (such as size, and coat, and color) to the Spanish Water Dog known today.

Many of the animals on O'Reilly covers are endangered; all of them are important to the world.

The cover illustration is by Karen Montgomery, based on a black-and-white engraving from *British Quadrupeds* (1845). The cover fonts are Gilroy Semibold and Guardian Sans. The text font is Adobe Minion Pro; the heading font is Adobe Myriad Condensed; and the code font is Dalton Maag's Ubuntu Mono.